## ANIMATION AND PRESENTATION

| Product | Page |
|---|---|
| Adobe Premiere | 302 |
| Animation Works | 306 |
| At Your Service | 320 |
| HookUp! | 330 |
| HyperCard | 282 |
| interFACE | 314 |
| MacroMind Director | 286 |
| MediaMaker | 295 |
| MediaTracks | 322 |
| Paracomp Magic | 326 |
| PROmotion | 333 |
| QuickTime | 345 |
| Studio/1 | 332 |
| SuperCard | 309 |

## MISCELLANEOUS

| Product | Page |
|---|---|
| Adventures in Musicland | 405 |
| After Dark | 397 |
| Kid Pix | 400 |
| Talking Moose | 402 |

# Computer users are not all alike.
# Neither are SYBEX books.

We know our customers have a variety of needs. They've told us so. And because we've listened, we've developed several distinct types of books to meet the needs of each of our customers. What are you looking for in computer help?

If you're looking for the basics, try the **ABC's** series. You'll find short, unintimidating tutorials and helpful illustrations. For a more visual approach, select **Teach Yourself,** featuring full-color, screen-by-screen illustrations of how to use the latest software.

**Learn Fast!** books are really two books in one: a tutorial, to get you off to a fast start, followed by a command reference, to answer more advanced questions.

**Mastering** and **Understanding** titles offer you a step-by-step introduction, plus an in-depth examination of intermediate-level features, to use as you progress.

Our **Up & Running** series is designed for computer-literate consumers who want a no-nonsense overview of new programs. Just 20 basic lessons, and you're on your way.

We also publish two types of reference books. Our **Instant References** provide quick access to each of a program's commands and functions. SYBEX **Encyclopedias, Desktop References,** and **A to Z** books provide a *comprehensive reference* and explanation of all of the commands, features, and functions of the subject software.

Sometimes a subject requires a special treatment that our standard series don't provide. So you'll find we have titles like **Advanced Techniques, Handbooks, Tips & Tricks,** and others that are specifically tailored to satisfy a unique need.

We carefully select our authors for their in-depth understanding of the software they're writing about, as well as their ability to write clearly and communicate effectively. Each manuscript is thoroughly reviewed by our technical staff to ensure its complete accuracy. Our production department makes sure it's easy to use. All of this adds up to the highest quality books available, consistently appearing on best-seller charts worldwide.

You'll find SYBEX publishes a variety of books on every popular software package. Looking for computer help? Help Yourself to SYBEX.

For a complete catalog of our publications:
SYBEX, Inc.
2021 Challenger Drive, Alameda, CA 94501
Tel: (510) 523-8233/(800) 227-2346 Telex: 336311
Fax: (510) 523-2373

SYBEX is committed to using natural resources wisely to preserve and improve our environment. As a leader in the computer book publishing industry, we are aware that over 40% of America's solid waste is paper. This is why we have been printing the text of books like this one on recycled paper since 1982.

This year our use of recycled paper will result in the saving of more than 15,300 trees. We will lower air pollution effluents by 54,000 pounds, save 6,300,000 gallons of water, and reduce landfill by 2,700 cubic yards.

In choosing a SYBEX book you are not only making a choice for the best in skills and information, you are also choosing to enhance the quality of life for all of us.

# The Audible Macintosh

# The Audible Macintosh®

David M. Rubin

SYBEX®

San Francisco ■ Paris ■ Düsseldorf ■ Soest

Acquisitions Editor: David J. Clark
Developmental Editor: Kenyon Brown
Editor: Richard Mills
Word Processors: Ann Dunn and Susan Trybull
Book Designer: Charlotte Carter
Chapter Art & Layout: Charlotte Carter
Technical Art: Delia Brown and Cuong Le
Screen Graphics: Arno Harris
Typesetter: Elizabeth Newman
Proofreader: David Silva
Indexer: Ted Laux
Cover Designer: Ingalls + Associates
Cover Illustrator: Hank Osuna

SYBEX is a registered trademark of SYBEX Inc.

TRADEMARKS: SYBEX has attempted throughout this book to distinguish proprietary trademarks from descriptive terms by following the capitalization style used by the manufacturer.

SYBEX is not affiliated with any manufacturer.

Every effort has been made to supply complete and accurate information. However, SYBEX assumes no responsibility for its use, nor for any infringement of the intellectual property rights of third parties which would result from such use.

Copyright ©1992 SYBEX Inc., 2021 Challenger Drive, Alameda, CA 94501. World rights reserved. No part of this publication may be stored in a retrieval system, transmitted, or reproduced in any way, including but not limited to photocopy, photograph, magnetic or other record, without the prior agreement and written permission of the publisher.

Library of Congress Card Number: 92-80313
ISBN: 0-7821-1045-2
Manufactured in the United States of America
10 9 8 7 6 5 4 3 2 1

# Acknowledgments

This book could not have been possible without the help of a great many companies and the generous efforts of the people who staff them. I sincerely thank the following companies for providing me with their products for review and for their technical assistance to ensure that this book is as up to date and accurate as possible:

Adobe Systems, Aldus Corp., Articulate Systems, Baseline Publishing, Berkeley Systems, Bright Star Technology, CD Technology, Claris Corp., Dynaware USA, Educorp, Electronic Arts, Five Pin Press, Gold Disk, Greytsounds, MacroMind/Paracomp, McGill University, MIDI Inn, Motion Works, Mus-Art Productions, New Sound Music, Olduvai Corp., PG Music, Phil Wood Consulting, Prosonus, Roland Corp., Sound Quest, Tran Tracks, Trycho Music International, Voyager Company, VPL Research, and the Works Music Productions.

Thanks also to these companies for providing me with information about their products: Acoustic Research, Altech Systems, E-mu Systems, International MIDI Association, JLCooper Electronics, Korg, Monster Design Group, and Yamaha International.

I'd also like to thank the following people for the extra efforts that they made in my behalf:

Keri Walker of Apple Computer; Bill Liu and Jim Armstrong of CD Technology; Paul Rice, Toby Richards, and Suz Howells of Digidesign; Stephen Thomas of Dr. T's; Trudy Edelson of Farallon; Robertson Reed Smith of the HyperCard Development Team; Susan Patalano of Mark of the Unicorn; Christy Gersich of Microsoft; Parker Adams of the Parker Adams Group; and Russ Jones and Bill Black of Steinberg/Jones.

I'm especially grateful to the following people for going well beyond the call of duty to help me with this book:

Nigel Redmon of EarLevel Engineering for patiently answering my endless questions about the more obscure aspects of MIDI; Harrison Rose of New Media Research for sharing with me his knowledge of QuickTime and its inner workings; Kord Taylor of Opcode Systems for tolerating my incessant phone calls and always displaying an accommodating, good-natured interest in this project; and Anastasia Lanier of Passport Designs for her enthusiastic support of my work and for being generous, responsive, and resourceful when I most needed it.

Many thanks as well go to the great people at SYBEX for taking a chance on my idea and giving me the opportunity to get this show on the road. In particular, I'd like to thank David Clark for getting the ball rolling, Ken Brown for keeping it rolling, and Richard Mills for his thoughtful and perceptive editing.

I would also like to thank New Media Research, Inc. for allowing me to include in this book several excerpts from my earlier writings for them. Additionally, I owe a real debt of gratitude to William Coggshall, editor for New Media Research, without whose help and encouragement the long path that ultimately led to this book would not have begun.

And finally, I must thank my wife, Katherine, for motivating me and providing me with help and support when the going got tough. And thanks to my son, Aaron, for understanding the importance of my work and for putting up with my absences even though he wanted to play with me some more.

Again, to all of the people behind the scenes whose combined efforts over these many months have helped make this book a reality: my sincere thanks.

This book is dedicated to my parents,
Louis and Gertrude Rubin, who were there when I heard my first sounds
and have always supported me in my varied pursuits
both audible and otherwise.

...She places the flute upon her lips,
and as the sunset fades and dusk settles,
she plays beneath the pale moon.

...The night is chill, her silken robes are thin, her fingers cold

...But music floats through frosty woods
and startled plums fall pattering down.

**—Chang Hsien**

# Contents at a Glance

Introduction     xxi

| | | |
|---|---|---|
| Chapter 1 | A Brief History of Sound for Presentations, or How We Got Here from There | 1 |
| Chapter 2 | Using Sound in Presentations: An Overview | 9 |
| Chapter 3 | An Introduction to MIDI | 17 |
| Chapter 4 | All about Sequencers | 35 |
| Chapter 5 | Sequencing at the Top | 45 |
| Chapter 6 | Sequencing on Easy Street | 97 |
| Chapter 7 | Instant MIDI | 119 |
| Chapter 8 | HyperCard Meets MIDI | 137 |
| Chapter 9 | Universal Editor/Librarians | 149 |
| Chapter 10 | An Introduction to Digital Audio | 169 |
| Chapter 11 | Digital Audio for the Masses (8-Bit) | 177 |
| Chapter 12 | Digital Audio for the Rich and Famous (16-Bit) | 199 |
| Chapter 13 | Sample-Editing Software | 225 |
| Chapter 14 | Digital Audio Meets MIDI | 243 |
| Chapter 15 | Adding Sound to Desktop Presentations | 281 |
| Chapter 16 | Sound and the System | 341 |
| Chapter 17 | Hardware | 353 |
| Chapter 18 | Adding Sound after Transfer to Video | 377 |
| Chapter 19 | Production Music and Sound-Effects Libraries | 385 |
| Chapter 20 | Just for Fun | 397 |
| Appendix A | Glossary | 411 |
| Appendix B | List of Companies | 421 |
| Appendix C | Bibliography | 427 |

Index     430

# Table of Contents

Introduction     xxi

**Chapter 1**     A Brief History of Sound for Presentations, or How We Got Here from There     **1**

    All the World's a Stage     2
    Mixing Music and Sound Effects     2
    Early Radio     3
    Not-So-Silent Movies     4
    Fear of Sound     4
    Modern Sound     5
    Final Thoughts     6

**Chapter 2**     Using Sound in Presentations: An Overview     **9**

    Voice of Reason     10
    Sound and Fury     11
       Sync Sounds     11
       Finding Sounds     13
    Music to My Ears     13
       Sources of Music     14
       Hardware and Software     14
    Audio for Video     15
    Helpful Hints     15

**Chapter 3**     An Introduction to MIDI     **17**

    What Is MIDI?     18
       Connections     19
       Channels     19

Modes   20
Messages   20
MIDI and the Mac   21
Sounds from Circuits   22
Getting Started with MIDI   23
　Speakers of the House   23
　All Systems Go   24
　Keys to Success   25
The More the Merrier: Expanding Your System   26
　More on Interfaces   27
　All Mixed Up   28
Samplers, Synths, and Cymbals   30

*Chapter 4*　**All about Sequencers**　**35**

Sequencer Anatomy   37
　Getting Around   38
　Fascinatin' Rhythm   40
　Command Performance   40
Through the Window   40
Sum of the Parts   43

*Chapter 5*　**Sequencing at the Top**　**45**

Performer   45
Vision   56
Master Tracks Pro 5   64
Beyond   73
Cubase   82
Final Thoughts   93

| | | |
|---|---|---|
| *Chapter 6* | **Sequencing on Easy Street** | **97** |
| | EZ Vision 97 | |
| | Trax 101 | |
| | Ballade 104 | |
| | DeluxeRecorder 109 | |
| | Encore 113 | |
| | Final Thoughts 115 | |
| *Chapter 7* | **Instant MIDI** | **119** |
| | In the Background 120 | |
| | Band-in-a-Box 122 | |
| | The Beat Goes On 124 | |
| | Out of Sequence 124 | |
| | General MIDI 125 | |
| | Losing Your Voice 130 | |
| | What's Out There 130 | |
| | Some Final Tips 134 | |
| *Chapter 8* | **HyperCard Meets MIDI** | **137** |
| | Hardware and Software 137 | |
| | SOUNDtraK 138 | |
| | HyperMIDI 143 | |
| | The Book of MIDI 145 | |
| *Chapter 9* | **Universal Editor/Librarians** | **149** |
| | How They Work 149 | |
| | X-oR 152 | |
| | Galaxy Plus Editors 156 | |

MIDI Quest   161
Final Thoughts   165

**Chapter 10   An Introduction to Digital Audio**                         **169**
The Analog World   169
The Digital Domain   170
Sound into Numbers   170
   Quantization   171
   Sampling Rate   172
   Westward Ho!   173
Playback   174

**Chapter 11   Digital Audio for the Masses (8-Bit)**                     **177**
MacRecorder   177
   SoundEdit   179
   HyperSound   186
   HyperSound Toolkit   188
Voice Impact Pro   188
   SoundWave   190
   Voice Record   195
Mitshiba StereoRecorder   196

**Chapter 12   Digital Audio for the Rich and Famous (16-Bit)**           **199**
Audiomedia   200
   Audiomedia's Software   201
   SoundAccess   209
Sound Tools   210
More about Samplers   211

       SampleCell   212
           SampleCell Editor   213
           Sampling with SampleCell   219
       More Sounds for SampleCell   220
           Digidesign   220
           Greytsounds   221
           McGill University Master Samples   221
           Prosonus   222

*Chapter 13*   Sample-Editing Software   **225**
       Sound Designer II   226
       Alchemy   230
       Final Thoughts   241

*Chapter 14*   Digital Audio Meets MIDI   **243**
       Audio Trax   243
       Deck   249
       Studio Vision   257
       Cubase Audio   267
       Digital Performer   271
       Final Thoughts   278

*Chapter 15*   Adding Sound to Desktop Presentations   **281**
       HyperCard   282
           HyperTalk and Sound   283
           External Commands and Functions   285
       MacroMind Director   286
           Overview   287
           Sound in Overview   288

　　　　Studio　289
　　　　　Sound in Studio　291
　　MediaMaker　295
　　　　Overall Structure　295
　　　　Mac-Based Sounds　297
　　　　External Sounds　299
　　　　Getting in Sync　301
　　Adobe Premiere　302
　　Animation Works　306
　　SuperCard　309
　　Voyager CD AudioStack　311
　　interFACE　314
　　　　Creating Actors　315
　　　　Speech Sync　318
　　　　At Your Service　320
　　MediaTracks　322
　　Paracomp Magic　326
　　HookUp!　330
　　Studio/1　332
　　PROmotion　333
　　Final Thoughts　339

## Chapter 16　Sound and the System　　341

Sound Manager　341
　　Sounding Off　342
　　Multiple Channels　342
　　MACE　343
　　Recording Sounds　343
QuickTime　345
　　How It Works　345

    Synchronization and Sound  347
      Requirements  348
   MIDI Manager  349
    What It Does  349
    How It Does It  350
    How It Affects Performance  351
    One Last Thought  351

**Chapter 17**  Hardware  **353**
   Sound Modules and More  353
    Roland  354
    E-mu Systems  362
    Yamaha  364
    Korg  366
   MIDI Interfaces  367
    Good  368
    Better  368
    Best  369
    Better Than Best  370
   Speakers  371
    Roland CS-10  371
    Roland MA-12C  372
    MacSpeaker  373
    Powered Partner 570  374

**Chapter 18**  Adding Sound after Transfer to Video  **377**
   Video Pros and Cons  377
   Production Music Libraries  378
   Original Music  379
   SMPTE Timecode  380

Working with a Composer   382
Other Sounds   383

**Chapter 19**  Production Music and Sound-Effects Libraries   **385**
Music and Sound Effects on Compact Disc   386
Music and Sound Effects on CD-ROM   392

**Chapter 20**  Just for Fun   **397**
After Dark   397
Kid Pix   400
Talking Moose   402
Adventures in Musicland   405

**Appendix A**  Glossary   **411**

**Appendix B**  List of Companies   **421**

**Appendix C**  Bibliography   **427**

Index   430

# Introduction

*E*verybody knows that the Macintosh can make sounds. Most Mac users have experimented, at one time or another, with changing their system alert beeps to a variety of entertaining sound effects and speech. But, until recently, most people treated the sonic potential of the Macintosh as a kind of novelty—to be sure, a novelty that humanized the computer and made it much more fun to use, but a novelty nonetheless.

As the popularity of electronic musical instruments flourished, the Macintosh took the lead as the computer of choice in professional recording studios across the country. And in recent years, the introduction of affordable CD-quality digital recording hardware has propelled the common Macintosh into the ranks of professional digital audio workstations.

Now that computer-based multimedia has emerged into the light of day, the Macintosh's multifaceted sound capabilities are suddenly assuming new importance. It is now *de rigueur* for animation programs to have some kind of sound support, and desktop presentations everywhere are boasting more sophisticated soundtracks as producers realize that the inept use of sound can undermine the impact of multimedia.

*The Audible Macintosh* grew out of my writings over the past couple of years for the *Desktop Multimedia Report* and *New Media Products*, where I have covered topics relating to the addition of sound and music for multimedia. I realized that there was a need for a single source that could gather together the seemingly disparate elements constituting the Macintosh's audio capabilities and present them in a comprehensive way that could benefit musicians, animators, and producers alike.

## Who Is This Book For?

This book is written for anyone who is interested in adding sound to the Macintosh. More specifically, it's for animators who may have a good background in working with visual elements, but who may lack a full understanding of how to use sound and music to bring their text and graphics to life.

This book is for musicians who want to explore and compare the composing, editing, and recording programs that they can use to integrate their craft into the field of multimedia.

This book is for desktop presentation producers of all kinds who want to know what their options are for adding sound to their projects.

And this book is especially for the average Macintosh users everywhere who find themselves mystified by the growing list of concepts and jargon that new developments in audio capabilities have brought.

## What's Inside?

The first two chapters of *The Audible Macintosh* are designed to provide a context and a starting point from which to explore the remaining chapters. Chapter 1 gives some historical background to help keep a sense of perspective about our place along the audio-visual evolutionary path. Chapter 2 gives an overview of sound and how it's being used today for presentations of various kinds.

The appearance of MIDI during the 1980s has permanently altered the way that musicians compose and perform with electronic instruments. More important, from the standpoint of multimedia, it has provided a way to add high-quality sound to presentations without necessarily breaking the bank. Chapters 3–9, therefore, are devoted to MIDI: what it is, how it works, and what programs are currently available to help you combine MIDI with multimedia.

Chapters 10–14 cover the topic of digital audio, and primarily, digital recording and editing. If you don't know anything about the principles of digital audio, Chapter 10 will fill you in on the basics. After that, I explore products ranging from the inexpensive and ever-popular MacRecorder all the way to pro-level hardware/software packages that let you record CD-quality sound directly to your hard disk.

In this section I have purposely narrowed the scope of the book to include only products that, in my opinion, are appropriate for most multimedia projects. This excludes exorbitantly priced dedicated workstations that use the Mac as a front end, and hardware/software combinations targeted primarily for professional recording studios and CD premastering facilities. Nonetheless, these products are often similar, in many ways, to those mentioned in this book, so you'll gain some insight into the workings of these top-end packages as well.

Chapter 15 deals specifically with animation and presentation software and how the different applications use sound. For animators and multimedia producers, this provides a way to compare the audio capabilities of most of the currently available presentation programs. If you're unhappy with the sound-handling features in your current application, Chapter 15 can help you find something more appropriate. If you're a musician interested in working with animators, this chapter can show you the different approaches to adding sound that are taken by the leading presentation programs. And if you're just starting out, this chapter can provide a good comparative guide to multimedia software and its audio potential.

The remaining chapters of the book—a potpourri of information covering a wide range of topics, both technical and nontechnical—will round out your understanding of adding sound to presentations.

Chapter 16 explores the Macintosh system software and how it handles sound. This chapter also examines the structure and capabilities of Quick-Time and provides some insight into its potential for bringing the elements of multimedia into countless new applications.

Chapter 17 discusses, in more detail, some of the hardware devices mentioned earlier in the book. Several sound modules that I feel are especially appropriate for low-to-medium-budget presentations are described along with a survey of MIDI interfaces of all types. I also describe a few examples of self-powered speakers that are specifically designed for desktop presentations.

Chapter 18 explains the process of adding sound and music to presentations that have been transferred to videotape. It provides information on tape formats, timecode, and working with a composer. If you can't find a composer or you need a source for new sounds, Chapter 19 lists more than 20 companies, both large and small, that offer production music libraries and sound effects for presentations of all kinds.

Finally, Chapter 20 describes some examples of inexpensive programs that use sound creatively to help make working and learning more fun for grown-ups and kids alike.

## The Companion Disk

To give you something to experiment with when you begin exploring sound and multimedia, I've included a companion disk with this book. On it you'll find several examples of professionally produced music that you can play with a simple MIDI system. I've also included a few digital music clips and sound effects to try out with your next presentation.

I hope this book serves you well, not only as a guide and a reference source but also as an inspiration that spurs you on to harness the power, the mystery, and the beauty of that often elusive phenomenon: sound.

# Chapter 1

# A Brief History of Sound for Presentations, or How We Got Here from There

Long before the dawn of civilization, wise people recognized the power and importance of adding sound to a presentation. No witch doctor worth his salt would try to cure a sick child by simply staring mutely off into space. No tribal leader could rescue his tribe from the fearsome effects of a solar eclipse or call forth rain from the dry, unyielding skies by gesturing silently toward the heavens. No, they shook rattles, beat drums, danced, chanted, and sang! Pretty much the same kind of thing we do today, only now we call it *multimedia*. Early man knew instinctively what modern man often forgets—that sound, when combined with visuals, extends the power of the individual and enables him to reach further into his environment and deeper into the psyches of those around him.

# All the World's a Stage

Taking the protean elements of music, speech, and sound effects and combining them with visuals in the form of live performance has yielded a rich legacy of theatrical art. Through the centuries, different cultures have produced plays with dialogue, but no music; music, but no dialogue; and dialogue and music together in combinations that have given birth to an extraordinary kaleidoscope of forms and styles.

The oft-neglected third member of this trinity, sound effects, has gradually gained in importance over the years as a means of heightening dramatic intensity, providing comic relief, or adding a note of realism to a scene to draw the audience more fully into the action. Writings from the time of Euripides and Sophocles describe a method for simulating thunder in Greek plays by bouncing leaden balls on stretched leather. Shakespeare often used sound effects in his plays to satisfy the ever-growing demands for realism and magic in his Elizabethan productions. In the following centuries opera achieved new levels of artistic expression by fusing music with dialogue and combining them with ever more elaborate stage settings. And let's not forget the great, majestic synthesizer of the Baroque era—the pipe organ—which reached its apogee of development long before the invention of the light bulb, yet did a very credible job of imitating flutes, oboes, cellos, and the other instrumental sounds of the period.

# Mixing Music and Sound Effects

At around this same time, in the Japanese Kabuki plays, the musicians were called upon to serve double duty by providing the atmospheric musical accompaniment as well as creating certain sound effects needed to heighten the dramatic peaks. This dual role is surprisingly similar to that of the later "trap" drummers who played in the musical theaters of America when vaudeville and burlesque were in their heyday. These versatile performers were not only the drummers for the house bands that played in these theaters but were also expected to provide an array of props, or "toys," as they're often called, to supply the shows with a variety of sound effects, usually with very little preparation time. Slide whistles, ratchets, gongs, and sandpaper blocks were all part of the arsenal of sounds that gave comic impact to this popular form of entertainment.

Now we've arrived at the 20th century, and this is where things get really interesting. By the mid-1920s, there were two parallel but soon-to-be-related performance phenomena. On the one hand there was radio, which was sound without pictures. And on the other hand there were silent movies, which were pictures without sound.

## Early Radio

Radio in its early days owed a great debt of gratitude to those trap drummers from the vaudeville theaters, many of whom made the natural transition to working in radio bands and orchestras. They brought with them the techniques necessary to enliven radio dramas and comedies by applying their knowledge of sound effects. Dialogue was treated much as it was in the theaters of the time, except that long dramatic pauses were not allowed since there were no corresponding visuals to carry the action. Music, in these early days, served primarily to fill in the "dead air" spaces left in the dialogue or from dramatic transitions, because it was feared that any significant gaps in the broadcast would quickly send people searching for another station.

By the time radio entered its "Golden Age" in the 1930s, full-time sound-effects creators appeared, busily working in large rooms filled with contraptions of all sorts, producing the sounds that gave life to the radio plays. Eventually, they began collecting sounds in advance and recording them on disks, which they often played from multiple turntables. Seeing a need, record companies adapted their equipment to capture sounds not easily created in the studios. These sound-effects libraries further raised the level of realism in radio dramas and freed the dialogue from being overly explanatory.

Throughout the 1920s and 1930s, radio served up a veritable smorgasbord of aural entertainment. Families could now get the news without reading the newspaper. They could enjoy comedies, dramas, symphonic concerts, and operas at the turn of a dial. All this attention to aural gratification fostered in the public an appetite for sound, which inevitably had an impact on the film industry.

## Not-So-Silent Movies

Most people realize that the so-called silent films were never totally silent. In the larger cities they were often accompanied by full orchestras that supplied lush background scores underlining the action and emotions on screen while supplying some sound effects as well. Smaller theaters made do with a single piano, while many other theaters across the country presented their films to the bellowing accompaniment of the "Mighty Wurlitzer" organ.

In Japan, rather than using written subtitles to provide the dialogue on screen, each theater employed a skilled actor and interpreter called a *benshi*. These highly popular men sat on stage, off to one side of the screen, and provided the voices and sound effects that brought to life the films of the day. At any given time they might be called upon to supply the voices of men, women, children, and animals, along with other vocal sound effects. The art of the benshi was so appreciated that often people came to hear them regardless of what films were playing. When movies with the novelty of sound appeared in Japan, the benshi could not compete and the art form gradually disappeared.

## Fear of Sound

The benshi were not the only ones to bemoan the advent of sound. It may seem hard to believe now, but in the late 1920s when movies finally acquired synchronized sound and dialogue, not everyone was thrilled. Charlie Chaplin feared that movies with sound would destroy the art of pantomime, and he complained that talkies would ruin "the great beauty of silence." To him the Little Tramp persona was inconceivable as a talking character.

The Russian expressionist directors Eisenstein and Pudovkin issued a statement expressing grave concerns about the effects of adding synchronous sounds to films, which they felt would bring the demise of the "montage" school of editing. Sound, they explained, should be used as a counterpoint to the image and not to convey strict realism. They were much more amenable to the use of music and asynchronous sounds. The French director

René Clair expressed apprehension that the addition of sound would turn movies into "canned theater" and cause the art form to lose the momentum it had gained during the past decade.

This initial resistance fortunately proved to be short-lived. The more aggressively artistic and experimental directors, such as Clair and the American Lewis Milestone, demonstrated that sound could be an immensely expressive component of the filmmaker's art and a valuable tool in expanding the meaning of the visuals. Suddenly the great advantages of sound became apparent. Acting styles became more natural, and sound effects began to take over some of the functions of furthering the story line and imbuing the plot with inner meanings. Later directors like Orson Welles and Alfred Hitchcock continued the exploration of creative applications of sound for cinema. In the late 1940s, radio finally got its picture and television was born. Television and film followed roughly parallel paths, with a fair amount of cross-pollination along the way, and this is where we find ourselves today.

## Modern Sound

In 1956, Louis and Bebe Barron created the first purely electronic music and sound-effects track for the movie *Forbidden Planet*. The landmark soundtrack, with its eerie effects, first brought to the attention of filmmakers the potential of electronic music. This fertile source of artistic expression has now blossomed beyond anyone's expectations. A new professional, the sound designer, has appeared. He combines sounds from various sources—electronic and acoustic—and creates the sonic landscapes that have captivated audiences everywhere.

Sound has become so important to our perception of reality that without it the visuals seem insubstantial and unreal. This brings up the philosophical question, "If a tree falls in the forest and there is no sound, did the tree really fall?" I think not. Reflect for a moment on *Star Wars* or *The Empire Strikes Back*. How many times have you seen explosions in outer space accompanied by a tremendous noise? Scientists will tell you that outer space is a vacuum, and because sound can't travel in a vacuum, the explosions would have made no noise. Didn't George Lucas know this? I'm sure he did. But he also knew something far more important: that those explosions would not have seemed convincing or substantive without the accompanying noise. Sound, it seems, can create a kind of hyperreality, and sound designers work long hours to bring that new dimension to the theaters.

## Final Thoughts

Computer-based multimedia is still in its infancy. The situation now is similar to that of the film industry in the mid-1920s; we can learn much from studying those who paved the way. The most important lesson here is that the power of sound is there to be harvested—now that the technology to apply it is accessible to everyone, there is really no excuse to be stuck producing silent "movies."

When that prehistoric painter drew his pictures on the cave walls at Lascaux, it may not have been the birth of modern animation. It certainly wasn't thirty frames per second. In fact, it was more like one frame per million years. But when that graphic was done, and he sat there looking at it with the rest of the tribe, you can be sure that someone began to sing and someone else started adding sounds.

# Chapter 2

# Using Sound in Presentations: An Overview

Now as we enter the mid-1990s, we find that the world of Hollywood has impinged upon the world of corporate computing and from this collision has sprung, full-blown, as from the head of Zeus, a new buzzword: *multimedia*. Today, expectations for compelling presentations run high, and a knowledge of sound and its applications is no longer only the domain of hobbyists and game programmers.

To sort out the field of audio for multimedia, let's go back to the original three categories of sound inherited from the movie industry and see how they relate to the somewhat different world of computer-generated presentations.

In the macrocosm of motion pictures, sound consists of three elements: dialogue (or voice), sound effects, and music. These components of the typical soundtrack are created separately, recorded on separate tracks, and kept separate throughout most of the postproduction editing process. This is due, mainly, to the differences in the way they are derived and later woven into the final aural fabric of the soundtrack. Taking these as a point of departure, let's explore some of the ways in which sound can add new dimensions to your presentations.

# Voice of Reason

The first category, voice, is most effective at conveying specific information as well as humanizing a presentation. Anyone who has seen the movie *2001* knows all too well how compelling a computer can be when it talks to you. Of course, a live speaker who talks into a microphone during a presentation adds a vocal element to a program, but generating speech from within the computer serves some other important functions. Self-running demonstrations, point-of-sale displays, and educational programs can benefit enormously from the addition of spoken words, and if the dialogue is tied to the software, the presentation can be mailed or carried around the country and reproduced with consistent results.

A speech synthesizer offers one way to add voice to your presentation. This usually comes in the form of software, such as MacinTalk, and typically requires that you type in words that it then converts into speech. The somewhat stilted and mechanical-sounding results may not be appropriate for serious presentations but may work well under some conditions. For a better solution, record speech with a digitizer: a hardware/software combination, such as MacRecorder or Voice Impact Pro, which takes the output of a microphone, converts it to digital data, and stores it as a sound file.

Although requiring a lot of memory, this excellent way to add speech to a program allows anyone to be the vocal source and results in clear and natural sound. The head of a company might, for instance, add his own voice to an interoffice memo or include a brief statement in a sales presentation to personalize his message to the audience. Alternate sound files, prepared in foreign languages by native speakers, can also allow quick and easy preparation of presentations for overseas clients. The new generation of word processors and business programs now offers voice notation capabilities, which should make these digitized messages increasingly commonplace. Apple's inclusion of digitizing hardware and software in the Mac Classic II, the LC, the IIsi, and the Quadra demonstrates undeniably the growing importance of this type of sound application to the evolution of Macintosh software.

In the field of education, the addition of speech to presentations offers enormous potential. Students can make more rapid progress in learning languages when they hear the words spoken correctly. Sight-impaired people can respond to prompts and questions in a program when presented audibly. Nearly every kind of educational program can benefit from the addition of an instructor's voice.

CD-ROM technology provides an important new application for the spoken word, when combined with a program like HyperCard, to access recordings of famous people. For instance, a program on World War II might include speeches by Winston Churchill or excerpts from newscasts of the period. Used extensively for educational and training applications, interactive CD technology has great potential for multimedia programs, allowing a presenter instant access to an impressive array of information.

## Sound and Fury

Sound effects fall roughly into two basic categories: synchronized sounds (those that appear to result from particular on-screen events) and background sounds (those that establish a sense of time and place). When used judiciously, they can make a presentation more compelling by focusing attention on specific actions or by creating a suitable background to work against. A presenter might have the sounds of a babbling brook and chirping birds running quietly in the background as he extols the virtues of a new resort development or presents the environmental policies of his corporation while showing appropriate visuals. Under the right circumstances, background sounds can add a subtle quality to your programs, but you must know your venue and your audience well. Don't expect background sounds to be anything but mush at a noisy trade show or other busy arenas.

### *Sync Sounds*

Synchronized sounds, by far the most compelling and widely used sound effects, make the actions on screen jump out at the audience. They have the great gift of entertaining the viewers while at the same time galvanizing their interest. Sound effects can be used to convey concepts in ways that words can't. One product developer, for example, asked to have the sound of electricity accompany the mouse clicks that appeared on his demo/presentation. He felt this would convey the sense of increased power that his product would bring the end user.

For a number of years, General Motors has distributed computer disks to potential customers that detail information on its latest line of Buicks. In earlier disks, HyperCard-like programs took you inside the car and introduced you to the instrumentation and other dashboard features. Revving the engine not only let you see the speedometer work but let you hear the motor. Clicking on the radio played the Buick jingle. Door locks, trunk slams, and other sounds embedded throughout the program made exploring these products both fun and memorable—a much more compelling presentation than a printed brochure.

Now we shift gears from one of the largest companies to one of the smallest. Celestial Wind Carillons of Eureka Springs, Arkansas, distributes its catalog of handmade wind chimes in the form of a HyperCard stack replete with graphics, buttons, animation, and sound effects (Figure 2.1). Clicking on the picture of each wind chime causes it to sway and lets you hear its unique sounds and tuning scale. Other buttons and icons let you explore each model in detail with pop-up fields providing definitions, historical background, technical information, descriptions, and even testimonials. You can also play the individual notes on each wind chime, so by the time you reach the Order Form page, you feel that you've actually tried out each model—a very clever and effective application of music, sound effects, and graphics. For another terrific example of a HyperCard stack with sound and graphics, see the description of The Book of MIDI in Chapter 8.

As with speech, the addition of sound effects holds great potential in educational and training programs. Can you tell the difference between the sound of a loose timing chain and a maladjusted rocker arm? An auto repair course that included sound effects could help. Doctors-in-training could study cardiac conditions by not only seeing but hearing the sounds of different types of arrhythmias. The inclusion of sounds in programs for children is especially effective because it adds an irresistible element of fun to their computing experience.

Using Sound in Presentations: An Overview 13

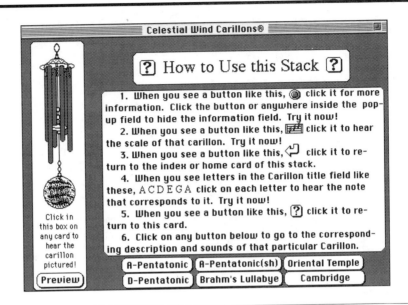

**Figure 2.1**
A sample HyperCard stack

## *Finding Sounds*

One way to add sound effects to your presentation is by installing a *music card* in your computer. Products such as Digidesign's MacProteus card, intended primarily for music applications, usually include a few dozen sound effects. Though offering very high fidelity, the sound-effects selection may be too limited for your needs. If so, you can record your own effects and save them as digitized sound files, just as you can for speech. The best way to get sound effects is to explore some of the numerous sound-effects libraries available on compact disc. Dozens of companies offer extensive libraries containing thousands of sounds intended primarily for the movie and broadcast industries.

## Music to My Ears

It might be argued that music is what really puts the *multi* in multimedia. Rapidly coming into its own as a powerful enhancement to computer presentations, music can capture the spirit of a product and carry an audience along through the most labyrinthian program. Music can establish moods, heighten transitions, and stress key points. Jingles and themes can impart a strong product identity in a way that printed text cannot.

## Sources of Music

Where can you get music for your presentations? The music industry releases records, tapes, and compact discs by the thousands each year, but beware of copyright violations! Production music libraries offer a better solution. Many of the same companies that offer sound-effects libraries produce collections of music designed specifically for broadcast and business applications. You can also get CD-ROMs filled with digitized production music ready to be edited and imported into a presentation program. But, for the very best solution, hire a composer to write a custom score for your project. In this way the music can accurately reflect your intentions and, with today's increasing number of small electronic studios, this may not cost as much as you think.

## Hardware and Software

Music can be incorporated into a presentation in much the same way as voice and sound effects. A digital audio add-on card, such as Digidesign's Audiomedia board, offers sound quality that rivals a compact disc, but the storage requirements are quite substantial. Less expensive digitizers like MacRecorder require considerably less storage, but for music purposes, they may not be of high enough fidelity for the more discerning end user.

You can obtain excellent sound quality from less memory with an add-on music card or an external MIDI sound module. A MIDI system (see Chapter 3) not only maintains high fidelity without the storage demands but it allows you to edit the music extensively with the appropriate software. If you're working with a composer, he will have to know your hardware/software configuration and write specifically for it to ensure optimum results. If you're not a composer, and you don't know one, there are many products to fill the gap, including MIDI production-music libraries offering music files that you can easily adapt to your project.

## Audio for Video

Adding sound to video presentations involves techniques more like the traditional methods used in film production. Voice, sound effects, and music are recorded on separate tracks and mixed during editing into the final product. The considerations of sound type and placement are still the same, but the approach differs somewhat from computer-generated presentations. Through the use of SMPTE *timecode* and a device that reads and writes it, many music software products can "lock" to a video picture, enabling the computer to handle the music performance while the video player supplies the visuals.

## Helpful Hints

In closing, let's review some helpful hints to keep in mind when adding sound to presentations. The most important rule is *don't overdo it*. We've all known amateur desktop publishers who one day discover changeable fonts and suddenly begin sending out newsletters that look like ransom notes. The same thing can happen with sound.

For better results follow the Zen-like maxim: Less is more. Ask yourself where the focus of the audience should be at various places throughout the presentation: text, narration, color, mood, graphics, etc. Add sound that enhances these points. Sound and visuals that are not synergistic make learning difficult. It's like trying to read a technical journal while your four-year-old son is lighting the television set on fire. Make sound effects, speech, and music work *for* you and you will be rewarded with more absorbing presentations and greater enthusiasm from your appreciative audience.

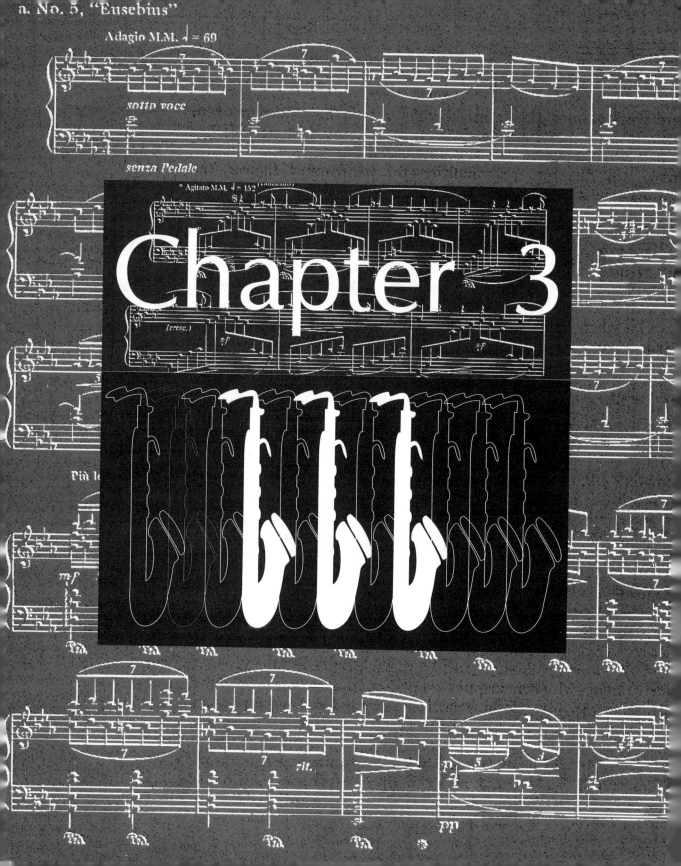

# Chapter 3

# An Introduction to MIDI

Back in the olden days—before about 1980—synthesizers were mostly analog devices. Pressing different keys on the keyboard sent different voltages to one or more oscillators, which produced the appropriate tones and pitches. Musicians discovered that by simultaneously triggering the same notes on two or more synthesizers with different settings they could create fuller, more compelling sounds. This practice, known as *layering,* led to attempts to interconnect synthesizers so that a controller keyboard—the master—could trigger sounds in another synthesizer—the slave. Unfortunately, there were no standards to ensure that one instrument would respond in the same way as another. Trying to connect a Roland drum machine to a Yamaha synthesizer or an Oberheim to a Korg was typically very troublesome and often simply impossible.

In an effort to break this technological logjam, Dave Smith, an American synthesizer maker, proposed an instrument hardware standard that he called the Universal Synthesizer Interface. Originally intended to allow the playing of two or more instruments from a single keyboard, it grew during the following year into a panoply of specifications that guaranteed a much higher level of versatility by including other functions and performance features.

In August 1983, at a meeting in Japan, the major synthesizer manufacturers, including Sequential Circuits, Yamaha, Roland, Korg, and Kawai, set aside their usually competitive instincts and established the MIDI 1.0 Specification. In the following year, MIDI became the hottest new item in the electronic music industry. Now it's virtually impossible to find any synthesizers or peripherals that don't have some MIDI capability.

## What Is MIDI?

MIDI stands for Musical Instrument Digital Interface. The MIDI Specification describes in detail the types of cables and connectors that must be used as well as the digital codes and commands that compatible instruments can transmit and receive. In other words, MIDI is a protocol for transmitting data between devices in a musical network. Furthermore, it is a serial interface transferring data at 31.25 kBaud and can transmit in two directions at one time, but not on the same cable. For this reason, a fully implemented MIDI device will always have at least two connectors in the back, labeled In and Out.

Most synthesizers also have a connector called MIDI Thru. This port sends out a direct copy of the data received at the MIDI In jack and provides a practical means of chaining together MIDI devices in a system with more than two components. Figure 3.1 shows the three MIDI ports.

The following sections describe some of the important features that MIDI devices incorporate into their designs.

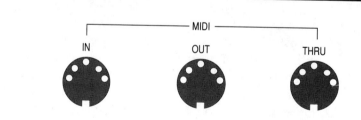

**Figure 3.1**
The three MIDI ports

## Connections

To transmit data between MIDI devices, you need a special type of serial cable. MIDI cables use a common five-pin DIN connector, the same kind often found on European hi-fi equipment. Pins 4 and 5 carry the digital signal, and pin 2 is used for grounding. The cables should not exceed 50 feet to prevent data transmission errors, although there are products that can extend this range.

To play one instrument from another, you simply connect the MIDI Out port on the master to the MIDI In port on the slave. To establish a bidirectional data flow, you must add a second cable connecting the MIDI Out of the slave to the MIDI In of the master. Then either instrument can transmit or receive performance information to or from the other (Figure 3.2).

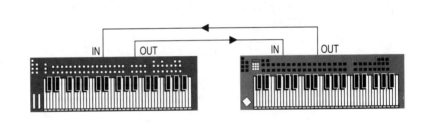

**Figure 3.2**
A simple bidirectional MIDI system

## Channels

In a setup involving several instruments, it is important to ensure that the data reaches only the appropriate devices or there will be a great jumble of noise as each synthesizer tries to respond to all the incoming information. MIDI, therefore, provides 16 channels to subdivide and organize the flow of MIDI data. It's important to remember that the MIDI cables are *not* carrying audio information, where different channels or tracks would require separate cables. MIDI cables carry digital data that has the channel information embedded in the computer code; all of it flows through a single line. The receiving instruments choose which data applies to them (according to their individual settings) as it comes through the cable.

The most common analogy is that of a television set receiving its signal from a cable TV company. A single cable is attached to the set and provides several channels simultaneously. You can determine which channel to watch by setting the channel selector on the television. If you have several different television sets connected to the same cable, you can have each one receiving a different channel.

## Modes

In addition to the 16 basic MIDI channels, there are also MIDI *modes*. These modes determine how the receiving device responds to the incoming channel data. In Omni mode all MIDI data on all channels is recognized. In Poly mode the receiving instrument responds only to a designated channel. In Mono mode individual voices (instrument sounds) respond to specific channels.

## Messages

When you create music on a MIDI keyboard, the performance is converted into digital information consisting of a series of messages that are sent to the MIDI Out port. There are many kinds of MIDI messages, but here are some of the most common ones.

The most important message is *note on*. This information goes out every time a note is played. The MIDI Specification provides for a range of 128 notes, numbered from 0 to 127. Middle C on a piano corresponds to MIDI note number 60. The lowest note on a piano (A1) corresponds to MIDI note number 21, and the highest note (C88) corresponds to MIDI note 108.

Most synthesizers also provide *velocity* data that tells how hard a key is struck. The *note off* message indicates that the key has been released. Many instruments also recognize *aftertouch* or *pressure data*, which describes how hard a key is pressed after it is played and until it is released. Aftertouch is an example of *continuous data* because its messages are represented as a string of values rather than a single event. Velocity and aftertouch data can be used to control certain aspects of a sound's parameters, such as loudness or timbre.

Another common type of continuous data, *pitch bend,* is usually produced with a wheel or lever on the keyboard. It allows you to slide pitches up or down to simulate instruments like the trombone or guitar that can "scoop" or "bend" notes. *Program change* messages tell a synthesizer to change sounds. *Clock* messages are used in synchronizing several MIDI devices during playback of a performance. *System-exclusive* messages enable you to transfer data to a specific brand of synthesizer to access the parameters of its internal architecture (see Chapter 9).

# MIDI and the Mac

It wasn't long before musicians discovered that the great power that MIDI conferred upon them for live performance was only the tip of the technological iceberg. The true power of MIDI came to the fore when MIDI instruments were coupled to computers. Because MIDI is a digital interface, and because computers speak digital all the time, it was truly love at first sight.

Macintoshes, however, don't come with MIDI ports as standard equipment. Therefore, the first thing you need to connect your computer to a MIDI system is a MIDI interface. This is a small box, sometimes as small as a pack of cigarettes. The larger units are often designed to mount in a standard 19-inch audio rack or to sit under the Mac much like an external hard disk. Different makes and models offer an array of features, with prices ranging from well below a hundred to several hundred dollars.

The MIDI interface attaches to the Mac's modem and/or printer port and provides one or more MIDI In and Out ports for connecting to the MIDI hardware. MIDI interfaces that connect to both the printer and modem ports can act as two independent units, allowing you to access the 16 MIDI channels through each cable, giving you a total of 32 channels. These interfaces typically offer a bypass switch so that you can use your printer and modem without disconnecting anything.

# Sounds from Circuits

To complete your basic computer-MIDI system, you need some kind of sound-generating device. Currently, there is a rich cornucopia of synthesizers available at your local electronic-music store, and because they invariably have MIDI capability, you can select any brand according to price and available features. The different manufacturers have devised different methods of generating musical sounds, using complex digital-processing schemes. Yamaha has championed FM (frequency modulation) synthesis. Roland uses linear arithmetic, or LA, synthesis. You may also encounter additive synthesis, digital resynthesis, wavetable synthesis, and interactive phase-distortion synthesis.

There are many ways of creating the varied timbres of musical sounds by algorithmically manipulating digital data. The important thing to remember is that no one method is necessarily any better than another. Your choice should be determined by the kinds of sounds you're looking for and how intuitive you find the instrument's user interface. Other considerations, in addition to price, might be availability of additional sounds and specific performance features.

*Sound modules* are essentially the same as synthesizers except that they lack the attached keyboard. They are the sound-producing component of a synthesizer mounted in a compact case. Many synthesizers come in a sound module version. I often use the terms *synthesizer* and *sound module* interchangeably since their functions in a MIDI system are usually the same.

Because of their attached keyboards and greater size, synthesizers may provide some benefits for live performances and stage shows, but for the average desktop multimedia producer or MIDI-Macintosh creator, collecting multiple keyboards is both cumbersome and space consuming. I recommend sticking with sound modules whenever possible. They are usually rack-mountable, require little space, and are easily transportable.

Many of the sound modules on the market today have *multitimbral* capability. This means that they can produce several different instrument sounds simultaneously. By assigning separate MIDI channels to the different sounds, you can create instrumental ensembles, such as a woodwind trio (flute, oboe, clarinet), a jazz combo (sax, guitar, piano, bass, drums), or any other combination of sounds available in that sound module.

*Polyphony* refers to the ability of an instrument to play more than one note at a time—an essential characteristic of all multitimbral instruments. When shopping for a sound module, be aware of the multitimbral and polyphonic capabilities of the instrument. For instance, an eight-voice multitimbral synthesizer with 16-note polyphony can play as many as 16 notes simultaneously spread over as many as eight different instrument sounds. It's easy to see that with one or two good multitimbral sound modules, you can have a veritable orchestra or big band on your desktop.

## Getting Started with MIDI

There are many ways to create a MIDI-Macintosh system. You must consider your intended use and anticipated needs as well as your budget when shopping for hardware. Do you have limited space in your office or studio? Will you need to carry the system around with you to trade shows, sales meetings, or public schools? Will you be composing your own music or using someone else's? Do you have to synchronize to videotape for film scoring or sound effects? And finally, what kinds of sounds most interest you: electronic, rock, commercial pop, or traditional? If you're like me you'll have a hard time limiting yourself to very specific criteria, so my first suggestion is to strive for versatility and flexibility.

### *Speakers of the House*

Any MIDI system needs some kind of amplifier/speaker arrangement for playback purposes. In some cases you can listen to your sound module with headphones, but this is obviously not suitable for presentations. Your home stereo will work just fine, but it may be impractical to locate it near your computer. There are also rack-mountable power amplifiers that will drive large speakers for presentations in auditoriums, but for most people, working in a limited space with limited resources, there is another choice.

Several companies now offer compact, self-powered, desktop speakers especially designed for use with your computer. These speakers have magnetically shielded cases to prevent stray magnetism from distorting the screen image, and they often come color-coordinated to match your Macintosh. Their built-in amplifiers, though not powerful enough for large audiences, should prove quite adequate for work at home or for presentations to small groups. If you have a single sound module, hookup is easy. Using standard audio cables, connect the audio outputs from the sound module to the speakers. At least one of the speakers will provide controls for adjusting the volume and balance.

## All Systems Go

The systems that I discuss in this section are intended to be cost effective, easy to set up, and if necessary, transportable. They are designed to work well with the kinds of desktop presentation programs mentioned later in this book. The simplest system consists of the Macintosh, a MIDI interface, and a sound module (Figure 3.3). This arrangement serves quite well as a playback system for presequenced MIDI music (see Chapter 7). Many multimedia producers are not interested in composing their own music, choosing instead to skip to the editing and playback stages of production. If you are one of these people, this setup should prove adequate. The sound module must be multitimbral, with no less than 16-note polyphony—twice that is much better.

Since this setup has no MIDI keyboard, it is difficult (though not impossible) to use it for composing music. To keep the same basic arrangement,

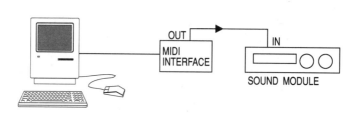

**Figure 3.3**
A basic MIDI playback system

# An Introduction to MIDI

but as a bidirectional system, you need to replace the sound module with a multitimbral synthesizer that has a built-in keyboard (Figure 3.4). Then you can play music into the Macintosh and have the computer send the data back to the synthesizer.

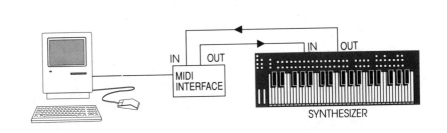

**Figure 3.4**
The simplest arrangement for recording and playing MIDI music with your Macintosh

## Keys to Success

If you have an interest in performing and composing music, you should consider a much better, though more expensive, alternative. Adding a MIDI keyboard controller to your setup (Figure 3.5) provides you with greater versatility and allows you to stick to using sound modules, which, in my opinion, are more suitable for desktop presentations and multimedia than are bulky synthesizers.

MIDI keyboard controllers send out MIDI data but do not make any sounds of their own. They offer several advantages over dedicated keyboards attached to synthesizers. For one thing you have a wide range of types and styles to choose from. Some keyboards have a soft, mushy feel similar to that of an organ, and others offer a heavier, more piano-like touch. There are keyboards with only a four- or five-octave range and others that provide a full 88 notes.

By selecting your keyboard separately, you can base your decision on the design and feel of the keyboard while selecting your sound modules according to their sounds and features. This way you can avoid being stuck with a combination you don't like. If you must travel with your MIDI system, the

**Figure 3.5**
Adding a MIDI keyboard controller

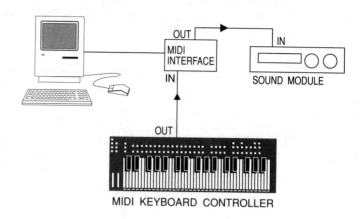

keyboard can stay at home because it is used only for composing the music, not for playing it back.

Incidentally, MIDI controllers come in forms other than keyboards. There are controllers for sax players, guitarists, and drummers, and there are retrofit kits for converting acoustic pianos into MIDI keyboards. Still, MIDI keyboard controllers remain the most precise and best-implemented devices for MIDI data input.

# The More the Merrier: Expanding Your System

Once you've acquired a MIDI keyboard and sound module, you may decide to expand the size of your desktop orchestra by adding one or more sound modules. This is easily done by chaining together the modules using their MIDI Thru connectors (Figure 3.6). For a system using several sound modules, it's a good idea to choose from different makes and models to provide a richer, wider palette of timbres when combining sounds. This can help to avoid a certain sameness of sounds that can occur with more limited systems.

**Figure 3.6**
Adding more sound modules to your system

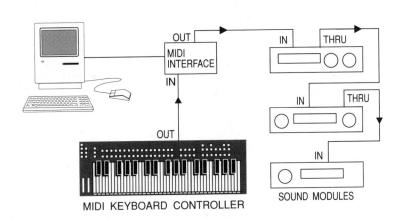

## *More on Interfaces*

If you think you'll be expanding your MIDI setup in the future with additional sound modules, or if you plan to combine your system with an audio or a video recorder, I recommend purchasing one of the more expensive MIDI interfaces. These units offer several important features. For one thing, they attach to both serial ports on the Macintosh, providing 32 channels of MIDI. The MIDI Time Piece from Mark of the Unicorn can expand that number to well over a hundred with the proper software. These interfaces also provide *timecode* reading/writing capabilities, which enable you to synchronize some brands of music software to an audio- or videotape recorder. Finally, these units provide multiple MIDI In and Out ports so that your system can be configured in a more efficient and flexible manner (Figure 3.7).

## All Mixed Up

If you use a basic system like the one shown in Figure 3.3, hooking up the audio lines should pose no problem. Most sound modules provide stereo output jacks that you simply connect to the stereo input jacks of your hi-fi or self-powered speakers. But what do you do if you have several instruments in your setup? Add an audio mixer to the system.

**Figure 3.7**
The best multi-instrument configuration

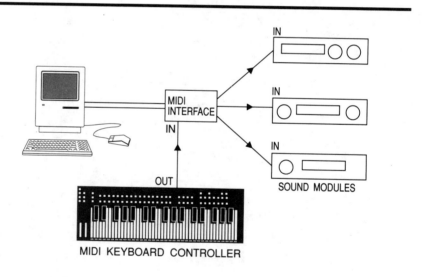

There are many kinds of mixers currently available, ranging in price from a few hundred dollars to many thousands of dollars. For the needs of most desktop multimedia producers, an inexpensive, rack-mountable *line mixer* works just fine. Then you can take the audio outputs from each instrument in the system and plug them into the inputs of the mixer (Figure 3.8). The mixer combines the individual signals into a stereo signal and routes it to the stereo output jacks. You simply take these outputs and connect them to the inputs of your hi-fi or self-powered speakers. Each audio input on the mixer has its own volume control, so it's easy to adjust the loudness of the different instrument sounds.

Some music programs (especially sequencers; see Chapter 5) provide on-screen *faders* that enable you to automate your mixes through the software by sending MIDI *volume* messages during playback (Figure 3.9). This way

**Figure 3.8**
Using a mixer to combine audio signals

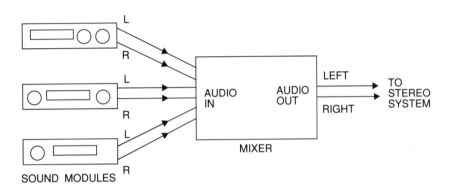

**Figure 3.9**
Typical on-screen faders

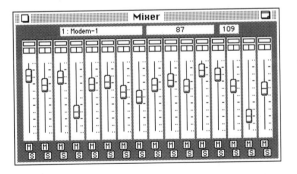

you can preset the line mixer and let the program handle the volume adjustments automatically during the performance. When the fader settings are saved along with the program's music file, you can re-create the identical mix anytime you want.

## Samplers, Synths, and Cymbals

In the broadest sense, electronic instruments fall into one of two large categories: synthesizers and samplers. Synthesizers create their sounds either by applying voltages to oscillators or by simulating the effects of oscillators by applying digital data to complex algorithmic formulas. They synthesize their sounds internally. *Samplers,* on the other hand, use a completely different approach to sound production. As with synthesizers, they are available in both keyboard and sound module versions. Samplers work by first making short digital recordings, or *samples,* of sounds. These sounds are then edited and *mapped* across the keyboard to create a performance setup that can be saved on a disk. Samplers are to music what scanners are to graphics: They take an external source, digitize it, and save it to be edited and applied as needed.

Each sample can be played over a specified range, with its pitch determined by the key that plays it. Because the sampler is a specialized digital recorder, it can use anything as the source for its sounds. If you take several samples of a section of basses, cellos, violas, and violins and map them across the keyboard, you can create a string ensemble. But samplers aren't limited to recording musical instruments. They can record vocal phrases, cars crashing, and glass breaking. If you sample several dogs barking and map the sounds across the keyboard, you can perform a barking-dog ensemble.

You can also experiment with altering sounds. For instance, you might sample the sound of a frog and play it down two octaves to produce an entirely new animal sound. Or you might turn the sound of timpani into the sound of toy bongos by playing the sample up three octaves. Samplers are a favorite tool of sound designers and other audio postproduction professionals, who use them extensively for sound-effects work. Musicians appreciate them for their ability to realistically re-create acoustic instrument sounds.

If a sampler lacks the ability to make its own samples, it is called a sample-playback module. In recent years, sample-playback modules have increased in popularity. Instruments such as E-mu's Proteus module are well suited to music production for desktop presentations. The Proteus lacks the disk drive common to most true samplers and instead stores its sounds in ROM. This reduces the cost of the unit and increases greatly the speed of accessing the sounds because disk-swapping problems are eliminated. Although you can't add new sounds to the unit, the sounds that it has are quite good. Similar products are sure to follow.

Samplers lack the extensive sound-creating capabilities that synthesizers possess, and they're not as effective at controlling and modifying sounds over time as synthesizers are. Unlike synthesizers, samplers also require a great deal of memory for their sounds. Samplers do, however, excel at creating certain types of sounds and can do things that no synthesizer ever could. Some instruments even combine sampled attack sounds with synthesized sustains to gain more realism with less memory.

The decision as to which type of module is right for you should be based on the kinds of music you'll be creating, the specific applications that you use, and your own personal tastes in sound-production techniques. Many musicians include both types of sound modules in their systems to gain the best of both worlds.

*Drum machines* are specialized sound modules that are designed specifically to create percussion sounds. These sounds may be either synthesized or sampled; some drum machines mix the two. In addition to the on-board percussion sounds (which include drums, cymbals, and Latin instruments), drum machines always have a dedicated sequencer that is optimized for producing rhythm patterns—typically, one to four measures long. You can then combine these patterns in various ways to create longer rhythm tracks.

Most drum machines come with a number of drum patterns already installed in memory, but you can create your own either by entering notes one at a time (step entry) or by playing the drum sounds in real time by tapping on the appropriate buttons or pads. You can also trigger the internal drum sounds from your MIDI keyboard if you prefer. Patterns and tracks that you create (by any method) can be transferred to your sequencer program for further editing.

Because drum machines have their own on-board sequencers, they are a little trickier to incorporate into the simple MIDI systems that I've discussed. To avoid conflicts between your software sequencer and the drum machine, I recommend working out your rhythm tracks on the drum machine first and then transferring them to the computer. The drum machine can then act as another playback-only sound module, providing high-quality percussion sounds to complement the other instruments in the system.

Many styles of music do not need a rhythm track, and many MIDI musicians will be quite satisfied with the drum sounds that come with their sound modules, so a drum machine is not an essential element for successful soundtrack production. Furthermore, many of the high-end sequencer programs covered in Chapter 5 offer drum-machine-style recording options that may preclude the need for a second device. Still, many people find that drum machines provide a valuable means of working out their ideas and creating background rhythms to build their other tracks on.

# Chapter 4

# All about Sequencers

The term *sequencer* goes back to the early days of analog synthesizers when circuits were created that could store and trigger a sequence of simple note events. Of course, there have been sequencer-like devices for hundreds of years if you count music boxes and other music-making machines. But, in my opinion, the early ancestor of the modern sequencer was surely the player piano. It was with the player piano that an important concept became widely appreciated. A musical performance can be captured and then reproduced *independently* of either the performer or the instrument.

When a musician sat at a specialized "recording" piano and played a piece of music, his performance was captured as a pattern of holes on a roll of paper. This was the equivalent of a floppy disk at the turn of the century, and it served its purpose quite well. If that paper roll was carried across town and installed in a compatible piano, those little holes could re-create the original performance by providing the host piano with information on notes, rhythms, pedaling, etc.

From our standpoint, though, the great significance of this development lies not so much in the reproduction of music but in the fact that the sound of the music could be changed while maintaining the performance. If you played that roll on a "tack" piano, it would sound like a harpsichord. If you played it on a piano with a piece of felt in front of the strings, it would sound soft and muted. And if you played it on a piano that was tuned a half-step flat, the music was re-created in another key.

It wasn't long before pianists and composers realized that you could edit (though not easily) the paper rolls to correct mistakes or create compositions unplayable by a single person. The ability to store performance data, to provide a means of editing that data, and to allow a variety of sounds to be associated with the data presaged the evolution of the modern MIDI sequencer by several decades.

I have taken this brief sojourn in history to stress an important fundamental concept: A sequencer does not record sounds the way a tape recorder does. It records performance data, which it stores in the form of MIDI messages: note on, note off, velocity, pitch bend, aftertouch, etc. The ability to choose which instrument sounds you'll attach to this data is what makes a sequencer such a powerful tool. It can be both a musical sketch-pad and an intensive editing environment for creating a finished product.

In addition to allowing you to reorchestrate your music easily, sequencers provide the power to correct rhythmic inaccuracies, change pitch, and alter dynamics and note durations. You can also make broad alterations to your pieces by transposing to other keys, changing tempos, or rearranging the sections of a composition. In this way a sequencer acts much like a word processor for music and even has many of the same menu items, such as Cut, Copy, and Paste.

A few years ago the companies that produced sequencer software took decidedly different approaches to the handling of MIDI data for editing. Over the past couple of years, however, the natural Darwinism of the MIDI marketplace has compelled manufacturers to adopt many of the features of their competitors. As consumers, we have benefited from this development because the current breed of sequencers have evolved into powerful, feature-rich editing environments, and even the less-expensive programs boast an impressive list of attributes. Nonetheless, there are differences in the architectural designs of these products, as well as some specific qualities, that will appeal to different people. First let's explore the characteristics that most sequencers share before examining individual programs more closely.

## ▣ Sequencer Anatomy

The main entity that you work with in a sequencer program is called, not surprisingly, a *sequence*. A sequence can consist of an entire composition or a few short fragments of music. In theory, its size can range from a single note to a seemingly infinite number of notes, limited only by the available RAM in your computer.

Sequences are divided into *tracks*, which resemble, in function, the tracks on a multitrack tape recorder. When you play a sequence, all the tracks associated with that sequence play together. The number of tracks provided for each sequence varies from one program to another. Inexpensive sequencers may provide as few as sixteen tracks, while high-end, pro-level sequencers often provide around a hundred.

Don't confuse tracks with channels. The term *channels* refers to the 16 MIDI channels that I discussed in Chapter 3. Channels determine which sound modules will respond to which MIDI data as it's transmitted through the cable. Tracks contain the performance data that forms the sequence.

Much of the time each track will be assigned a single MIDI channel. The flute part, for example, could be recorded onto track 1 and assigned to play on channel 6, which would trigger the appropriate flute sound from the corresponding sound module. The oboe might be track 2, channel 3, and the clarinet might be track 3, channel 5.

Most sequencers also allow you to assign more than one MIDI channel to a single track. If you assign MIDI channels 3, 6, and 7 to track 1, you can have three different instrument sounds responding to the performance data on track 1. This is an easy way to combine, or *layer*, sounds to fatten an orchestration.

On the other hand, you will often want to assign several sequencer tracks to a single MIDI channel. This is especially useful for creating "exploded" drum parts, where the hi-hat is on track 1, the ride cymbal on track 2, the snare drum on 3, the kick drum on 4, etc. You then assign these tracks to a single MIDI channel to trigger the drum sounds from your sound module. Separating the different parts of the drum set enables you to edit each part quickly without affecting the others. You might also want to separate the right and left hands of a piano part, for instance, and send them to a single piano sound on a single channel. It should be clear from these examples that a complex orchestration can easily consume a great many tracks in a sequence.

To compose music on a sequencer, you usually start by recording a track and assigning it to an instrument sound. Next, while listening to that track, you record a second track. You then listen to both tracks while adding a third and repeat the procedure until the composition is complete. The process is very similar to the way you might record a composition on a multi-track tape deck.

## Getting Around

To facilitate the process of maneuvering around in a composition, all sequencers have a *controls window* that is modeled after the transport controls of a conventional tape deck (Figure 4.1). These controls, however, are a significant improvement over the buttons on a mechanical tape recorder because they produce precise and instantaneous results at the click of a mouse.

**Figure 4.1**
A typical controls window

Closely associated with the controls window, the *counter window* (Figure 4.2) provides information about your location in a sequence. Most commonly, this takes the form of a readout indicating the current measure, beat, and fraction of a beat as the music progresses. All sequencers divide their beats into subdivisions called ticks, clocks, or pulses. The greater the number of these subdivisions, the higher the sequencer's timing resolution. A higher resolution means a more accurate reproduction of the rhythmic nuances in a performance. Most pro-level sequencers use a resolution of 480 pulses per quarter note (ppqn). Other common figures are 240 and 192 ppqn. In addition to the measure/beat indicator, more advanced programs provide an elapsed-time readout, and some also offer a SMPTE timecode display for working with external devices.

**Figure 4.2**
A counter window showing the three types of displays

Most sequencers offer two methods to enter music into the computer. The first method, called *real-time recording,* I have already described. The second method, called *step entry,* enables you to enter notes, one at a time, by selecting each pitch and assigning it a rhythmic value and velocity. Because the notes entered this way all have precise rhythmic placement, the resulting music often tends to sound a bit robotic. But this method can be useful in situations where a passage would be difficult or impossible to perform.

If you record in real time, you can use the metronome option (Figure 4.3) that all sequencers provide. Most of the time you can choose between having the Macintosh produce the clicks internally or having your MIDI sound module play a note that you specify. You can also elect to have a one- or two-measure count-off before the sequencer begins recording.

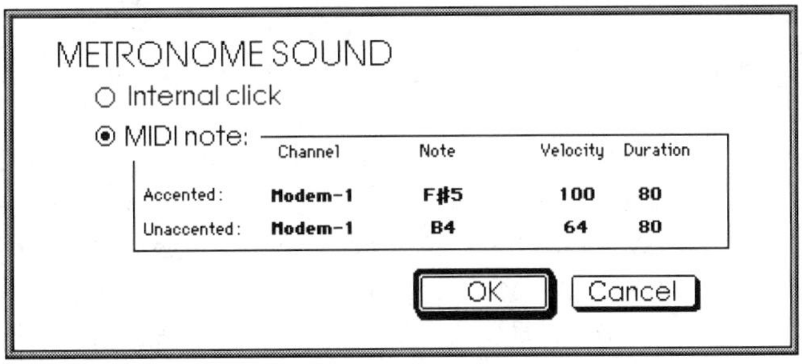

**Figure 4.3**
A metronome options dialog box

## Fascinatin' Rhythm

Once you have recorded some music onto a track, you can edit the placement of the notes to correct for any rhythmic inaccuracies or to tighten up the performance. This process, known as *quantization,* involves moving the notes to align them with the nearest specified beat. Any rhythmic value, such as quarter note, eighth note, sixteenth note, etc., may be chosen. If you select eighth-note quantization, for example, all notes in the selected region will be moved to the nearest eighth-note beat.

Quantization can be a double-edged sword, however. Overly quantized passages can sound mechanized and lifeless. To counteract this situation, many sequencers now offer a *humanize* function, which introduces a small degree of random inaccuracy to music that has been step-entered or heavily quantized. Some programs also offer a range of quantizing strengths that allow you to select how rigidly the quantization will be applied and to which notes.

## Command Performance

In addition to quantization, there are a number of other global editing commands that are now commonplace in sequencer programs. The *transpose* function enables you to change the key of any selected area by raising or lowering all the notes in the region by a specified amount. The more sophisticated programs also allow you to change from major to minor or vice versa. In a similar manner, sequencers can change the *velocity* and *duration* of a group of notes according to various user-defined criteria.

## Through the Window

Whether you're selecting groups of notes for global editing or trying to change the value of a single note at the microscopic level, you need an intuitive and versatile editing environment to achieve the best results. To this end, sequencers offer one or more of three different types of windows to display MIDI data for selection and editing.

The *event list window* (Figure 4.4) is the most common and the best suited to making precise alterations of individual MIDI event parameters. The window displays events alphanumerically in a vertical list, using small icons or abbreviations to indicate the kinds of events being represented. Each line on the list includes the measure and beat of each event followed by the relevant data. A note event, for instance, would include the pitch name along with values for the velocity and duration. Any value can be changed with precision by selecting it and entering a new number. You can select groups of notes quickly by clicking and dragging across several lines, and some programs allow selection of noncontiguous events as well.

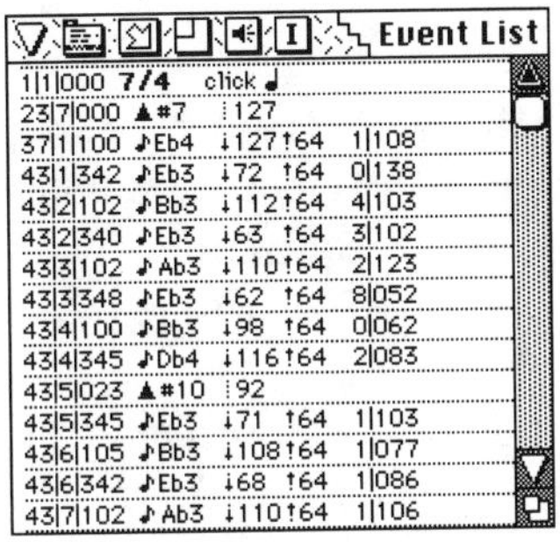

**Figure 4.4**
A typical event-list window

Many sequencers base their editing on a *graphic display window* commonly referred to as a "piano-roll" display (Figure 4.5). In this approach, notes appear as bars or lines of varying lengths—the longer the line, the longer the note duration. The note events are superimposed on a grid that represents pitch along the vertical axis and time along the horizontal axis. The appearance is reminiscent of the old paper piano rolls.

Graphic displays offer the advantage of a much more intuitive user interface, which more closely resembles the appearance of written music. Event lists, although allowing for great accuracy, do not provide a very good sense of elapsed time or note relationships the way a graphic display does. By selecting a note, you can drag it up or down to change its pitch and left or right to change its position in a measure. Groups of notes can be selected and moved together to a new location. Duration is altered by grabbing and

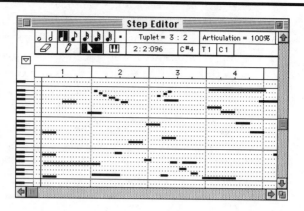

**Figure 4.5**
A graphic editing window, often called a piano-roll display

extending or shortening the length of the note line. Many editing activities lend themselves more readily to one or the other type of display. For this reason, most sequencers provide both types of windows, with any changes made in one window reflected instantaneously in the other.

The third and least common display, the *notation window*, represents notes in the form of standard musical notation (Figure 4.6). This is the least accurate and least versatile of the window displays, because standard notation does not indicate precise rhythmic placements or durations. It is a much more general view of the music that, nonetheless, offers some unique benefits for those who read music. For example, music notation provides the best way to analyze a passage harmonically. If you hear a wrong note in a chord in measure 7 on beat 3, the mistake will stand out more clearly when seen in the context of musical notes rather than lines on a grid or numbers on a list. For similar reasons, it's also easier to work with melodies in this format.

One disadvantage of the notation display is that it takes up a lot of space horizontally on the screen to show a relatively small amount of elapsed time. This can make it difficult to get an overview of large sections of music. Many people, though, feel more comfortable working with standard notation and will appreciate the option of seeing their music with notes, flags, beams, and clefs.

**Figure 4.6**
A few programs also display notes in standard musical notation.

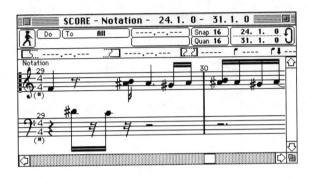

## ▬ Sum of the Parts

Sequencer programs use two different approaches to structuring and assembling sequences. Some programs favor the *linear-style,* or "through-composed," approach, in which a sequence is seen as one long continuous unit. Others favor the *pattern-song* approach, in which you create sequences out of smaller sections that are combined into a larger sequence.

In truth, the two styles are often not as different as they once were. Many pattern-song-style sequencers allow you to create sections of any length so that one long block can be an entire sequence. On the other hand, some linear-style sequencers now offer options that enable you to assemble several shorter sequences into one large composition. Different companies, however, have different philosophies about the best way to compose music. It would pay to examine this aspect of the programs before you purchase one, especially if you write exclusively in one style.

In Chapter 5, we'll take a look at some of the leading software sequencers currently on the market.

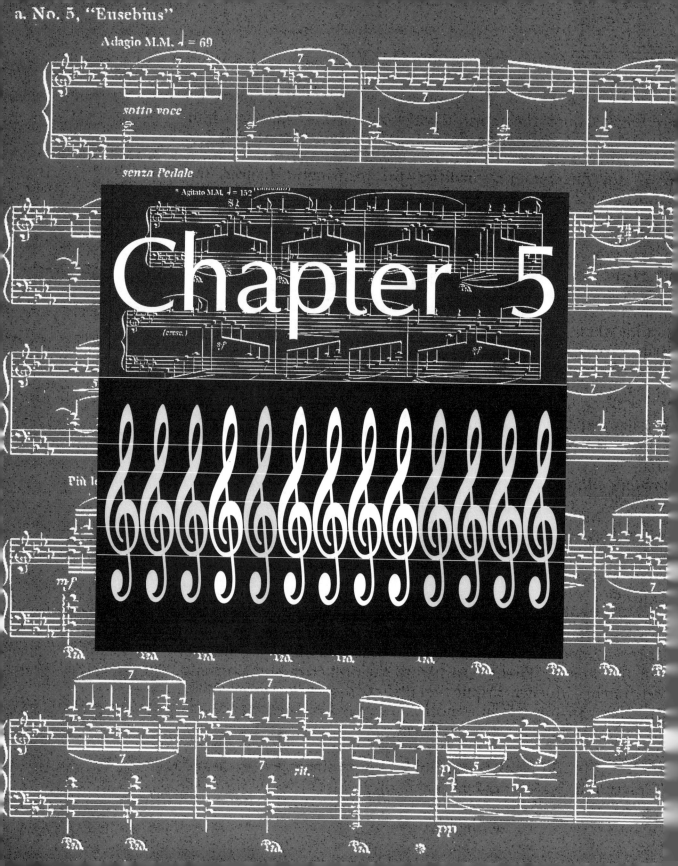

# Chapter 5

# Sequencing at the Top

The programs discussed in this chapter—Performer, Vision, Beyond, Master Tracks Pro 5, and Cubase—represent the highest level of sequencing software currently available. They are intended to satisfy the demands of professional composers, but will serve equally well for less advanced users or those whose interests lean more toward precise, flexible editing than simply capturing performances. At an average retail price of around $500 (except for Beyond), they are clearly aimed at the serious MIDI user who doesn't want to be limited by software lacking power and control. High-end sequencers all provide at least two or three different editing environments, support for SMPTE timecode, real-time editing capability, and several modes for recording data. They can handle complex MIDI configurations and are structured to accommodate the most intricate musical compositions. Many of these programs are large and require at least two megs of RAM and a hard disk—be sure to check the system requirements before buying.

## ▬ Performer

Performer, from Mark of the Unicorn, is one of the oldest and most popular of the professional-level sequencers. Its impressive list of features combined with its jazzy-looking, monochrome graphics has made it a kind of benchmark of the music industry. Although Performer is one of the most powerful sequencers on the market, its layered structure and thoughtfully designed, intuitive user interface make it relatively easy to navigate the program.

Performer centers its activities on its Tracks window, which is actually two different windows (Tracks List and Tracks Overview) integrated into a single work area that allows you to create, define, and organize the contents of each sequence (Figure 5.1). The Tracks List displays the names of, MIDI channels for, and other important information about the instruments and sounds that form your composition. Performer lets you create as many tracks as you need, limited only by the available memory in your computer. Furthermore, both the modem and printer ports can be used at the same time and performance data can be recorded simultaneously on several tracks from multiple MIDI channels. If you prefer, you can list the "devices" (synths, modules, etc.) by name with their associated "patches" (instrument sounds) rather than by MIDI channel numbers. A Comments column provides space to annotate each track with information concerning the details of your setup and performance.

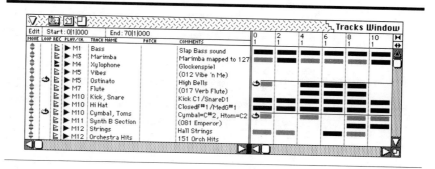

**Figure 5.1** Performer's Tracks window shows the presence of MIDI data in a graphic format along with a list of the instruments and settings in a sequence.

The Tracks Overview displays MIDI data as equal-sized segments, each representing a user-defined number of measures. Black segments represent measures with a large number of MIDI events. Gray segments represent measures with a small number of events. Measures with no data are left white.

This overview of track activity makes it easy to determine which instruments are playing and when they start and stop. Once you find an area that requires closer examination, you can click on the appropriate segment and immediately enter the editing window of your choice, which will display that segment's data in greater detail.

Above the tracks, the Time Ruler provides a reference for locating your position in the sequence. Typically, this appears as a series of measure numbers, but Performer can also display elapsed time and SMPTE timecode numbers if you are working with film or video.

Recording and playback in Performer are initiated in the Controls window (Figure 5.2), which emulates the transport-control panel of a conventional tape recorder. Aside from the usual Play, Record, Rewind, Pause, and Stop buttons, there are a number of buttons along the bottom of the window that activate certain automating functions involving recording, rewinding, shuttling between points, and auto punch-in/out capability. Between the main transport controls and the auxiliary buttons, a scroll bar with a movable indicator follows the progress of the sequence. By dragging the indicator to a new position, you can immediately begin recording or playing back from that point.

**Figure 5.2** Performer's Consolidated Controls Panel combines its transport controls with its Metronome and Counter windows.

Performer allows you to access all of the above transport controls and many of the auxiliary functions from the Macintosh keyboard or a MIDI controller keyboard. The Remote Controls window (Figure 5.3) displays the available functions and allows you to designate which MIDI notes or Macintosh keys will trigger them. Unnecessary controls can be deleted and others can be combined into subgroups. Having remote-control capability enables you to access the essential operating controls of Performer without having to reach for the mouse or take your hands away from your MIDI keyboard. Depending on your studio setup, this can be a valuable feature.

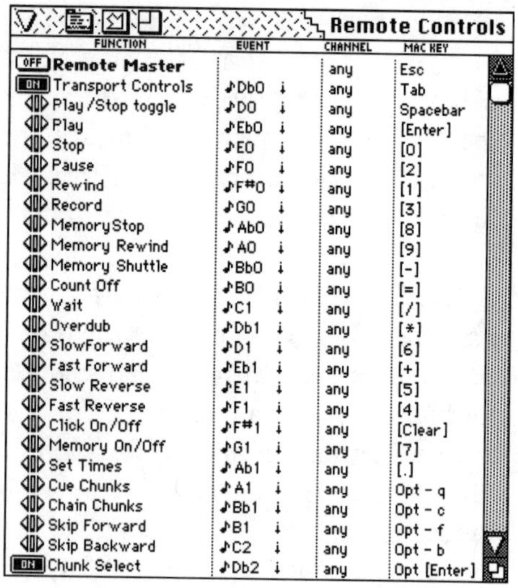

**Figure 5.3**
The Remote Controls window lets you assign a MIDI note or Macintosh key equivalent to any of numerous transport functions.

| FUNCTION | EVENT | CHANNEL | MAC KEY |
|---|---|---|---|
| [OFF] Remote Master | | any | Esc |
| [ON] Transport Controls | ♪Db0 ↓ | any | Tab |
| Play/Stop toggle | ♪D0 ↓ | any | Spacebar |
| Play | ♪Eb0 ↓ | any | [Enter] |
| Stop | ♪E0 ↓ | any | [0] |
| Pause | ♪F0 ↓ | any | [2] |
| Rewind | ♪F#0 ↓ | any | [1] |
| Record | ♪G0 ↓ | any | [3] |
| Memory Stop | ♪Ab0 ↓ | any | [8] |
| Memory Rewind | ♪A0 ↓ | any | [9] |
| Memory Shuttle | ♪Bb0 ↓ | any | [-] |
| Count Off | ♪B0 ↓ | any | [=] |
| Wait | ♪C1 ↓ | any | [/] |
| Overdub | ♪Db1 ↓ | any | [*] |
| Slow Forward | ♪D1 ↓ | any | [6] |
| Fast Forward | ♪Eb1 ↓ | any | [+] |
| Slow Reverse | ♪E1 ↓ | any | [5] |
| Fast Reverse | ♪F1 ↓ | any | [4] |
| Click On/Off | ♪F#1 ↓ | any | [Clear] |
| Memory On/Off | ♪G1 ↓ | any | [7] |
| Set Times | ♪Ab1 ↓ | any | [.] |
| Cue Chunks | ♪A1 ↓ | any | Opt - q |
| Chain Chunks | ♪Bb1 ↓ | any | Opt - c |
| Skip Forward | ♪B1 ↓ | any | Opt - f |
| Skip Backward | ♪C2 ↓ | any | Opt - b |
| [ON] Chunk Select | ♪Db2 ↓ | any | Opt [Enter] |

Working in conjunction with the Controls window, the Counter window shows the current location in the sequence. Usually this is represented in terms of measures, beats, and ticks, but Performer also provides the option of displaying elapsed time and SMPTE time. By clicking on any number in the display, you can type in a new location and instantly start from that spot. With a timing resolution of 480 ticks per quarter note, this allows for extremely precise positioning within the sequence.

Below the Counter display, four buttons lead directly to the different editing windows while a fifth sets loops within a selected region. Closely allied with the two windows above, the Metronome window displays the current meter and tempo of the music. In the middle of the window, a graphic slider can be dragged toward its plus or minus indicators to change the tempo in real time. By switching from manual to auto mode, you change the slider to a moving indicator that responds to the programmed tempo changes in the sequence. Along the bottom of the window, several buttons access additional windows for combining and marking sequences and for creating sliders.

Sequencing at the Top

The Control, Counter, and Metronome windows can all be displayed as separate entities but are put to best advantage when combined into what Mark of the Unicorn calls the Consolidated Controls Panel, which integrates the three into a large unified display. This display, along with the Tracks window, provides access to nearly everything necessary for recording and playing sequences. To edit a performance, you can enter one of three editing environments that offer a wealth of features to handle the most demanding tasks.

By double-clicking any track name, you can directly enter the Event List window (Figure 5.4). This display shows all MIDI events in a sequence along with the associated data. The traditional event-list format shows the time location in measures, beats, and ticks followed by an icon indicating the type of MIDI event being represented (Figure 5.5).

**Figure 5.4**
The Event List window uses numbers, text, and icons to represent MIDI data.

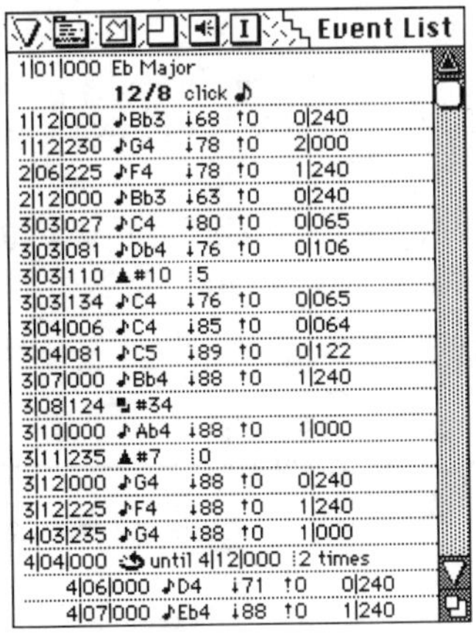

All data pertaining to these events can be clicked on and edited by typing in the new values. For MIDI note data you can also click on a parameter and change its value by playing the note from your MIDI keyboard. For example, to change a wrong note, simply click on the note name in the window and play the correct note from the MIDI controller. Velocity and

**Figure 5.5**
A pop-up window showing the types of data that you can include in the Event List

other parameters can also be changed in the same way. By clicking on the speaker button, you can hear each note as you select it, and another button enables you to insert a MIDI event of any kind, anywhere in the list.

Since MIDI systems and editing requirements vary from one situation to the next, Performer provides a View Filter (Figure 5.6) that allows you to customize your event lists by selecting which parameters will appear in the window and which will be excluded.

Although the Event List provides an excellent means of editing individual note values, the Graphic Editing window (Figure 5.7) offers an alternative that you may find more intuitive. Here the notes appear as elongated black

**Figure 5.6**
The View Filter lets you select what MIDI data can appear in the Event List.

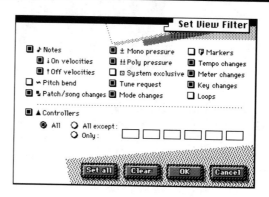

bars against a grid, marked with measures or the same time-related options as in the other windows. In typical piano-roll style, a keyboard along the left edge provides a pitch reference, and time is indicated along the top. Beneath the note grid, an additional area displays the corresponding velocity, aftertouch, or other continuous data with tiny icons in a graphlike setting.

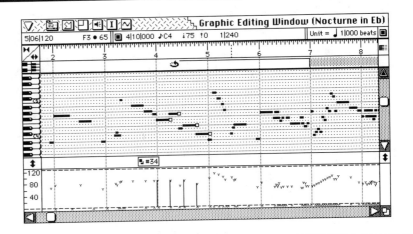

**Figure 5.7**
Performer's Graphic Editing window. Notice the four selected notes in the center.

Notes can be selected individually or in groups. Many editing conventions common to paint programs apply to this window as well. For instance, you can drag a selection box over a group of notes for editing or option-drag to copy a note to another location. A zoom in/out box allows you to see either a greater area of the performance or to get a very close look at the individual notes for making precise placements.

When you select a note, its event parameters appear above the grid in the Event Information box, where they can be edited as in the Event List. At the same time a small grab-handle appears on the right side of the note bar, which allows you to shorten or lengthen the note to affect its duration. The same speaker button as in the Event List appears in the Graphic Editing window along with the ability to insert notes (or other data) individually anywhere on the grid.

For those composers who prefer to see their music in standard notation, Performer provides a Notation Editing window (Figure 5.8), which displays the MIDI data on a staff with notes, rests, and ties. Editing here is similar to editing in the graphic display, although it's a little more awkward. Unquantized music may fill the display with an excessive number of ties and rests, which can make editing cumbersome. Nonetheless, some types of editing situations are especially well suited to a standard notational display.

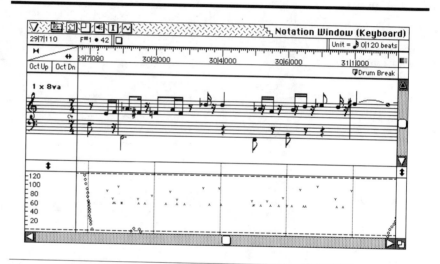

**Figure 5.8**
The Notation window displays MIDI data using standard musical notation.

As in the graphic display, notes can be selected and dragged to new positions to change their pitches and location in the measure. Notes can be inserted and deleted, and the speaker button allows you to hear the notes as they're selected. Both the Graphic Editing and the Notation windows provide a moving cursor while the sequence is playing, which helps in following the music. These windows along with the Event List also offer an auto-scroll option that keeps the display current with the sequence as it plays.

In Performer, a sequence can be a single composition from beginning to end, but for those who are less oriented to a linear approach to composing and prefer a more sectional approach, Performer offers another option.

Sequencing at the Top

Several sequences can be combined into a larger piece. When treated this way, the smaller sequences are called Chunks, and the larger structure is called a Song.

The Song window (Figure 5.9) graphically represents the arrangement of the Chunks, showing their order and allowing you to change the structure of the song by dragging the Chunks around and repositioning them where you want. Adjacent Chunks are played one after the other, and Chunks arranged vertically are played simultaneously. When you play a song, the Skip button in the Controls window (Figure 5.2) will jump playback to the next or previous Chunk shown in the Chunks window.

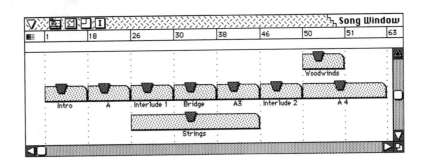

**Figure 5.9**
Performer lets you create arrangements by assembling Chunks in the Song window.

As part of its extensive editing capabilities, Performer boasts many sophisticated global commands. Its Quantize dialog box (Figure 5.10) offers a number of variables affecting not only note resolution but also the strength and sensitivity of the quantizing effect. By changing these variables, you can tighten up a performance without ruining the feel of the music or making it sound mechanical.

The velocities of selected notes can be altered in a number of ways through the Change Velocity dialog box (Figure 5.11), which offers enough options to accommodate almost any situation. The Change Duration dialog box has a similar number of options for altering note durations.

**Figure 5.10**
The Quantize dialog box offers several options to adjust rhythmic placement while retaining musicality.

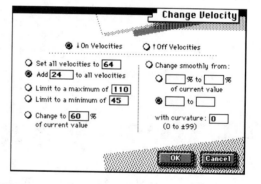

**Figure 5.11**
Performer lets you change note velocities in a variety of ways—a similar dialog box affects durations.

Performer's Transpose command brings up a window that includes a Transpose Map along with several options for changing keys. You can transpose diatonically or by interval. You can change keys from any root to any other or from any mode to any other. You can also transpose into or out of any custom scale of your own design and up or down by any number of octaves. This is clearly a very powerful feature.

# Sequencing at the Top

Performer also provides an amazing array of on-screen, graphic faders, or *sliders* (Figure 5.12). You can use these sliders to control any kind of continuous MIDI data, such as volume, pitch bend, panning, and filtering. You create your own custom panels in a variety of formats (such as large, small, vertical, or horizontal), label each control, and assign it to perform a function. During recording or playback, you can move the slider handle to generate MIDI data, or the sliders can respond automatically to data already in the sequence. You can also combine several sliders into subgroups to create sophisticated mixing consoles for more elaborate compositions.

**Figure 5.12**
Performer lets you create a number of slider consoles in any configuration to control any kind of continuous MIDI data.

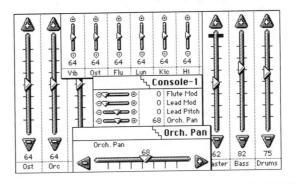

To help you keep track of the MIDI data flow in your system, Performer offers the MIDI Monitor (Figure 5.13). This handy display indicates incoming MIDI data according to channel, port, and general type. The MIDI Monitor provides a valuable source of visual feedback to aid you in troubleshooting problems in your MIDI setup and reminds you of where the current activity is taking place.

One final feature worth noting, Tap Tempo, allows you to create a tempo map in real time before, after, or during recording by tapping the tempo from your MIDI keyboard. This allows you to include accelerandos and ritards in the music while still maintaining the proper relationship to the measures and beats in the sequence.

**Figure 5.13**
The MIDI Monitor lets you see the presence of MIDI activity on each channel in your setup.

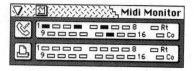

As you can see, Performer is a very impressive program. When Mark of the Unicorn adds new features it goes all the way, providing numerous options, great flexibility, and powerful implementations. It's no wonder this sequencer has garnered such a large and loyal following among professional musicians.

# Vision

When Opcode Systems introduced Vision in 1988, it created quite a stir in the music industry. With a 480-ppqn resolution and later, with its support for color as well, here was a program with myriad features, designed to compete directly with Performer. Since then it has more than lived up to its promise and continues to evolve as Opcode refines its capabilities.

Providing such a plethora of features, however, comes at some cost. The initial setup and many of the functions are not quite as intuitive as they might be, so the learning curve is a bit steeper than for some other sequencers in this class. Still, once you know your way around this program, you'll be surprised at some of the unique and powerful options that it offers.

One of the important concepts behind Vision's design is that it act not only as a recording, editing, and playback system but also as an environment for extensive MIDI-management capabilities, including integration with Galaxy, Opcode's editor/librarian program (see Chapter 9). To this end, Opcode includes a system extension (INIT) called the Opcode MIDI System (OMS), which must be installed before you use Vision.

With OMS you create a Studio Setup document by defining all of the instruments in your system (along with their MIDI connections) and entering the information graphically in the Studio Setup window (Figure 5.14).

**Figure 5.14**
The Studio Setup window represents your MIDI system with icons connected by cables.

Once you've done this, your MIDI devices will appear in a pop-up menu in Vision so that you can refer to them by name rather than by MIDI channel and port.

Vision's output mapping assignments are displayed in the Instruments window (Figure 5.15), which lists the devices in your MIDI system along with their MIDI output channels. Here you can mute or solo a track, scale its velocity, transpose its output, and establish its keyboard range. An instrument using more than one MIDI channel will have more than one line along with the attendant parameters.

When you first open Vision, you are presented with three windows. At the top of the screen, the Control Bar window (Figure 5.16) displays a number of buttons for controlling and editing sequences. The transport controls are

**Figure 5.15**
The Instruments window in Vision shows your MIDI devices along with their channel assignments and several other parameters.

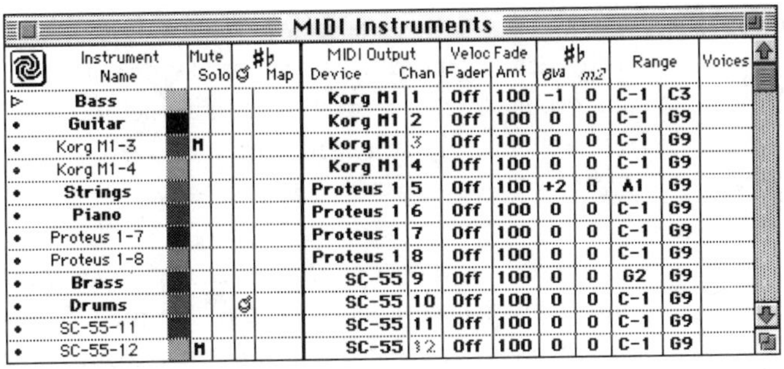

| Instrument Name | Mute Solo | ♯♭ Map | MIDI Output Device | Chan | Veloc Fader | Fade Amt | ♯♭ 8va | m2 | Range | | Voices |
|---|---|---|---|---|---|---|---|---|---|---|---|
| Bass | | | Korg M1 | 1 | Off | 100 | -1 | 0 | C-1 | C3 | |
| Guitar | | | Korg M1 | 2 | Off | 100 | 0 | 0 | C-1 | G9 | |
| Korg M1-3 | M | | Korg M1 | 3 | Off | 100 | 0 | 0 | C-1 | G9 | |
| Korg M1-4 | | | Korg M1 | 4 | Off | 100 | 0 | 0 | C-1 | G9 | |
| Strings | | | Proteus 1 | 5 | Off | 100 | +2 | 0 | A1 | G9 | |
| Piano | | | Proteus 1 | 6 | Off | 100 | 0 | 0 | C-1 | G9 | |
| Proteus 1-7 | | | Proteus 1 | 7 | Off | 100 | 0 | 0 | C-1 | G9 | |
| Proteus 1-8 | | | Proteus 1 | 8 | Off | 100 | 0 | 0 | C-1 | G9 | |
| Brass | | | SC-55 | 9 | Off | 100 | 0 | 0 | G2 | G9 | |
| Drums | | ♂ | SC-55 | 10 | Off | 100 | 0 | 0 | C-1 | G9 | |
| SC-55-11 | | | SC-55 | 11 | Off | 100 | 0 | 0 | C-1 | G9 | |
| SC-55-12 | M | | SC-55 | 12 | Off | 100 | 0 | 0 | C-1 | G9 | |

similar in function to those in other sequencers. In Vision, the Record button displays the current sequence by letter name. The Play button becomes a Pause button once the sequence starts and becomes a Continue button while in Pause mode. All of the transport controls are labeled with their Macintosh keyboard equivalents. To the left of the Record control, the Step Record button opens the Step window, which provides a number of options for entering notes one at a time.

**Figure 5.16**
The Control Bar window

To the right of the transport controls, the Counter display gives the usual readout in measures, beats, and "units." By clicking on the thin rectangle beneath the counter, you can change the display to indicate SMPTE timecode. A second click brings up a combination display with both sets of numbers.

The three buttons on the far left of the Control Bar open the List window, the Graphic window, and the Sequence window, respectively. The Wait for Note button prevents the sequencer from beginning to record until it receives its first MIDI note. This button can be changed to provide a specified number of measures for a count-off. Below this button, a control for initiating loop-recording mode gives you the option of recording with a drum-machine approach, where a number of measures repeat over and over while new material is layered onto old. Like Performer, Vision offers several other recording options, which include Replacement mode (new notes replace the old), Punch in/out, and Overdub, in which new notes can be added to a previous recording.

On the far right of the Control Bar, you will find a separate area that displays information about the available memory, synchronization settings, master tempo and, at the top, the Thru Instrument and Program settings. The Thru Instrument setting indicates which synthesizer you will hear, and record into the sequence, when you begin. The Program setting tells you which specific *patch*, or sound, is selected for that device.

The second window in the group, the File window (Figure 5.17), appears below the Control Bar. The File window displays all of the sequences that make up a particular file—you can have up to 26 sequences in a file, each designated by a letter of the alphabet. A clever feature in Vision allows you to play your sequences in real time, in any order, by typing the appropriate letters on the Macintosh keyboard. This is a great way to experiment with the structure of a piece by trying different combinations.

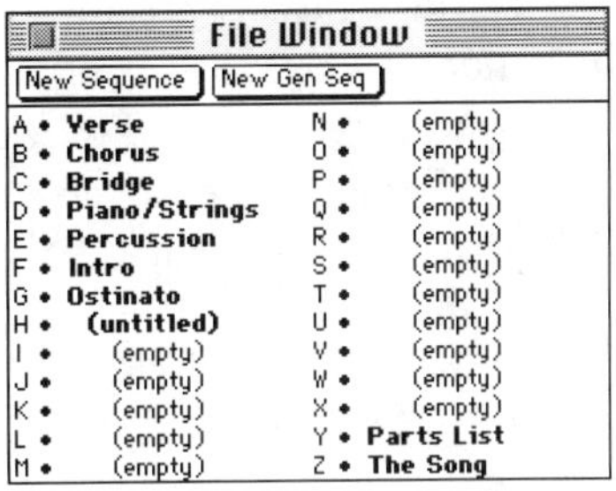

**Figure 5.17**
The File window lists the sequences by letter, allowing easy playback of up to 26 sequences in a file from the Macintosh keyboard.

```
================ File Window ================
[New Sequence] [New Gen Seq]
A • Verse           N • (empty)
B • Chorus          O • (empty)
C • Bridge          P • (empty)
D • Piano/Strings   Q • (empty)
E • Percussion      R • (empty)
F • Intro           S • (empty)
G • Ostinato        T • (empty)
H • (untitled)      U • (empty)
I •   (empty)       V • (empty)
J •   (empty)       W • (empty)
K •   (empty)       X • (empty)
L •   (empty)       Y • Parts List
M •   (empty)       Z • The Song
```

You can also play sequences in a specific order by using the Queue mode in the Control Bar window. You type the sequence letters into the Queue box in the order that you want them to be played. Each sequence then waits for its turn as Vision plays them one after the other. Additionally, up to nine sequences can be played simultaneously by using the Players option.

The third part of the opening screen display is the Sequence window (Figure 5.18), where you can change most of the parameters of a sequence except for the actual notes themselves. This window displays and allows you to edit such things as meter, tempo, sequence length, looping, and instrumentation. Here you designate which of the tracks to mute, solo, or record-enable. Each sequence can have up to 99 tracks, and much of the information in each track can be changed while the sequence is playing. Sequences can be combined into larger sequences at which point the smaller parts become known as Subsequences—the equivalent of Chunks in Performer.

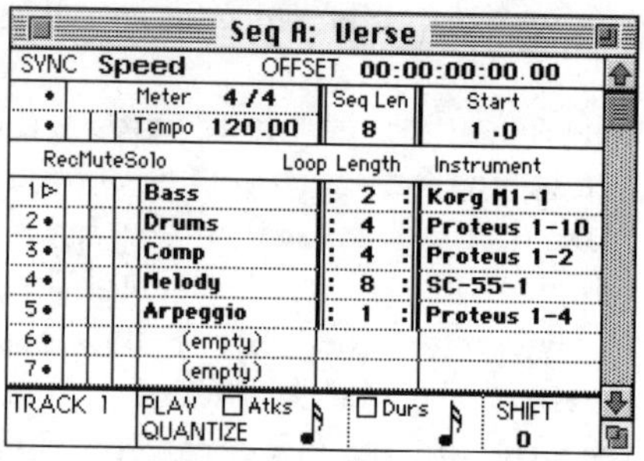

**Figure 5.18**
The Sequence window lets you specify the parameters of a sequence, such as meter, tempo, length, and instrumentation.

Vision provides another great feature: Play Quantization. This form of quantization occurs only during playback and does not alter the note data. It allows you to try several different note resolutions without changing your original performance. Once you decide on a resolution, you can make the change permanent by using Edit quantization, with its more versatile implementation.

Vision also offers a sophisticated feature for creating *generated sequences*. By applying a number of variables to some prerecorded track data, you can create a new performance that is different from, but related to, the original. This can produce some very interesting and useful musical material.

Vision provides two types of windows for editing MIDI events. The first type, the Graphic window, displays track events in the standard piano-roll configuration (Figure 5.19). Along the top of the window, several buttons enable you to access various editing options.

The first button allows you to zoom in to gain greater precision or to zoom out for a larger overview of the grid. The next button, the Quantize Resolution button, opens a pop-up menu displaying the 21 different note values that you can choose for quantizing your music. Next to this is the Quantize Cursor button, which limits the cursor's selection range to increments that match the note value set in the Quantize Resolution menu. For instance, if you choose a half-note quantization value, the cursor will jump in half-note blocks when you select regions for editing.

# Sequencing at the Top

**Figure 5.19**
Vision's Graphic window displays both note events and continuous controller data.

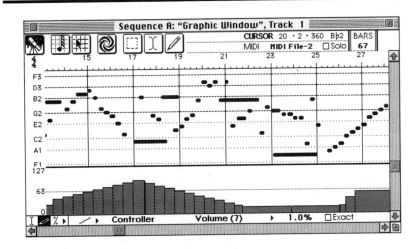

The middle button in the group, the Mogrify button, displays a pop-up menu that contains most of the commands from the Edit and Do menus (Figure 5.20). The Marquee button lets you drag a selection box over a group of notes as you would select an area in a paint program. The I-beam button allows you to select regions of the grid in two ways: Dragging the I-beam horizontally selects all notes that fall within the selected area of time, regardless of pitch. Dragging vertically along the left margin selects all notes within the desired pitch range.

**Figure 5.20**
Clicking the Mogrify button opens this pop-up menu for quickly selecting editing options.

| | |
|---|---|
| Redo Legato | Transpose Selection... |
| | Quantize Selection |
| Cut Selection | Set Up Quantize... |
| Copy Selection | Modify Notes... |
| Paste Selection | Set Instrument... |
| Clear Selection | Reassign... |
| | Substitute... |
| Merge Selection | |
| Insert Clipboard | Reverse Time |
| Repeat Paste... | Scale Time... |
| Clone | Change Tempo... |
| Get Times from Clipboard | |
| | Play from Selection |
| Insert Blank Time | Play Selection |
| Delete Time | Jump to Selection |
| Move Events... | Select by Rule... |
| | Select All |
| Unmerge Track->Seq | Split Notes... |

The Pencil button enables you to insert notes into the grid. At the top of the window, the Cursor Position display gives numerical information concerning the location of the cursor to help you position new notes. In some views of the note grid, a treble and bass clef provide a sort of hybrid note display that attempts to combine some features of standard notation with the piano-roll display—a useful addition, though not as versatile as a separate notation window.

Vision, like Performer, offers an audible feedback option that plays a note when it's selected or dragged up and down the grid. But Vision also provides a "note-scrubbing" feature that lets you drag a vertical line across the grid to manually play sections of the sequence out of tempo—a very useful tool for pinpointing an exact spot in the music.

Directly below the piano-roll display lies the Strip Chart. This area displays a variety of information that pertains to the notes above. Note velocity, continuous controller events, program changes, fader events, and even text such as lyrics and copyright notices are graphically displayed in the Strip Chart. You can edit this data easily using the same drawing and selecting tools as above. You can also quickly redraw and reshape continuous controller data graphs using several tools and menu options.

The List window (Figure 5.21) contains the same information as the Graphic window, except now it is displayed in a chronological list. Measure and beat numbers are followed by note names, duration, velocity, and other types of data in a standard event-list format. At the top of the window, four buttons provide access to several display and editing options.

Clicking the Insert Event button opens a pop-up menu that allows you to insert any kind of data into the list (Figure 5.22). The Quantize Resolution and Mogrify buttons function the same as in the Graphic window. The last button allows you to include a SMPTE timecode display with each event.

Vision supports up to 32 graphic faders arranged in a single- or double-column format in its Faders window (Figure 5.23). The faders can send tempo and MIDI controller data in real time that you can record into your sequence. On playback they act as automated faders, moving and displaying the current values as the sequence progresses. Although Vision doesn't

**Figure 5.21**
Vision's List window is similar to Performer's—without the icons.

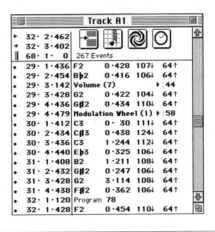

**Figure 5.22**
Clicking the Insert Event button opens a pop-up menu offering a large selection of MIDI and non-MIDI data.

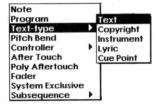

offer the great number of fader types and console configurations that Performer does, its faders, nonetheless, provide the same basic functions as the sliders in Performer.

Another feature, common to both programs, is the ability to control the operations of the sequencer remotely from a MIDI keyboard. Vision calls this feature MIDIKeys. To use MIDIKeys you enter a MIDI event into the MIDIKeys window and assign it to play the Macintosh keyboard equivalent for each sequencer operation that you want to control. Although this approach is slightly less direct than that used by Performer, the result is essentially the same. MIDIKeys can also be used to trigger a keyboard equivalent for the Tap Tempo feature that lets you record and play back

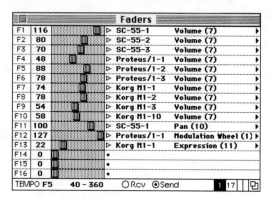

**Figure 5.23**
Vision supports up to 32 graphic faders in its Faders window.

while the Master Tempo changes in real time to reflect the speed of your key taps.

Vision has gained steadily in popularity during the past two years mainly because of its great power and the number of options that it offers. It has led the way in the introduction of new features, which has helped establish its solid foothold in the pro-level sequencer market and has helped set the stride for the future of sequencing software.

## Master Tracks Pro 5

While other high-end sequencer programs have distinguished themselves by adding an ever-growing list of sometimes arcane features, Master Tracks Pro 5, from Passport, has built its reputation on its simple, straightforward, intuitive design. Though it lacks some of the more sophisticated but esoteric editing options, it is still very much a professional-level sequencer, with the ability to read timecode, map instruments, edit continuous controller data, and scale time.

The Transport window provides the standard tape-deck controls in a clear and logical arrangement (Figure 5.24). To the left of the controls, a counter field displays the current location in the sequence with measures, beats, and "clocks." Pro 5 has a timing resolution of 240 clocks per beat—not as high as many of its competitors but certainly adequate for most applications.

Below the measure indicator, a second display provides an elapsed-time reading, which can be adapted for use with SMPTE timecode. Selecting and changing any number in the measure display will move you to that position in the sequence.

The transport controls are mostly self-explanatory. The Rewind button moves you back in one measure increments each time you click it. Clicking and holding the button moves you back continuously by measures, and double-clicking returns you to the start of the sequence. Fast Forward is similar to Rewind, except in the other direction. Double-clicking the button moves you to the end of the sequence. You can operate all of the transport controls from the Macintosh keyboard by using their keyboard equivalents.

**Figure 5.24**
Pro 5's Transport window provides "tape-deck" controls in a clear and logical arrangement.

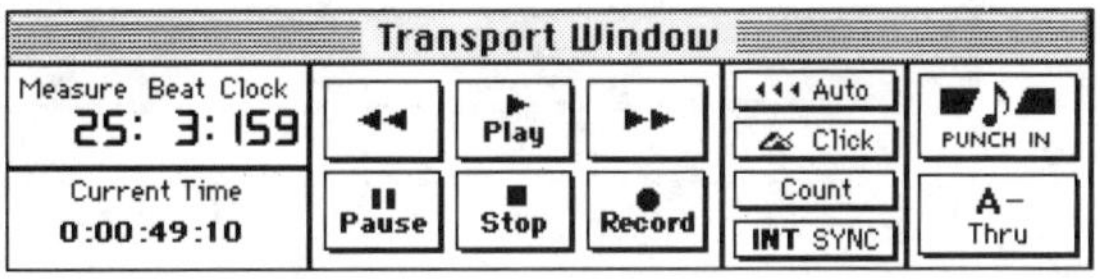

To the right of the transport controls, there are six additional buttons, which supplement the main controls. When Auto is activated, it automatically returns you—after stopping the sequence—to the point at which recording or playback last began. The Thru control allows you to set the MIDI port and channel (or channels) that the computer will pass on to your sound modules from the MIDI controller keyboard. This determines what sound you'll hear while performing during the recording.

The Count In button provides you with a one-measure metronome lead-in before recording or playback, and the Click button toggles the metronome on and off, which can be set to play internally from the Macintosh or from a MIDI device. Sync determines whether or not the sequencer will synchronize to an internal or external timing source.

The Record Mode button selects and displays one of four Special Record modes: Overdub, Punch-in, Looped Record, and Looped Overdub. Overdub and Punch-in work essentially the same as in the other sequencers.

Looped Record repeats a designated section and replaces the previously recorded data with the current performance each time the section repeats. Looped Overdub provides drum-machine-style recording by retaining and playing back the previous material while adding in the current performance.

The Tempo window, which resembles its counterpart in Performer, provides a slider for making temporary changes to a sequence's tempo, while displaying the current tempo, meter, and beat.

The Track Editor window (Figure 5.25) is Pro 5's main window for viewing, organizing, and setting the parameters of each sequence. The left half of the window provides names and settings for the individual tracks, and the right half indicates with a graphic display the presence of MIDI data in those tracks.

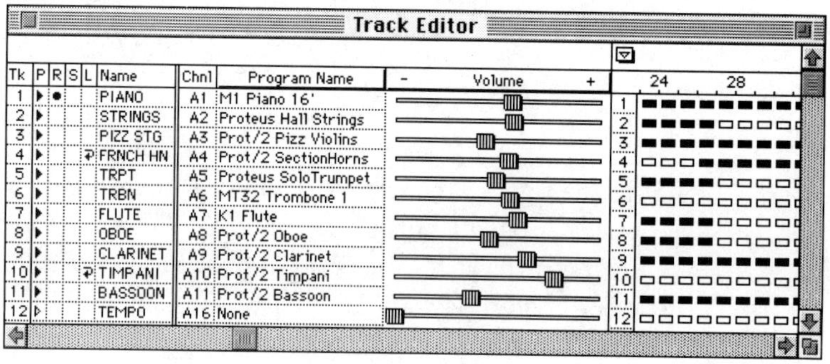

**Figure 5.25**
The Track Editor window combines a list of tracks with a graphic display showing the presence of MIDI data in the sequence. Shown here in its fully expanded form, it indicates patches by name and displays the automated volume faders.

The first column in the left half of the window lists the 64 tracks provided in Pro 5. Next to that are columns for selecting Play, Record, Solo, and Looping, respectively. Each of these categories uses one or more small icons to indicate the status of the selected functions. The Channel column lets you set the MIDI port and channel (or combination of channels) for each track's playback, and the Program Number column displays the MIDI program number for the instrument sound in the corresponding synthesizer. Clicking on the heading of the Program Number column brings up the Device menu, listing several popular synthesizers and sound modules.

Selecting an instrument fills a window with the program names that correspond to that device. The Program Number column—now the Program Name column—lists the selected instrument sounds by name rather than number.

The Volume column lists the volume setting for each track either with a simple numerical display or optionally with a set of real-time volume faders that can display, adjust, record, and play back MIDI volume settings for each track. Additionally, a pop-up, variable-mode Master Fader lets you control the other faders as a group.

Pro 5 offers a Multi-Track Record option, which allows you to record on more than one track at a time, and a Multi-Channel option, which lets you record up to eight channels per track. You can also loop different tracks independently, but the loops must always end on a measure boundary. Like Vision and Performer, Pro 5 lets you place markers at important points throughout the sequence. The markers, which look and act like the tab stops in MacWrite, can appear in all of the editing windows just below the title bar. Similar markers are also available for placing Program Change commands in each track throughout the sequence.

The right half of the Track Editor window shows the structure of the sequence by indicating the presence of MIDI data on a measure-by-measure basis. Here you can cut, copy, and paste sections of tracks, insert measures, and create new tracks from sections of other tracks. The display is very much like the Tracks Overview in Performer, which followed Master Tracks Pro in adopting this feature.

To view and edit individual note data, you must open the Step Editor window (Figure 5.26). This is the same kind of graphic, piano-roll display that the other sequencers use. It doesn't include continuous controller data, though; instead, it provides separate windows for this type of information.

Pro 5 does, however, offer a very useful Show Velocity feature, which displays velocity values in the Step Editor window as thin vertical lines attached to the front of each note (Figure 5.27). Longer lines indicate greater velocities, and you can edit each value by clicking on the note and dragging up or down to change the line's length.

**Figure 5.26**
Pro 5's Step Editor Window is a typical piano-roll display.

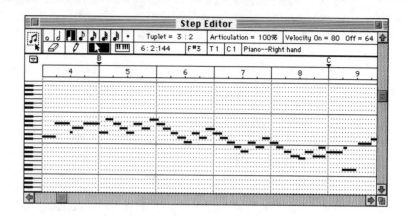

**Figure 5.27**
Pro 5's Show Velocity feature displays velocity values as thin vertical lines that can easily be edited.

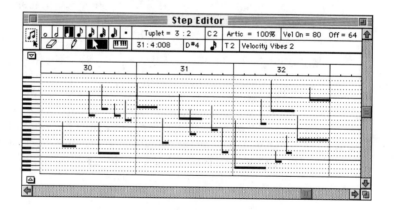

In the upper-left corner of the window, just to the left of the menu bar, there's an icon depicting two eighth notes. This lets you determine whether edits made to selected regions in the Step Editor window will affect only note data or will include continuous controller data as well—even though it may not be visible at the time.

The top row of fields and icons in the menu bar apply to the entering of new notes onto the grid. To insert a note into a track, you first select the

Pencil tool and choose a note value from the menu bar. Then you simply choose the desired pitch and time location and click the mouse. Subsequent positioning and clicking will enter additional notes. By clicking the small keyboard icon, you activate step-time, note-entry mode—Pro 5's version of step recording. Now you can select the rhythmic values of the notes from the computer and enter the velocities and pitches from your MIDI keyboard. Each time a note is entered the cursor advances to the next insertion point. Pro 5 recognizes and inserts chords in the same way.

*Articulation* refers to the actual duration of a note—expressed as a percentage—as opposed to its indicated rhythmic value. For example, adjusting the articulation down from 100 percent will produce a more staccato passage than if the notes all received their full rhythmic values.

Holding down the Command key turns the cursor into a hand with a pointing finger, which sounds the notes on the grid as it passes over them. This is a good way to preview notes when inserting and editing them and can help you locate drum sounds while compiling rhythm tracks. The arrow icon in the menu bar is used for selecting regions for editing, and the eraser icon deletes notes when you click on them. The other items indicate the measure/beat location of the cursor or selected note, the note name, the MIDI channel, the track number, and the patch name. A note remapping feature lets you select all notes of a specific pitch and move them over the grid to a new pitch location.

Pro 5 also has a Keyboard Setup feature that lets you assign MIDI keyboard equivalents to all of the transport controls and allows you to select note durations while working in the Step Editor window.

Like the sequencers already mentioned, Pro 5 provides an Event List Editor window (Figure 5.28), which displays track data in the traditional event-list format. Along the top of the window, several icons representing the different types of MIDI events allow easy and direct insertion of new data. To insert an event, simply click on the appropriate icon and type in the location. The icons represent note events, program changes, pitch bend, controller data, aftertouch, and polyphonic aftertouch. The Filter button lets you eliminate certain types of data from the display for easier viewing and to allow for better discrimination of events for editing.

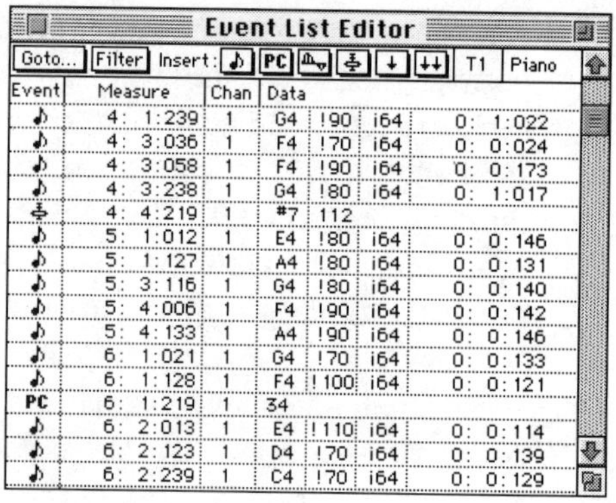

**Figure 5.28**
Pro 5's Event List, similar to the others, also includes a column for MIDI channel.

Since the Step Editor window includes only note and velocity data, Pro 5 offers several additional MIDI Data windows to graphically display other types of events for editing. These windows are similar in appearance and layout to the Step Editor display except that they are optimized for the types of data that they contain. MIDI events appear as vertical lines ("skyline" mode) or as a series of points whose heights correspond to the numeric values. Data displays can be redrawn with the Pencil tool, and the eraser and arrow cursors work in a similar manner to their Step Editor counterparts.

The Channel Pressure, Key Pressure, Modulation, and Controller windows are all the same in appearance, with the vertical axis representing values from 0 to 127 and the horizontal axis indicating measures and beats (Figure 5.29). Changes made in one window do not influence the data in the others.

The Pitch Bend window is similar to the others except that it represents both positive and negative values, ranging from −127 to +127. The center horizontal line represents a pitch bend value of zero. To better correlate controller data with note events, you can toggle on the Ghost Notes option, which superimposes a transparent view of the Step Editor's notes over the controller event displays in the MIDI Data windows (Figure 5.30). The grayed-out notes act as a valuable guide when you create or edit the different kinds of controller data.

**Figure 5.29**
The Modulation window is typical of several graphic displays that let you create and edit continuous controller data.

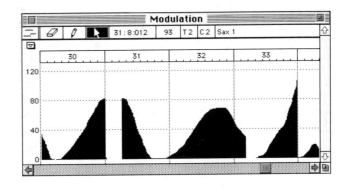

**Figure 5.30**
The Pitch Bend window displays both positive and negative values. It is shown here with the Ghost Notes option toggled on, which superimposes note events over the continuous controller data.

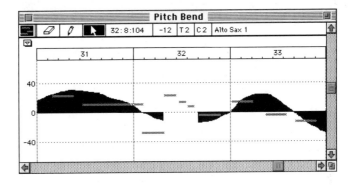

If you prefer an alternate method for editing velocity, you can open the Velocity window, which displays the same note and velocity data as the Step Editor but now in a dedicated window where the Pencil tool can be used to draw velocity curves.

The Tempo Map window (Figure 5.31) displays the meter and tempo for a track. Horizontal lines graphically depict the changes in tempo as the sequence progresses. You can use the Pencil tool to insert new tempos on any clock or the Eraser tool to delete them.

**Figure 5.31**
Pro 5's unique Tempo Map window graphically depicts tempo changes and lets you edit them with the Pencil tool and the Eraser tool.

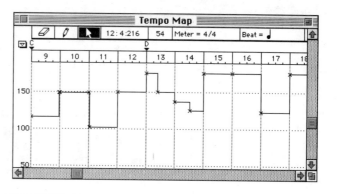

Master Tracks Pro 5 provides the same types of global editing capabilities as most other sequencers. Commands affecting duration, velocity, transposition, quantizing, humanizing, and time scaling are found on the Change menu. In most cases, these are similar in implementation to the programs mentioned above. One interesting feature in Pro 5 is the Change Filter (Figure 5.32), which enables you to restrict the effects of the Change menu's commands. This can be very useful in isolating specific types of data by making your global commands less global.

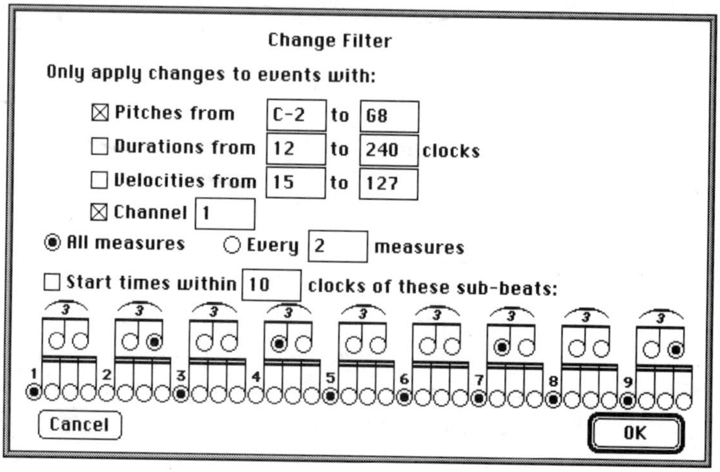

**Figure 5.32**
The Change Filter lets you set limits for several editing operations.

For playing several sequences in succession, Pro 5 offers an option similar to Vision's Queue feature. The Song Playlist window (Figure 5.33) lets you construct a list of sequences and determine parameters that affect playback. The Playlist itself is only a list and does not contain the actual sequence data, which is saved in separate files.

Master Tracks Pro 5 has gained a well-deserved reputation for being an intuitive, uncomplicated program while still maintaining its status as a professional-level sequencer. Its graphic implementation of step-recording mode, velocity and continuous controller editing, and tempo mapping make this a very appealing program.

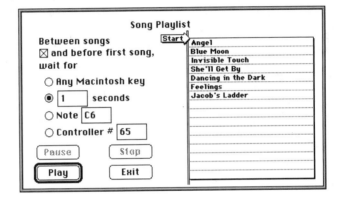

**Figure 5.33**
The Song Playlist window lets you construct a list of sequences that can be played back one after another.

# Beyond

Beyond, from Dr. T's Music Software, occupies a unique position in the sequencer market. Priced well below the other high-end sequencers, yet above the less expensive programs, it straddles the fence between performance and cost. Beyond, however, offers extensive real-time editing capabilities, numerous graphic displays, and several distinctive features that clearly place it in the same league with the other pro-level sequencers and, in spite of a few shortcomings, it compares very well with the more expensive programs.

When you first open Beyond, three windows appear for displaying and organizing MIDI data and for operating the sequencer itself. The Tracks window (Figure 5.34) looks and acts much like the comparable windows in other programs. Down the left side of the window, the 99 available tracks are numbered along with their assigned names. On either side of the Name column, check boxes allow you to enable recording, muting, soloing, and looping options. Clicking on an instrument name brings up a list of your available synthesizers for quick substitutions.

Beyond also provides a graphic display of track activity much like the Track Overview windows in Performer and Master Tracks Pro 5, but this incarnation has a twist. The Multitrack page (Figure 5.35) displays MIDI note data in solid black and continuous controller data in gray. Subsequences and system-exclusive data can be included as well and everything can be cut, copied, pasted, and edited.

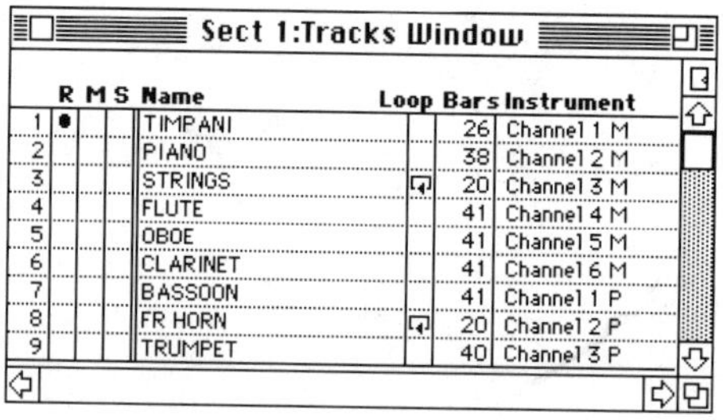

**Figure 5.34**
Beyond uses a standard format in its Tracks window, which lists the names for each track opposite the corresponding MIDI channels.

**Figure 5.35**
Beyond's unusual Multitrack page displays MIDI note data in black and continuous controller data in gray.

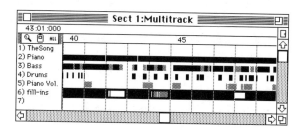

To view and edit individual note data in greater detail, you must open the Note Editor window (Figure 5.36). This is the standard piano-roll graphic display that most sequencers use, with a keyboard along the left side and measures along the top. The first three icons above the display are for selecting and editing. The arrow cursor selects all pitches in a given time frame. Clicking on a black measure marker selects that measure. You can select a fraction of a measure or several measures by dragging through the desired area. The Pencil tool inserts and deletes notes, and the Forceps tool can be used to draw a selection box over a group of notes or to select and move an individual note to a new pitch and/or location. Option-clicking on a note brings up a dialog box that lets you change parameters like measure, beat, clock location, velocity, duration, and channel.

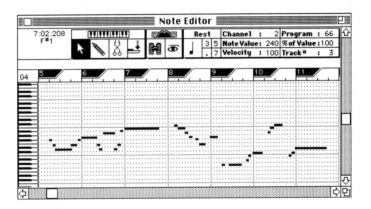

**Figure 5.36**
The Note Editor window uses a typical piano-roll design.

Another of Beyond's useful display options allows you to graphically edit velocity data by including "velocity stems" on each note (Figure 5.37). These stems (similar to those in Master Tracks Pro 5) depict velocity values; the longer stems represent the higher numbers. Selecting the Edit Velocity Stem icon (to the right of the forceps) produces a small tool that can clip off a stem to lower the velocity of a note or grab and stretch a stem to increase the velocity. This is a great way to quickly edit the velocity data in a musical passage where great precision is not necessary.

**Figure 5.37**
Beyond offers the useful option of displaying note velocities with adjustable stems that indicate relative values.

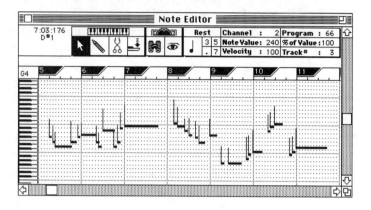

For viewing pitch-bend data, Beyond offers yet another unusual display. By clicking on the Pitch Bend Enable button (above the binoculars), you can replace the velocity-stemmed notes with notes that graphically portray the presence of pitch bend. In this mode, any note that has pitch bend applied to it will appear with a curved nose or tail that shows both the direction and approximate amount of pitch bend (Figure 5.38). This is a handy way to easily correlate pitch-bend events with individual notes and to focus on specific locations that need further editing in the Continuous Data window.

**Figure 5.38**
Beyond offers another unique display option that graphically depicts the presence of pitch bend.

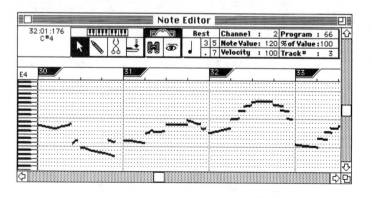

For graphically editing continuous controller events, Beyond provides a single window that can be switched from one data type to another by clicking in a row of buttons. Along the top of the Continuous Data window (Figure 5.39), several icons provide access to displays for pitch bend, other controllers, average velocity, aftertouch, program change events, polyphonic aftertouch, and tempo. Opening each display automatically changes the scale markings to reflect that type of data. You can copy and paste the display from one window into another to translate one kind of data into another kind.

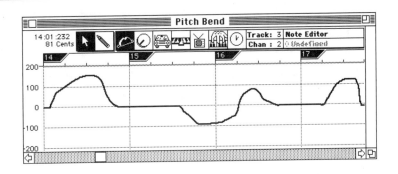

**Figure 5.39**
The Continuous Data window lets you create and edit pitch bend, aftertouch, modulation, and other kinds of MIDI data.

As with most other sequencers, Beyond provides a list of MIDI events in its Display List window (Figure 5.40). This event list is not as fully implemented as those from the programs mentioned earlier. For instance, there is no provision for displaying markers or SMPTE timecode, and editing options are limited. Still, this window does offer information in a basic list format, which is often useful for displaying and changing data.

Beyond refers to sequences as *Sections*, so the window that lists sequences is called the Sections window (Figure 5.41). This looks like the sequence windows in many other programs but most closely resembles the Chunks window in Performer in terms of how it works. Beyond lets you assemble compositions by dragging Sections from the Sections window into one of the graphic displays used for editing tracks (Figure 5.42). Once dragged to this new location, the Section becomes a SubSection—a sort of independent clone of the original Section.

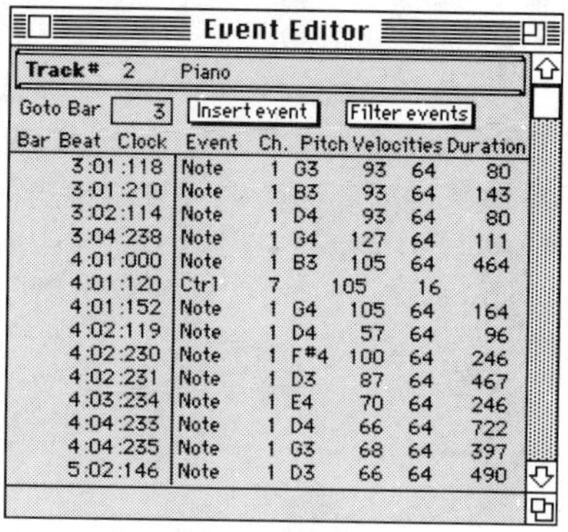

**Figure 5.40**
Beyond's Display List window is not as fully implemented as the event lists in other programs.

**Figure 5.41**
Sequences in Beyond are listed in the Sections window.

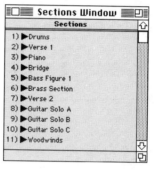

The SubSections can be combined in a number of ways and subjected to a variety of editing functions. Alterations and edits made to a SubSection do not affect the Section and vice versa. You can have up to 16 different SubSections per track, but copies of a SubSection don't count as being different since edits made to a SubSection are reflected in its copies.

You can create new Sections by combining and editing SubSections. Having done that, you can convert all of the SubSections back into regular note

**Figure 5.42**
Beyond lets you assemble complete compositions by dragging Sections into a graphic display where they can be combined and further edited.

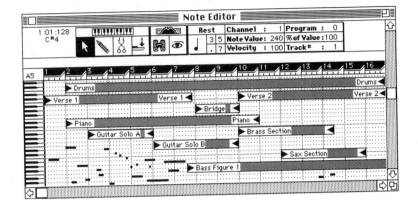

data by using the Expand SubSections function, which places the expanded data in the next available track. Clearly the handling of sequences and the combining of sequence material into larger forms is uniquely implemented in Beyond. Similar options in other programs are more limited in terms of editing capabilities for these subgroupings and don't allow you to graphically display blocks of data alongside individual note events.

The transport controls for Beyond appear in the Bridge display (Figure 5.43), which provides the usual control buttons for operating the sequencer. The Return button positions you back at the beginning of the sequence, while Fast Forward scans rapidly ahead. Beyond offers a feature that lets you specify and play back up to four distinct regions called *Cues*. You can play a Cue by selecting its number from the buttons to the right of the Time display and then clicking on the Cue transport button. Cues can also be looped for repeated playback.

To the left of the transport controls, the Meter and Tempo displays let you specify both of these parameters. The Tempo display is similar to the one in Performer except that you can move the tempo indicator in real time and record the tempo changes on any available track.

**Figure 5.43**

Beyond's transport, metronome, and counter functions are grouped together in the Bridge display.

To the right of the transport controls, the Counter display gives the current location in measures, beats, and clocks as well as SMPTE time. You can begin recording or playback from any point in the sequence by clicking on the measure number and typing in the appropriate value. Unlike many other sequencers, however, this is the only variable allowed. You cannot enter a precise location in measures, beats, and clocks or by indicating an exact SMPTE time to position the start of the sequence.

Beyond has a maximum resolution of 480 ppqn, but that number is variable, allowing you to select from three other values: 192, 240, and 384 ppqn. This helpful feature allows users with one of the slower Macs (i.e., Plus or SE) to optimize performance by reducing the processor work load. This should improve your timing accuracy and reduce wait time during operations, although the timing resolution itself will no longer be as high.

The remaining buttons on the right of the Bridge are used for setting the MIDI Thru channel, the punch-in/out parameters, the metronome, the countdown parameters, and the timing source. Pop-up menus provide the options for easy selection.

Recording in Beyond is pretty much as it is in other programs, with a few special options. Step recording takes place in the Note Editor window in a manner very similar to that in Master Tracks Pro 5. Note parameters are selected from the menu in the upper-right corner, and the Pencil tool places them in the grid. Clicking the keyboard icon at the top of the display allows you to enter notes from your MIDI keyboard. As each note is entered, the cursor jumps to the next entry point.

Beyond offers two types of loop-recording modes: Song Building mode and Multiple Take mode. In Song Building mode each recorded pass is placed on a separate track while the previous overdubs continue to play. This is a variant of drum-machine-style recording except that it places each overdub on the next available track and, therefore, allows you to mute or solo tracks at any time while you build up your sequence. Song Building mode is especially well suited for creating drum patterns and other kinds of rhythmic recordings.

Multiple Take mode is similar to Song Building mode in that each overdub is placed on its own track. But now the tracks are muted after they are recorded so that you can perform a passage over and over until you get it right. You can also create a composite track by cutting and pasting the best parts from several takes. This mode is perfect for recording solos against a background since it allows you to record several passes without unnecessary interruptions and without losing any of the previous performances.

Like the other sequencers discussed earlier, Beyond offers a number of graphic faders that can be assigned to record various types of continuous controller data. The Instruments window (Figure 5.44) provides 32 moving faders, although only 10 at a time can actually be seen—an unfortunate shortcoming. Each fader is assigned an instrument and controller number. There is also a box for including program change numbers while the sequencer is stopped or running. Faders can also be grouped and a Master Fader can be used to scale the settings of other faders.

Beyond has all the same kinds of global commands that other sequencers use, such as quantizing (with adjustable strength), changing duration and velocity, "humanizing," transposing, and time scaling. Additionally, there are two types of harmonizing options: Chromatic and "Intelligent" harmonizing. Chromatic harmonies consist of one to four parallel lines that maintain a specified interval from the original melody, and Intelligent harmonies retain the key and scale relationship as the new lines are generated.

Beyond is an unusual program in several ways. It is priced moderately but still provides a high level of performing and editing capability. It also boasts a number of distinctive features that set it apart from other sequencer

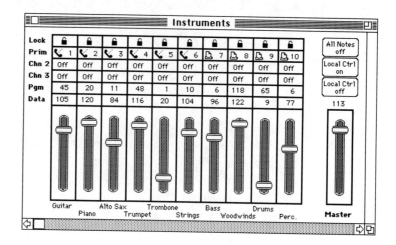

**Figure 5.44**
The Instruments window provides up to 32 graphic faders assignable to various types of data.

designs. Whether these features will be of benefit to you largely depends on the type of composing you do and the methodology that you employ in constructing your sequences. Since any Section in Beyond can be a complete sequence containing up to 99 tracks, you can certainly compose in a linear fashion if you like. But many of the features in this program, and their specific implementations, suggest a strong bias toward the sectional or pattern-song approach to composing. Some people, especially those who compose in commercial and pop styles, may find this aspect of the program attractive.

# Cubase

Cubase, from Steinberg/Jones, is a unique product. Based on the popular sequencer for the Atari, it provides more ways of creating and editing music than any other program mentioned so far. With its surprising array of graphic displays and MIDI-manipulating environments, it's a button-pusher's, knob-tweaker's, fader-slider's delight—once you figure out how it all works. Right from the start you're confronted with a bewildering list of

Sequencing at the Top

terms describing the hierarchal structure used in Cubase: Arrangements, Tracks, Parts, Groups, Group Parts, Group Tracks, Songs, and more. For the beginner this may seem a bit daunting, but spending some time with the program should get you over the initial learning curve and open the door to some very intriguing features.

The first window to appear when you start the program is the Arrange window (Figure 5.45). Cubase refers to sequences as *Arrangements,* and the Arrange window provides up to 64 tracks, which it displays along its left side. Several Arrange windows can be open at one time to facilitate cutting, copying, and pasting between displays. The Tracks list also provides columns for muting Tracks, selecting MIDI channels and ports, and setting program numbers and volume at the start of the sequence.

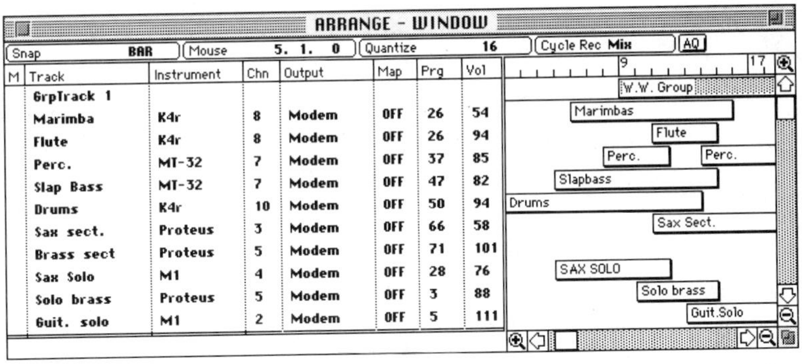

**Figure 5.45**
Cubase displays a sequence in its Arrange window, which lists the Tracks on the left side and graphically represents Parts on the right.

Just as Arrangements are made up of Tracks, Tracks are made up of Parts. At the simplest level, Parts resemble drum-machine "patterns" in that they are smaller sections of music that can be edited and combined to create tracks. But Parts, which can be any length, are much more than drumlike patterns since they can consist of a number of different types of data and can be extensively edited, lengthened, shortened, cut into pieces, and combined with other Parts.

The right side of the Arrange window displays Parts graphically as small rectangles with the Part's name on each rectangle. When you make a recording, the data appears as a Part in the Part display opposite its corresponding Track. The Position Bar indicates the location in measures or SMPTE timecode.

You can select Parts individually or in a group by dragging a selection box over them. A Part can be duplicated or deleted, and any Part that is moved to another Track adopts that Track's MIDI channel and port setting. If you drag one Part onto another, a copy of the dragged Part will either merge with or replace the data in the other Part depending on the Record Mode setting. The Parts need not have equal lengths either. You can merge a small Part into the middle of a larger one if you like.

An individual Part can be muted and its length can be changed by grabbing the rectangle and stretching or shortening it. The Scissors tool enables you to cut a Part in two, and the Scrubbing tool lets you hear the music in a Part by dragging over its rectangle. When Parts are joined, areas with overlapping data will be merged without losing any events.

Parts can also be combined into a Group—a collection of Parts that play simultaneously and are treated as a separate entity. Since each of the component Parts retain their individual MIDI assignments, Groups appear in a separate Group Track, which is created at the top of the Parts display. Groups are treated as distinct blocks of music and as such are subject to a number of editing options unique to them. Groups can be useful for composing music with recurring elements or for assembling larger works from smaller sections.

Recording and playback operations in Cubase are initiated from the Transport Bar (Figure 5.46). Here you'll find all the usual controls, like Play, Record, Fast Forward, Rewind, etc. To the right of these buttons, two small displays show the current location in measures/beats/ticks and SMPTE time. Cubase uses a timing resolution of 384 ppqn—not the highest in this group but respectable nonetheless. You can store up to six Song Position settings for cueing important parts of the sequence from the Mac's keyboard. The two adjacent displays show meter and tempo.

The Click button toggles the metronome on and off, Master deactivates the existing tempo changes, and Sync provides options for timing sources. On the far right, two rectangles marked In and Out indicate the presence

**Figure 5.46**
Recording and playback operations are initiated from the Transport Bar.

of MIDI data flow—sort of a poor man's version of Performer's MIDI Monitor—a feature that all sequencers should have for diagnosing problems. On the left of the Transport Bar are several controls for soloing, cycling (looping), selecting recording modes (overdub and replace), and activating Punch In/Out recording. Cubase provides all of the standard recording methods along with Multi Recording, which lets you record up to four tracks simultaneously—fewer than most other programs of this caliber.

You use the Left and Right Locator boxes to set the boundaries of a region for editing, looping, or automated punch in and out. The numbers from the Transport Bar are reflected in the Part display, along the top, much like tab markers in a word processor. You can also change their positions by dragging them to new locations. Cubase lets you store ten of these sets of location markers, which you can access by typing one of the number keys on the Macintosh keyboard. You can then call up often-used sections of your music instantly for playback, looping, or editing.

For graphic editing of individual note events, Cubase provides a Key Edit window (Figure 5.47). This is the same piano-roll graphic display that by now you have come to know and love. You can drag and edit notes in the upper part of the display. The lower part—the Controller display—shows continuous controller data in a manner similar to the Strip Chart display in Vision. A button to the left of the display lets you select from several types of continuous controller data, such as pitch bend and aftertouch, as well as other kinds of non-note values like velocity and program numbers.

Along the top in the Functions Bar, you'll find several boxes indicating the current cursor position, quantize setting, snap (cursor quantize) setting, and loop boundaries. The Speaker icon activates note monitoring, and the remaining buttons are used in step-entry recording, which can be done with

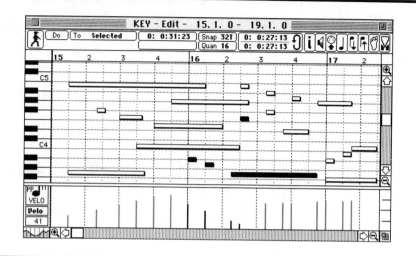

**Figure 5.47**
The Key Edit window displays notes graphically in the familiar piano-roll format and includes a lower section for continuous controller and other types of data. Notice the four selected notes in the center.

the Pencil tool from the Tools menu or from a MIDI keyboard. Selecting the Paint Brush tool allows you to "paint" new notes onto the grid by dragging the brush around (Figure 5.48). Although the results are seldom very musical, it's still fun to play with. One other unique feature in this window deserves mentioning: the Chord display. This box shows the current names of chords as you record them and again when you play them back—very useful for analyzing your music.

Cubase's version of the Event List display is the Grid Edit window (Figure 5.49). This multipart window combines the listing of events with two types of graphic displays. On the left you'll find the typical chronological list of MIDI events along with the corresponding data. You can display the start position of each event in either measures or SMPTE timecode, and you can insert, delete, and edit notes in the same ways that most other programs allow. Cubase, however, puts a unique twist on the old event-list format by including a graphic representation of the same data.

The middle section of the Grid Edit window displays measures along the top—much like the Key Edit window—but now the vertical axis corresponds to the chronological position of the MIDI events displayed in the adjoining list. Notes and other events appear as white rectangles with duration represented graphically. You can change the length of a note with the

# Sequencing at the Top 87

**Figure 5.48**
The Paint Brush tool allows you to "paint" new notes onto the grid.

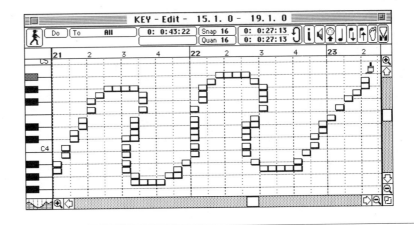

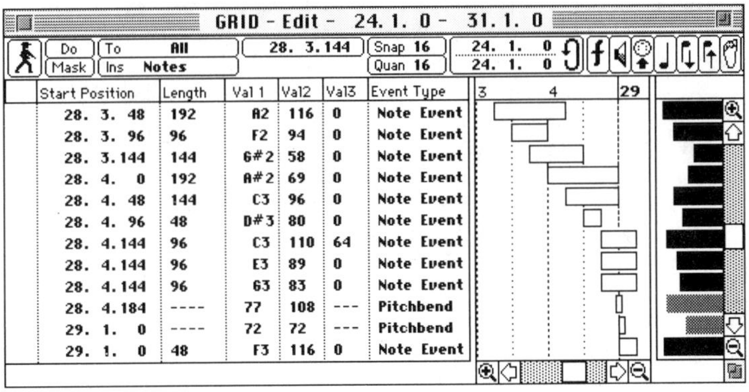

**Figure 5.49**
Cubase's unique Grid Edit window combines an event list with two additional graphic displays.

Pencil tool by dragging its rectangle into a longer or shorter shape. You can also move an event to another location in the list by dragging its rectangle to a new position.

On the far right of the window, the Bargraph display represents note velocities (and some other types of data) as a series of black horizontal bars. You can adjust velocity values quickly by dragging the bars to the left or right to lengthen or shorten them. Most of the same recording, editing, and playback features found in the Key Edit window are available in the Grid Edit window as well. Global commands, looping, step-entry recording, quantizing, note monitoring, etc., can all be accomplished within this environment if you prefer.

Cubase is the only program in this group, other than Performer, that offers a display in standard musical notation. The Score Edit window (Figure 5.50), however, goes one step beyond Performer by allowing you to display several staves at once. If you select a number of Parts to be edited in the Score Edit window, each Part will be assigned a staff although only one Part at a time will be active. You may have to scroll up or down to see all of the staves if you are editing many Parts, but the ability to compare the music on several lines is a very valuable feature.

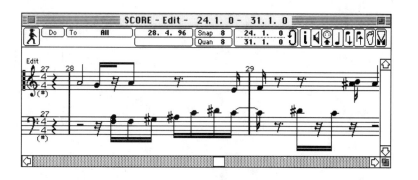

**Figure 5.50**
The Score Edit window lets you view and edit your music using standard notation.

As in the other graphic displays, you can select notes singly or in groups and drag them to new locations or new pitches. Several options allow you to adjust the display to eliminate unnecessary ties, automatically select an appropriate clef, change key, or split parts into a bass and treble clef as in piano notation. This window also has the Chord display mentioned above, along with the same editing, looping, and step-recording functions shared by the other windows.

If you have an insatiable appetite for graphic editing displays, Cubase offers yet another way to record and edit music. The Drum Edit window (Figure 5.51) is designed specifically for creating and editing drum and percussion parts. The format makes it especially well suited to the requirements of drum-machine-style recording while allowing you to refer to individual percussion sounds by name rather than MIDI note number. If you're familiar with Upbeat (Dr. T's Music Software), or you've used a Roland drum machine, this display should make you feel right at home. The left side of the display lists the different drum sounds in your drum machine or sound module, which you assign to the appropriate MIDI note numbers. In the other columns you set the quantization values, note lengths, and MIDI channels. These settings comprise the Drum Map, which can list up to 64 drum and percussion sounds and their corresponding parameter values. Different drum maps can be saved for different sound modules and different compositions.

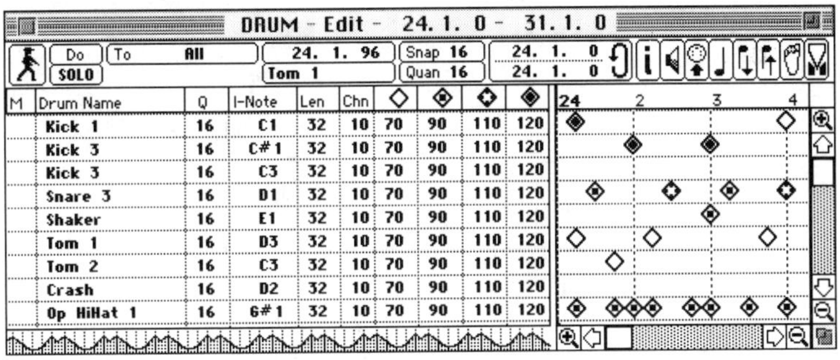

**Figure 5.51**
Cubase's Drum Edit window lets you create and edit rhythm parts.

| M | Drum Name | Q | I-Note | Len | Chn | ◊ | ◈ | ◊ | ◈ | 24 | 2 | 3 | 4 |
|---|-----------|----|--------|-----|-----|----|----|----|----|----|----|----|----|
|   | Kick 1    | 16 | C1     | 32  | 10  | 70 | 90 | 110| 120| ◈  |    | ◊  | ◊  |
|   | Kick 3    | 16 | C#1    | 32  | 10  | 70 | 90 | 110| 120|    |    |    |    |
|   | Kick 3    | 16 | C3     | 32  | 10  | 70 | 90 | 110| 120|    |    |    |    |
|   | Snare 3   | 16 | D1     | 32  | 10  | 70 | 90 | 110| 120| ◈  | ◊  | ◈  | ◈  |
|   | Shaker    | 16 | E1     | 32  | 10  | 70 | 90 | 110| 120|    | ◈  |    |    |
|   | Tom 1     | 16 | D3     | 32  | 10  | 70 | 90 | 110| 120| ◊  | ◊  |    | ◊  |
|   | Tom 2     | 16 | C3     | 32  | 10  | 70 | 90 | 110| 120| ◊  |    |    |    |
|   | Crash     | 16 | D2     | 32  | 10  | 70 | 90 | 110| 120|    |    |    |    |
|   | Op HiHat 1| 16 | G#1    | 32  | 10  | 70 | 90 | 110| 120| ◈  |◈◈◈| ◈◈ | ◈ ◈|

The graphic display uses little diamond shapes to indicate the individual drum-sound events along a grid marked horizontally with measures. You enter notes by first selecting the Drumstick tool and then simply clicking where you want to add each drum sound. By selecting different Macintosh key combinations before clicking each note, you can set one of four user-defined velocity values represented by different patterns inside the diamonds. Looping a 2–4 measure section allows you to build up rhythm patterns in a drum-machine-style, but more easily with the benefit of visual feedback. Recording can also be done from your MIDI keyboard and any results, from either method, are subject to the same graphic editing capabilities as in the other editing windows. In addition, a Controller display like the one in the Key Edit window provides non-note event editing.

If you feel that five editing environments are not quite enough for your taste, Cubase offers still another way to affect your MIDI data. The Logical Edit display provides the opportunity to alter MIDI events in a variety of ways by selecting parameters from a large dialog box (Figure 5.52). This serves a function similar to the Change Filter display in Master Tracks Pro 5, but in a more elaborate and powerful, though much less intuitive, form. Logical Edit lets you set up Conditions and Operations or specify Results to make certain kinds of alterations, within certain ranges, to the designated kinds of events. In fact, other programs like Performer and Vision provide many of the same kinds of variable parameter settings for their global editing commands, but Cubase has focused these operations into a single, though somewhat abstruse, display.

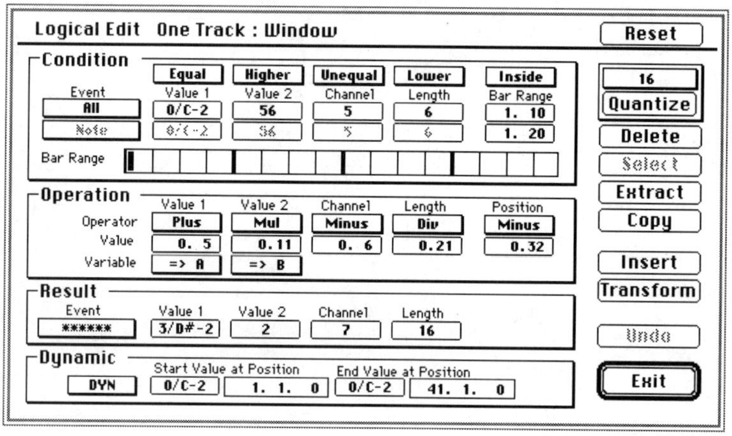

**Figure 5.52**
The Logical Edit display lets you alter MIDI events by assigning parameters to achieve certain kinds of results.

Since all of the other sequencers mentioned in this chapter provide a graphic display with faders or sliders, it's no surprise that Cubase also offers this feature. But what is surprising is the variety and flexibility of controls that Cubase provides. Rather than predefining the number and style of faders, the MIDI Mixer window lets you create your own customized control panel with faders, knobs, numerical displays, and switches (Figure 5.53). You then assign these "Objects" to control the kinds of MIDI data that you want.

**Figure 5.53**
Cubase's MIDI Mixer window lets you create your own control panels by grouping various "Objects" and assigning them to different kinds of MIDI data.

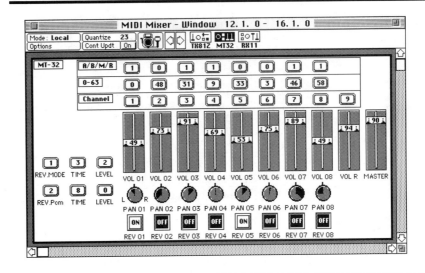

With the MIDI Mixer you can create mixing consoles, switch boxes, or "virtual" front-end panels for your sound modules. You can group controls in a variety of ways and record their actions into a Part. Any configuration with up to 128 objects can be easily assembled by creating, moving, and sizing the graphic controls.

Most of the sequencers in this group offer an option that enables you to generate new music from old. In its most basic form, this can be simply a function that takes a melody and inverts or reverses it. More advanced applications, like the one in Vision, separate the components of the music and algorithmically recombine them. Not to be outdone, Cubase introduces yet another window, which it calls the Interactive Phrase Synthesizer (Figure 5.54). This music-generating feature models itself after a synthesizer that creates music, not sounds, in real time.

The IPS uses three modules—Phrase Input, MIDI Input, and Interpreter—to modify a recorded section of music. The phrase is a copy of the original recorded material—the basic building blocks. By playing from your MIDI keyboard, the MIDI Input module interacts with this data in a way determined by the Interpreter module. The new music output from the Interpreter gets further split into its three components—Rhythm, Pitch, and

**Figure 5.54**
The Interactive Phrase Synthesizer combines real-time MIDI input with prerecorded material to create algorithmically generated new music.

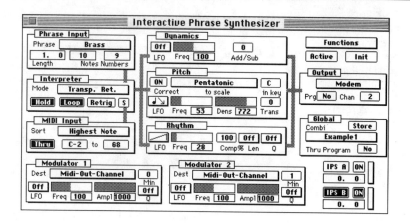

Dynamics—represented by individual on-screen modules. The output from these modules is then summed together and sent to the Output module. The ability to interact with recorded data in real time to make algorithmically generated new music offers great potential for creating a variety of useful musical ideas that can be recorded or performed live.

If you like, you can also use the MIDI Processor (Figure 5.55), Cubase's MIDI equivalent of an audio signal processor, to produce MIDI echo, chorus, pitch shifting, and other effects. Of course, Cubase also offers several quantizing options, as well as a MIDI-keyboard remote-control feature.

**Figure 5.55**
Cubase provides the MIDI equivalent of an audio signal processor in its MIDI Processor window.

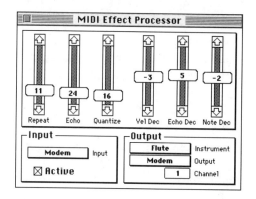

Cubase is an exceptional program. The developers have thrown in everything but the kitchen sink to provide the most comprehensive sequencer possible. The number of options and editing displays is very impressive, and the heavy emphasis on graphics and modular composing techniques will appeal to many users. The trade-off is that often you'll be confronted with unfamiliar terms and a hierarchal structure that can be confusing to work within. Still, if you like manipulating MIDI data, this program should keep you busy for a very long time.

## Final Thoughts

All of the sequencers in this chapter are intended for people who demand the highest levels of power and control for working with MIDI compositions. Although competition has caused them to acquire many of the same kinds of features, there are still very clear differences in the look and feel of the programs, as well as differences in their overall architectures.

The appearance of the program on the screen is more than just cosmetics —it is the environment that you must work within on a regular basis. Performer has an exceptionally nice, well-designed appearance that makes using it feel natural and intuitive. Vision supports color and allows you to assign different colors to different kinds of information. This can be extremely helpful in keeping yourself organized and dealing with the many kinds of data that you will be using. Beyond uses color for some of its windows and monochrome for others. Whether or not you have a color system, you should always consider the clarity and design of a program as one important criterion for selection.

User friendliness also varies from one sequencer to another. Performer and Vision provide online help—a feature that many will appreciate—while Master Tracks Pro 5 tries to keep the program itself as simple as possible. The documentation in this group is generally very good, with Performer and Vision topping the list for thoroughness and usability. Pro 5's manual is concise and well structured. Beyond's is also concise but lacks the same level of clarity, while Cubase's is very thorough but occasionally a bit confusing.

If you're using one of the slower Macintoshes (Plus or SE), you might consider the size and processing demands of the programs. Master Tracks Pro 5 and Beyond may work more smoothly and cause fewer delays than some of the other sequencers, depending on your specific configuration.

Finally, you should consider the structure of the program. All of the sequencers in this chapter allow you to create a piece of music as one long continuous work. All of the programs also offer ways of combining sections of music into larger forms, but there are definitely differences in the emphasis placed on these two styles of writing. It's important to consider your compositional needs and the flexibility of the software to avoid being forced into a writing or editing approach that does not ideally suit you.

# Chapter 6

# Sequencing on Easy Street

All the sequencers described in Chapter 5 are powerful, complex, and rather expensive. While professional composers will run these programs through their paces, many other users only need something to meet more modest demands. If your interest lies in playing MIDI files along with presentations and your editing requirements are not extensive, or if you're a relative newcomer to MIDI and you want a program that's not too daunting and not too expensive, then one of the sequencers in this chapter should be just the ticket.

## EZ Vision

EZ Vision is Opcode's scaled-down, budget-priced version of its popular high-end sequencer. Although many of Vision's more sophisticated features are missing in EZ Vision, this program offers some unique options and surprises of its own and the result is a highly intuitive, well-designed sequencer that will satisfy the needs of a great many users.

EZ Vision shares many qualities with its bigger brother, such as a respectable 480-ppqn note resolution and the ability to establish a communication link with Galaxy, Opcode's universal editor/librarian (covered in Chapter 9). By creating this link you can transfer patch names directly from Galaxy to EZ Vision, where they will appear in pop-up windows for you to select. If you're concerned about your future sequencing needs, Opcode provides an upgrade path to Vision, which directly imports EZ Vision files.

To simplify this sequencer, several choices had to be made concerning where to trim the program. As a result, several features present in Vision are absent here. EZ Vision, for example, does not support SMPTE timecode and also doesn't show elapsed time in its counter display. You can only record on one track at a time in EZ Vision since there is no MultiRecord provision allowing input from several channels into several tracks simultaneously. The graphic editing display has been simplified, and there is no event-list editing capability.

Both Vision and EZ Vision share the same quantizing categories—note quantize, cursor quantize, and playback quantize—but EZ Vision lacks the additional note-quantizing options, such as Strength and Sensitivity, that Vision offers.

Each sequence in EZ Vision can have up to 16 tracks, which are assigned as a default to the 16 MIDI channels. If you like, you can change the assignments by selecting from any of the 16 channels on either the modem or printer port. You can create and save up to 25 sequences in EZ Vision, which, as in Vision, can be played by typing the designated letter from the Macintosh keyboard.

Notes and other MIDI events are displayed and edited in a large integrated window that also incorporates the transport controls and counter. The Edit window (Figure 6.1) shares a number of features with Vision, including the Strip Chart, which allows you to edit note velocity, duration, and several other kinds of MIDI events. EZ Vision also offers the same recording options—Overdub, Replace, and Loop—that are found in Vision, and similar step-recording and note-inserting features are available as well.

Along the left side of the window, you'll find a column listing the tracks by number and color. EZ Vision offers one of the best color implementations of any sequencer on the market. Each track can be assigned a color, and the note events displayed in the Edit window appear in the appropriate color for each track. Down below, the Strip Chart also shows its data in the corresponding color.

This use of color is, itself, a useful feature for reducing confusion when viewing track data, but it becomes even more extraordinary when combined with another powerful feature: multiple-track display. EZ Vision lets you

# Sequencing on Easy Street

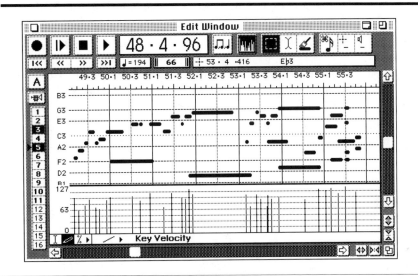

**Figure 6.1**
EZ Vision's Edit window combines a piano-roll display with the same kind of Strip Chart that Vision uses.

view and edit any or all of a sequence's 16 tracks simultaneously, with each track's data designated by a different color. Watching a sequence scroll by with the different instrument sounds appearing in different colors is quite a treat, as well as an invaluable tool for analyzing music and diagnosing compositional problems. This is one feature that every sequencer should have.

Once you have recorded your data onto a track, EZ Vision provides a good assortment of editing options. You can select notes with the Marquee tool by dragging over a region of limited pitch and time, whereas the I-beam tool selects all pitches in a region limited only by time. At the top of the window, the status bar changes to display information that is appropriate to the editing task being performed.

Inserting notes in EZ Vision is a breeze. Aside from the usual note-inserting procedures, there is an option that lets you "paint" a note in by clicking where you want it and dragging the cursor to establish its duration—very fast and intuitive. EZ Vision also provides an Audible Feedback option, which lets you hear each note as it's selected, and two excellent Scrubbing features for listening to the whole track (or group of tracks) out of tempo. The Shuttle button (in the transport controls) lets you scan with variable speeds through your music. This works well even at extremely slow speeds. If you prefer, you can press the Command key to turn the cursor into a speaker icon that allows you to scrub manually with the mouse.

EZ Vision's Strip Chart resembles the one in Vision and displays the same kinds of non-note MIDI events. Selecting the Pencil tool makes editing this data quick and easy by simply drawing a line where you want the new values. Seven Edit Tools and five Edit Curves allow you to modify note properties in a variety of ways, such as determining minimum or maximum amounts and applying a variety of shapes or curves to the data display. Tempo changes can also be displayed and edited in the Strip Chart, and the Tap Tempo feature lets you set the sequence tempo by tapping on the Quote key at least three times.

In EZ Vision you can string together several sequences into a "Song" by employing a window that resembles a simplified version of the Chunks display in Performer. The Arrangement window (Figure 6.2) provides a large field on which you can display and organize your sequences and includes its own set of transport controls. It uses graphic representations called *blocks* to symbolize the different sequences. To enter a sequence you can type its letter or select it from a pop-up menu. The sequence block then appears in the Arrangement window with its name and letter. Sequences can only play serially and cannot overlap or play simultaneously. They can, however, be cut, copied, dragged, lengthened, shortened, and rearranged within the window.

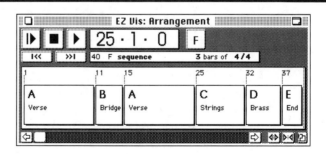

**Figure 6.2**
With the Arrangement window, EZ Vision lets you string together several sequences into a Song.

To allow you to adjust the volume and the pan settings (stereo positioning) of the individual instruments in your sequences, EZ Vision provides a Mixer window (Figure 6.3). Unlike the mixers in the pro-level programs, these faders control only volume (or velocity) data, which can be further edited in the Strip Chart display. Above each volume fader, a Pan controller produces a pop-up display that lets you adjust the stereo position of each track. Above that, an activity indicator shows the presence of MIDI information on each track much like the MIDI Monitor in Performer. Faders can also be grouped, and individual tracks can be soloed or muted.

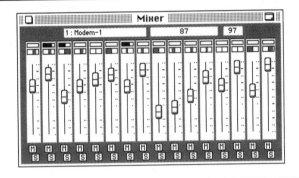

**Figure 6.3**
The Mixer window allows you to adjust the volume and pan position of each track.

Opcode Systems has managed to strike a very good balance between simplicity and power in its design of EZ Vision. Most operations are logical and straightforward, and the addition of color, as a functional feature, provides an extra bonus. Some users may be concerned about the 16-track limit for sequences and the inability to assign multiple channels to a single track, but for many people these limitations should not pose a serious problem. With its 480-ppqn note resolution and online help, EZ Vision deserves serious consideration as an entry-level sequencer.

## Trax

Although Trax is the least expensive sequencer in this group, it still retains many of the features that characterize its parent program, Master Tracks

Pro 5. Passport has taken the structure and layout of its popular pro-level sequencer and trimmed away several features to provide a product with the same straightforward design but at a fraction of the cost.

Like Pro 5, Trax boasts a generous 64 tracks per sequence along with the same 240-ppqn note resolution. The Track Sheet in Trax (Figure 6.4) corresponds to the left side of the Track Editor window in Master Tracks Pro 5. A quick comparison of the two reveals the same columns for Record and Playback functions, device and patch names, MIDI channel assignments, and graphic volume faders. Although the two windows differ slightly in appearance, the essential functions are the same.

The right half of Pro 5's Track Editor (which shows sequence data in measure units) has become the Song Editor window in Trax (Figure 6.5). These two displays, which look nearly identical, provide the same kinds of Cut, Copy, Paste, and regional editing capabilities.

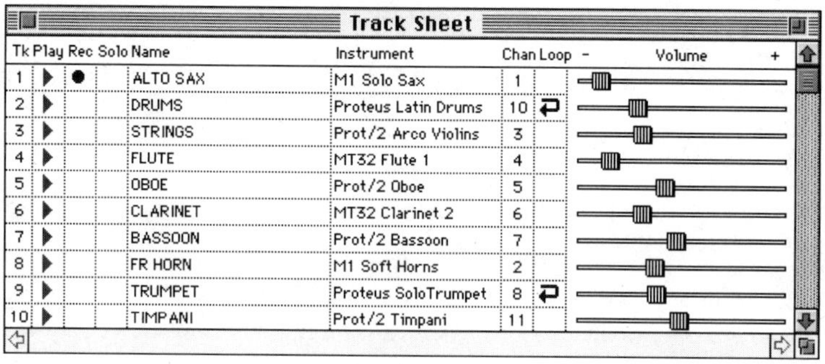

**Figure 6.4**
Trax provides a clearly designed Track Sheet listing instrument names and channel assignments along with graphic faders for volume adjustments.

| Tk | Play | Rec | Solo | Name | Instrument | Chan | Loop | Volume |
|----|------|-----|------|------|------------|------|------|--------|
| 1  | ▶    | ●   |      | ALTO SAX | M1 Solo Sax | 1 | | |
| 2  | ▶    |     |      | DRUMS | Proteus Latin Drums | 10 | ↵ | |
| 3  | ▶    |     |      | STRINGS | Prot/2 Arco Violins | 3 | | |
| 4  | ▶    |     |      | FLUTE | MT32 Flute 1 | 4 | | |
| 5  | ▶    |     |      | OBOE | Prot/2 Oboe | 5 | | |
| 6  | ▶    |     |      | CLARINET | MT32 Clarinet 2 | 6 | | |
| 7  | ▶    |     |      | BASSOON | Prot/2 Bassoon | 7 | | |
| 8  | ▶    |     |      | FR HORN | M1 Soft Horns | 2 | | |
| 9  | ▶    |     |      | TRUMPET | Proteus SoloTrumpet | 8 | ↵ | |
| 10 | ▶    |     |      | TIMPANI | Prot/2 Timpani | 11 | | |

The Step Editor window in Trax (Figure 6.6) is almost an exact clone, in both appearance and function, of Pro 5's display of the same name. The one noticeable omission from Trax's window, the note icon in the upper-left corner, reveals one of the biggest differences between these two products: Trax does not display or provide for the editing of continuous controller data. As a result, the various MIDI Data windows in Pro 5 are missing in Trax. Passport has also eliminated the Event List window from its less expensive program. In spite of having fewer displays, Trax still provides most of the global editing commands and quantizing options (except Humanize and Time Scaling) that its high-end counterpart offers.

Sequencing on Easy Street

**Figure 6.5**
The Song Editor window displays the presence of MIDI data in measure units.

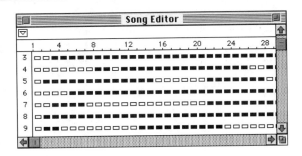

**Figure 6.6**
The Step Editor window in Trax is nearly identical to the same display in Master Tracks Pro 5.

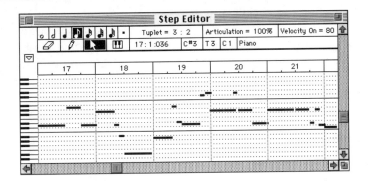

Not surprisingly, the Transport window in Trax (Figure 6.7) matches very closely its equivalent in Pro 5. Although the counter display shows elapsed time below the measure indicator, Trax does not recognize SMPTE timecode. On the right side of the Transport window, the absence of a Record Mode button points out that Trax also does not provide the same recording options that are found in Pro 5, such as Overdub, Loop Recording, and Multi-Track Recording. Trax also lacks a Song Playlist feature that lets you string sequences together and doesn't provide a MIDI-keyboard remote-control option. Both programs do share the same kind of tempo window for displaying and changing meter and tempo.

For a more detailed exploration of the things that Trax can do and how it does them, you should read the relevant descriptions of the Master Tracks Pro 5 features in Chapter 5. The general operating procedures and the look

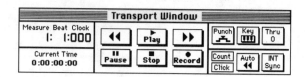

**Figure 6.7**
The Transport window in Trax is very similar to its equivalent in Pro 5.

and feel of the two sequencers are remarkably similar considering that Trax costs less than a third as much as Pro 5.

With Trax, Passport Designs has successfully brought quality sequencing to the masses by combining many of the features from its high-end sequencer into a package that is very easy to use and cost-effective. Many people will be concerned about the lack of overdub and loop-recording options as well as the conspicuous absence of continuous controller editing, but for most beginners and those with modest needs, Trax should serve quite well. Pro 5 and Trax sequences use the same format, so they can read each other's files, and Passport Designs offers an upgrade path for Trax users who find they need the features of Pro 5.

## Ballade

Ballade, from Dynaware, is a fascinating product that approaches sequencing from a slightly different angle than most programs. It is also a product filled with apparent contradictions. Although it's a moderately inexpensive program, clearly targeted at beginning users, it requires a substantial 1.5 megabytes of memory for the application and its files. Additionally, it records with a surprisingly meager 48-ppqn note resolution (to avoid slowing its data processing), yet supports several formats of SMPTE timecode—most unusual for this type of product. Apple's MIDI Manager, which must be used with Ballade, is included with the program.

If you want to use Ballade, you must be able to read standard musical notation since the only display for editing note data (except for the rhythm track) uses this system. Some people will find this appealing, but as I've pointed out earlier, standard notation has its drawbacks. For one thing, it's hard to see more than two or three measures at a time, and for another thing, musical notes don't accurately reflect the subtleties of a performance. Ballade makes the most of these limitations by providing ways to slightly adjust the playback performance and by allowing you to print one or more tracks of your music.

The main editing display, the Score Editor window (Figure 6.8), requires most of the screen to be fully useful. But, to enter note data, you'll also need at least three or four additional palettes or displays. This creates an instant on-screen clutter that often requires shuffling windows to see all parts of the main display.

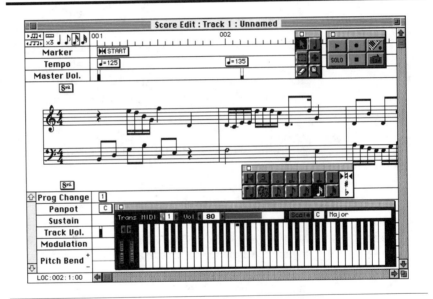

**Figure 6.8**
Ballade's Score Editor window uses standard musical notation along with several horizontal fields for other types of MIDI data.

To enter notes on the staff, Ballade offers three step-recording approaches: You can enter notes from your MIDI keyboard, you can insert notes using the mouse, or you can select notes using the "Virtual Keyboard." In any case, you first select a note value from the Note Palette. Playing notes from your MIDI controller or the on-screen keyboard places the notes on the staff in succession as the rests disappear to accommodate the entries. You can also enter chords in this way.

If you enter a wrong note with the mouse, you can undo the entry, but if you enter a wrong note from the MIDI keyboard, you must choose another cursor and select the note before you can clear or cut it—not very conducive to rapid step-entry. The Eraser tool is faster, but only a little.

The Transport display that appears with the Score Editor provides buttons for Play, Stop, Record, Step Entry, and Auto Scroll. Noticeably absent, however, is a Rewind button to quickly return you to the start of the track. This must be done by scrolling with the scroll bar at the bottom of the window or by setting the Auto-Return feature. Similarly, to view the other tracks in the sequence—there can be as many as 16—you must use the vertical scroll bar to skip from track to track. Only one track can be active at a time.

Selecting the magnifying-glass icon and clicking on a note produces a pop-up window that lets you change certain note parameters. You can also shift the attack of the note forward or backward, in a limited way, to keep the music from becoming too mechanical sounding.

Above and below the staff, several horizontal fields display markers, tempo and volume changes, modulation and pitch-bend events, and program changes.

To control the different instrument sounds in your sequence, Ballade provides an impressively realistic, full-color mixing console. The Mixer window (Figure 6.9) has faders for each of the 16 possible tracks in a sequence, which are assigned to the MIDI channels with the same numbers. In spite of its many limitations, this window is a lot of fun to watch, with its pulsing, two-color, VU-style meters, its flashing indicators, and its readouts that mimic the appearance of LCD displays. Clicking on the panel's buttons changes their color, and the faders move during playback to reflect the volume settings on each track.

In the upper-right corner a measure indicator shows the current sequence location, but only by measure number, not by measure, beat, and unit as in all other sequencers. You are left to deduce the current beat within the measure by studying a line of flashing triangles beneath the numerical display. This may be entertaining to watch but not very practical for serious editing.

# Sequencing on Easy Street

**Figure 6.9**
Ballade's colorful Mixer window provides faders for 16 MIDI channels along with pulsing meters and numeric displays that mimic LCD readouts.

The small windows for SMPTE time, Tempo, and Transpose are more useful, and the Master Volume fader is handy for adjusting the overall volume.

Ballade, in its current incarnation, is optimized for use with Roland sound modules (MT-32, CM-32L, CM-64, and SC-55)—a fact only obliquely mentioned in the documentation. This becomes apparent when viewing the default settings in the Mixer window. The rhythm track has been assigned to channel 10, there is no Reverb button for track 1, and the program numbers refer to Roland default settings. Furthermore, the Reverb button above each slider sends system-exclusive messages that are only readable by Roland modules. If you are using another brand of hardware, you can create your own list of patch names and assign the program numbers to the appropriate tracks. You can also move the rhythm track to another location.

When you enter the Mixer window, you are provided with a Transport Palette that differs from the one in the Score Editor. This display supplies the missing Rewind button along with a Fast Forward control to help you maneuver through the sequence. To record in real time, you click on the desired Track button in the Mixer and press the Record button in the Transport Palette. Ballade provides options for Loop, Overdub, Normal, and Punch-in recording, as well as a multi-record mode for entering data into several tracks at once. There are also limited quantizing and time-scaling options and a Chain Play feature that lets you define a list of sequences to play back jukebox-style in a specified order.

To step-record drum parts, Ballade provides a Rhythm Track editor (Figure 6.10). This allows you to build drum tracks by selecting "sound symbols" from the Rhythm Palette and placing them on a grid. These diamond shapes determine the loudness of the notes by depicting higher velocities with larger diamonds. The editing commands from the Score Editor are available here as well.

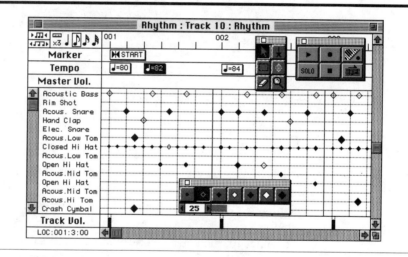

**Figure 6.10**
Ballade's Rhythm Track editor lets you build drum tracks by placing small diamonds on a grid.

Ballade lets you print your scores (using the Sonata font) with a number of options. You can select the whole score or specify one or more tracks. A Score Preview feature lets you see (but not alter) the layout of the page before you print.

It's hard to summarize Ballade—a program with some high-end features, like SMPTE timecode recognition, time scaling, and MIDI-keyboard remote control, but lacking in several other areas. Its 48-ppqn note resolution does not meet current sequencer standards, although it can read Standard MIDI Files from other programs with higher resolutions and retain those resolutions during playback. Step recording and editing are often cumbersome, the displays, although nice to look at, are sometimes awkwardly implemented, and the program lacks a consistently true Macintosh feel.

If you prefer working with standard musical notation but are not inclined to invest in a pro-level sequencer, you may find Ballade a viable alternative. If your primary interest lies in playing back Standard MIDI Files, especially in conjunction with a video presentation or an audiotape recording, the SMPTE timecode capability may be a significant plus. If your system includes a color monitor and one or two Roland sound modules, so much the better. In any case, the Mixer window is always fun to watch and fiddle with.

## DeluxeRecorder

DeluxeRecorder, from Electronic Arts, provides a commendable assortment of MIDI data displays while still keeping the overall structure of the program appropriately simple for an inexpensive sequencer. Its two primary windows manage to handle the tasks of setting up, recording, and editing data with enough flexibility to accommodate most circumstances. It also offers its own unique approach to performing various operations and combines that with several features not commonly found in other similar products.

DeluxeRecorder's Console window (Figure 6.11) consists of two components: the Control Panel, with its familiar transport-style buttons and indicators, and the Track List, which displays the 16 available tracks per sequence along with their related settings. The Channel column lets you assign any MIDI channel from either port to any track and, if you like, list tracks, devices, and instrument sounds by name. Clicking on an entry in the Volume, Pan, or Transpose column pops up a thermometer-style indicator that you can set quickly and easily by dragging with the mouse. DeluxeRecorder also provides a Split Channel command, which allows multi-channel recording by separating incoming data into separate tracks.

On the right side of the Control Panel, a counter display shows the current location in measures, beats, and ticks with a resolution of 480 ppqn. By

**Figure 6.11**
DeluxeRecorder's Console window combines the Control Panel with the Track List.

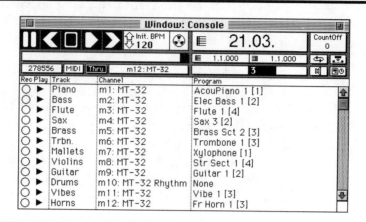

clicking in the window, you can change the display to indicate elapsed time. The CountOff button allows you to set any number of beats as a lead-in for recording. Below that, four additional buttons activate the looping, auto punch-in, metronome, and MIDI timing-source functions.

Next to the transport controls, a tempo indicator lets you set the initial tempo for the sequence by entering a specific value or by tapping on the mouse or spacebar to determine the tempo. In the lower-left corner, two indicators show available memory, the presence of MIDI input data, and the MIDI Thru channel.

The transport controls, themselves, are similar to those in other programs except that you can click and drag on the Fast Forward button to speed up or slow down the playback as much as you want until you release the button and automatically return to the initial tempo setting. You may be surprised to discover that the Control Panel doesn't include a Record button. That's because DeluxeRecorder approaches the recording process in a unique way.

To record music from your MIDI keyboard, you simply click the Play button in the Control Panel and begin your performance. The program does not immediately place the data in a selected track but rather stores the contents of the recording in a buffer. When you click Stop, the Reel icon flashes, indicating the presence of data in the buffer. Then the Post Record dialog box appears, asking what you would like to do with the recording (Figure 6.12). Clicking Play without assigning the data to a track replaces the contents of the buffer with the new recording. This way you can try a passage of music several times until you get something you like and then decide where to place it.

**Figure 6.12**
The Post Record dialog box lets you decide where to put each recording.

If you find the dialog box bothersome, you can simply drag the flashing Reel icon to the track where you want the recording placed. If you prefer a more traditional approach, you can also click one of the Record buttons in the Track List to record directly onto that track. Once you make a recording, a scrolling Cue Bar, similar to the Position Bar in Performer, shows your progress through the sequence during playback.

Double-clicking on a track name in the Track List opens DeluxeRecorder's Edit window (Figure 6.13). This display can contain as many as 11 "staves" to depict graphically the MIDI data in each track. The note events, themselves, appear on a Grand Staff—the kind used for piano music—only this display does not use standard notation. The Edit window employs a very effective hybrid system of notation that combines the best features of piano-roll displays and standard musical notation. The notes are depicted as black bars, with duration represented by length rather than stems, flags, and beams. The black-key notes appear as bars preceded by sharps or flats, and ledger lines extend the note range outside the staff area. This system works well under most circumstances and offers a notational method that allows precise adjustments of notes while still maintaining a visual familiarity for those used to working with printed music. If you prefer, you can have the notes appear on a Chromatic staff, which more closely resembles the standard piano-roll display.

The tear-off Tools menu provides several cursor options that allow you to select notes in various ways, to change their positions, durations, and velocities, and to add new notes and accidentals. Of course, the usual Cut, Copy, and Paste commands are available as well, but DeluxeRecorder also offers another option that is both interesting and unique. The Scale Paste command lets you copy a selected area of notes and then specify an area of any length (larger or smaller) into which you want the selection pasted. For instance, you could past a two-measure phrase into an area four measures long, thereby doubling the note values as well as the phrase length without affecting the pitch. You can also apply Scale Paste to graphically displayed continuous controller data to create both useful and unusual effects.

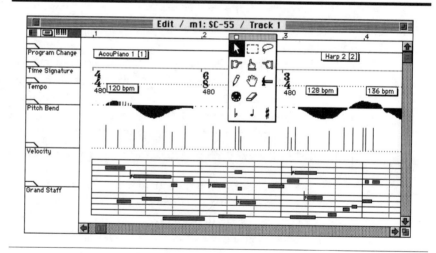

**Figure 6.13**
DeluxeRecorder's Edit window uses a unique hybrid display that combines a piano-roll format with musical notation. Additional "staves" show other kinds of MIDI data.

Selected regions can also be transposed up or down by a half step, a scale step, or an octave and quantized fully or halfway. Another useful feature in DeluxeRecorder lets you make a Rubato recording, playing freely without the metronome; afterward, you can establish the correct barline positions (relative to the music) with the Fit Music to Beat Lines option. This aligns the measures with the program's internal clock and displays the resulting tempo changes on the Tempo staff. Step recording in DeluxeRecorder is similar to that in other sequencers where note values are selected from a menu and placed on the staff by playing from a MIDI controller, with the degree of legato or staccato determined by the specified Duration value.

Aside from the Grand Staff, you can include any combination of additional staves in the Edit window. These are actually single lines or horizontal fields that display a variety of non-note MIDI data. The Edit window allows graphic displays of continuous controller data, pitch bend, tempo changes, time signature changes, velocity, and program-change numbers, among others. Data in these staves can be inserted and edited by using the same tools that are available for note editing. Changing parameters is easy and intuitive, often making use of pop-up windows and dialog boxes.

DeluxeRecorder represents yet another effort to bring affordable sequencing to the masses. Its unusual approach to recording, along with its clearly designed graphic displays, gives it a character all its own. It doesn't have a mixer window nor does it provide an option for chaining sequences, but it does offer high resolution, several unique options, an excellent manual, and a note event display that many will find quite functional and intuitive.

## Encore

Encore, from Passport Designs, has long enjoyed a reputation for being a smart and intuitive notation program that, with the right printer, can produce publisher-quality sheet music without imposing an arduous learning curve. But many people are unaware of Encore's other side. Technically speaking, Encore is also a sequencer since it enables you to record, notate, edit, and play back MIDI performances. To be sure, it does have its limitations. You can only view data in standard musical notation, you can't edit continuous controller events, there is no mixer window, and you can't edit program changes. Quantizing options are similarly limited and there are none of the sophisticated recording and editing features that some sequencers provide.

On the other hand, Encore does have a lot to offer even aside from its manuscript-layout capabilities. With it you can create a piece of music with up to four voices per staff and as many as 64 staves per sequence. The music can be played back on any of 32 MIDI channels (16 from each port) and can import Standard MIDI Files as well as files from Master Tracks Pro 5 and Trax, which share its 240-ppqn note resolution. Unlike the other programs in this group, Encore costs more than the high-end sequencers in Chapter 5. It is included in this section because its sequencing abilities more nearly match the products in this chapter, rather than those in the previous one. You must decide, therefore, whether the music manuscript editing and printing capabilities justify the additional cost for your particular application.

Nearly all of the operations in Encore are centered on the Edit window (Figure 6.14), which contains the Record and Play buttons, the cursor options, and the musical staves. Seven palettes of symbols can be accessed for selecting note values along with a plethora of markings and musical devices.

**Figure 6.14**
Encore's Edit window combines its basic transport controls with multistaff display capabilities.

Aside from importing MIDI files, you can enter music into the program in several ways. Step-recording options in Encore resemble those in other programs. You can select note values from the Notes Palette and deposit them anywhere on the staff with the mouse, or you can play the notes one at a time from your MIDI keyboard. If you prefer, you can perform the music in real time while Encore displays the note heads on the staff as you play. Since your performance will not likely be metrically perfect, Encore uses its Guess Durations command to make an educated guess about your musical intentions from a notational standpoint. It then supplies the appropriate flags, stems, and beams to transform your performance into written music. In most cases, this feature works surprisingly well, eliminating the blizzard of 32nd rests, tied notes, and illegible clusters that mar the functionality of many other sequencers using standard notation.

Regardless of the method of note entry chosen, you can adjust the appearance of the score as well as the music's playback characteristics by choosing one of several editing options. Selected areas can be cut, copied, pasted, deleted, and mixed. Additionally, you can transpose the music and change its key, meter, tempo, note durations, velocities, and accidentals. If you're printing the music, you can also add chord symbols, lyrics, and text.

In truth, it's a little unfair to compare Encore—designed to record and edit music for creating printed scores—with a more traditional sequencer—designed to record, edit, and play performances. Still, there is an undeniable overlap in capabilities here. If you have academic training in composition, Encore is the closest you're likely to come to combining MIDI with the traditional pencil and manuscript paper.

One problem encountered in displaying MIDI data as standard notation is that most sequencers let you see only a few measures at a time. Encore does not suffer from this problem. It offers the opportunity to view several staves at once, and if you are using a 13- or 14-inch monitor, it is not impossible to view 30 or more measures per screen. On the other hand, Encore's MIDI editing and organizing capabilities are basic. If you like working with on-screen manuscript paper and your recording and editing requirements are not too demanding, this program deserves consideration, especially if you work with singers and instrumentalists who need printed music. Encore's logical, intuitive design, combined with its excellent documentation, makes it a pleasure to use.

## Final Thoughts

The sequencers in this chapter offer a surprising range of styles and features considering their modest prices. They are often marketed to MIDI neophytes but are actually quite suitable for anyone who doesn't need or can't afford the power and complexity of the high-end sequencers. Multimedia producers, in particular, should find these programs adequate for playing and adjusting Standard MIDI Files for inclusion in presentations.

These programs are not without their limitations, however. All but one lack SMPTE timecode capabilities, and they all provide fewer types of editing environments and fewer editing and recording options. Still, they represent a good, though variable, balance between features and price.

EZ Vision is clearly the strongest contender in this group. It offers high resolution, the ability to chain sequences, graphic display and editing of continuous controller data, and a logical, intuitive design. Furthermore, it's hard to beat its color support, multitrack display, and online help.

Trax offers its own combination of strong points. Rather than the 16-track limit in EZ Vision, Trax provides up to 64 tracks per sequence and allows you to assign any MIDI channel to any track. It also boasts a multi-record option that lets you record on several tracks from several MIDI channels simultaneously.

Ballade has some especially nice graphics, SMPTE support, and a time-scaling feature, while DeluxeRecorder offers unique recording options combined with its hybrid note-event display and continuous controller editing. Finally, Encore brings together the worlds of traditional notation and MIDI performance in a program that is elegant and logical, though a bit pricey.

Since many of these programs are aimed at beginners, their documentation becomes especially important. Top honors go to EZ Vision, Encore, and DeluxeRecorder for manuals that are lucid, comprehensive, and well designed. The Trax manual is concise and readable but loses points for the inexcusable absence of an index. The Ballade manual looks much better than it is but may be improved in future revisions.

# Chapter 7

# Instant MIDI

As presentation programs acquire more sophistication and visual displays become more advanced, an ever-increasing need arises for music-production quality to keep pace. Several programs can trigger external devices, such as compact disc players, and this will certainly add high-fidelity music to your presentation. But this arrangement offers little flexibility and no real editing capability. Digitized audio provides greater editing potential as well as more flexibility, but to produce CD-quality stereo sound requires enormous amounts of memory and usually involves additional plug-in cards. To capture that elusive combination of great flexibility, high fidelity, and reasonable cost, multimedia producers are turning in growing numbers to MIDI music sequences.

MIDI sequences, as I explained in Chapter 4, are simply files containing the performance data needed to re-create a musical composition via MIDI. To add sequenced music to a presentation, you'll need a synthesizer or sound module, a sequencer program, and a MIDI interface. In a later chapter we'll examine a line of computer-music peripherals offered by Roland Corp., which attests to the burgeoning popularity of this hardware/software solution to music production.

Unlike digitized audio, music sequences do not require large amounts of memory, and since the music is re-created in real time directly from the sound modules, there won't be any degradation of sound quality associated with some recording processes. Most significantly, with any of the current crop of professional-level sequencer programs, you can apply music editing capabilities ranging from the most infinitesimal alterations to the most global of commands. With a few mouse clicks you can change the tempo of a melody, shift the attack of a chord forward or backward by milliseconds, or transpose an entire piece down a half step. Sections of a song can be extracted and recombined and in many other ways a piece of music can be customized to fit your presentation. Although digital audio lets you cut, copy, and paste, only MIDI lets you select the third oboe part in measure 17, beat 3, and change it to an alto sax. The ability to tailor a piece of music to a specific purpose by reorchestrating gives MIDI music an irresistible appeal.

Once you decide to use MIDI sequences for your presentation, you have to consider the next logical step—acquiring good music. There are several possibilities to weigh: 1. You can hire a composer to write the music and deliver it in the form of MIDI files on a floppy disk. 2. You can use a MIDI keyboard along with a sequencer to create the music yourself. Or if these options seem too daunting then fear not! Third-party vendors have jumped in to fill the void by providing *presequenced MIDI music.* These MIDI files are to music what clip art is to the world of graphics—prefabricated works that can be edited and customized to suit your final application. But before we take a more detailed look at this rapidly growing resource, let's examine a few products that can give you a head start in putting together your own music sequences for presentations.

## In the Background

One of the simplest and least expensive offerings comes from New Sound Music. Its **Background Rhythm Patterns** come as a collection of 157 popular rhythm tracks in a wide variety of musical styles, including Rock, Pop, Funk, Heavy Metal, Fusion, Blues, Latin, Jazz, and many more. There are no melodies here, simply drums, keyboard, and bass combined to form a professional-sounding rhythm section for those who want to do their own composing but may lack extensive training in popular music styles. These 4-, 8-, and 12-bar phrases use chord progressions and accompaniment techniques that perfectly capture the flavor of the different musical styles. As a reference tool alone, it provides a great way to acquaint yourself with the myriad styles coexisting in the world of popular music today, but it also serves as a great source of inspiration when you need some help generating new ideas. Simply choose the pattern you want, loop it with your sequencer, and start performing. If you want to build longer sequences you can cut, copy, and paste the patterns and your sequencer will let you add key and tempo changes as needed. For more professional arrangements the library also includes 35 breaks, intros, and endings, and an additional 130 drum patterns in various styles.

New Sound Music also offers a second library of background patterns dedicated entirely to Latin and Afro-Cuban rhythms. This volume includes 70 rhythm patterns along with breaks, intros, fills, and endings. Some sequences even include piano and percussion solos, and the documentation provides notes on constructing and playing original Latin songs.

New Sound's Background Rhythm Patterns come in the form of Standard MIDI Files using channels 1, 2, and 3 for drums, piano, and bass respectively, so they'll work with any multitimbral sound module having on-board drum sounds. The manual includes complete chord charts for all sequences as well as general information.

If you're especially interested in jazz and would like to improve your understanding and technique, New Sound offers **Jazz Through MIDI**, a course in jazz improvising for all levels. Jazz Through MIDI includes 60 professionally arranged, solos or riffs, accompanied by the same piano, bass, and drum setup mentioned above. Each sequence consists of 8-, 12-, 16-, or 32-bar phrases transmitted on MIDI channels 1 through 4, in an impressive array of styles including Bebop, Modal, Blues, Fusion, Swing, and Jazz Waltz. From a pedagogic standpoint, this product has a wealth of information for the study of jazz, but it's also a great source of short, professional-sounding sequences for use with presentations. The jazz phrases can be edited, combined, and looped into longer sections, and you can add more parts if you like. The documentation shows all of the solo parts and includes explanations, lessons, and tips for learning more about jazz.

If you're looking for a library of dramatic or background music, more in the vein of traditional film scoring, New Sound Music offers a third product of particular interest. **Soundtracks for MIDI** is a collection of over 90 sequences designed specifically for multimedia, film, and video. They are labeled generically by type and include titles like Industrial/Sports, Nature,

Comedy, Action/Suspense, Drama, TV News, Fantasy, and more. These come orchestrated in a variety of ways using as many as seven parts.

The sequences are actually phrases ranging from one to ten measures that you can loop or combine with other phrases to create a customized soundtrack. Your sequencer program will also let you adjust the tempo and pitch, and you can add or subtract parts and change the orchestration to suit your taste. Soundtracks for MIDI comes with a manual that includes chord charts for all sequences and additional information on setting up.

## Band-in-a-Box

Another approach to creating background accompaniments comes from PG Music's Band-in-a-Box. With this "intelligent" software, you type in the chords to any song, choose one of the 24 musical styles (Figure 7.1), and Band-in-a-Box generates professional-quality drum, bass, piano, guitar, and string parts complete with fills, variations, and embellishments.

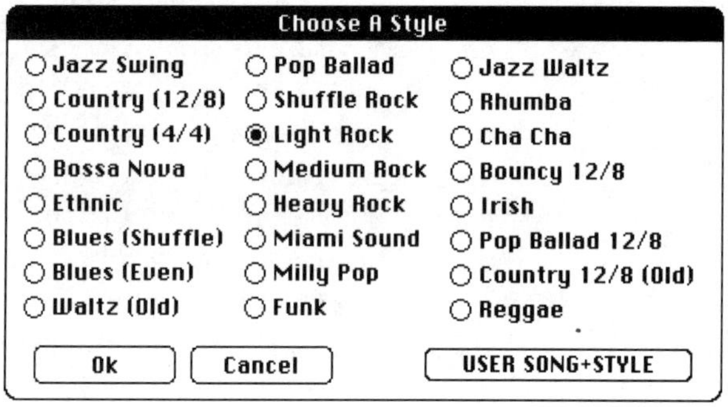

**Figure 7.1**
Band-in-a-Box lets you choose from a long list of styles for your accompaniments.

Creating new songs is easy. After opening the main window (Figure 7.2), you just enter chords where you want (up to four per measure) by typing in standard chord symbols. You can also indicate the structure of the song by placing markers at the start and end of the intro and each chorus and verse. Band-in-a-Box uses these markers to add appropriate drum fills, just like a live drummer, to set up each section and add momentum to the piece.

**Figure 7.2**

To create an arrangement in Band-in-a-Box, just type your chord changes into the main display. You can also use markers to indicate the structure of your song.

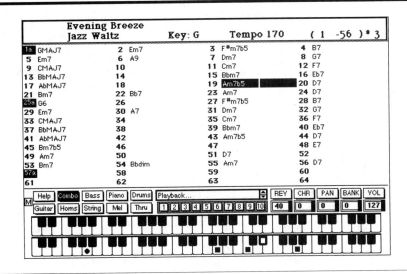

For variety, each of the styles has two "substyles," which you can also select for the different sections of your song. In the Jazz Swing style, for example, the "a" substyle plays a two-beat feel, while the "b" substyle plays in swing. Jazz styles can gain even more authenticity when you toggle on the Chord Embellishment option, which "intelligently" adds occasional 9ths and 13ths to the appropriate chords to enrich the harmonic texture.

Once you have chords and markers, all you have to do is choose a style, set the tempo, and push Play. When you're familiar with the program, entering the parameters for a typical song shouldn't take more than about two or three minutes. You can make up your own chord progressions or choose harmonies from your favorite tunes.

For more choices, the Band-in-a-Box Professional Edition adds over 75 additional styles to the program for an impressive collection of more than 100 different musical styles for your palette. If that's not enough to suit you, Band-in-a-Box also provides an elaborate and sophisticated StyleMaker feature, which lets you create your own styles and add them to the list. If you want to add a melody to your arrangements, the program provides a simple, built-in sequencer, and the Pro Edition also includes 100 jazz standards complete with melody and chord changes.

Band-in-a-Box supports the General MIDI Standard, with specific support (optional) for the Roland Sound Canvas (see below). You can store hundreds of songs on a floppy disk or convert them into Standard MIDI Files, which you can import into your sequencer for editing or adding other parts. The great advantage of this software lies in its ability to easily change musical styles while retaining the original chord progression and song structure. This gives you the opportunity to capture the right musical feel for your presentation without destructive editing or additional rewriting.

## The Beat Goes On

If you can't afford or don't want a drum machine, but still need help writing rhythm parts, Five Pin Press has just the thing to get you started. Its **260 Instant Drum Patterns** come on a disk as Standard MIDI Files in a wide variety of styles, including Afro-Cuban, Blues, Boogie, Disco, Latin, Jazz, Funk, Rock, Reggae, etc. The program defaults to the Roland D-110 drum note assignments (similar to MT-32, CM-32L, and SC-55), but any sound module with built-in drum sounds will work (conversion tables are provided). The patterns, each one measure long, were written by drummer Rene-Pierre Bardet and appear in his book *260 Drum Machine Patterns* (Hal Leonard Publ.), which is included with the software. In the book you'll find all of the patterns from the disk written out in musical notation and grid form, allowing you to study and compare the rhythms. To use the patterns, you import them into your sequencer and copy, paste, or loop the measures into longer sections. Your sequencer will let you adjust the tempo and edit the patterns to create new rhythms.

For many people, writing professional-sounding drum tracks is the most difficult part of composing popular music. 260 Instant Drum Patterns can give you an inexpensive helping hand in creating your background rhythm sections. The documentation is clear and helpful, and the accompanying book makes it easy to see and analyze each pattern.

## Out of Sequence

The programs above illustrate ways in which sequenced music can facilitate MIDI music production by providing a good starting place for those who plan to do their own composing and/or arranging. Many multimedia producers, however, will want to skip the composing stage altogether and go directly to editing the music. This is really what presequenced MIDI music is all about. These arrangements are complete, professionally performed and edited renditions of popular music with heavy representation in the areas of Top 40s hits, Oldies but Goodies, Country & Western, and Standards. Many of the songs are note-for-note reproductions of the original full arrangements while others may be scaled down to accommodate smaller systems.

The music sequences arrive in the form of Standard MIDI Files, which all of the software sequencers mentioned in Chapters 5 and 6 can convert into their own formats for full access to their editing capabilities. When you open a file in the program of your choice, you will see a list of instruments with their corresponding tracks and MIDI channel numbers. To run a sequence you simply select the appropriate instrument sounds from your multitimbral sound module and assign them to the corresponding MIDI channels. Push "start" and there you have it—instant big-band MIDI!

Well, maybe it's not quite that simple. There are a few additional considerations that must be taken into account. For one thing, it's assumed that you are already familiar with the pieces you'll be using before you begin. If you have never heard a particular Top 40 song, for instance, you may run into difficulties attempting to reconstruct an accurate rendition of it based upon the one- or two-word descriptions given for each instrument. Some companies might list a track simply as BASS. This leaves it up to you to decide if it should be a funky bass, slap bass, electronic bass, acoustic bass, Fender bass, etc. Your choice will affect the stylistic accuracy of the final arrangement even though most sequences will allow for some latitude. For best results, try to listen to the original recording of a piece to determine the best selections for each instrument sound. Remember that you will always be limited by the available sounds in your particular sound module.

## General MIDI

The problem of assigning appropriate instrument sounds to a sequence has plagued producers of MIDI music products for some time now. The birth of the Standard MIDI File was an important first step in providing complete exchangeability of MIDI data between dissimilar systems. Using this standardized file format, a composer could perform a piece of music on a Korg M1 and record the data using Vision. He might then send the sequence to a friend, who could use Performer to re-create the piece on a Kawai K4. Everything should work just fine and dandy except for one thing—the music won't sound the same to both people. That's because different synthesizers use different methods for creating their sounds and use different internal architectures for numbering and organizing those sounds. Program change commands become impractical to use since the piano sound in one MIDI device, for example, is not likely to use the same program number as another device. Furthermore, each synthesizer or sound module has its own distinct collection of sounds, so you can't automatically assume that the shakuhachi melody you recorded in measure 6 won't end up being played by a tuba or a marimba when the time comes.

To professional musicians this lack of universality is annoying but not insurmountable. It's viewed as a necessary by-product of the rich pluralism that characterizes the world of MIDI. Nonetheless, as MIDI continued to evolve, it was clear that some needs were not being met. To this end Warner New Media recommended to the MIDI Manufacturers Association a few years ago that a new standardized subset of the MIDI protocols be established. Although initially met with indifference, the proposal, supported by Passport Designs and several other companies, was finally adopted and *General MIDI* was born.

The purpose of General MIDI is to introduce a level of predictability in the way that certain "consumer" sound modules respond to MIDI. This, in turn, opens the way for true plug-and-play MIDI systems, with little or no setup time and few unexpected results. Multimedia producers, in particular, can benefit enormously from the combination of Standard MIDI Files and General MIDI and indeed, the original aim of General MIDI was for use with CD+MIDI—a format that combines MIDI data with CD audio.

General MIDI works by describing the physical requirements that a GM-compatible sound module must have. It specifies, for example, that an instrument must respond to all 16 MIDI channels with at least 24-voice polyphony and with middle C corresponding to note number 60. General

MIDI reserves channel 10 for percussion parts and also specifies that velocity, aftertouch, pitch bend, panning, volume, and several other continuous controller messages be implemented.

The core of General MIDI, however, lies in the Instrument Patch Map—a list of 128 sounds along with their assigned program numbers (Figure 7.3). The sounds are divided into 16 categories, each containing eight related entries and covering a broad sonic spectrum ranging from orchestral instruments, vocal ensembles, and keyboards to ethnic instruments, electronic timbres, and sound effects. By dictating the presence of certain kinds of sounds and standardizing their arrangement numerically, General MIDI effectively provides a template for manufacturers to follow in designing their instruments.

To standardize the placement of drum notes for rhythm parts, General MIDI provides a Percussion Key Map, which lists the specified percussion sounds and assigns them to individual MIDI notes (Figure 7.4). These two MIDI maps are not intended in any way to limit the potential for new sound modules but rather to ensure that a basic set of instrument sounds will be present and organized in a predictable manner. Furthermore, General MIDI does not specify how the sounds are synthesized or how well they sound, so manufacturers will continue to produce distinctive and uniquely characteristic instruments. General MIDI does, however, offer the opportunity to play a GM-compatible Standard MIDI File on several different General MIDI devices and have the music sound approximately the same—at least without any shocking surprises.

Roland Corp. recently introduced the first General MIDI sound module: the SC-55 (Sound Canvas). It represents a significant improvement over Roland's enormously popular MT-32 module, which had become a sort of de facto standard for many producers of presequenced music. To maintain a level of compatibility with these sequences, the SC-55 provides an MT-32 mode that mimics the patch-list arrangement of the earlier instrument, although its system-exclusive messages won't be recognized.

Some companies still offer their sequences configured in advance to play on the default settings of the Roland MT-32 (also on the CM-32L and CM-64), as well as other brands of synthesizers. This is helpful for those

**Figure 7.3**
The General MIDI Instrument Patch Map (printed by permission of the International MIDI Association)

## General MIDI - Level 1 Sound Set

| #   | Instrument              | #   | Instrument            | #    | Instrument           |
|-----|-------------------------|-----|-----------------------|------|----------------------|
| 1.  | Acoustic Grand Piano    | 44. | Contrabass            | 87.  | Lead 7 (fifths)      |
| 2.  | Bright Acoustic Piano   | 45. | Tremolo Strings       | 88.  | Lead 8 (bass + lead) |
| 3.  | Electric Grand Piano    | 46. | Pizzicato Strings     | 89.  | Pad 1 (new age)      |
| 4.  | Honky-tonk Piano        | 47. | Orchestral Harp       | 90.  | Pad 2 (warm)         |
| 5.  | Electric Piano 1        | 48. | Timpani               | 91.  | Pad 3 (polysynth)    |
| 6.  | Electric Piano 2        | 49. | String Ensemble 1     | 92.  | Pad 4 (choir)        |
| 7.  | Harpsichord             | 50. | String Ensemble 2     | 93.  | Pad 5 (bowed)        |
| 8.  | Clavi                   | 51. | SynthStrings 1        | 94.  | Pad 6 (metallic)     |
| 9.  | Celesta                 | 52. | SynthStrings 2        | 95.  | Pad 7 (halo)         |
| 10. | Glockenspiel            | 53. | Choir Aahs            | 96.  | Pad 8 (sweep)        |
| 11. | Music Box               | 54. | Voice Oohs            | 97.  | FX 1 (rain)          |
| 12. | Vibraphone              | 55. | Synth Voice           | 98.  | FX 2 (soundtrack)    |
| 13. | Marimba                 | 56. | Orchestra Hit         | 99.  | FX 3 (crystal)       |
| 14. | Xylophone               | 57. | Trumpet               | 100. | FX 4 (atmosphere)    |
| 15. | Tubular Bells           | 58. | Trombone              | 101. | FX 5 (brightness)    |
| 16. | Dulcimer                | 59. | Tuba                  | 102. | FX 6 (goblins)       |
| 17. | Drawbar Organ           | 60. | Muted Trumpet         | 103. | FX 7 (echoes)        |
| 18. | Percussive Organ        | 61. | French Horn           | 104. | FX 8 (sci-fi)        |
| 19. | Rock Organ              | 62. | Brass Section         | 105. | Sitar                |
| 20. | Church Organ            | 63. | SynthBrass 1          | 106. | Banjo                |
| 21. | Reed Organ              | 64. | SynthBrass 2          | 107. | Shamisen             |
| 22. | Accordion               | 65. | Soprano Sax           | 108. | Koto                 |
| 23. | Harmonica               | 66. | Alto Sax              | 109. | Kalimba              |
| 24. | Tango Accordion         | 67. | Tenor Sax             | 110. | Bag pipe             |
| 25. | Acoustic Guitar (nylon) | 68. | Baritone Sax          | 111. | Fiddle               |
| 26. | Acoustic Guitar (steel) | 69. | Oboe                  | 112. | Shanai               |
| 27. | Electric Guitar (jazz)  | 70. | English Horn          | 113. | Tinkle Bell          |
| 28. | Electric Guitar (clean) | 71. | Bassoon               | 114. | Agogo                |
| 29. | Electric Guitar (muted) | 72. | Clarinet              | 115. | Steel Drums          |
| 30. | Overdriven Guitar       | 73. | Piccolo               | 116. | Woodblock            |
| 31. | Distortion Guitar       | 74. | Flute                 | 117. | Taiko Drum           |
| 32. | Guitar harmonics        | 75. | Recorder              | 118. | Melodic Tom          |
| 33. | Acoustic Bass           | 76. | Pan Flute             | 119. | Synth Drum           |
| 34. | Electric Bass (finger)  | 77. | Blown Bottle          | 120. | Reverse Cymbal       |
| 35. | Electric Bass (pick)    | 78. | Shakuhachi            | 121. | Guitar Fret Noise    |
| 36. | Fretless Bass           | 79. | Whistle               | 122. | Breath Noise         |
| 37. | Slap Bass 1             | 80. | Ocarina               | 123. | Seashore             |
| 38. | Slap Bass 2             | 81. | Lead 1 (square)       | 124. | Bird Tweet           |
| 39. | Synth Bass 1            | 82. | Lead 2 (sawtooth)     | 125. | Telephone Ring       |
| 40. | Synth Bass 2            | 83. | Lead 3 (calliope)     | 126. | Helicopter           |
| 41. | Violin                  | 84. | Lead 4 (chiff)        | 127. | Applause             |
| 42. | Viola                   | 85. | Lead 5 (charang)      | 128. | Gunshot              |
| 43. | Cello                   | 86. | Lead 6 (voice)        |      |                      |

**Figure 7.4**
The General MIDI Percussion Key Map (printed by permission of the International MIDI Association)

## General MIDI - Level 1 Percussion Map (Channel 10)

| Key # | Drum Sound | Key # | Drum Sound | Key # | Drum Sound |
|---|---|---|---|---|---|
| 35 | Acoustic Bass Drum | 51 | Ride Cymbal 1 | 67 | High Agogo |
| 36 | Bass Drum 1 | 52 | Chinese Cymbal | 68 | Low Agogo |
| 37 | Side Stick | 53 | Ride Bell | 69 | Cabasa |
| 38 | Acoustic Snare | 54 | Tambourine | 70 | Maracas |
| 39 | Hand Clap | 55 | Splash Cymbal | 71 | Short Whistle |
| 40 | Electric Snare | 56 | Cowbell | 72 | Long Whistle |
| 41 | Low Floor Tom | 57 | Crash Cymbal 2 | 73 | Short Guiro |
| 42 | Closed Hi Hat | 58 | Vibraslap | 74 | Long Guiro |
| 43 | High Floor Tom | 59 | Ride Cymbal 2 | 75 | Claves |
| 44 | Pedal Hi-Hat | 60 | Hi Bongo | 76 | Hi Wood Block |
| 45 | Low Tom | 61 | Low Bongo | 77 | Low Wood Block |
| 46 | Open Hi-Hat | 62 | Mute Hi Conga | 78 | Mute Cuica |
| 47 | Low-Mid Tom | 63 | Open Hi Conga | 79 | Open Cuica |
| 48 | Hi Mid Tom | 64 | Low Conga | 80 | Mute Triangle |
| 49 | Crash Cymbal 1 | 65 | High Timbale | 81 | Open Triangle |
| 50 | High Tom | 66 | Low Timbale | | |

unfamiliar with the arrangement of a particular song or for those seeking instant gratification with zero setup time. It's important to remember that some inexpensive sound modules may not provide enough polyphonic capability to play a full-blown band arrangement by themselves. Because of this, any sequence directed toward a specific module may be scaled down to accommodate the hardware limitations.

Most companies offer only generic sequences, preferring not to compromise their arrangements, but some offer both an MT-32 version and a fuller, more complete, generic version for those users with more than one sound module or synthesizer. With a little editing, however, most of the currently available sound modules can be made to work well with most sequences. Many producers of sequenced music, recognizing the vast potential of General MIDI, now offer either all or most of their libraries in that format as well. Some target their sequences specifically for the Roland SC-55, which they feel is destined to become another immensely popular industry standard.

# Losing Your Voice

One final caveat. Some companies intend their sequences to be used as accompaniments during live performances and, therefore, don't include the melody or vocal line in the sequence. They assume that a singer will cover that part. These sequences can still work as general background music for some presentations, but if you want the tune included, you will have to perform it into the sequencer yourself. Most of the products include a melody track for reference, which you can assign to the instrument of your choice.

# What's Out There

The following is an alphabetical listing of most of the currently available presequenced music products along with brief descriptions:

***Bach Songbook*** A single disk containing a nice collection of Bach's keyboard works, including all of the two-part inventions, several three-part sinfonias, and a couple of four-part fugues. They arrive as Standard MIDI Files in a generic format with parts indicated by channel numbers only. There is no documentation. You can produce your own "Switched on Bach" arrangements by applying a little creative orchestration to these files. (Dr. T's Music Software)

***DTP & Multimedia CD*** This CD-ROM, designed to be a collection of materials for desktop publishing and multimedia, contains 39 MIDI sequences in addition to its clip art, fonts, and digital audio files. The sequences come in the form of generic MIDI files, with mostly original works in various pop styles and a few classical transcriptions. The minimal documentation isn't much help. The performances are fair. (Olduvai Corp.)

***MIDI Hits*** Approximately 200 titles in the usual categories: Top 40s, Oldies, Country/Western, Big Band, Jazz, and Classical. These come as Standard MIDI Files preconfigured for the Roland MT-32, but can be easily adapted to other sound modules. Most are also available in General

MIDI format and support the Roland Sound Canvas. Melody parts are usually present. The documentation is exceptional and exemplary. (Passport Designs, Inc.)

***MIDI Hits*** The MIDI Hits library is very large (1,000-plus titles) and impressive in its range of musical styles. It includes the usual Top 40 hits, Oldies but Goodies, and Country/Western favorites, as well as Big Band Jazz, Jazz Combos, Jazz Fusion, Show Tunes, Standards, Wedding Music, Piano Music, Dixieland, Classical, Patriotic music, and more. Many of the sequences are note-for-note reproductions of the original recordings, and most of the titles include the melody. Several pieces also contain choir tracks to represent background vocal parts. The sequences come as generic files. The documentation is minimal, consisting of a printout of the instrument and drum note assignments. (Phil Wood Consulting)

***MIDI Inn*** MIDI Inn offers a substantial library of over 450 titles in a variety of styles, including Top 40s, Big Band, Motown, and Jazz Standards (arranged for small combos). The sequences, which support the General MIDI Standard, include the melody lines. The documentation is very good.

***MIDI Jukebox*** Over 150 titles in the usual categories of Top 40s, Oldies, Big Band, Country Western, etc. All support the General MIDI Standard, with particular support for Roland's Sound Canvas (SC-55) sound module. A separate catalog of titles is also available under the name **Multimedia Artists Sequences**. It includes the following categories: Christian, Jazz/Big Band, Classical, and Pop/Top 40s. These are fuller, more complex arrangements designed to take full advantage of the SC-55—also available in General MIDI format. Sequences include a melody part but little documentation. Parker Adams also offers a **Wedding Package,** which includes approximately 100 wedding songs and a MIDI Wedding Guide manual. Membership in several user groups is also offered supporting the Sound Canvas, the MT-32, the Proteus, and several other sound modules. (Parker Adams Group)

***MIDIclips*** This product consists of a single CD-ROM with at least 140 "clips" of original production music, in various styles, designed specifically for desktop presentations and multimedia. The music comes in the form of 8-bit digital audio files along with the same pieces in Standard MIDI File format. The sequences support the General MIDI Standard and come with some documentation. A database function lets you search for pieces according to various criteria. Additional volumes will be available. (Opcode Systems, Inc.)

**MIDIFile Tunes**   Four dozen musical arrangements on a single disk, including movie and TV themes, Top 40 hits, and others. These arrive as Standard MIDI Files, but in the less common Format 0, which combines all channels onto a single track. When you import these into your sequencer, there won't be any indication as to which instruments are on which channels. Only some of the sequences come with text files showing the instrument/channel assignments. Performances range from fair to good. Many of the sequences seem to be targeted toward the Roland MT-32. There is no additional documentation. (Educorp)

**MultiMedia HANDisc**   The MultiMedia HANDisc is designed to be a resource collection for multimedia producers. It includes artwork, HyperCard stacks, product demos, tutorials, QuickTime movies, and more. In its Sounds folder you'll find both digitized audio and a few dozen MIDI files. The MIDI music comes from a variety of sources. There are some samples from Opcode's and Passport's MIDI libraries along with several miscellaneous sequences of original music. Some of these additional files come with documentation; others don't. They range in quality from fair to good. There's also a demo of Passport's AudioTrax program, which lets you combine digital audio with MIDI. (CD Technology)

**Mus-Art Productions**   Mus-Art offers a very large catalog listing over 1200 titles, including Top 40s, Oldies, Standards, Big Band, Country, and Christmas. The sequences adhere to the General MIDI Standard, and about half of the songs include a melody part. Documentation consists of a track sheet showing instrument names and channel assignments. Mus-Art also operates its own BBS.

**QuikTunes**   The QuikTunes collection comes on a single CD-ROM. The pieces are all original production music in styles such as Sports, Jazz, New

Age, Travel, Nature, Industrial, etc., along with intros, stings, and fanfares. The music comes in various lengths designed specifically for multimedia, film, and video. The CD contains about an hour of music in 8-bit digital audio with the same pieces also offered as MIDI sequences. These files support the General MIDI Standard, and the whole package includes excellent documentation along with a HyperCard browser that lets you locate and preview the different song files. Additional volumes will also be available. (Passport Designs, Inc.)

**Tran Tracks**   A substantial offering of over 500 titles, including the following categories: Rhythm & Blues, Rock & Roll, Pop/Dance, Oldies, Big Band, Classical Piano, and Country/Western. These come as generic sequences—a large number do not have melody parts. Tran Tracks also offers MIDI Pacs—five-song collections set up for instant playback on the MT-32 (CM-32L/CM-64). These songs have melody parts. The generic sequences include an octave test to ensure that each track plays back at the proper register—a handy feature. The documentation is excellent.

**Trycho Tunes**   One of the largest libraries of MIDI sequences available. Over 1400 titles from several categories, including Top 40s, Oldies, Standards, Big Band, Country, and Christmas. The sequences come in a variety of formats, including support for the General MIDI Standard. The songs are programmed with a "live band" concept, typically using four to eight channels. Many songs include a melody track. The documentation is excellent and has track lists and other information on instruments and setups. Trycho also sells sheet music and songbooks to go with its sequences. (Trycho Music International)

**The Works Music Productions, Inc.**   A large catalog offering over 500 songs in categories including Top 40s, Oldies, Country/Western, Rhythm & Blues, Standards, Big Band, and Christmas. The sequences arrive in a generic format and include a melody part. The documentation is very good.

# ▤ Some Final Tips

If you are considering using sequenced music for your presentations, but have not yet purchased any hardware, here are some suggestions:

- Give preference to sound modules and synthesizers with the greatest maximum polyphony. Roland's popular MT-32 or the similar CM-32L are fine for many of the products listed here, but the CM-64 with its doubled maximum polyphony is much better and less limiting.

- Check your local music store for sound modules by other manufacturers, such as Yamaha, Kawai, E-mu Systems, Ensoniq, and Korg. These companies all offer multitimbral modules with different user interfaces and different sounds.

- You can combine two or more MIDI devices from the same or different manufacturers to expand your available palette of sounds and to increase your maximum polyphony. Be sure that at least one of them has internal drum sounds.

- Most of the MIDI-sequence companies listed above will send a demo tape or disk on request. Be prepared to accurately describe your hardware/software configuration, and don't hesitate to ask questions.

# HyperCard Meets MIDI

Remember when HyperCard made its world debut and quickly became the talk of the town? It seems like a long time ago, doesn't it? In those days having a button go "boing" when you pushed it or hearing a fragment of scratchy-sounding digitized speech when you clicked on a picture was exciting stuff. Well, times have changed. New combinations of hardware and software can transform a simple Macintosh into a "digital audio workstation" producing CD-quality sound from the desktop. Meanwhile, multimedia programs like MacroMind Director have reached maturity by combining the production of dazzling animation with access to a variety of external devices.

While all of this was going on, MIDI evolved in some unexpected ways. Originally conceived as a means of tying together electronic instruments for performance and recording, it expanded laterally into areas of postproduction audio and even some nonmusical applications. It is, therefore, not surprising that a growing demand for low-cost, high-quality, interactive multimedia would eventually bring together accessible, flexible HyperCard and spontaneous, real-time MIDI.

## ▣ Hardware and Software

To incorporate MIDI music into a HyperCard presentation, you'll need one of the basic setups described in Chapter 3. An inexpensive MIDI interface and a sound module will work just fine for starters. The great thing about MIDI is that it divides the responsibility for making music between the computer and an external instrument. This means that the load on the Mac's processor is low and the files don't require much memory compared to digital audio. In fact, a few minutes of CD-quality, stereo, digital music would require the same disk storage as hundreds of MIDI files representing hours of music. And with one of the sequencer programs described in Chapters 5 and 6, you can edit the music in a great variety of ways, changing such things as orchestration, tempo, and key. The products discussed in this chapter all combine HyperCard and MIDI in different ways to provide information, programming tools, or postproduction editing capabilities.

## SOUNDtraK

SOUNDtraK, from Opcode Systems, is itself a HyperCard stack that helps you make the MIDI-HyperCard connection quickly and painlessly. It comes on a CD-ROM packed with over 100 pieces of production music from Opcode's MIDIclips library. This gives you a wealth of new material right out of the box, but you can add any Standard MIDI Files that you want to expand the list—keeping SOUNDtraK an open-ended resource tool for scoring any kind of HyperCard presentation. In fact, SOUNDtraK's Library card (Figure 8.1) consists of a File Management section and an easy-to-use but powerful database to help you organize your ever-growing list of titles and to help you find the ones you want when you need them.

On the right side of the card, the Search/Define section provides three boxes with scrolling lists of labels describing the music in your library according to style, descriptive adjective, and time period. Each time you add a new MIDI file to your library, you can define its characteristics with these lists. When you select a word from each of the three boxes, the selections appear in the Current Description column. Clicking the Set Information for Selection button in the Music Library attaches your descriptive words to the selected MIDI file. From then on, you can search for that piece of music by entering any or all of those labels into the Current Description column and clicking the Search for Matches button. Not only can you label new pieces this way but you can change the labels for old pieces anytime you want.

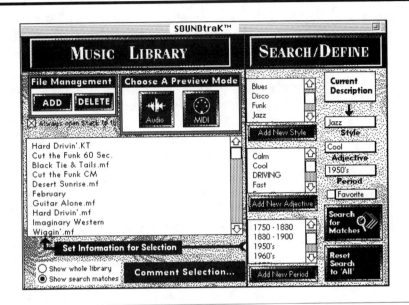

**Figure 8.1**
SOUNDtraK's Library card includes a section for maintaining and organizing your files and an easy-to-use but powerful database for locating selections.

If you don't like the labels that come with the card, you can add your own by typing in a word and clicking the appropriate Add button found under each list. To help make SOUNDtraK instantly usable, Opcode has included descriptive words for all of the MIDIclips files included with the stack. If you feel that using three descriptive categories is too restrictive for your needs, you can use the Comment Selection button to open a field where you can add comments to each file. SOUNDtraK will then take key words from your comments and use those to help locate selections.

The large list on the left side of the card represents the available MIDI files in your library. You can add or delete files by choosing the appropriate button under the File Management heading. When you select a file in the Music Library, its current description appears in the Search/Define area on the right. This makes it easier to remember pieces if the titles alone don't jog your memory, but when you're dealing with a large list of titles, general labels usually don't provide an accurate-enough sense of the music. To address this problem, Opcode has included a unique and powerful feature: Preview mode.

By clicking the MIDI button in the Preview Mode box, you can audition a MIDI file directly from the Library card. This should work well if you're using one of the supported MIDI devices (Roland CM-32L, Proteus/1) or a General MIDI sound module, but for most other sound modules, you'll have to spend a bit of time setting up channel, track, and instrument assignments. If you're trying to preview many files or you're working against a deadline, you may find the process too cumbersome to be practical with an unsupported MIDI device. As an alternative, SOUNDtraK provides an Audio preview button.

With each of the Standard MIDI Files that come in the MIDIclips collection, Opcode has included a corresponding digital audio version of the piece. These 8-bit, 22-kHz soundfiles are kept in an audio stack that SOUNDtraK accesses when you want to audition your selections. The concept here is that you can use the audio files to get a feeling for how the pieces sound and what instrumentation and styles they use. You can even try running the audio file against your video or desktop presentation to see if the two go together well and which parts of the composition work best. When you have a selection that you want to use, you can click on the Edit/Mixer button in the Navigation Panel (Figure 8.2) to open a card that provides the tools to mix and edit the selected file to fit your visuals precisely.

**Figure 8.2**
The Navigation Panel takes you from one card to the next.

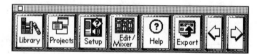

SOUNDtraK divides its Edit/Mixer card (Figure 8.3) into two distinct halves. The lower half is a 16-track mixing board with faders, Solo and Mute buttons, a Pan control, and fields for displaying instrument names and numbers, and MIDI channels. When you select a file from the Music Library and click the appropriate button in the Navigation Panel, the file appears in the Edit/Mixer card with the corresponding channel and instrument settings and any fader positions that have been saved with the file.

# HyperCard Meets MIDI

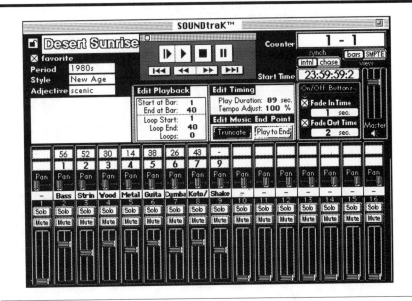

**Figure 8.3**
SOUNDtraK's Edit/Mixer card combines a mixing board with several tools for tailoring music to picture.

To prepare a piece of music for use with a presentation, you first use the transport controls to play back your MIDI file while you set the fader level and pan position for each instrument sound. If you don't like the orchestration, you can change the instrument assignments with a pop-up chart showing the internal sounds for the assigned MIDI device. When the music sounds right, you can turn your attention to the editing half of the card.

In the upper-right corner, a large Counter display indicates the current sequence location in measures and beats. Clicking the SMPTE button changes the display to read out in timecode numbers. You can elect to have the sequence play by itself by using the Macintosh's internal clock as a timing source, or you can click the Chase button to have the sequence synchronize to an external source, like a VCR or tape deck, by using SMPTE timecode. The Start Time display lets you enter the timecode location where the music will begin playing. SOUNDtraK also provides a Fade In option and a Fade Out option, which let you set the length, in seconds, of each fade.

To fit your music to animation or other time-related presentations, SOUNDtraK provides adjustments for both playback and timing parameters. The Edit Playback area lets you assign start and end points for your sequence along with a looped section if needed. The Edit Timing box lets you specify either a playback duration (in seconds) or a tempo—expressed as a percentage of the original. The Truncate and Play to End buttons determine how the sequence will be handled. Play to End ensures that the entire sequence will be played. Truncate stops the music when you reach the specified duration.

Changing a parameter in one of the Edit areas automatically changes the other related settings. For instance, if you change the duration, the tempo setting changes. If you change the length of the sequence, the duration changes. This makes fitting music to visuals easy, even for nonmusicians, because you can work with the parameters that best suit your needs.

You can save the results of your SOUNDtraK editing sessions as separate files. The Export card provides buttons for including these files in any HyperCard stack. You have the option of exporting a button, along with the file, to initiate playback of your music, or you can choose to have the music begin when a specific card is opened.

Because many SOUNDtraK users work in environments where other people will want access to the same library of music, the stack includes a Project card. This allows several people to use and customize their SOUNDtraK libraries—by designating them as separate Projects—without destroying other people's descriptions or settings. To complete the list of features, SOUNDtraK includes a Help stack that provides useful information about using the program. In addition to HyperCard, SOUNDtraK also works with SuperCard and MacroMind Director.

SOUNDtraK has a lot to offer multimedia producers who use MIDI music with their presentations. The database features alone make it useful in maintaining an ever-growing collection of MIDI files. The MIDIclips library, with its audio-preview versions of the music, gives you the opportunity to get started with MIDI and HyperCard right away, and SOUNDtraK's intuitive, graphical approach makes the process easy.

## ▤ HyperMIDI

HyperMIDI, from EarLevel Engineering, is a difficult product to characterize. It's not so much a specific application as it is a tool kit of powerful external commands (XCMDs) and external functions (XFCNs) that enable you to produce your own interactive MIDI stacks. These routines include utilities for manipulating MIDI data, for creating real-time MIDI controls, and for sending and receiving MIDI data.

You can create almost any kind of MIDI-based stack from scratch, or you can start with the sample stacks provided and modify them to your liking. You might, for instance, create a MIDI-sequence recording and playback stack that could import and export Standard MIDI Files and run in the background of a multimedia presentation. But this only scratches the surface. With HyperMIDI you can create your own editor/librarian stacks for your favorite sound module. Or you can invent your own real-time effects processors, such as the Delay FX sample stack, which enables you to input a note and process it to produce an echo, a chord, or an arpeggio output. Another stack, a fractal music generator, creates sequences based on user-defined parameters that you apply to formulas, and the Algorithm stack (Figure 8.4) lets you set up musical criteria to create algorithmically generated music. The Key Strummer stack (Figure 8.5) allows you to create guitar chords with an on-screen fingerboard that you can "strum" to play. Other stacks appropriately illustrate the range and potential of HyperMIDI for real-time processing, experimentation, and education.

Unlike SOUNDtraK, however, HyperMIDI does have a bit of a learning curve. Although its creator, Nigel Redmon, states that you don't need "a lifetime of programming experience" to use HyperMIDI, you do need at least some experience to explore this product in a meaningful way. For starters, it's assumed that you have a working knowledge of HyperTalk (HyperCard's programming language) and a good grasp of MIDI and how it works. It's not altogether surprising, therefore, that the tutorial section in the owner's manual doesn't appear until Chapter 7—following much introductory and background material. Nonetheless, the documentation is well written and achieves a good level of clarity and completeness.

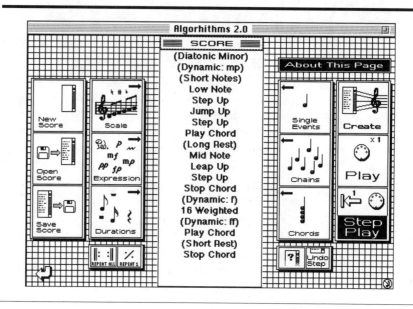

**Figure 8.4**
The Algorithm stack lets you establish musical criteria to create algorithmically generated music.

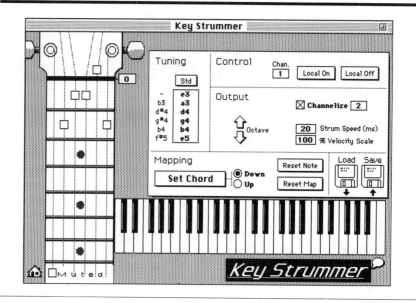

**Figure 8.5**
HyperMIDI's Key Strummer stack lets you play an on-screen guitar.

For those whose needs go beyond the limitations of SOUNDtraK and for those more advanced users interested in doing their own programming, HyperMIDI should provide enough power and flexibility to create a useful array of HyperCard-MIDI applications.

## The Book of MIDI

No discussion of HyperCard and MIDI would be complete without mentioning The Book of MIDI, from Opcode Systems. This HyperCard stack makes learning the ins and outs of MIDI easy and entertaining. For beginners it includes basic information on the nature of MIDI and also provides diagrams to help you set up different MIDI systems—with or without a computer.

There are chapters that explain how MIDI works and others that answer questions about using MIDI. The chapter on hardware compares various synthesizers, past and present, and uses digitized soundfiles to let you hear them (Figure 8.6). The chapter covering software describes and illustrates the different kinds of MIDI programs on the market today and includes an animated demo of EZ Vision. MIDI neophytes will enjoy setting up and playing Pachelbel's Canon in D (Figure 8.7) to get a feel for using and adjusting MIDI files.

For more advanced users, The Book of MIDI is a valuable reference source containing MIDI specifications, a glossary of computer music terminology, a bibliography, and numerous context-sensitive references to articles and reviews. An excellent index and a nice collection of buttons make it easy to navigate this comprehensive stack, which has been assembled with a good dose of humor and a flair for entertaining animation.

Listen to the sounds of classic synthesizers, test your knowledge of MIDI in the MIDI Game, or use your sound module to play and modify a MIDI file. There are many things to discover here in a program that is itself a model for wonderful, interactive HyperCard-MIDI programming.

**Figure 8.6**
The Book of MIDI describes famous synthesizers from the past and present. You can hear what they sound like by clicking the ear icon.

**Figure 8.7**
After setting up and playing Pachelbel's Canon in D, you can try changing some of the playback parameters.

a. No. 5, "Eusebius"

# Chapter 9

# Universal Editor/Librarians

The many benefits of using a MIDI system for multimedia sound production have encouraged a growing number of producers to explore this promising trend. Handling music and sound-effects reproduction outside of the computer reserves valuable disk-storage space for other memory-intensive activities without sacrificing sound quality. The MIDI system itself can be as simple as a MIDI interface and a sound module or as elaborate as setups involving MIDI patchbays, effects devices, and numerous synthesizers and modules.

If you want to extend your musical horizons by expanding your available palette of sounds, you have essentially two options: You can buy more synthesizers, or you can change the internal sounds of the synths and modules that you own. If you like to keep your options open, a relatively new class of software addresses both of these situations—the universal editor/librarian, or ed/lib for short. Universal ed/libs, however, are definitely not for everyone, so to help illuminate this subject let's examine some of the most popular of these products; but first a little background.

## How They Work

Most MIDI instruments on the market today support MIDI System Exclusive (sys/ex) commands. This type of MIDI data provides access to the internal parameters that are specific to a given manufacturer's instrument or family of instruments. Editor/librarian programs use system-exclusive messages to send and receive data involving the internal sounds in a particular synthesizer and to modify, store, and reorganize these sounds. However, different manufacturers handle sys/ex information in different ways, and different synthesizers have widely varying internal architectures, so in the past you needed a separate ed/lib program for each synthesizer in your setup. Switching between instruments was cumbersome, and if you added a new sound module to your system, you had to buy a new editor/librarian to access it.

Universal ed/lib programs, on the other hand, are open-ended and designed to cover a wide range of MIDI devices. To accomplish this they employ a separate *driver* for every device that the ed/lib supports. Each driver then communicates with the unique internal operating system and corresponding protocol of a given instrument.

With an appropriate driver in place, the ed/lib program can exchange patches (sounds, or "presets") between the computer and the MIDI device. The term *patch* goes back to the early days of electronic music studios when synthesizers consisted of separate modular components. Sounds were created by connecting the components with patch cords so that a specific configuration of knob settings and patch cords produced a specific sound called a "patch." Although modern synthesizers no longer use patch cords to create their sounds, the term has stayed with us. Patches can be sent back and forth individually or as groups called *banks*.

To edit your sounds you need an additional communication interface called a *template*. Templates are graphic representations of the controls and the edit parameters for specific synthesizers. They typically consist of a variety of buttons, sliders, knobs, graphs, and fields designed to reproduce visually the internal architecture of a synthesizer with the variables needed to modify its sounds.

Drivers and templates exist separately in some ed/libs while others link the two together to simplify installation and configuration procedures. Templates vary considerably in layout and appearance from one ed/lib to the next. Even within the same program, quality and functionality can vary since different programmers may be responsible for individual templates and different synthesizers lend themselves to the particular graphic formats with varying degrees of success.

In any case, for a universal editor/librarian to be truly universal, there must be some provision for creating new drivers and templates. All of the products mentioned below have that capability. This enables users and third-party developers to create custom templates and drivers for existing devices as well as future products. Writing your own drivers and templates, however, is not for the faint of heart. You will need a good understanding of computer programming and MIDI system-exclusive code along with a fair dose of time and effort. For the rest of us, there are drivers available for downloading from several bulletin board services supported by the ed/lib companies.

By now it should be clear that these programs are both powerful and complex, and it therefore comes as little surprise that they can also be both confusing and frustrating to use. For starters, the installation procedures are not always as simple and straightforward as the manufacturers would like to believe, although these problems generally occur only in the initial setup stage.

Terminology is another possible source of confusion. To make these ed/libs generic in nature, the programmers have had to choose terms that can be applied in the broadest possible way to a widely varying group of devices. The result is that new terms are often invented and old terms redefined. The end user must then decipher this nomenclature and correlate it with the particular instruments in his or her MIDI system.

Comparing products is similarly difficult since terms like patch, bank, and library can mean somewhat different things in different programs. If possible, try to get a demo of the program before buying it to see if the design of the templates suits your taste and to see how intuitive the program seems for your setup. Generally speaking, these programs are not well suited to rank amateurs. As one company rep explained, they are not intended for beginners with little understanding of MIDI and how it works.

# X-oR

X-oR, from Dr. T's Music Software, offers a number of powerful features that can help you organize, find, and edit your sounds whether you have a large, complex system or a much simpler setup. Its many operations are based on its Performance window (Figure 9.1), which lists the current patch data and sound bank information for each synthesizer, sound module, and MIDI device in your system. If you have a MIDI patchbay, its settings can also be included.

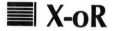

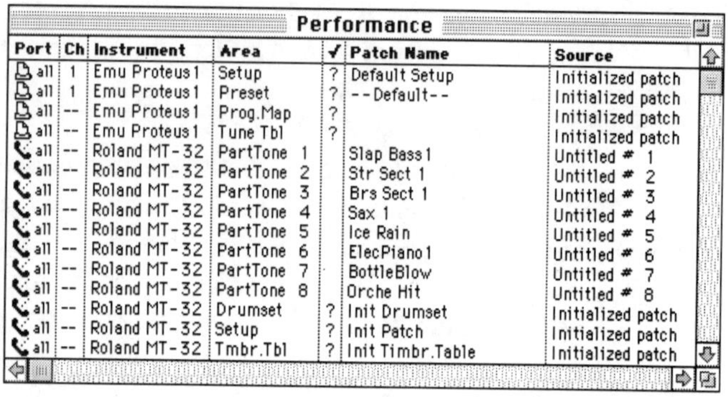

**Figure 9.1**
X-oR bases its many operations on the Performance window, which lists patch and sound bank data for each device.

Once you've entered the setup information, X-oR uses this "snapshot" of the system to re-create an entire MIDI configuration, including all settings, channel assignments, and relevant information each time you load that Performance File. From there you can open new sound bank files and initiate data transfers or begin an editing session by selecting an appropriate driver/template combination called a *Profile*. If you have any trouble using a certain Profile, you can open the Profile Help window to get specific information about any device supported by X-oR. A Monitor window is also available to troubleshoot transmission problems while you send or receive data.

X-oR allows any number of windows of any type to appear on the screen at one time, making it easy to switch between different libraries and data

# Universal Editor/Librarians

banks. Once you have transferred a bank of patches from your MIDI device into X-oR, you can add any or all of the patches to a library file by dragging them to the appropriate Library window, where they can be listed in order by name or date. Libraries are simply collections of patches with the same type of data. They can hold virtually unlimited numbers of entries for storage and cross-referencing.

X-oR boasts some truly outstanding features for organizing and searching through its libraries. Every entry in a Library window can have up to eight keywords associated with it. You can choose these quickly and easily from a number of pop-up menus designed around a flexible, hierarchal system. The selected keywords along with a descriptive comment appear opposite each patch name in a Library window to give you an overview of the sounds in each library (Figure 9.2).

To locate a specific sound or type of sound, X-oR provides a sophisticated Find command, which lets you enter a combination of keywords, text, and logic to search all open libraries for patches that meet certain criteria (Figure 9.3). This full-featured, database approach to sound bank management makes X-oR worth considering if you have an extensive MIDI system and/or large numbers of patches to organize.

**Figure 9.2**
The Library window lists patches by name, followed by a comment and/or up to eight keywords.

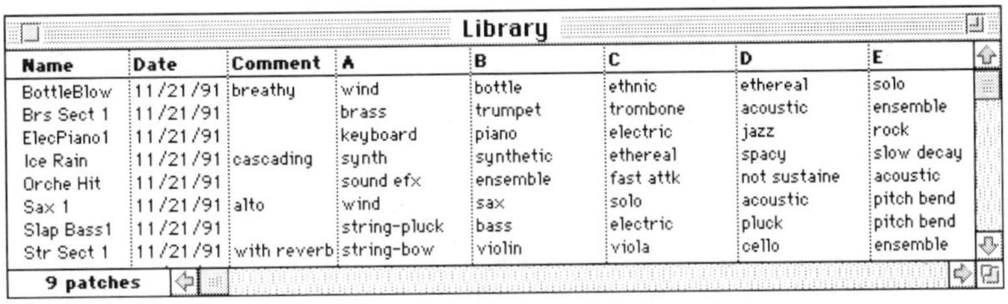

| Name | Date | Comment | A | B | C | D | E |
|---|---|---|---|---|---|---|---|
| BottleBlow | 11/21/91 | breathy | wind | bottle | ethnic | ethereal | solo |
| Brs Sect 1 | 11/21/91 | | brass | trumpet | trombone | acoustic | ensemble |
| ElecPiano1 | 11/21/91 | | keyboard | piano | electric | jazz | rock |
| Ice Rain | 11/21/91 | cascading | synth | synthetic | ethereal | spacy | slow decay |
| Orche Hit | 11/21/91 | | sound efx | ensemble | fast attk | not sustaine | acoustic |
| Sax 1 | 11/21/91 | alto | wind | sax | solo | acoustic | pitch bend |
| Slap Bass1 | 11/21/91 | | string-pluck | bass | electric | pluck | pitch bend |
| Str Sect 1 | 11/21/91 | with reverb | string-bow | violin | viola | cello | ensemble |

9 patches

To audition sounds from within the program, X-oR offers no less than four options. By selecting ScreenKeys from the Play menu, you can use your mouse to play notes from an on-screen keyboard (Figure 9.4), which responds to velocity information according to where you click each key front to back. Two sets of octave buttons let you select the keyboard range. ScreenKeys will work even when it's not the front window.

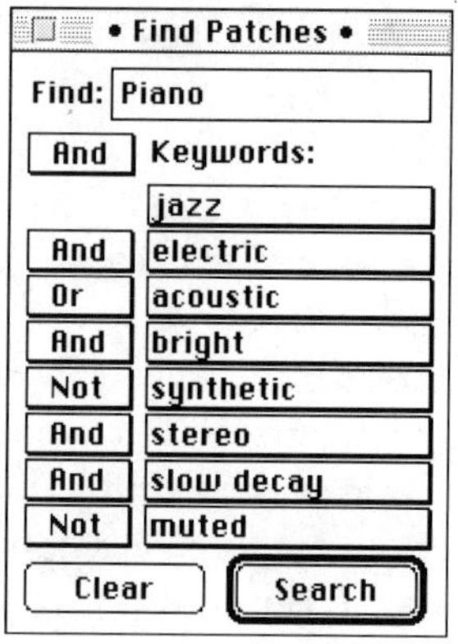

**Figure 9.3**
X-oR's Find command uses keywords and modifiers to establish the criteria for a search.

**Figure 9.4**
Selecting ScreenKeys lets you audition sounds from an on-screen keyboard.

For more fun in triggering your MIDI devices, X-oR offers MousePlay. This option doesn't use a keyboard; instead, the position of the mouse left to right determines which note is played, and the position top to bottom affects the velocity. You trigger notes by pressing the Option key on the Macintosh keyboard. The MousePlay Preferences window lets you select whether typing the Option key will produce single notes or mouse-controlled glissandos, as well as which of 13 scales (major, minor, Hungarian, chromatic, whole tone, etc.) your triggered notes will adhere to. Moving the mouse with the Command key pressed turns it into a pitch-bend controller, with movements left or right bending notes up or down. Combining the Control key with the Option key lets you send one of several kinds of MIDI controller messages that you can also choose from the MousePlay Preferences window.

If you prefer a more traditional approach to auditioning sounds, X-oR's Echo function lets you play your MIDI keyboard controller to hear each patch. And finally, if you want a more musical and/or polyphonic context to hear your sounds, you can play sequences from another program, through X-oR, by using Apple's MIDI Manager.

X-oR's editing operations take place in the Patch Edit windows (Figure 9.5). These templates are very well designed, clear, and easy to use. The displays for many of the templates, however, take up more room than a single screen provides, so the additional display area must be accessed by scrolling—a minor annoyance. To help mitigate this problem, X-oR provides a Jump feature (in the lower-left corner of the window), which produces a small pop-up menu that you can use to "jump" to any part of the display.

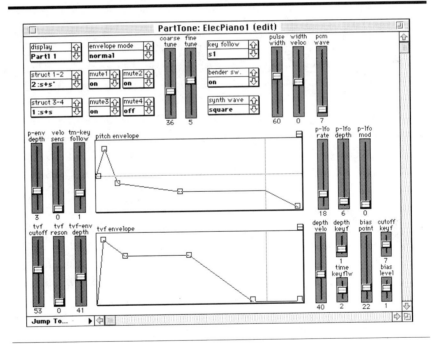

**Figure 9.5**
X-oR's templates are very clear and well designed.

The Envelope Graphs let you quickly change envelope parameters by dragging little grab handles to change the envelope's shape. There's also an option for displaying the corresponding numerical values below each envelope's graph.

To eliminate patches with the same or similar parameter settings, X-oR provides a Compare Patches command on the Edit menu. This feature produces a detailed comparison list between any two patches to help you weed out duplicate sounds with or without the same names.

As with the other programs, X-oR provides a function that takes certain parameters from existing patches and mixes them together to create new sounds. The Blend & Mingle command combines selected parameters from two source patches to create a new bank of sounds by interpolating values between the patches according to one of four different algorithms. A Randomize command also lets you generate a bank of new patches by randomly varying the parameters of a single patch.

If you are interested in creating custom drivers and templates, you will need a separate "Profile Development System" called **E-oR**. The owner's manual warns that E-oR is definitely not for the "casual user" and requires substantial knowledge of computer programming and MIDI sys-ex data.

X-oR is a nicely designed and intuitive program. The owner's manual, except for a very weak index, is likewise excellent. The clearly written documentation offers plenty of help for getting started and for troubleshooting problems. Dr. T's also provides BBS support and new Profiles on GEnie.

# Galaxy Plus Editors

Galaxy Plus Editors (Opcode Systems, Inc.) combines the universal librarian features of the original Galaxy (still available) with the many excellent dedicated editors that Opcode has produced for the Macintosh during the past few years. The result is a powerful, feature-laden program offering flexibility, online help, and an excellent look and feel.

Galaxy Plus Editors comes packaged with **Opcode MIDI System** (OMS), a Mac system extension (INIT) that provides an environment allowing multiple MIDI applications to run concurrently. OMS incorporates a setup application that enables you to store information about your MIDI system configuration, which it supplies to each of your OMS-compatible MIDI programs (such as Vision). The OMS Setup display resembles an Apple

Universal Editor/Librarians

MIDI Manager window, with various devices (shown as icons) connected by "cables" representing the signal path and direction (Figure 9.6).

OMS is designed to be either an alternative to MIDI Manager or an adjunct to it, depending on the requirements of the programs in use. Unlike MIDI Manager, OMS does not slow down your computer, but neither does it manage timing information or allow interapplication communication. The OMS Setup procedure for Galaxy is longer and more labyrinthian than the other ed/lib setups, but the abundant and well-written documentation should get you through the process without a hitch. To install Galaxy itself, Opcode provides an Easy Configuration feature, which finds and installs the appropriate drivers and templates automatically and painlessly.

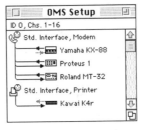

**Figure 9.6**
The OMS Setup display uses icons to represent the instruments and connections in your MIDI system.

To begin working in Galaxy, you first open a Bundle window, which can contain different types of patch banks from different types of instruments (Figure 9.7). Once you select a particular patch bank, the exchange of data can occur in much the same way as in the other ed/lib programs. You can change names and create libraries by using the usual Cut, Copy and Paste commands.

Like X-oR, Galaxy boasts a wealth of powerful searching and organizing functions, which are centered on names, keywords, and comments that you can attach to any patch for describing its characteristics. The General Find dialog box lets you type any word, or part of a word, which Galaxy uses to search through any open Bank, Library, or Bundle window. If the specified text appears in the name, keyword, or comments for a patch, it becomes

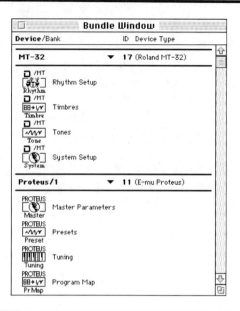

**Figure 9.7**
Galaxy's Bundle window can contain different types of patch banks from different instruments.

highlighted in the window where it's found. The Find Again command lets you continue the search.

For a much more sophisticated option, you can use the Specific Find dialog box to indicate separate text entries for names and comments. Keywords are selected using a hierarchal, menu-based approach similar to that in X-oR (Figure 9.8). Highlighting an entry in the Categories column generates a list of available options in the Keywords menu. Keywords selected here are then added to the Find list on the right until an appropriate number of keywords are shown to narrow the search. You can further alter the scope of the search by adding *And* and *Or* after each entry or adding *Not* before selected keywords. Complex keyword-combinations can further be saved as macros so that you can apply often-used search specifications without tedious reentry. Galaxy also gives you the option of cutting or copying the patches as they're found and pasting them into another window to create a new library.

Both Galaxy and X-oR let you customize your lists of categories and keywords, and Galaxy also offers a function that searches for patches with

# Universal Editor/Librarians 159

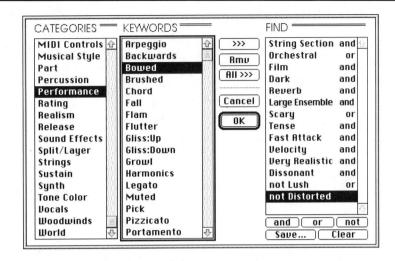

**Figure 9.8**
Galaxy's Specific Find dialog box lets you search for patches using numerous keywords chosen from several categories. Modifying words help narrow the search.

duplicate parameter information to eliminate redundant patches with different names. Many synthesizers use patches that derive some of their parameters from other patches. To avoid losing this shared parameter data when moving patches from one location to another, Galaxy provides a useful Attached Patch feature, which keeps track of these related entries and moves them together to maintain the necessary parameter references when you reorganize your sounds.

The sound-auditioning section of Galaxy offers both a sequencer and a mouse-triggering option. To use the mouse feature, you open the Mouse-Keys window (Figure 9.9), where an on-screen keyboard allows you to play notes by clicking on the appropriate keys. The location of the cursor front to back on each key determines volume, and the range of the keyboard can be shifted up or down by octaves. If you prefer, you can use the Macintosh keyboard to trigger sounds with its velocity set from the MouseKeys window as well.

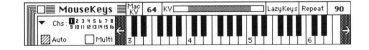

**Figure 9.9**
Galaxy lets you audition sounds by playing notes from an on-screen keyboard.

For those circumstances where a sequence playback would be preferable, Galaxy provides the option of recording and saving a small sequence that will play when chosen, or automatically when you select a patch—very useful for reviewing banks of sounds. To extend its sequencer option even further, Galaxy also allows you to play back prerecorded sequences stored as Standard MIDI Files. This means that sequences recorded in other programs can be imported into Galaxy for patch-auditioning purposes. Of course, as with the other ed/libs, you can always use an external MIDI keyboard to audition patches.

Galaxy's editing templates (Figure 9.10) are designed and implemented extremely well. The layout is very clear, with excellent detail. The envelope graphs appear initially in miniature giving a general view of the envelope shape, but clicking on one brings up a matrix of numbers showing all of the parameter settings for quick adjustment by keyboard or mouse. Another click and the miniature graph becomes a much larger window, with grab boxes to change the envelope's shape by dragging with the mouse. The use of these and other types of pop-up windows enables Galaxy to display the entire main editing template on a single screen, thereby eliminating the need for scrolling or page turning. This, in turn, creates a more efficient work environment.

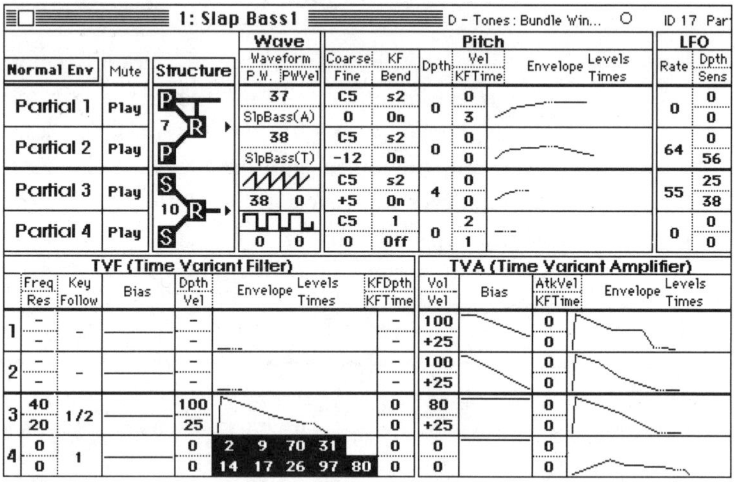

**Figure 9.10**
Galaxy's templates fit a lot of information on a single screen without losing clarity. Clicking on a miniature envelope graph produces a larger window with grab handles for changing the envelope's shape.

As might be expected, Galaxy also offers several means of generating new patches from old. Options include Constrained Random (random generation with parameter limits), Shade Two (gradual transitions between two patches), and Shuffler (totally random combinations). Each option can generate a new bank of any specified number of patches.

If you're interested in creating custom drivers and templates, Galaxy includes **PatchTalk**, its programming language. This is intended for those with a working knowledge of programming and MIDI system-exclusive code. The documentation is clear and well written, and there are several examples of custom modules included with Galaxy.

Finally, the owner's manual must be mentioned. In short, it is outstanding. It is lucid, complete, organized, and filled with helpful illustrations and tutorials. This is an excellent example of thoughtful and well-designed documentation.

## MIDI Quest

MIDI Quest, from Sound Quest, Inc., offers yet another approach to organizing and editing your instrument sounds. It has variations on many of the options found in other ed/lib programs along with a few intriguing features of its own.

After a rather convoluted decompression/installation procedure, you begin the program by building a Driver List. The Driver List window that emerges (Figure 9.11) has entries for each instrument in your system along with the appropriate settings. Selecting a driver from the Driver List window and clicking on the Edit button loads a bank of patches into the computer, where it appears in a Bank Editor window. This window lets you display, organize, and name your sounds. You can exchange patches with other windows by using commands such as Cut, Copy, Paste, Swap, and Delete.

MIDI Quest offers three ways to generate new sounds from the patches in a Bank Editor window: Mix randomly selects parameters from two different patches, Blend randomly combines large parts of two patches, and Mix

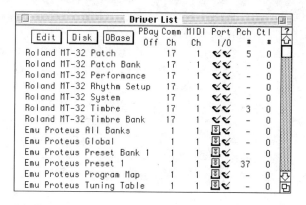

**Figure 9.11**
MIDI Quest's Driver List window displays the instruments in your system along with their settings.

All randomly selects parameters from several patches. In all cases, a new bank is created containing the resulting sounds. This approach to patch generation doesn't offer the same level of control and flexibility as in the other ed/libs but may still yield some worthwhile results.

For collecting and organizing your patches into larger groups, MIDI Quest provides a good array of librarian functions, centered on its Library window. You can easily drag patches from the Bank Editor windows into the Library window to create a master list of sounds or other types of data for each instrument in your system. Once it appears in the library, a patch can have a keyword and a comment attached to it, and the library can then sort your sounds alphabetically by name, keyword, or comment.

The Choose command opens a display within the Library window that provides several useful options for searching through your lists of sounds (Figure 9.12). MIDI Quest lets you launch a general search of the library to locate duplicate patches with or without the same names. You can also search for patches with similar parameter settings based on a selectable "percentage of similarity." Additionally, you can locate patches by specifying a name or keyword.

To shorten the search time, the Use Select command lets you choose a patch in advance with which the various criteria will be compared. The And button ensures that only patches meeting all of the selected criteria will be chosen, while the Or button allows selection based on any one of the

**Figure 9.12**
The Choose command in MIDI Quest offers several useful options for locating patches.

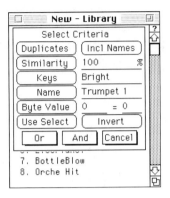

criteria. The Library window also offers a Mix All command to generate a new library of 32 sounds by randomly picking parameters from several selected patches.

MIDI Quest's Sound Checker feature offers a number of excellent ways to audition your sounds. The MIDI Sequencer window (Figure 9.13) lets you import Standard MIDI Files to play while you edit your sounds or try out other patches. You can load up to 10 different sequences into the MIDI Sequencer window, which provides 10 buttons for file selection and 16 additional buttons for disabling any MIDI channel during playback. Tempo can also be adjusted and the Loop button lets you set the sequence to repeat.

To view MIDI activity at either your MIDI In or Out port, MIDI Quest includes a MIDI Monitor window (Figure 9.14), which displays MIDI data graphically or in text form. If you choose not to use a Standard MIDI File

**Figure 9.13**
The MIDI Sequencer window lets you store and play up to ten Standard MIDI Files for auditioning your sounds.

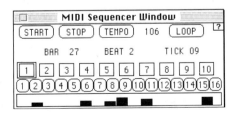

to test your sounds, you can use the Tones window to create a chord or sequence of up to 16 notes, which can be triggered from any window. You can also use the MIDI Controller window to generate several types of MIDI messages, including Aftertouch, Program Change, Poly Pressure, and Pitch Bend.

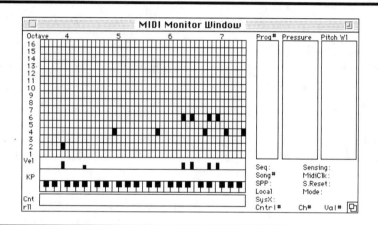

**Figure 9.14**
The MIDI Monitor window displays MIDI activity graphically or in text form.

Editing activities take place in MIDI Quest's Patch Editor windows (Figure 9.15). These templates are not always as clean or visually well designed as those in the ed/libs mentioned above, but they provide a satisfactory environment for quickly adjusting parameters to fine-tune your patches or to create new sounds. Many of the templates require more than one screen to accommodate their displays, so you'll have to use the scroll bars or the "jump" buttons in the lower-right corner to access the additional information.

MIDI Quest's Data Base feature lets you store information from the different instruments in your system so that you can save a "snapshot" of your device settings. Several Data Bases can be displayed simultaneously and any one can be used to reconfigure your entire MIDI system in a single step.

For the more technically minded users, MIDI Quest provides the Driver Creator window. This utility lets you write your own drivers for instruments that are not already supported. Newly created drivers can then be

# Universal Editor/Librarians

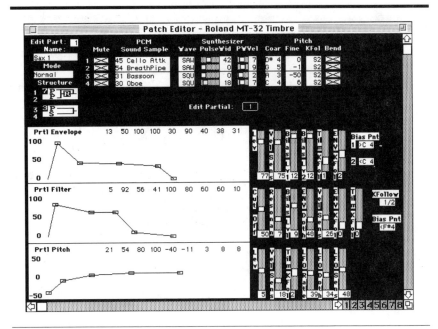

**Figure 9.15**
Editing activities take place in MIDI Quest's Patch Editor windows.

added to the Driver List window. Sound Quest does not include information on the use of the Driver Creator window but does offer documentation through its BBS.

MIDI Quest has several features that make it worth considering. Although its templates are a bit coarser-looking than its competition and may require much scrolling or page turning, other aspects of the program are stronger. The Sound Checker features are noteworthy. The ability to import and access up to ten different MIDI files and to monitor MIDI activity during playback are especially appealing. The online help and the useful search, sort, and compare options add to the program's strength. The documentation is concise but occasionally confusing, and it suffers further from the lack of an index.

## ≣ Final Thoughts

Of the programs covered in this chapter, the strongest contenders are clearly Galaxy Plus Editors and X-oR. These two ed/libs combine powerful features, excellent graphics, and well-written documentation. MIDI Quest is very close behind with several good features to recommend it.

During the past few years there has been an ongoing trend by synthesizer manufacturers to produce devices with fewer and fewer front panel controls. The inevitable result of this trend can clearly be seen in Roland's CM-32L sound module, which has virtually no controls except a power switch and a volume knob. Many hardware companies now assume that anyone interested in serious sound designing will use an ed/lib program of some kind, but the landscape of MIDI hardware devices changes constantly along with the requirements of multimedia music producers. All of the programs above are powerful and refined enough to tackle today's archiving and editing problems while still leaving the door open to embrace future products and developments.

# An Introduction to Digital Audio

With the tremendous success of the compact disc, the burgeoning demand for DAT (digital audiotape) recorders and the myriad new computer-based RAM and hard-disk recording systems, the future of digital audio has by now been very well established. When you go shopping for hardware and software, though, you'll inevitably find yourself facing a confusing array of specifications involving varying costs, memory requirements, and cryptic claims for performance. An understanding of the digital audio process is, therefore, essential to assess your needs and to evaluate the plethora of new products entering the marketplace. If you're a digital audio novice, this introduction (though it gets a little technical) should provide some basic information that can help you grapple with the new terminology that you'll certainly encounter. To keep from drifting too far afield, I'm assuming that you have a basic understanding of simple audio concepts so that I can focus on the world of digits, disks, and dynamics, and the new concepts brought by this exciting technology.

## ▦ The Analog World

From the beginning, and for the past several decades, recording techniques have involved analog procedures. The typical process is straightforward and relatively simple: Sound waves impinging on a microphone get converted into continuously fluctuating voltages that, by way of the record head, become stored on tape as patterns of magnetization. The changing signal and the resultant magnetic patterns are directly analogous to the original sound waves. In other words, an increase in sound level produces a corresponding increase in voltage and it's this analog that you preserve on tape. Playback takes place when you reverse the process so that the fluctuating voltages produce sound waves after passing through an amplifier and speakers. The analog relationship is thereby preserved throughout the procedure.

## The Digital Domain

In the past five years, as computer components have gained in speed and power, digital audio has become a viable alternative in both the professional and consumer markets. Simply stated, digital audio describes a method of recording that takes sound waves and converts them into numbers, which you can then store as data in a variety of media, including hard disks, compact discs, digital audiotape, and computer RAM. In addition to the potential for greatly improved sound quality, digital recording offers a quantum-leap improvement in the areas of editing capability, signal processing, mixing, and networking. In short, it brings a new level of power and flexibility to the recording process, which does not exist in the world of analog tape recording.

To begin understanding digital audio, you must first realize that sound consists of two elements: amplitude (level) and frequency (events over time). In digital audio these elements are addressed through quantization and sampling, respectively. Now let's examine in greater detail the important roles of these fundamental processes.

## Sound into Numbers

The digital recording chain begins in the analog world with sound waves reaching a microphone, which converts them into fluctuating voltages. This analog signal reaches the *sample-and-hold circuit,* which grabs and freezes the signal momentarily as a discreet voltage whose measurement represents a snapshot, at a specific point in time, of the continuously fluctuating voltage. The sample-and-hold circuit has the responsibility of retaining each snapshot just long enough for the next component in the chain, the *analog-to-digital converter,* to do its work. The A/D converter obtains each voltage reading from the sample-and-hold circuit, evaluates it, and outputs a series of numbers (1's and 0's), which represents the amplitude of the signal for that precise moment in time. Once done, the sample-and-hold circuit releases its grip and the process begins again—tens of thousands of times each second. The number of times per second this conversion process occurs is called the *sampling rate.* As you'll see, it's an important factor in evaluating digital audio hardware.

## *Quantization*

The process above by which fluctuating electricity, representing sound waves, gets converted into a series of number values is called *quantization.* This term refers to the *amplitude* component of digital audio recording. The A/D converter after receiving each voltage reading outputs a series of binary numbers (bits) that represent the signal amplitude at that moment. These bits are grouped into "words," and the sizes of the words determines the number of quantization levels available to represent the incoming voltages. Since larger words can carry more information, they consequently allow for greater resolution. Common word sizes include 8-bit, 12-bit, and 16-bit. MacRecorder and other similar voice digitizers typically provide 8-bit resolution, while compact discs, DAT recorders, and most professional-level products, like Digidesign's Audiomedia card, incorporate 16-bit technology.

Every time another bit is added to a word the number of available combinations that can represent the incoming signal levels is increased by a factor of two. This means that an 8-bit number has 2 to the 8th power (256) discreet values possible. A 12-bit number has 2 to the 12th power (4096) combinations, and a 16-bit number has 2 to the 16th power or 65,536 possible values! The greater the number of combinations there are, the finer the resolution will be and the less inaccuracy will occur. This results in a lower degree of *quantization noise*—a type of distortion occurring when the digitally represented waveform does not accurately match the original analog signal. Additionally, a higher resolution produces a wider *dynamic range.* This is the difference, expressed in decibels, between the loudest and the quietest possible audio levels of a recording.

## Sampling Rate

So far we've focused on the amplitude component of an audio signal. Now let's examine the matter of *frequency response* in a digital system. As mentioned above, the sampling rate is the number of times per second that the digital audio circuitry examines and converts the incoming voltages. Logically, the lower audio frequencies, with their larger cycles and slower changes, can be represented reasonably well with fewer samples per second than the higher frequencies, with their small, rapidly changing patterns. Therefore, the greater the sampling rate, the greater the available range of frequencies, or *bandwidth*, that the digital recorder can handle adequately.

To represent a given signal with any accuracy, the digital circuitry must obtain a minimum of two samples for each audio cycle so that both the positive and negative motion of the waveform can be represented (Figure 10.1). If the signal isn't sampled at least twice during each cycle, the resulting numbers will appear to represent a frequency that is much lower than the actual frequency being examined (Figure 10.2). This unwanted variant of the original tone is called an *alias frequency*, and its appearance in the audio chain is referred to as *aliasing*.

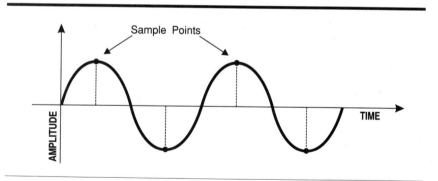

**Figure 10.1**
The digital circuitry must obtain at least two samples per audio cycle so that both the positive and negative parts of the waveform can be represented.

To avoid this type of harmonic distortion, you must adhere to the restrictions of the Nyquist theorem, which states that the sample rate must be at least twice as high as the highest frequency recorded. In other words, the highest frequency that you can record without aliasing will be one-half of the sample rate—a limit known as the *Nyquist frequency*.

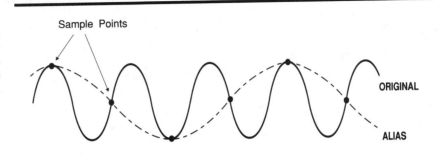

**Figure 10.2**
Aliasing occurs when too few samples are taken to describe the audio signal accurately.

To ensure that frequencies beyond the Nyquist limit do not enter the recording chain, a *low-pass filter* with a steep cutoff slope, often referred to as an anti-aliasing filter, is placed just before the sample-and-hold circuit (Figure 10.3). Customarily, the cutoff frequency of this input filter is set slightly lower than the Nyquist limit to provide a guard band so that, in practice, the upper frequency response is not quite half of the sampling rate. Compact discs use a sampling frequency of 44.1 kHz, and DAT recorders typically incorporate a rate of 48 kHz. It's clear that in both cases you'll have ample room to accurately reproduce the full audio bandwidth of 20 Hz–20 kHz.

## Westward Ho!

Digital audio recording and filmmaking share many similarities. Films are made when a movie camera "samples" the world at a rate of 24 frames per second. Even though in real life there are no such things as frames per second, the action on screen appears natural because the sampling rate is high enough to fool our eyes. Occasionally, an event on screen reminds us that we are watching a sampled reproduction of life. Such is the case with the well-known "wagon wheel" effect, which most people have noticed while watching old westerns. Even though the on-screen wagon is clearly moving and the wheels are turning, the spokes appear to be stationary (or sometimes even turning backward). This is an example of aliasing. In this case the sampling rate of the camera is too slow to represent accurately the forward rotation of the wagon spokes. If the spokes keep arriving at the same position each time the camera shutter opens, the movie will include the confusing alias image of the nonmoving wheel along with the other

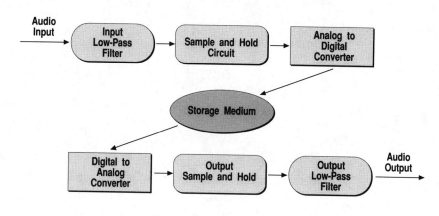

**Figure 10.3**
The basic components of a digital audio system

images of movement. The visual sampling frequency is, therefore, insufficient to reproduce convincingly the real-life action. In a like manner, unwanted, spurious tones may appear in a digital recording if the sampling rate doesn't prove sufficient for the program material or other steps aren't taken to eliminate aliasing.

# Playback

As might be expected, the digital audio playback process simply reverses (more or less) the recording process. The digital numbers are output from storage to a *digital-to-analog converter*, which, logically, transforms the digital "words" back into voltages. The analog signal then encounters an *output sample-and-hold circuit*, which produces a more stable and regular output. The reconstructed analog voltages next pass through an *output low-pass filter*, which eliminates the unwanted, additional high frequencies that result from the conversion process. This final component performs an important function since it must smooth out the irregularities created by the digital circuitry and, therefore, will determine the quality of the end result. The analog signal, by now, should very closely resemble the original fluctuating voltages that began the process, and you can finally send it to an audio amplifier and speakers for listening.

Digital audio recording eliminates many of the problems, such as tape noise, that have plagued similar analog processes for many years. Its most important aspect, however, lies in the fact that, once an audio signal enters the digital domain, you can subject it to an astounding array of editing capabilities never before possible. In the following chapters we'll examine some of the hardware/software products that provide this editing power and enable you to incorporate this new technology into multimedia presentations.

# Chapter 11

# Digital Audio for the Masses (8-Bit)

Nearly every presentation can benefit from the addition of sound, and MIDI goes a long way to fill that potential. But MIDI isn't always well suited to every kind of audio requirement. Some things, especially narration (and even some kinds of music), are better handled with digital audio. The products covered in this chapter all have several things going for them: They're inexpensive, their recordings can be distributed with disk-based presentations, they don't need additional hardware for playback, and they work with any model of Macintosh from a Plus on up. In other words, they offer universal digital audio for the Mac user on the street.

## ▤ MacRecorder

It seems like MacRecorder (from MacroMind/Paracomp) has been around as long as the Macintosh itself. True, the Mac has always been able to produce digitized sounds, but when Farallon Computing first released MacRecorder in January 1988, the whole world began to tap into this addicting capability. Soon bulletin boards everywhere were sprouting lists of sound effects, music clips, and pithy quotes from favorite movies to enliven our everyday computing tasks. Business users discovered that less "off-the-wall" sounds could improve communications, and finally Apple took the next logical, evolutionary step and included digitizing hardware and software in its Mac LC, IIsi, Classic II, and Quadra models. Today,

MacRecorder is still the most popular product on the market for adding digitized sounds to desktop presentations and low-budget multimedia.

The MacRecorder Sound System consists of a hardware/software combination that includes a sound digitizer and three applications. **SoundEdit** lets you record, edit, process, play, and store sounds. **HyperSound** is a stack that you can use to record and play sounds in HyperCard. And a second stack, the **HyperSound Toolkit**, contains external commands and functions that enable you to record and play sounds from any stack.

The MacRecorder digitizer—a little larger than a pack of cigarettes—plugs into the Mac's modem or printer port. It has a small built-in, omnidirectional microphone and a line-level input jack for recording from a radio, tape deck, or CD player. If you prefer your own microphone, MacRecorder provides a second minijack for an external mic input. On the side, a small thumb wheel lets you adjust the input for setting proper recording levels.

MacRecorder defaults to a record mode with 8-bit resolution and a 22-kHz sampling rate. Its anti-aliasing filter eliminates frequencies over 11 kHz, so from a practical standpoint you can capture frequencies up to about 10 kHz with reasonable accuracy. It has a dynamic range of 48 db. With these settings, you can store approximately 45 seconds of monaural sound per megabyte of memory. If you have a second digitizer, you can plug both into your Macintosh and record in stereo. This, of course, requires twice as much memory.

To fit more sound into less memory, MacRecorder provides two methods of altering sounds: downsampling and compressing. A downsampled sound is one that has been recorded at or converted to one of three lower sampling rates: 11, 7, or 5 kHz. An 11-kHz sound, for example, requires half the memory of the same recording at 22 kHz. It also reduces the frequency response and sound quality. A compressed sound also requires less memory, but achieves this reduction by storing the sound using less than 8-bit resolution. Although this doesn't reduce the frequency response in quite the same way that downsampling does, it still noticeably degrades sound quality. SoundEdit and HyperSound support compression ratios of 8:1, 6:1, 4:1, and 3:1, with each ratio expressing a comparison between the size of a compressed sound and its normal-size equivalent.

## SoundEdit

At the heart of MacRecorder, the SoundEdit application provides an impressive number of features for recording, displaying, and editing sounds. To begin recording you first open the SoundEdit window (Figure 11.1), which provides a large area for displaying waveforms. A waveform is a two-dimensional representation of a sound, with amplitude indicated along the vertical axis and time shown along the horizontal. The Display Options command lets you choose whether the waveform appears as a series of dots or vertical lines. Beneath the waveform display, several buttons enable (from left to right) recording, playing, zooming in or out, monitoring input levels, and showing the Spectrum Analysis display. To the right of these buttons, six variable-mode "report boxes" give information about the waveform or a selected region within it.

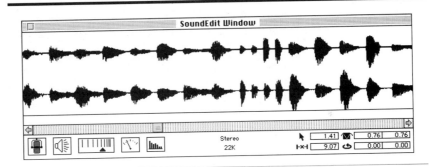

**Figure 11.1**
MacRecorder's SoundEdit window shows your recording as a waveform display.

Before you start recording, it's a good idea to check your input levels to establish an optimum setting. Clicking on the Input Level button starts the input level test. Speaking into the microphone (or starting playback from an external source) produces a real-time waveform display that lets you see the sounds you're making. Ideally, the loudest sounds should nearly fill the display from top to bottom. Proper level setting is critical in digital recording since a waveform that is too narrow will not only sound too soft when recorded but will also produce an unnecessary amount of quantization noise (Figure 11.2). If you record the waveform at too high a level, the tops and bottoms of the waveform peaks will get cut off—a characteristic known as "clipping"—and the recording will be distorted (Figure 11.3).

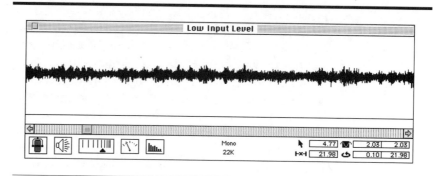

**Figure 11.2**
This sound was recorded at too low a level. It will have an unnecessary amount of quantization noise.

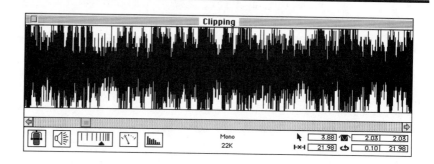

**Figure 11.3**
This sound was recorded at too high a level. It will have distortion from clipping.

To obtain the proper input level, you can adjust the microphone placement or turn the input-level thumb wheel on the side of the digitizer until the waveform looks right. Once you've set your level, recording is easy. Just click the Record button to start and click the mouse to stop. Your recording will then appear in the waveform display, where you can play back the entire soundfile or any selected portion of it. Clicking and dragging through a part of the waveform selects a region for editing, and you can then subject it to the usual Cut, Copy, Paste, and Delete commands, along with labeling and color identification options and a multitude of digital effects.

Three of the effects don't require any recording since they generate sounds themselves. You can mix together the results to create new sounds and use them alone or paste them into other recordings. The Noise command generates "white noise," which resembles static from a radio or television. The

Tone Generator produces three types of waveforms—sine wave, square wave, and sawtooth wave—each with its own characteristic sound. Once you select the wave type, you can specify the frequency, amplitude, and duration. The FM Synthesis effect allows you to turn MacRecorder into a simple synthesizer that creates sounds through the interaction of one frequency with another, as determined by a number of variables.

MacRecorder lets you apply one or more of 11 effects to modify any noncompressed waveform or selected portion. Amplify increases the amplitude of a selected region; Backwards plays it in reverse. The Smooth effect removes harsh-sounding upper frequencies and noise by simulating a low-pass filter, and the Flanger effect adds a whooshing sound like a jet plane to selected regions. The Echo effect simulates a digital delay device to generate a repeating sound that decays over time like the echoes you hear when you yell into a canyon. You can adjust both the delay time, in fractions of a second, and the echo strength, which determines how quickly the repetitions die away. MacRecorder provides a time-scaling feature in its Tempo effect, which changes the playback speed of a sound without altering its pitch. Selecting Speed Up from the dialog box doubles the speed and Slow Down halves it. Using Tempo is most useful for extending or shortening sections of dialog in a presentation.

Two of MacRecorder's effects apply only to stereo recordings. The Ping Pong effect creates the illusion that a sound is moving from left to right or vice versa by gradually interchanging the amplitudes of the left and right channels (Figure 11.4). The Swap Channels effect simply exchanges the right and left channels as long as they are the same length.

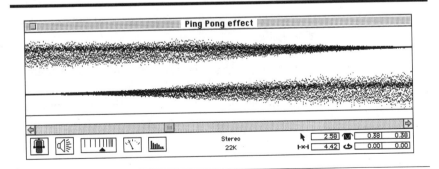

**Figure 11.4**
With MacRecorder's Ping Pong effect, you can create the illusion that a sound is moving from left to right or vice versa.

MacRecorder also provides an easy yet powerful way to create envelopes for your sounds. The Envelope effect lets you determine the amplitude of a sound by an amount that can vary over time. Choosing Envelope from the Effects menu superimposes an "amplitude adjustment line" over the selected waveform area (Figure 11.5). Clicking anywhere on the line creates a handle that you can drag up or down to increase or decrease the waveform's amplitude. In appearance, these envelopes resemble those described in Chapter 9, except that here you can choose how many handles to create and where. This enables you to quickly produce any kinds of fade-in or fade-out effects as well as more complex envelope shapes.

**Figure 11.5**
The Envelope effect lets you vary a sound's amplitude over time.

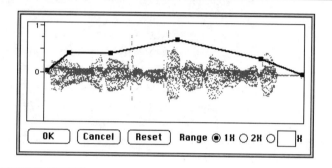

The Bender effect works the same as the Envelope effect, only here you adjust the pitch of a sound over time. The "pitch adjustment line" works the same way as its amplitude counterpart, letting you create handles anywhere along the line and drag them to new locations (Figure 11.6). Dragging the line upward raises the pitch and dragging it downward lowers the pitch. This produces an effect much like using the pitch-bend wheel on a synthesizer. MacRecorder allows you to choose between a one- or two-octave range above and below the zero line.

The Filter effect is one of MacRecorder's most useful features. It looks and acts much like the graphic equalizers common on many home stereo systems, with sliders adjusting the amplitudes of different frequency bands (Figure 11.7). This equalizer, however, lets you drag the dividers between

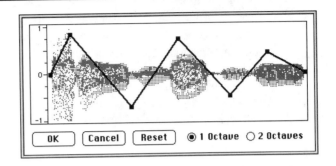

**Figure 11.6**
The Bender effect lets you vary a sound's pitch over time.

its five frequency bands to the right or left to change the frequency ranges affected by its sliders. This makes it function more like an on-screen parametric equalizer, with amplitude along the vertical axis and frequency along the horizontal axis.

Of course, no digitizing program would be complete without reverb, and MacRecorder's Reverb effect comes in four flavors: Empty Room, Concert Hall, Stadium, and Outer Space. You can apply reverb to the entire waveform or to any selected portion, in case you want to emphasize a single word in a narration, for instance.

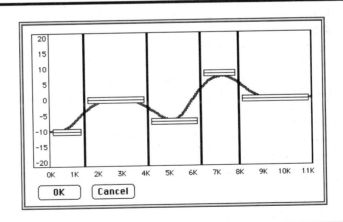

**Figure 11.7**
MacRecorder's Filter effect combines the best features of a graphic and parametric equalizer.

Looping is another essential feature in a digital editing program. MacRecorder's Loopback option lets you repeat any selected region over and over to extend its duration without requiring additional memory. Used often in music applications, looping lets you create sustained sounds from short segments. This works well with certain kinds of sound effects and musical instrument tones, but you can also put it to good use with spoken words and even entire musical passages. And speaking of music, there's also a Set Pitches command, which allows you to raise or lower the playback pitch of a recording in half-step increments.

In addition to the waveform itself, MacRecorder provides three other displays for viewing your sounds. Clicking the Spectrum Analysis button produces a real-time graph showing the different frequencies reaching the computer through the microphone (Figure 11.8). This can help you decide if you're using the best sampling rate for the sound source.

**Figure 11.8**
MacRecorder provides a real-time Spectrum Analysis display, which lets you view the incoming frequencies.

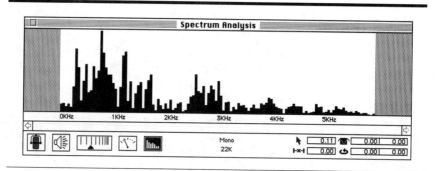

If you're using a Mac that supports color QuickDraw, you can use the Sonogram effect to show a map of the relative strengths of the frequencies in your recording (Figure 11.9). The Sonogram represents frequencies in 16 colors or gray scales, based on relative strength, on a two-dimensional graph showing frequency and time.

The Spectrogram effect also shows the relative strengths of frequencies in a recording, only this time the frequencies are represented in a series of two-dimensional graphs (Figure 11.10). The vertical axis indicates the power in decibels, and the horizontal axis indicates the frequencies. Each graph in the series represents a different time interval. You can use this map to examine the frequency content of a sound and how it changes over time.

**Figure 11.9**
The Sonogram display shows the relative strengths of the frequencies in your recording.

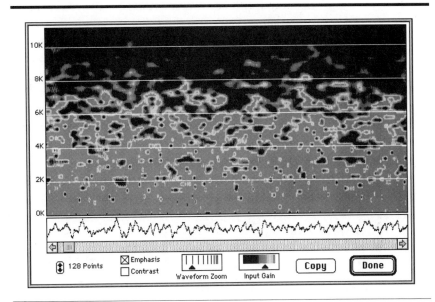

The Mixer window (Figure 11.11) is one of MacRecorder's most important features. It lets you combine up to four recordings and save the result in a specified destination. Any noncompressed sound or selected portion can appear in one of the four channel displays, where it can have its amplitude

**Figure 11.10**
The Spectrogram display shows the frequency content of a sound and how it changes over time.

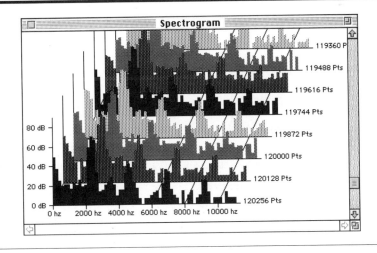

adjusted with an envelope effect like the one mentioned earlier. This window allows you to combine dialog, sound effects, or music into a final mix for your presentation.

SoundEdit supports three file formats: SoundEdit format (used in many Macintosh applications), Instrument format (used in some music programs), and Audio Interchange File Format (Audio IFF), a standard audio format supported by Apple Computer and by sample-editing programs such as Alchemy. Additionally, SoundEdit supports both Format 1 and Format 2 sound (SND) resources.

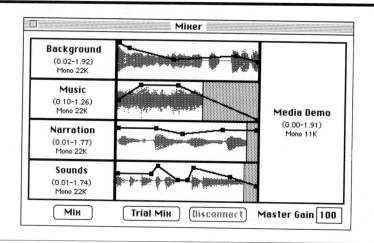

**Figure 11.11**
The Mixer window lets you combine up to four recordings, each with its own envelope effect.

## *HyperSound*

In addition to SoundEdit, MacRecorder provides a HyperCard stack that allows you to record and play monaural sounds using a variety of sampling rates and compression ratios. With HyperSound, you can copy sounds to other stacks or transfer sounds to SoundEdit for further editing. The HyperSound stack (Figure 11.12) consists of a number of "tape-deck" controls along with several buttons, controls, indicators, and information fields.

Digital Audio for the Masses (8-Bit)

**Figure 11.12**
With Mac-Recorder's HyperSound you can record sounds and add them to HyperCard stacks.

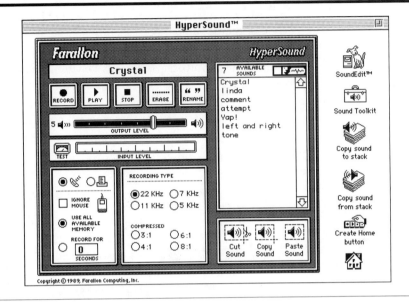

To test your input level before recording, HyperSound provides a bar-graph level meter that you activate by clicking the Test button. After setting the input level and choosing a sampling rate or compression ratio, simply click the Record button to begin. When you do, a pop-up window appears with a thermometer-style gauge, which fills as you record, to indicate the remaining time available for the recording. You can then play back your soundfile and adjust the volume using the Output Level slider.

Along the right side of the window, several icons help you integrate your work in HyperSound with other applications and stacks. Clicking the first icon closes HyperSound and opens SoundEdit; clicking the second button opens the HyperSound Toolkit. The third icon lets you copy the current sound and export it to another stack. If you like, you can choose Paste Button from the Edit menu to create a button that will play your new sound. The next icon lets you copy sounds from another HyperCard stack into HyperSound, and the fifth icon lets you create a button on the Home card that will take you directly to the HyperSound stack.

## HyperSound ToolKit

The HyperSound Toolkit consists of a number of HyperTalk external commands (XCMDs) and external functions (XFCNs) that you can use to record and play monaural sounds or noncompressed stereo sounds in other HyperCard stacks. At the top of the stack, an Index card (Figure 11.13) represents each XCMD and XFCN with an icon. Clicking any button produces the installer card for that external command or function. With the HyperSound Toolkit you can customize your stacks and use sounds in a variety of ways, but you must first be familiar with the structure, syntax, and usage of the HyperTalk language to get useful results.

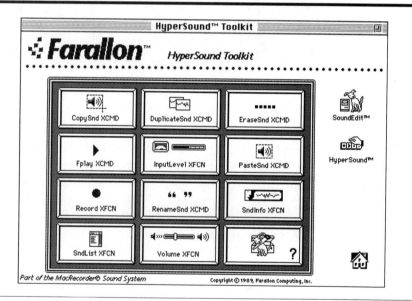

**Figure 11.13**
The HyperSound Toolkit provides XCMDs and XFCNs for more advanced HyperCard users.

## ▄ Voice Impact Pro

As with MacRecorder, the Voice Impact Pro package from Articulate Systems consists of a hardware/software combination that digitizes sounds for recording, editing, and saving. Although the two products share much common ground, Articulate Systems has introduced a number of design improvements yet has sacrificed other features in the process. The two products also part company somewhat in terms of their intended use. MacRecorder serves effectively as a general-purpose recording system while Voice Impact Pro, through its design and literature, stresses its capabilities at fully integrating with a number of business software products, such as Microsoft Excel and Mail, CE QuickMail, FullWrite Professional, Mathematica, WordPerfect Office, and other programs that support sound or voice annotation.

Voice Impact Pro's hardware comes in a thin, modern-looking, 7.5" × 3" rectangular box, which Articulate Systems describes as an "ergonomically designed black case." It comes with a clip for mounting on the side of your monitor, or you can use it as a hand-held unit. The bottom of the device provides an unmarked input-level adjustment slider and a small, unmarked switch for selecting between the Voice Impact Pro recording mode or a mode that emulates the MacRecorder. The rear panel includes a minijack for use as either a monaural, line input or an external microphone connection.

Aside from the standard digitizing components, Voice Impact Pro includes a built-in digital signal processor as well as on-board digital compression circuitry that enables it to perform real-time compression even on older Macintosh models. The more complex nature of Voice Impact Pro requires an external AC power supply (unlike MacRecorder), which plugs into the back panel below the minijack.

The top section of the plastic case houses a nicely designed, unidirectional microphone that slides forward to activate recording functions. The front panel provides two LEDs: The first indicates that the power is on and the microphone is extended, while the second shows that recording is in progress.

Voice Impact Pro records with 8-bit resolution at any of three sampling rates: 22, 11, and 7.4 kHz. It also offers two compression ratios: 3:1 and 6:1. The software side of the product consists mainly of two applications for recording and editing sounds. **Voice Record** can be used as a desk accessory or accessed directly from within several business applications. You would most likely use it to add voice messages to various kinds of documents. **SoundWave** more closely resembles MacRecorder's SoundEdit application since it provides graphic displays, additional editing options, and sound-processing features.

## SoundWave

To begin recording in SoundWave, you first select Record from the File menu, which opens a dialog box containing transport-control buttons, an available-time indicator, a VU-style peak-hold meter (for monitoring input levels), and an options box for setting the sampling rate (Figure 11.14). If you change the sampling rate, the available-time indicator (which fills from left to right during recording) reflects the change. When you've finished your recording, click the Stop button and then choose Done. This immediately opens the Sound Editing window, which incorporates two different displays of your recorded sound (Figure 11.15).

**Figure 11.14**
Voice Impact Pro provides a dialog box to record and play back sounds.

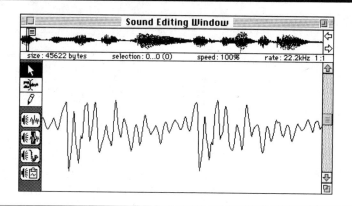

**Figure 11.15**
The Sound Editing window shows your recording as a waveform display with an overview of the entire soundfile above it.

Along its top section, the editing window provides a reduced view of the sound wave for the entire recording. This gives a good overview to help you locate specific sections while retaining a sense of the overall context. Beneath this display, a bigger area provides an enlarged view showing, in much greater detail, a small, selected area of the sound wave. You determine the area to show in the enlarged view by dragging a small rectangle, called a Scroll window, through the upper display to the desired location. The Scroll window changes size in proportion to the length of the recorded sound that can be shown in the enlarged view. In other words, short recordings produce a larger Scroll window since more of the total waveform can fit in the enlarged view and vice versa. These settings are otherwise not user-definable.

Along the left side of the window, a palette of tools offers three cursor options for editing and four buttons for playing sounds. You use the Pointer to scroll, select menu items, and choose options. The I-beam cursor selects segments of sound for editing by dragging through them, and you can make modifications to the waveform in the enlarged display by drawing with the Pencil tool.

The first of the playback buttons plays the entire sound from beginning to end, and the second button plays any selected area. The Play Instrument button is used when working with Studio Session sounds, and the last button plays whatever sound was last copied to the Clipboard. This lets you preview a copied sound before you paste it into another recording—a handy feature.

SoundWave's editing options are not as extensive as SoundEdit's, but you'll still find plenty to keep you busy. The Mix command lets you combine a sound on the Clipboard with the contents of the Sound Editing window. When you select Mix from the Edit menu, a dialog box appears with two sliders for adjusting the amplitude of the Clipboard sound and the original sound before initiating the mix.

You can adjust playback speed for each of your recordings by selecting Play Options from the Edit menu. Although it doesn't modify the sound itself, the Speed scroll-bar lets you increase or decrease the playing speed of a sound and save the setting with the soundfile. This is not the same as MacRecorder's Tempo effect, which increases or decreases playback speed without changing pitch. SoundWave's command produces an effect more like playing a record at the wrong speed—both pitch and speed change together. A Volume control also lets you set the volume for each soundfile independently of the Macintosh Control Panel.

By selecting Filter from the Wave menu, you can access SoundWave's on-screen, digital filter, which resembles a six-band graphic equalizer (Figure 11.16). Double-clicking on a slider handle produces a dialog box that lets you reset the range of that slider's frequency band. To create echo effects, SoundWave offers a Delay option that uses sliders in a dialog box to set the Delay Time, Delay Amplitude, and Final Amplitude for a sound or selected portion. The Amplify option enables you to adjust the amplitude of a selected sound segment from 1 percent to 400 percent of the original. Although SoundWave doesn't provide the same advanced envelope-shaping features as MacRecorder, it does offer a Fade In option and a Fade Out option to create simple and limited kinds of amplitude modifications.

**Figure 11.16**
SoundWave's digital filter lets you set the range of each slider's frequency band.

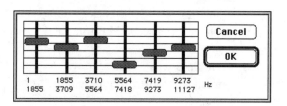

SoundWave's Reverse effect lets you play sounds (or selected portions) backward. The Smooth command averages out sudden amplitude changes, causing a muted effect, while Resample and Compress let you downsample your recording or apply compression to conserve storage space.

To further analyze your sounds, SoundWave includes a Spectrum window that resembles SoundEdit's Spectrogram feature. This window graphically displays the amplitudes of frequencies and how they change over time by showing a series of 1-kilobyte segments of sound (Figure 11.17). The Spectrum command brings up a dialog box giving you the opportunity to set the range of frequencies shown in the display and whether or not the graph will appear in three dimensions. Although the Spectrum window is not as well implemented as its MacRecorder counterpart, its graphics are clearer and easier to read.

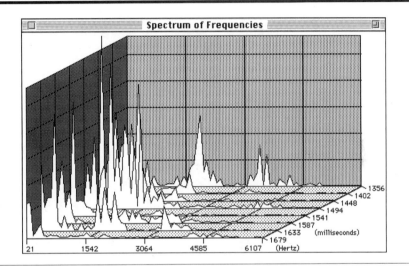

**Figure 11.17**
The Spectrum window shows the amplitudes of frequencies and how they change over time.

SoundWave provides a very helpful feature with its Connect-the-Dots option under the Display menu. When you select this command, the program draws lines between the amplitude dots in the waveform, making it much easier to interpret what you see in the window (Figure 11.18).

If you like synthesizing your own sounds, the Tone Generator feature (Figure 11.19) may interest you. You can use it to produce a tone by specifying and mixing up to four sine waves, each with its own period and amplitude. You can then combine the result with a recorded sound for special effect or use it as a signal tone.

SoundWave allows you to display up to four waveform windows at a time. To facilitate comparison, it provides two viewing options. The Stack Windows command displays all open windows stacked on top of one another with a slight offset, while the Tile Windows command arranges the windows in a side-by-side configuration.

**Figure 11.18**
Using the Connect-the-Dots option makes interpreting some waveforms much easier, as shown here in a before-and-after comparison.

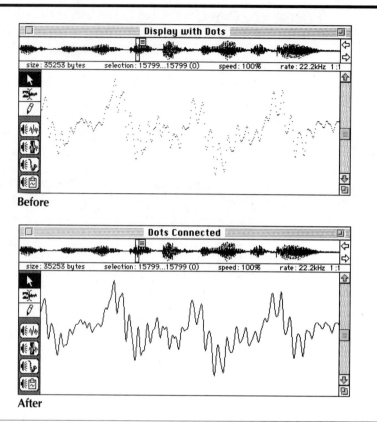

**Figure 11.19**
The Tone Generator lets you synthesize your own sounds by mixing up to four different sine waves.

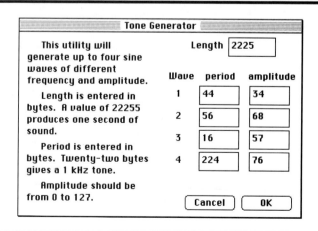

## Voice Record

The primary strength of the Voice Impact Pro system lies in its ability to integrate its recording and editing features into other programs. The application that accomplishes this, Voice Record, can be used independently as a desk accessory (if there is no host application) or from within any program that supports sound recording. When used in this manner, Voice Record replaces the often-limited transport-control panel of the host program with its own, more advanced display, which provides recording and editing options not otherwise available. As mentioned previously, this will mainly interest users of business software that supports digitized voice annotation along with its text and graphics files; but those who own one of the newer Macintosh models (LC, IIsi, etc.) can benefit as well, since Voice Record can override the limited recording capabilities offered with these machines.

To begin using Voice Record, you must open it from within the supporting application or select it from the Apple menu. This brings up the Voice Record dialog box, which contains the transport-style buttons, a level meter, and a pie graph that shows the available recording time (Figure 11.20).

**Figure 11.20**
Voice Record can replace the often-limited control panels provided with other programs that support sound. It is shown here in its expanded version, which includes a waveform display and additional buttons.

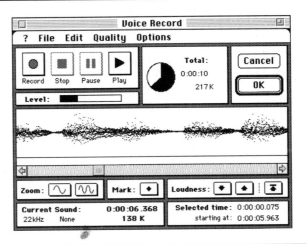

When you've made your recording, you can view the sound by selecting Show Editing from the Edit menu. This expands the window to its full size, revealing the waveform display along with several additional buttons. The Zoom In and Out buttons let you adjust the level of detail that you see in the sound display. The Mark button lets you place little diamond shapes at key places along the display as an aid in identifying and relocating important parts. The Loudness buttons allow you to adjust the amplitude of selected areas. Any selected portion of a waveform can be cut, copied, pasted, deleted, or merged. If you need to do additional editing, you can import the sound into SoundWave.

Voice Record and SoundWave support a number of file formats, including SoundWave format (similar to FSSD), usable with many applications, including SoundWave and SoundEdit; Audio IFF, used by Apple Computer and others for storing audio files; Audio IFF-C, a format based on Audio IFF that allows for compression; and Resource (SND) format, used for storing sounds inside an application, a document, or a file.

For HyperCard users, the Voice Record disk includes a stack providing you with all of Voice Record's capabilities from within HyperCard. Additionally, the software lets you install external commands (XCMDs) that enable you to use Voice Record in other stacks that you create.

## Mitshiba StereoRecorder

Olduvai Corporation has recently entered the digital audio marketplace with the introduction of the Mitshiba StereoRecorder. As its name clearly states, this 8-bit sound digitizer differs from those mentioned above in its ability to record in stereo with a single unit. The 5" × 7" box comes with cables that attach to both of the serial ports on you Macintosh and includes jacks that allow you to keep your printer and modem connected. The front panel provides two Port Select buttons to switch between the StereoRecorder and your peripherals.

You can record from line-level sources like CD players and tape recorders by using the stereo RCA-type input jacks on the rear panel. On the front panel there are three inputs for microphones—one for a monaural electret microphone and two for a stereo dynamic microphone. The digitizer can simultaneously handle line-level signals and input from a microphone to record, for example, background music and narration at the same time.

StereoRecorder comes packaged with a monaural, omnidirectional electret microphone and its **SoundMan** application, which provides a control panel for recording and playing sounds. The software lets you control the amplitude and speed of playback, and it also provides a waveform display and looping feature. SoundMan supports all of the standard sample rates, like 5, 11, and 22 kHz, as well as any other sample rate that you choose—up to 44 kHz. It also provides compression ratios of 6:1 and 3:1 and supports Audio IFF and SND file formats in addition to its own SoundMan File Format.

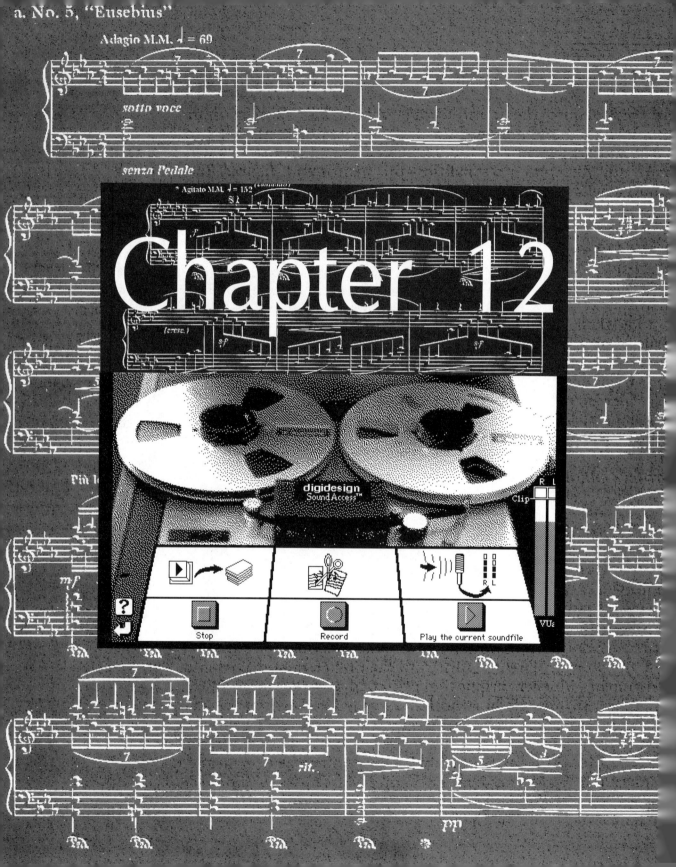

# Digital Audio for the Rich and Famous (16-Bit)

The recording systems described in the previous chapter make good use of the Macintosh's inherent ability to handle sound. But, to do that (without slowing the processor or demanding too much memory), they've had to limit themselves to 8-bit resolution and reasonably low sample rates of up to 22 kHz. With those numbers you can expect sound that's about as good as an inexpensive AM radio—not too bad for dialog but not great for music and many kinds of sound effects.

With movie theaters offering improved sound systems, video recorders producing hi-fi stereo playback, and compact discs rapidly becoming the audio norm, many multimedia producers have raised their expectations to meet the new demands for improved clarity and realism in their presentation soundtracks. The jump from 8-bit, 22-kHz audio to true high fidelity, however, is no small step. It requires substantially more processing power and, therefore, more sophisticated hardware, which in turn costs much more money. All the products in this chapter yield impressive results, which should please even the most demanding audiophiles and open the door, for many, to true Mac-based professional audio.

# Audiomedia

Like the products covered in Chapter 11, the Audiomedia system, from Digidesign, consists of a hardware/software combination for recording and editing digital sound with your computer. Unlike those products, however, Audiomedia brings CD-quality sound to the Macintosh with its 16-bit resolution and sampling rates of up to 44.1 kHz. To achieve this level of performance, Audiomedia incorporates its own Motorola processing chip into an add-on NuBus card that will work in any available Mac II slot. The card, combined with the Audiomedia application, turns your computer into a powerful direct-to-disk recording system that can record both monaural and stereo sounds and save them in a variety of file formats.

When it comes to high-quality, direct-to-disk recording, you might say there's good news and there's bad news. The good news is that Audiomedia requires very little RAM to operate. Digitizing systems like MacRecorder use the computer's RAM for recording and playback and only use the hard disk for storing files. This means that your computer needs enough memory to hold the System, Finder, and any applications that you want to use along with the sounds that you'll be playing. It's clear that very long sounds are impractical with this approach.

Audiomedia, on the other hand, records directly to your hard disk and playback is direct-from-disk. The Audiomedia's microprocessor board significantly enhances the audio capabilities of your computer and simultaneously frees the Macintosh's processor to handle other work-intensive tasks, like animation. In practical terms this means that with no more than about 50 kilobytes of available RAM, you can play back a sound of virtually any length—limited only by the size of your hard disk. In theory, then, a 1-megabyte Macintosh could play back an hour-long sound.

The bad news is that to record that one-hour soundfile, you'll need a hard disk with a 600-megabyte capacity, since 16-bit, 44.1-kHz stereo recording requires 10 megabytes per minute. A large-capacity hard drive—with an access time of 28 milliseconds or less—is an essential component of this direct-to-disk recording system. You'll also need a high-impedance microphone to record vocal parts and acoustic instruments.

The back panel of the Audiomedia card houses five jacks for connecting inputs and outputs. The ¼-inch jack at the top provides a microphone input and the two RCA-type jacks below it allow line-level input connections. If you like, you can use all three together to record voice and stereo audio simultaneously. The bottom two RCA-style jacks—the stereo outputs—connect to your amplifier for playback.

## Audiomedia's Software

Recording and playback activities in Audiomedia are centered on the Tape Deck Panel (Figure 12.1), which includes the standard transport-style controls in a clearly designed, straightforward display. A small pop-up menu lets you select an appropriate sample rate, while the Input Level slider and the Input Level meters enable you to set the incoming signal for optimum results without clipping. To initiate recording, click on the Record button and then click Stop when you're finished. The RTZ (rewind to zero) button returns you to the beginning of the track, and Play yields instant playback. If necessary, you can rerecord your performance by returning to the start and repeating the procedure.

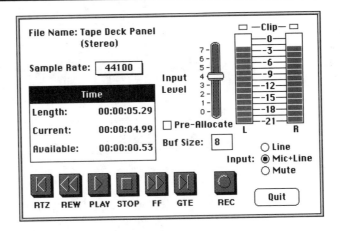

**Figure 12.1**
Audiomedia's Tape Deck Panel

When you're satisfied with your work, selecting Quit opens the Soundfile window, where your recorded sound appears as a waveform in a graphic display (Figure 12.2). The Soundfile window actually consists of two different displays. The Overview display shows either the entire recording in a single waveform picture or a simple time line (without the waveform) representing the length of the recording. Below the Overview display, the Right and Left Channel waveforms appear in a magnified view that you can edit. In these displays the horizontal axis shows elapsed time in seconds, and the vertical axis shows the percentage of maximum amplitude of each waveform.

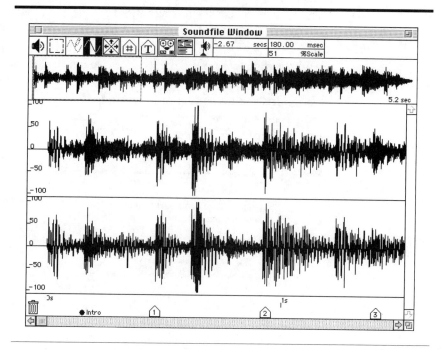

**Figure 12.2**
The Soundfile window, showing the Overview display above the Right and Left Channel waveforms

Along the top of the Soundfile window, several icons provide access to a number of recording, editing, and playback functions. The Speaker icon plays the entire soundfile (or any selected portion of it) directly from disk. The Zoom Box icon lets you draw a selection box over any part of the Overview or Waveform display, enlarging that area to fill the Right/Left Channel view.

The Pencil icon lets you redraw small sections of the waveform to eliminate jagged edges from edit points or to smooth over transient clicks and pops. The Selection icon changes the cursor into an I-beam for selecting regions of the waveform to edit, with commands such as Cut, Copy, Paste, Reverse, and Fade Out. The Display Scale icon, with its four arrows, provides different ways to adjust the viewing scale in the waveform display. The up and down arrows let you adjust how tall the waveform appears so that you can achieve the best resolution when viewing amplitude differences. The right arrow zooms the display in to view more detail, and the left arrow zooms out to gain a greater overview of the waveform.

The Soundfile window lets you place two different kinds of markers along the bottom of the waveform display. You can use the Numbered Marker icon to place an unlimited number of markers in any soundfile, tagging important areas for later recall. You can quickly locate the first nine markers by typing their numbers on the Macintosh keyboard. Additionally, the Text Marker icon lets you place text notes in a soundfile to help label or identify significant events.

The Tape Deck button opens the Tape Deck Panel, where recording takes place, while the Playlist button opens the Playlist window, where nondestructive playlist edits are assembled (see below). Finally, the Scrub icon switches the window into Scrub mode so that you can locate exact spots in the waveform by slowly dragging the playback cursor back and forth across the display as you listen to the soundfile.

In the upper-right corner of the Soundfile window, the Data Indicator boxes provide relevant information about such things as the insertion point and cursor position, while the Trash Can in the lower-left corner lets you throw away both kinds of markers. Additionally, for users with color or gray-scale monitors, the Set Colors command lets you assign different colors to the various components in the Soundfile window for easier identification.

Aside from its high-level recording quality, Audiomedia's greatest strengths lie in its extensive editing capabilities. These fall into two distinct and important categories: *destructive* and *nondestructive*.

Destructive editing, with commands like Smooth, Mix, and Reverse, changes the way a recording sounds by permanently altering the actual data that constitutes the waveform. In so doing, you cause the Macintosh to manipulate and/or rearrange files that are often very large and this can take some time to process. But destructive edits offer the only way to produce a finished soundfile that you can then export to another application for playback.

Nondestructive editing, on the other hand, allows you to slice, dice, and rearrange the parts of a soundfile to your heart's content, *without altering the original recording*. Audiomedia calls this approach "Playlist editing," and it's one of the program's most powerful features. It involves selecting various subdivisions of a soundfile and playing them back in whatever order you want. Rather than changing the source material itself, the Playlist acts like a map that assigns a playback sequence to the parts of the soundfile, allowing you to create a virtually unlimited number of arrangements from a single recording. Creating a new structure from the parts of a soundfile involves editing only the "playback map," not the recording, so aside from being nondestructive, it also demands far less processing.

To assemble a Playlist, you first must define the various Playlist Regions (such as Chorus, Verse, and Interlude) by selecting the appropriate areas from the waveform and choosing the Capture Region command for each. Once you've named the regions, you can open the Playlist window (Figure 12.3), where they will appear in the upper half of the display. Creating a Playlist is easy—just drag the names from the Regions area down into the Playlist area to form the proper playback sequence.

To produce the smoothest results where the regions are joined, Audiomedia lets you choose from a plethora of different transitions. The Playlist defaults to the Splice transition, which simply connects the adjacent regions. If you find this edit too abrupt, you can choose one of several crossfade types, including Linear crossfade, Equal Power crossfade (which compensates for a possible volume drop at the transition point), Linear pre-crossfade (which crossfades before the transition), Equal Power pre-crossfade, Slow-in/Fast-out crossfade, and Fast-in/Slow-out crossfade. Two types of Overlap transitions round out the list.

Once you assemble and save a Playlist, you can always open, play, and edit it, and you can even modify a Region itself by reselecting the waveform

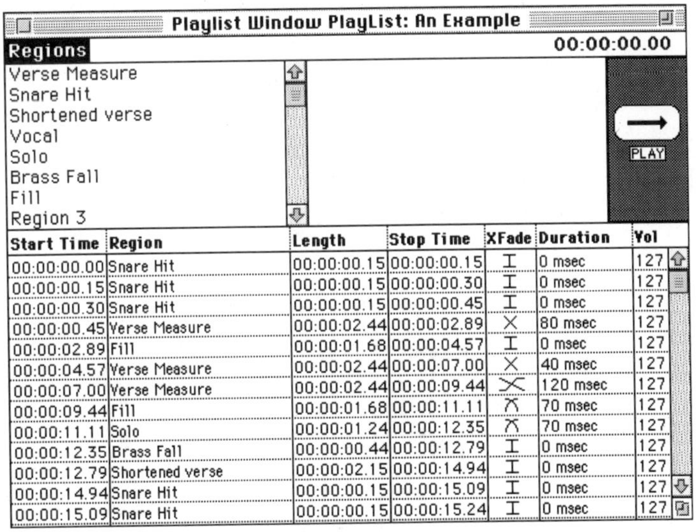

**Figure 12.3**
Audiomedia's Playlist window lets you use nondestructive editing to create new recordings by rearranging the parts of a soundfile.

| Regions |
|---|
| Verse Measure |
| Snare Hit |
| Shortened verse |
| Vocal |
| Solo |
| Brass Fall |
| Fill |
| Region 3 |

00:00:00.00

| Start Time | Region | Length | Stop Time | XFade | Duration | Vol |
|---|---|---|---|---|---|---|
| 00:00:00.00 | Snare Hit | 00:00:00.15 | 00:00:00.15 | I | 0 msec | 127 |
| 00:00:00.15 | Snare Hit | 00:00:00.15 | 00:00:00.30 | I | 0 msec | 127 |
| 00:00:00.30 | Snare Hit | 00:00:00.15 | 00:00:00.45 | I | 0 msec | 127 |
| 00:00:00.45 | Verse Measure | 00:00:02.44 | 00:00:02.89 | X | 80 msec | 127 |
| 00:00:02.89 | Fill | 00:00:01.68 | 00:00:04.57 | I | 0 msec | 127 |
| 00:00:04.57 | Verse Measure | 00:00:02.44 | 00:00:07.00 | X | 40 msec | 127 |
| 00:00:07.00 | Verse Measure | 00:00:02.44 | 00:00:09.44 | X | 120 msec | 127 |
| 00:00:09.44 | Fill | 00:00:01.68 | 00:00:11.11 | X | 70 msec | 127 |
| 00:00:11.11 | Solo | 00:00:01.24 | 00:00:12.35 | X | 70 msec | 127 |
| 00:00:12.35 | Brass Fall | 00:00:00.44 | 00:00:12.79 | I | 0 msec | 127 |
| 00:00:12.79 | Shortened verse | 00:00:02.15 | 00:00:14.94 | I | 0 msec | 127 |
| 00:00:14.94 | Snare Hit | 00:00:00.15 | 00:00:15.09 | I | 0 msec | 127 |
| 00:00:15.09 | Snare Hit | 00:00:00.15 | 00:00:15.24 | I | 0 msec | 127 |

area that it's derived from. Unfortunately, you can't use Playlists directly in other applications. To circumvent this limitation, Audiomedia provides a Save Playlist as Soundfile command that creates a copy of a Playlist performance and saves it in a format usable by other programs.

Aside from those already mentioned, Audiomedia boasts an impressive list of other editing options. In addition to the usual Cut, Copy, and Paste commands, you can reverse or invert a waveform area, insert silence, or trim away unwanted data from outside the selected range. You can also fade in or out and adjust the amplitude of a waveform range to achieve optimum levels. The Smoothing command automatically eliminates the transient clicks that often appear at edit points, the Merge command lets you set the parameters for crossfades, and the SR Convert command allows you to change a soundfile to another sample rate.

For those users with MIDI equipment as part of their computer systems, Audiomedia provides the MIDI Preview command, which enables you to turn your Macintosh into a rudimentary instrument-playback device that you can trigger from a MIDI controller. This is not intended as a substitute for a full-featured sampling keyboard—a job handled quite well by Digidesign's SampleCell (see later in this chapter)—but rather as a way to audition music-oriented soundfiles by playing them over a range of notes, using a MIDI keyboard controller or similar device.

With Audiomedia's digital mixing function, you can take up to four soundfiles (mono or stereo) and blend them together into a new mono or stereo soundfile. Choosing the Mix command opens the Mix window, which provides controls for specifying the fader levels, pan positions, and delay settings (if any) for each input channel (Figure 12.4).

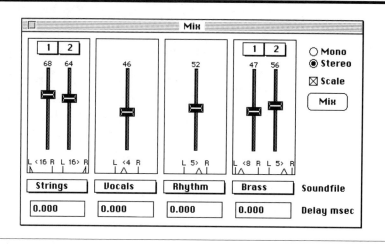

**Figure 12.4**
The Mix window lets you combine up to four mono or stereo soundfiles.

As you might expect, Audiomedia offers a versatile and well-implemented graphic equalization feature. The Programmable Graphic EQ window (Figure 12.5) includes a master volume control and ten frequency sliders, which are used together for mono recordings or divided into two groups of five for stereo. You can customize each frequency band by double-clicking on the frequency number below each fader. This opens a dialog box that lets you specify both the center frequency and the bandwidth for the selected control. You can also save any EQ configuration along with its soundfile or as a general setup in Audiomedia.

The Graphic EQ window provides even more versatility by letting you use it either destructively or nondestructively. In other words, you can apply the EQ effect to a recording and permanently alter the soundfile to

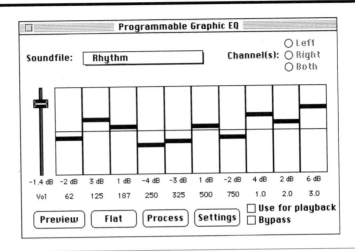

**Figure 12.5**
The Programmable Graphic EQ window allows you to customize each slider by specifying its center frequency and bandwidth.

reflect the new frequency curve, or you can use the EQ controls as a real-time, nondestructive equalizer during playback without changing the actual soundfile data.

To analyze your waveforms, Audiomedia provides a 3-D, Fast Fourier Transform (FFT) display that shows the frequency content of a sound and how the different amplitudes change over time. The FFT window (Figure 12.6) allows you to adjust its display parameters by setting such things as the frequency range, the time interval, and the type of scale. You can also select from one of four types of displays, each of which emphasizes specific aspects of the data.

Of particular interest to multimedia producers, the Time Compression/Expansion window (Figure 12.7) lets you adjust the duration of a recording (or any selected portion) without altering its pitch. This is especially useful for fitting narration (or an instrumental solo) into a given time period—as long as you keep the adjustment within reason. The window provides boxes for specifying either the desired length or a ratio between the new version and the old. You can also specify the sound's relative complexity, which channel to use as a guide track, and whether or not to process percussive attacks.

**Figure 12.6**
The FFT window shows the frequency content of a sound and how it changes over time.

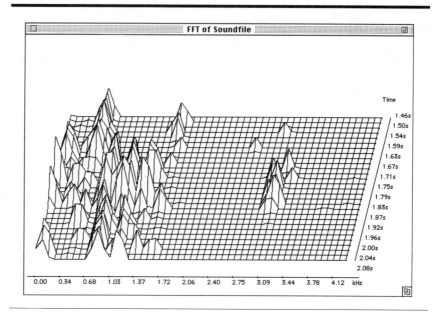

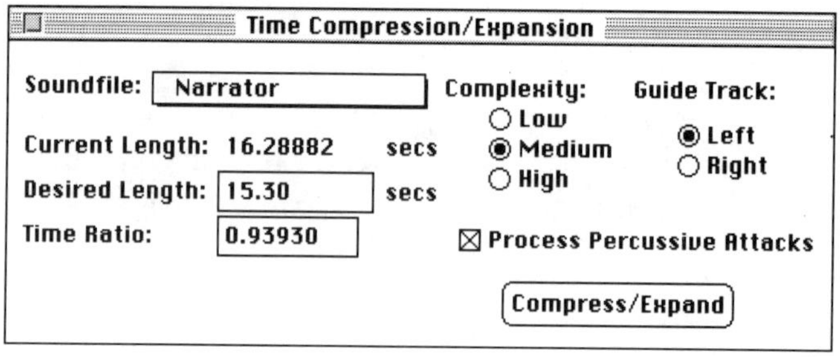

**Figure 12.7**
With Audiomedia's Time Compression/ Expansion window, you can adjust the duration of a soundfile without changing its pitch.

Audiomedia supports several soundfile formats, including SoundEdit format (created by MacRecorder), both 8-bit and 16-bit SND resources, Audio IFF format, and mono or stereo Sound Designer formats (created by Digidesign's Sound Designer program). If you need the disk space, you can also choose either a 2:1 or a 4:1 compression ratio.

Digital Audio for the Rich and Famous (16-Bit)     209

## *SoundAccess*

Audiomedia provides a second application, SoundAccess, that allows you to record, edit, and play back hard-disk-based soundfiles from within Hyper-Card. The current version of SoundAccess supports HyperCard versions 1.2.2 and later—up to, but not including, HyperCard 2.0. If you're still using one of these earlier versions of HyperCard, you can incorporate Audiomedia sounds into your stacks. Clicking on the Recording Workshop button produces a card (SoundAccess is itself a stack) that depicts an open-reel tape deck (Figure 12.8). Below the picture, several icons let you set levels, and record, play, and edit your sounds.

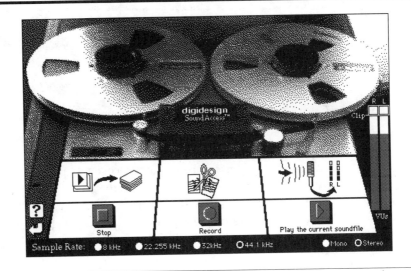

**Figure 12.8**
The Recording Workshop card in SoundAccess provides the controls for recording HyperCard sounds.

If you understand HyperTalk, the SoundAccess Installer Card (Figure 12.9) provides you with the tools to copy XCMDs and XFCNs into your own stacks. With SoundAccess you can create buttons to play sounds and create interactive HyperCard presentations that include high-fidelity audio.

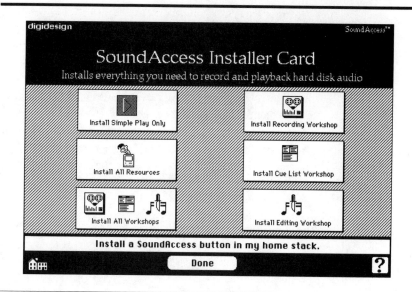

**Figure 12.9**
The SoundAccess Installer Card supplies several tools for working with HyperCard.

## Sound Tools

Digidesign's Sound Tools, another hardware/software combination for direct-to-disk recording, preceded Audiomedia in the marketplace and soon gained an avid following. The system costs more than three times as much as Audiomedia, but offers several additional features that make it more suitable for professional recording applications, such as CD premastering, film scoring, sound-effects editing, and ADR (automatic dialog replacement).

The recording/editing system consists of three components. The Sound Tools NuBus card resembles Audiomedia's except that it only provides a single stereo output jack. The card attaches to one of three external hardware interfaces: the standard Analog Interface for recording line-level signals, the bidirectional Digital Interface for digital-domain recording and mastering capability, and the Professional Analog Interface for meeting the higher demands of professional recording studios and sound engineers.

**Sound Designer II** represents the third part of the package. It's nearly identical to the software that comes with Audiomedia except that it also offers a number of useful looping features, as well as several powerful DSP (digital signal processing) functions.

Sound Tools boasts a slightly better signal-to-noise ratio than Audiomedia and (with the Pro I/O or Digital Interface) a top sampling rate of 48 kHz. Of particular interest to those working with film and video, Sound Tools supports all major SMPTE timecode formats and also offers continuous resync and chasing capabilities.

## More about Samplers

While Audiomedia and Sound Tools excel at recording, editing, and saving digital audio, they are not appropriately designed to play back sounds in a way that you can use for real-time musical performance. If you want to use digital recording technology to compose and perform your music, you'll need a device called a *sampler*. As I described briefly in Chapter 3, samplers typically come in keyboard and sound module versions and sport a wide variety of features and specifications. They typically provide resolutions ranging from 8-bit to 16-bit with prices that vary accordingly. In spite of all the seeming diversity of hardware, samplers all employ the same basic approach to producing instrumental sounds: A short digital recording, called a *sample*, is used as the basic source material and its pitch is raised or lowered by half-step increments when triggered from a MIDI keyboard.

In theory, you should be able to take a single sample of a piano sound and re-create the entire keyboard range by extending it up and down over several octaves. Unfortunately, it doesn't work that way in the real world. Individual samples begin to sound strained and unnatural when they're stretched more than a few half steps in either direction above or below the original pitch. To avoid this problem, samplers use several samples taken at strategic points along the range of an instrument. When these *multisamples* are "mapped" across the keyboard, they not only solve the problem of over-stretched samples but they better capture the inherent changes in timbre that acoustic instruments exhibit as they play from one register to another.

# SampleCell

Until recently, samplers were mainly external hardware devices that connected to a MIDI system, in the usual way, along with the other components in the setup. Digidesign, however, now offers a significant alternative to that approach with SampleCell: a hardware/software combination that turns your Macintosh into a powerful stereo sample-playback system with 16-bit resolution, 16-note polyphony, and a maximum 16-voice multitimbral capability. The hardware consists of an add-on NuBus card that works in any Macintosh II computer with at least 2 megabytes of RAM and a 13-inch (or larger) monitor. The back panel of the SampleCell card provides eight audio output channels configured as four stereo ¼-inch jacks. To expand the system, you can combine up to five SampleCell cards (if you have the slots), with each contributing another 16 notes of polyphony and another eight audio outputs.

SampleCell has also been designed to work closely with Audiomedia to create a fully integrated sampling system that allows you to record sounds onto your hard disk, edit them, and then import them into SampleCell, where they can be mapped across the keyboard and further edited for performance. If you're not interested in doing your own sampling, you needn't worry. The SampleCell package includes a CD-ROM library with hundreds of high-quality samples ready for performance, and several third-party vendors offer CD-ROMs with more excellent sounds (see "More Sounds for SampleCell" later in this chapter). Of course, this means that if you don't already own one, you'll need to buy a CD-ROM player to effectively use SampleCell since all of its current libraries come in CD format.

Aside from this possible hidden expense, there are several additional requirements that you must address before you can put SampleCell to good use. For starters, although you can get by with only 2 megabytes of RAM in your computer, I recommend at least twice that amount to avoid problems when running SampleCell with other programs. And speaking of RAM, SampleCell uses its own on-board memory—up to 8 megabytes—to configure and play back its samples, but Digidesign ships the NuBus card without the RAM installed. Although you can buy the board fully loaded with eight 1-megabyte SIMMs (single in-line memory modules), most people prefer to save several hundred dollars by installing their own memory; Digidesign encourages this approach. You'll need Macintosh-compatible 1-megabyte SIMMs with no more than an 80-ns (nanosecond) rating.

Many of the multisampled instruments in the SampleCell libraries are surprisingly large—often ranging in size from 1 to 5 megabytes. Some even use almost the entire 8 megabytes for a single instrument. Trying to put together a multitimbral setup with a single SampleCell can be frustrating since you'll often find yourself short of memory for the instruments that you want. To mitigate this situation, the SampleCell CD-ROM offers "Lite" versions of several of its instruments. Nonetheless, many of these scaled-down variations still demand 1–3 megabytes of RAM. Although, technically speaking, the SampleCell card will work with a minimum of 2 megabytes of installed RAM, I strongly recommend buying 8 megabytes since anything less would severely limit its usefulness.

You should also have a hard disk with a minimum capacity of 40 megabytes. If you'll also be using Audiomedia, the recommended minimum increases to 100 megabytes with an average access time of 28 milliseconds or less. To use SampleCell for performing music, you'll need a MIDI keyboard controller (or other device) and a MIDI interface. You can use SampleCell with most sequencers and other compatible music programs by installing Apple's MIDI Manager software in your system.

## *SampleCell Editor*

SampleCell uses a straightforward, logical hierarchy for organizing its data. The individual raw samples that it uses as its building blocks are contained in a Samples folder. By taking one or more samples and assigning them to specific keyboard areas, you can create a multisampled Instrument. The Instruments folder contains only the data necessary to re-create the settings and sample combinations that are used to build an Instrument, but not the sample data itself.

Similarly, grouping several Instruments together as a performance setup forms a Bank. When you save a Bank, you are actually storing the information needed to reconfigure a group of Instruments with their corresponding settings, but not the Instruments or samples themselves. Since it's the sample data that demands the lion's share of the memory, you can save Instrument and Bank files on your hard drive or even on floppy disks with little trouble.

To begin using SampleCell, you must first open a Bank and fill it with the Instruments that you want to use by selecting the Open Instrument command from the Edit menu. After waiting for them to load (SampleCell is no speed demon), the Instruments that you've chosen appear in the Bank window, which resembles a mixing console with a vertical panel for each Instrument (Figure 12.10).

**Figure 12.10**
The SampleCell Bank window represents each Instrument with a vertical panel.

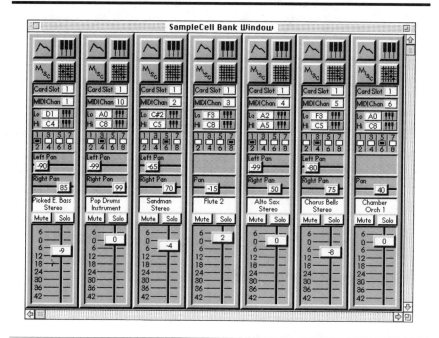

Each Instrument panel has a volume fader and a mute and solo button. Monaural Instruments have a single panning control while stereo Instruments use two sliders—one for left and one for right. In the middle of the display, you can set the MIDI channel and the keyboard range that the Instrument will respond to as well as the output channel where you want the audio signal to appear. At the top of each display, you'll find four buttons that open the doors into SampleCell's powerful editing displays, where you can modify a variety of Instrument parameters to customize your sounds.

Clicking on the button with the keyboard icon opens the Sample Map window (Figure 12.11). This window lets you assign each sample in a multi-sample Instrument to a specific range of notes, called a Key Group. You can have a Key Group that covers the entire keyboard, or you can have up to 20 smaller areas that range in size down to a single note. Samples appear by name in the Sample Map window with thin vertical lines indicating the boundaries of the assigned Key Groups. You can easily change the range of a Key Group by dragging a line to a new position, which automatically enlarges one area while shrinking its neighboring area.

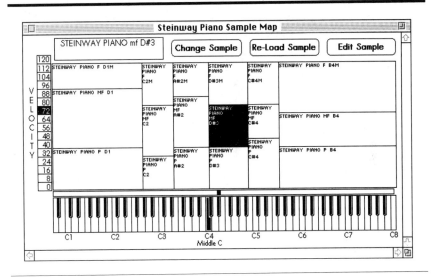

**Figure 12.11**
The Sample Map window with a sample selected for editing

SampleCell lets you have as many as three samples per Key Group, with each sample responding to a different Velocity Zone. This means that when you play a note, any one of the assigned samples will sound depending upon how hard you strike the key. Many acoustic instruments have different tonal qualities when they're played loudly as opposed to quietly or moderately. By capturing these differences with individual samples and assigning them to the appropriate Velocity Zones, you can create an Instrument that not only gets louder when you play harder but also reflects the corresponding tonal character. Of course, there's nothing that says you have to use similar samples in your Instruments. If you like, you can have the different velocities trigger entirely different kinds of sounds.

The horizontal lines in the Sample Map window show the assigned Velocity Zone boundaries for each sample, and you can drag the lines to new positions just like with the Key Groups. The combination of the vertical and horizontal lines encloses each Sample in a square or rectangle that delineates its key and velocity range. Clicking in an enclosed area selects that sample and lets you delete or change the sample as needed.

Aside from its function as a mapping grid, the Sample Map window also acts as a MIDI monitor that highlights incoming notes on the keyboard display along the bottom and the velocity scale on the left. The currently triggered sample also appears highlighted to help you in analyzing your Instruments. Double-clicking a sample opens the Sample Parameters dialog box (Figure 12.12), which allows you to make adjustments to such things as the pan position of each Key Group, the direction and start point of playback, and the volume and pitch of each sample.

**Figure 12.12**
The Sample Parameters dialog box

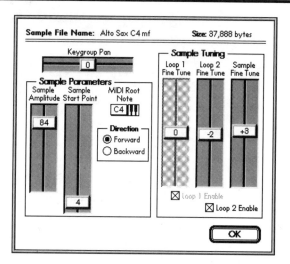

Clicking the Misc button in the Bank window opens the Misc window (Figure 12.13), where you can set several different kinds of parameters for an Instrument. On the left side of the window, the Aux Sends display lets you assign any two of SampleCell's eight outputs to act as auxiliary sends for use with outboard processors, such as reverbs and digital delays. The controls (one for left and one for right) have faders to adjust the amount of signal that feeds the Aux outputs, but you can bypass each fader by clicking the appropriate Pre/Post-Fader check box.

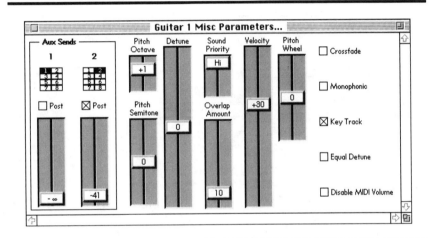

**Figure 12.13**
SampleCell's Misc window lets you set several of an Instrument's parameters.

The Misc window also provides three controls for changing the Instrument's tuning: Octave and Semitone sliders for coarse settings and Detune for finer adjustments. If you play more notes than SampleCell can respond to, the Sound Priority slider for each Instrument lets you prioritize the Instruments in a Bank to determine where the excess notes will be dropped. The Overlap Amount slider lets you adjust the length of a note's release stage when the same note is retriggered, such as when a cymbal is repeatedly struck in a rhythm part. The Velocity and Pitch Wheel sliders let you adjust how an Instrument will respond to those MIDI messages, and the check boxes along the right determine how SampleCell will respond to your keyboard controller.

Back in the Bank window, the Matrix Modulation button (the one with the grid icon) opens one of SampleCell's most powerful features. The Matrix

Modulation window (Figure 12.14) allows you to control or influence any destination parameter with any available control source. The matrix itself, located in the top-center of the window, can have up to 16 "paths" per Instrument. Each modulation path (represented horizontally) consists of a source control and a destination, along with a gate switch and a modulation-amount setting. You can quickly select the source and destination parameters from the corresponding pop-up menus, and the Amplitude setting establishes the range of the modulation effects. The Gate button lets you determine if each modulation option will be effective continuously or only while a note is held.

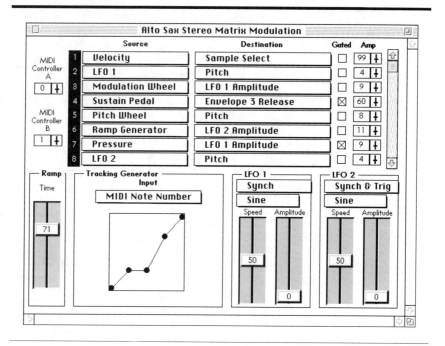

**Figure 12.14**
SampleCell's powerful Matrix Modulation window allows you to control any destination parameter with any available control source.

In the lower-right corner of the window, SampleCell provides controls for setting up two LFOs (low-frequency oscillators) that can use any of seven different waveforms to affect a destination parameter. For example, you can create a vibrato effect by assigning an LFO with a sine wave to control pitch. A square wave produces a trill-like effect. The Tracking Generator lets you create a graph with five adjustable points to act as a modulation source, which can itself be affected by other sources, and the Ramp Generator lets you apply a ramplike control signal to a modulation path for additional effects.

In the Bank window, each Instrument also has a fourth editing button, which opens the Envelope window (Figure 12.15). An *envelope* is a common modulation source that produces a control signal that changes over time. This window displays envelopes in a standard graphlike form, but if you prefer, you can have them appear as a group of parameter sliders. SampleCell provides up to three envelopes per Instrument with each envelope consisting of five parts: Attack, Decay, Sustain Level, Sustain Decay, and Release. Typically, you use envelopes to control amplitude, but the program allows great flexibility for creatively applying envelope effects.

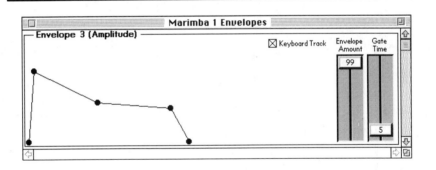

**Figure 12.15**
The Envelope window can have up to three envelopes per Instrument.

The Gate Time slider lets you set a minimum time that a note will sound before the Release stage. This can prevent very short notes (as in some rhythm parts) from being abruptly cut off. The Envelope Amount slider lets you adjust the overall output of the envelope, and the Keyboard Track button causes the envelope times to shorten as the pitches go up and to lengthen as they go down. This feature is especially useful when you work with some acoustic instrument sounds.

## Sampling with SampleCell

Although SampleCell is technically a sample-playback device, you can turn it into a full-featured sampler by using Audiomedia or Sound Tools as a sample-recording "front-end." To use Sound Tools, you record a short sound, edit and loop it as needed, and save it in Sound Designer II format within your Samples folder on your hard disk. SampleCell can then load your sample, and you can include it in any Sample Map window as long as there's enough RAM available.

To use Audiomedia instead of Sound Tools, you follow the same procedure except that you can't loop a sound because Audiomedia doesn't support looping. If your sample needs looping, you can use the Sound Designer II SC software that's included with SampleCell. After saving your recording to disk with Audiomedia, use Sound Designer to set the loop points and import the sample into SampleCell. If you own another Sound Designer-compatible sampler, you can also import its samples into SampleCell to greatly expand your potential library of sounds. SampleCell supports Sound Designer, Sound Designer II, and Audio IFF file formats. For more on Sound Designer II, see Chapter 13.

## More Sounds for SampleCell

A number of companies, recognizing SampleCell's potential, have released CD-ROMs that complement and greatly expand the original library that comes in the package. Here are several excellent collections that offer a wide variety of instrumental sounds. Let's begin with the one that comes with SampleCell.

### *Digidesign*

Digidesign has wisely included this disc as part of the SampleCell package to allow owners to begin using SampleCell in a meaningful way right from the start. As a first library of sounds, it succeeds quite well in illustrating both the variety that's possible with SampleCell and the complexity of some of its Instrument configurations. It is by no means a comprehensive library, however, since it lacks several important orchestral instruments.

A number of the Instruments are quite large, making them difficult if not impossible to use in a multitimbral setup. Several "Lite" versions help. The library includes various types of acoustic and electronic basses, guitars, pianos, organs, and drums. There are brass ensembles, solo trumpets, female voices, and some woodwinds, and the library also offers acoustic and electronic strings, synthesizers, and sound effects. The disc, produced by Prosonus, shows a close attention to detail and has excellent sound quality and very smooth looping.

## *Greytsounds*

The Greytsounds CD-ROM, Volume 1 for SampleCell, offers a good assortment of sounds that can be applied to many styles of music and writing situations. Greytsounds has chosen to fill its library with Instruments that consume far less memory than most of those found in other collections. This means that many of the Instruments don't display the same level of complexity in their multisample configurations as some of the others, but the lower RAM requirements for each Instrument allow you to assemble all kinds of Bank setups, making this collection far more suitable for multitimbral applications. With this library it's quite possible to put together a Bank with eight or nine Instruments in it and still have RAM left over. For working on ideas or sketching out an arrangement, this can be very useful.

The CD has a wide variety of sounds with good representation in the areas of brass, keyboards, percussion, woodwinds, and guitars (both acoustic and electric). There are also many electronic sounds, several vintage keyboards, and miscellaneous synthesizers, including the Fairlight. A large section of sound effects completes the list.

## *McGill University Master Samples*

If your interests lie in the area of orchestral scoring, you should definitely look into this CD-ROM. This library offers no saxes, electric guitars, or synthesizers, but rather a unique and varied collection of symphonic instruments, including orchestral percussion, classical guitars, harps, pianos, and organs. There's a complete assortment of woodwinds (including fluttertongued flute), with several reeds that are especially clean and sweet sounding and several solo brass instruments. For you historical types, the library also includes a number of Baroque and Renaissance instruments, such as archlute, crumhorn, recorder, shawm, and harpsichord. To round out the list, there are several solo and ensemble string sounds with various effects.

The documentation that comes on the disc is exceptional. It gives more information than most people could possibly want about the individual instruments used in the recordings (where, when, and by whom they were made), the recording techniques employed (number, placement, and types of mikes), and the production process itself. There are also descriptions of the Instruments and Banks and some general advice for beginners. It's clear that this collection represents a lot of dedication and hard work, and its combination of high-quality sounds, good orchestral variety, and reasonable cost makes it well worth considering.

## *Prosonus*

This collection (entitled Volume Two) is designed to function as a companion to the original SampleCell disc that Prosonus produced for Digidesign. Although it offers no additional woodwinds, saxes, orchestral percussion, or vocals, it does provide a significant supplement in the area of stringed instruments, both ensemble and solo. There are also several new brass instruments, some piano effects, additional synthesizer sounds, more basses, drum kits, harps, and sound effects.

Clearly this library is intended to appeal to those who do film scoring, postproduction, and studio work, especially in conjunction with popular music. Over the past few years, Prosonus has maintained a reputation for offering high-quality audio products for musicians, and this collection of samples is no exception. It's a clean, well-produced library, which nicely complements SampleCell's abilities.

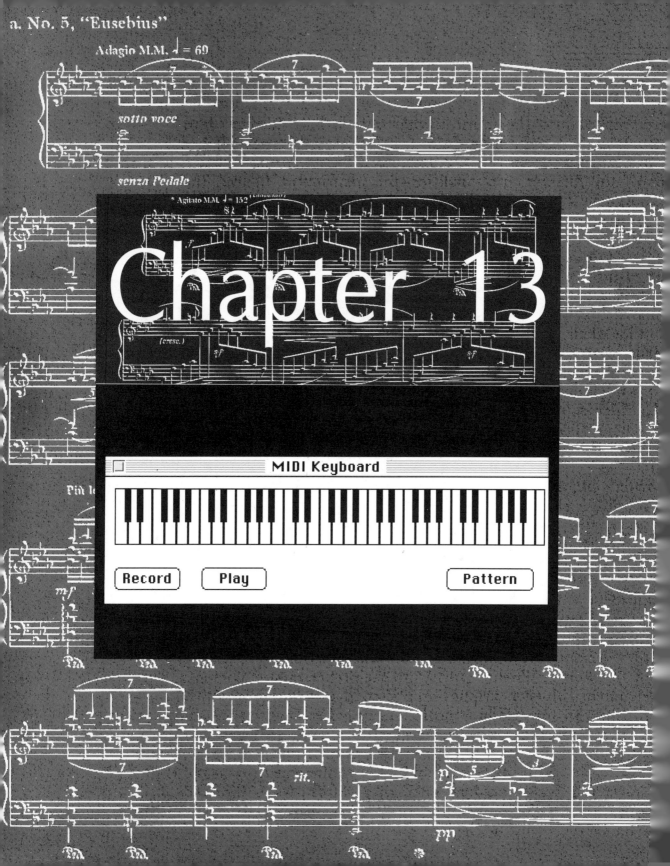

# Sample-Editing Software

Using digital audio technology to capture samples of sound has proven to be an invaluable tool for creating effective soundtracks for film, video, and multimedia. Aside from SampleCell, there are numerous external, hardware samplers that work well as part of a MIDI system, allowing you to play back sounds at specific points in time. And those sounds don't have to be just musical instrument sounds. Sound effects and short sections of dialog work equally well. By taking a sample and assigning it to a MIDI note number, you can use one of several sequencing programs to trigger the sound, with single-frame accuracy, at the appropriate time in a presentation. Of course, samplers lend themselves extremely well to musical applications, but many people don't realize how extensively samplers are used in postproduction for sound designing and dialog editing.

Nonetheless, in spite of their capabilities, samplers need help in achieving their maximum potential. To apply intricate editing functions and sophisticated digital signal processing (DSP), you'll have to use an editing program. The Macintosh, with its intuitive, graphical interface, provides the perfect environment for manipulating and saving sound data for use with a variety of hardware devices. In this chapter I'll examine the two most popular sample-editing programs for the Mac to see what they have to offer.

# Sound Designer II

Sound Designer II is the new, improved stereo successor to Digidesign's popular Sound Designer software. In fact, it has lately assumed a bit of a split personality since it now appears in several incarnations depending on how you intend to use it. The Sound Designer II that comes with Sound Tools represents the fully implemented parent program, which provides all of the features found in the other versions. The Audiomedia application is actually a slightly scaled back version of Sound Designer II, which lacks only the looping functions, a few additional DSP options, and the ability to transfer files between the Mac and external samplers.

If you have a MIDI sampler and you want to edit its samples with your computer, **Sound Designer II SK** provides the necessary tools, and for SampleCell users, Digidesign provides a special version—**Sound Designer II SC**—that's been modified to work with that product. Sound Designer II SC (included with SampleCell) functions as a companion to the SampleCell Editor by providing the ability to transfer files between the Macintosh and other samplers. If you're using Audiomedia with SampleCell to record new sounds, Sound Designer II SC also supplies the looping functions missing from the Audiomedia program. On the other hand, both the SK and SC versions of Sound Designer lack the Tape Deck and Playlist buttons found elsewhere, since they are designed to function as sample editors and not as direct-to-disk recording programs. And finally, only the Sound Designer that comes with Sound Tools supports SMPTE timecode.

All versions of Sound Designer II center their activities on the Soundfile window (Figure 13.1). The SK and SC versions don't display the Tape Deck and Playlist icons found in Audiomedia, but provide instead an additional button in the upper-left corner. Clicking on this Mac-to-Sampler icon produces a dialog box that lets you transfer the current soundfile (after configuring the program) to any selected MIDI sampler. The File menu provides a Sampler-to-Mac command for importing samples from your MIDI sampler to the Macintosh for editing.

The appearance and structure of the Soundfile window is essentially the same as described in Chapter 12. The Speaker icon plays the entire soundfile, or any selected portion, directly from disk if you're using Sound Tools.

**Figure 13.1**
Sound Designer II uses the same kind of Soundfile window as Audiomedia. The SC version (shown here) lacks the Tape Deck and Playlist icons but adds the Mac-to-Sampler button.

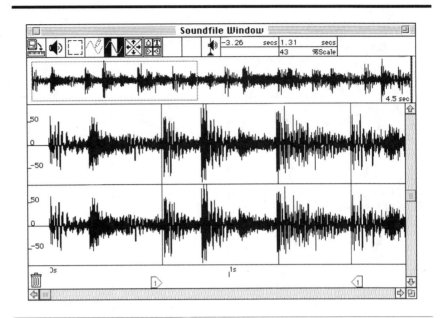

Otherwise it plays back as much of the soundfile selection as the available RAM will hold. The Zoom Box, Pencil, Selection, and Display Scale icons all work identically to their counterparts in Audiomedia.

The Numbered Marker and Text Marker buttons in Audiomedia have been consolidated in Sound Designer II into a single icon that incorporates four different kinds of markers. The Numbered Marker and Text Marker icons work as described in Chapter 12. Below them, two additional icons—the Loop Start Marker and the Loop End Marker—let you determine where to begin and end a waveform section for looping.

Once you've dragged start and end markers onto the Soundfile display, you can listen to your looped sound by using the Speaker icon for playback. At this point the odds are extremely high that your loop will need further editing to eliminate clicks, pops, or other anomalies that occur at the transition point where the looped section repeats itself. To handle these problems, Sound Designer II provides a Loop window (Figure 13.2) that offers several options for making precise adjustments to your loop's parameters. The window consists of two waveform displays divided by a vertical line. The left side shows the loop end and the waveform immediately preceding it, while the right side shows the loop start point and the waveform that follows. The vertical line represents the actual splice point where playback jumps from loop end to loop start.

**Figure 13.2**
The Loop window shows the splice point between the loop end and loop start. The arrows at the bottom help you create a smooth transition.

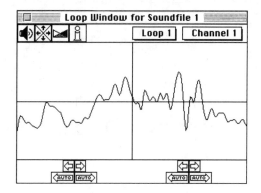

To create an effective, natural-sounding loop, you must match the waveform slopes and general shapes on both sides of the display, paying particular attention to the transition between the waveforms that occurs at the splice point. This must have a smooth, continuous appearance to avoid unwanted noise or other problems that can result from an abrupt waveform change at the splice.

For help in fine-tuning your start and end points, the Loop window provides a set of arrows beneath each half of the display. These arrows let you slide either of the waveforms forward or backward to precisely maneuver the two displays (and their corresponding markers) into a position for optimum looping. To increase your speed and efficiency in finding good loop points, the Loop window also provides a second set of arrows marked Auto. Each of these controls skips the waveform forward or backward to the next available point in the sound wave that produces a smooth-looking transition with the other display. Although this doesn't always produce a perfect loop, it's an effective tool for quickly and easily finding useful loop points.

Clicking the Speaker icon in the upper-left corner of the Loop window lets you play back your loop. The Display Scale arrows work the same as the

View Adjustment arrows in the Soundfile window. The third control, the Crossfade icon, provides an important option for creating smooth loops, especially with difficult soundfiles. Sound Designer's Crossfade feature takes some of the waveform's characteristics before and after the splice point and blends them together in equal amounts to "smooth over" the transition area. The Crossfade button produces a dialog box that lets you select the type of crossfade (linear or equal power), the type of loop (forward or backward/forward), and the length of the crossfade region. The Information icon rounds out the Loop window's panel of buttons. Through its dialog box, it provides you with relevant information about the current loop and soundfile and lets you change some of the parameters directly.

Sound Designer II and Audiomedia share the same Graphic EQ feature (Figure 12.5) described in the previous chapter. But Sound Designer also provides a Parametric EQ window (Figure 13.3) for more flexibility in setting equalization effects. With this window you can select and adjust one of five different equalization filters: High Pass, Low Shelf, Peak/Notch, High Shelf, and Low Pass. The equalization curve that you create with these filters can be saved either with the program or with a specific soundfile and can apply to one or two channels.

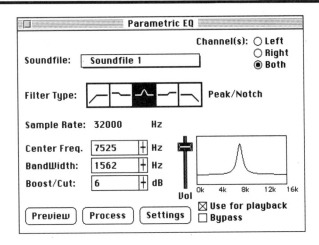

**Figure 13.3**
Sound Designer II's Parametric EQ window offers several filter options.

If you want to try out a soundfile over a range of notes, but you don't have an external MIDI controller handy, you can use Sound Designer's MIDI Keyboard window (Figure 13.4). This on-screen keyboard lets you play individual notes by clicking the appropriate keys. You can record a simple sequence or, if you prefer, you can use the Pattern button to play each note sequentially from left to right across the keyboard.

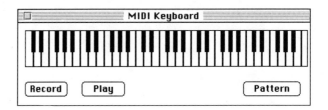

**Figure 13.4**
The MIDI Keyboard window lets you play individual notes by clicking on its keys.

Most of the Audiomedia features described in Chapter 12 also can be found in Sound Designer II. The Mix window (Figure 12.4), the FFT Window (Figure 12.6), the Time Compression/Expansion window (Figure 12.7), the Merge and SR Convert commands, and the MIDI Preview option all work the same. However, some of the features, such as Graphic EQ, SR Convert, MIDI Preview, and the Scrubbing tool, work only with Audiomedia and/or Sound Tools. On the other hand, all of the basic editing commands, such as Cut, Copy, Paste, Reverse, Trim, Invert, Fade In/Out, and Normalize, are available in all versions of the program. In addition to its own stereo format, Sound Designer II supports Sound Designer (mono), Audio IFF, and SND Resource file formats.

## Alchemy

Passport Designs describes Alchemy as "multimedia sound and sample editing software," which points out the two tasks that this program addresses. It is both a sample storage/distribution environment and an advanced sound design/editing system. Alchemy can act as a central library for storing 16-bit stereo samples and previewing them direct-from-disk. In addition to a long list of supported samplers, Alchemy is also compatible with the Studer Dyaxis digital recording system and the Digidesign NuBus cards used in Sound Tools and Audiomedia, which provide 16-bit stereo playback of Alchemy soundfiles directly from your hard disk. On most Macs (other than the Plus, SE, and Classic), Alchemy can also play stereo soundfiles from RAM using 8-bit resolution—without additional hardware. Aside from Dyaxis, Sound Designer, and Sound Designer II files, Alchemy supports 8-bit and 16-bit Audio IFF, SoundEdit, and SND Resource files.

The ability to import and export so many dissimilar file formats enables Alchemy to function as the hub of a versatile storage environment providing fast access and editing of audio material. Furthermore, through the use of its sophisticated Sample-Rate Conversion algorithm, Alchemy can convert soundfiles to any desired sample rate (up to 100 kHz) without altering the pitch. This allows you to import a file from one sampling device, resample the waveform to convert it to another sampler's specifications, and export the file to that sampler. In addition to resampling, you can easily convert monophonic samples into stereo and vice versa so that a common sound library can be shared by numerous devices, with Alchemy tying all branches of the system together into what Passport calls a Distributed Audio Network.

Importing, exporting, and resampling soundfiles is really only the tip of the Alchemy iceberg, and for many multimedia producers this will be the least exciting aspect of the program. For those who derive their audio material from only one or two sources, by far the most important part of this software lies in the realm of editing and digital sound-processing functions.

Choosing the Open Special command from the File menu brings up a dialog box (Figure 13.5) with a list of available soundfiles and a Listen button that lets you preview any selection directly from your hard disk. If you have an Audiomedia card installed, you can audition files in 16-bit stereo. In the lower part of the dialog box, an information display provides pertinent data about each selected soundfile to help you make a choice.

When you open a soundfile in Alchemy, it appears as a standard waveform display in the Waveform window (Figure 13.6). On the left side of the screen, the Alchemy Tool Palette with its myriad icons, buttons, and indicators provides direct access to most of Alchemy's editing functions. At the bottom of the Palette, four rectangular fields, grouped into a box, supply

**Figure 13.5**
Alchemy's Open Special dialog box provides you with important data about each selected soundfile. The Listen button lets you preview sounds direct-from-disk.

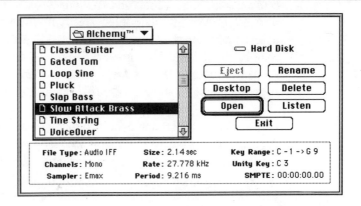

information about the cursor position, selection parameters, insertion point, and more—depending on the current display. Above this Numeric Display box, the View Memory buttons let you save up to eight separate views or ranges for each open Waveform window. The memories not only retain the selected range or insertion point but also the Zoom level for each view, making it easy to navigate your waveform and to return quickly to previous editing points with only a single mouse click.

**Figure 13.6**
Alchemy's Tool Palette and Waveform window showing a region selected for editing

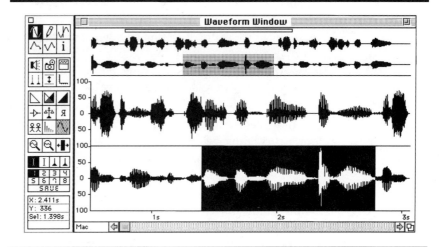

Above the View Memory buttons, four Cursor Locator icons let you move directly to the beginning or end of the currently selected range or loop and automatically center the view in the waveform display at that point—without changing the magnification level. The three Waveform View icons, above this group, let you zoom in and out or resize any selected range to fill the Waveform display.

The middle of the Palette holds a group of nine Process icons that enable you to initiate, with a single mouse click, many of the editing commands from the Process and Edit menus. The six Display icons above them allow you to change the characteristics of the Waveform window and play back the current soundfile or any selected part of it. At the top of the Palette, the Mode icons let you establish the basic cursor or display mode that you'll use for each editing task. The Tool Palette itself, though not resizable, can be moved to any position in the window. Its large selection of icons creates a graphical interface that makes many of Alchemy's editing operations both direct and intuitive.

As in Sound Designer, the Waveform window in Alchemy is divided into two sections: the Waveform display itself, and the Overview display, which shows the entire soundfile in a reduced view. Although you can toggle the Overview display off, most of the time you'll want to use it since it acts as an effective navigational map to help you locate regions for editing.

Dragging a selection box over a region in the Overview display causes the Waveform display to show that region, automatically sized to fill the window. Furthermore, whatever part of the soundfile that currently appears in the Waveform display is always indicated above in the Overview display with a thin, white rectangle that keeps you properly oriented by showing you the area that you're viewing in terms of the total picture. When you select a region for editing (by dragging across the waveform), the selected region appears with inverse video in the lower display, while the Overview display shows the selection with a grayed-out area.

Alchemy offers all of the standard editing features found in other programs, such as Cut, Copy, Paste, Delete, Insert, and Mix. The Blend option, when toggled on, automatically crossfades any edit points from the Cut, Paste, and Insert commands, while Extract works like Sound Designer's Trim feature by eliminating everything outside of the selected area. Both programs offer commands to invert and/or reverse a waveform (or any selected portion), and they also both provide the same kind of Pencil tool, which allows you to draw in waveform alterations.

To help smooth transitions at edit points, Alchemy provides icons for executing its Fade In, Fade Out, and Crossfade functions. Clicking the appropriate icon accomplishes the fade using one of several "fade slopes" that you select ahead of time from a dialog box. All fade types will continue to use the same fade-slope value until you choose another at a later time.

The Amplitude Scaling function increases or decreases the amplitude of a waveform (or selected region) by a uniform amount over its duration. This is an important tool to help you avoid clipping when you mix two sounds together or to ensure a smoother transition when joining soundfiles that have different volume levels. Alchemy uses an effective, graphical approach to making its amplitude changes.

Clicking on the Threshold Bars icon in the Tool Palette produces two horizontal dotted lines, one above and one below the Waveform display. As you drag these lines up or down, the Numeric Display indicates the percentage of maximum amplitude represented by their positions. When you arrive at the desired setting, you simply click the Scale icon to produce the change.

In addition to its Amplitude Scaling feature, Alchemy offers several powerful and impressive Amplitude Enveloping options. When you click on the Amplitude Envelope Mode icon, the waveform becomes grayed out and a horizontal "amplitude envelope line" appears at the top of the display. You can click anywhere on this line to produce a grab handle, or "knob," that you can drag to any position in the display for creating the desired envelope shape (Figure 13.7). This is similar to MacRecorder's envelope feature in its Mixer window, but Alchemy also offers another option. By clicking the Knob/Draw icon, you can toggle off the envelope knobs and toggle on the Envelope Draw mode. Then you can use the Pencil tool to hand-draw any envelope shape that you like, including one with curved lines.

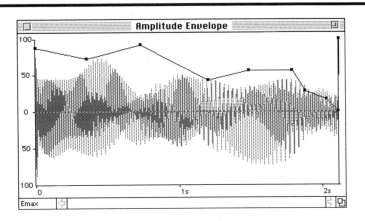

**Figure 13.7**
The Amplitude Envelope window lets you create an envelope in almost any shape.

As if these options weren't enough, Alchemy offers another, even more intriguing, way to change a sound's envelope. Clicking on the Trace Envelope icon lets you copy the envelope of any sampled sound and superimpose it on the waveform of another. You might, for instance, capture the envelope shape of a plucked instrument, like a guitar, and apply it to the sound of a trumpet or clarinet to create an entirely new kind of instrument. Recombining envelopes and sounds offers an interesting way to experiment with soundfiles and provides a useful tool for quickly capturing the envelopes of certain kinds of acoustic sounds.

Once you've created your new envelope (by whatever means), you have two further options for completing the process. The Amplitude Fit icon automatically adjusts the waveform to fit the new envelope by increasing or decreasing the appropriate parts of the sound. The Amplitude Scale icon fits the waveform to the new envelope by making only downward adjustments to the amplitude, which produces better results with low amplitude sounds or those with areas of silence.

The same kinds of options that Alchemy provides for its Amplitude Enveloping mode are also available for modulating the frequency of a sound. Clicking the Frequency Modulation Mode icon causes the waveform to appear grayed-out, as in Amplitude Enveloping mode. The vertical axis now becomes the frequency scale, which indicates your selected range in semitones, and a horizontal "frequency envelope line" appears at the center of the display (Figure 13.8). You can drag this line into any shape you want by using as many grab handles as needed, or if you prefer, you can use the Pencil tool to draw in a modulation curve that will change your sound's pitch. This "frequency profile" controls the amount of pitch bending that's applied to your soundfile, with lines sloping above the zero point causing the pitch to rise and negative values causing it to drop.

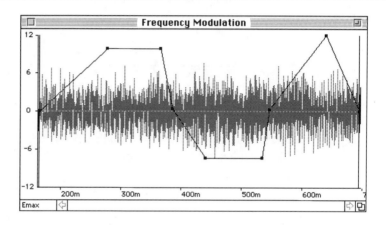

**Figure 13.8**
In Frequency Modulation mode, an adjustable line determines how a soundfile's pitch will change.

Since Alchemy treats sound data and wave data the same, you can copy the waveform from one sound and use it as an envelope to modulate another sound's frequency or amplitude. If, for instance, you copy a simple sine wave into the Clipboard and paste it as a frequency envelope over a second sound, that sound's pitch will rise and fall in a regular pattern as described by the sine wave's shape (Figure 13.9). The same sine wave used as an amplitude envelope would cause the sound to increase and decrease in volume with the same pattern.

Any waveform can act as an envelope, giving you endless opportunities for creating interesting and unusual effects. Since Alchemy doesn't distinguish between waveforms used for envelopes and those used for sound, you can establish a large library of natural and artificial envelopes by pasting them into windows and saving them in a file. Clearly, the unique enveloping features in Alchemy offer great potential for sound designers, musicians, and experimenters of all kinds.

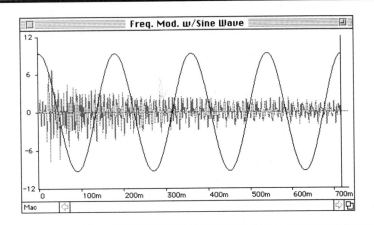

**Figure 13.9**
Using a sine wave to modulate the frequency of a soundfile

As you might expect, Alchemy provides a number of useful tools for creating effective, smooth-sounding loops. The Loop Cursors icon displays the loop beginning and end points with solid vertical lines that you can drag to any position in the Waveform display. For fine-tuning your loops, the Loop Splice Mode icon changes the Waveform window to a display that, in many ways, resembles the Loop window in Sound Designer II (Figure 13.10).

The dark vertical line down the center of the window represents the loop splice point. To the left of this line, you see the loop end and to the right, the

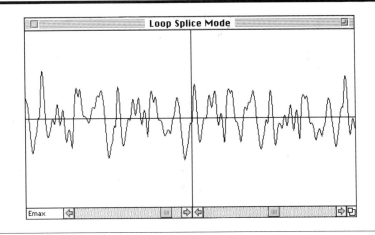

**Figure 13.10**
Alchemy's Loop Splice Mode window shows the beginning and end of a looped section, with the splice point in the center.

loop start. A scroll bar beneath each half of the window lets you move the loop points slowly in either direction. By clicking in the gray areas of either scroll bar you can advance the loop point to the next zero crossing. Since zero crossings often make good loop points, this feature can save you a lot of time when searching for promising splice locations.

In some cases, you can clean up a loop splice point by choosing the Pencil tool and drawing a smooth transition between the two halves of the window. You can also achieve an effective loop by using Alchemy's Crossfade Loop command. Before initiating the process, a dialog box lets you specify the percentage of the whole loop that you want involved in the crossfade. This feature often produces usable results even with otherwise difficult waveforms.

Alchemy and Sound Designer take decidedly different approaches to analyzing the harmonic content of waveforms. Although they both use Fast Fourier Transforms to generate harmonic spectrum displays, Sound Designer uses a 3-D display to show the frequency components of a waveform as they evolve over time. Alchemy, on the other hand, displays its harmonic spectrum with a two-dimensional bar graph that shows the harmonic content of the entire selected waveform range.

The Harmonic Spectrum Display window (Figure 13.11) indicates amplitude in decibels along the vertical axis and frequency bands along the horizontal axis. The scroll bar at the bottom of the window lets you view more of the frequency range since it may take quite a few screens to show all of the frequency bars. Whereas Sound Designer's display is perhaps more visually interesting and provides some insight into the changing characteristics of a sound, Alchemy's display offers one very important and powerful advantage: editing.

In Alchemy's Harmonic Spectrum display, you can select any of the frequency bands by clicking on them, producing a small grab handle at the tip of each selected bar. Dragging across a range in the window selects a group of frequencies, and using the Shift key lets you select noncontiguous bands. Once you have selected one or more frequency bars, you can apply the familiar Cut, Copy, Paste, Clear, and Mix commands to perform very precise and sophisticated editing.

**Figure 13.11**
The Harmonic Spectrum Display window shows the frequency components of a selected waveform range. Several frequency bars on the left show the small grab handles, which indicate they're selected for editing.

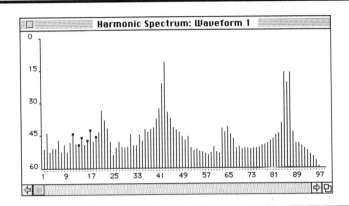

For starters, you can drag the tip of any selected bar up or down to change that frequency's amplitude. You can also choose one or more frequencies and cut or clear them, in effect, creating a versatile and highly accurate notch filter. Cutting more bands produces a filter with a wider notch, while cutting a single frequency allows you to edit your waveform's harmonic content with surgical precision. Additionally, the Clear Above command removes frequencies above the selected band, and the Clear Below command does the opposite. With these two commands, you can create a variety of razor-sharp low-pass and high-pass filters to further shape your waveforms.

In some situations, the exacting nature of the Harmonic Spectrum display may not make it the best choice for creating digital-filtering effects. As an alternative, therefore, Alchemy offers a digital EQ option that provides a more gentle-walled cutoff to produce a smoother equalization curve. Although the Digital EQ dialog box (Figure 13.12) lacks the high-pass and low-pass options found in Sound Designer's EQ window, the Harmonic Spectrum display handles these two filter types well enough.

Of particular interest to sound designers and postproduction engineers, Alchemy's sophisticated time-scaling algorithms let you change the duration of a selected waveform range—without altering its pitch. With the Time Scale dialog box (Figure 13.13), you can type in a desired end time, duration, or scale factor describing the relationship between the scaled and the original versions of the file.

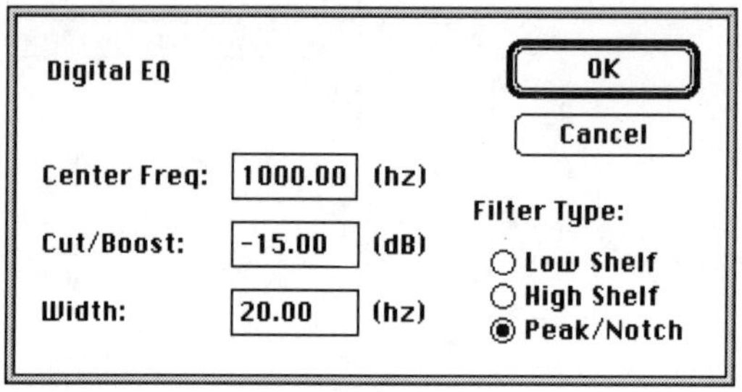

**Figure 13.12**
Alchemy's Digital EQ dialog box

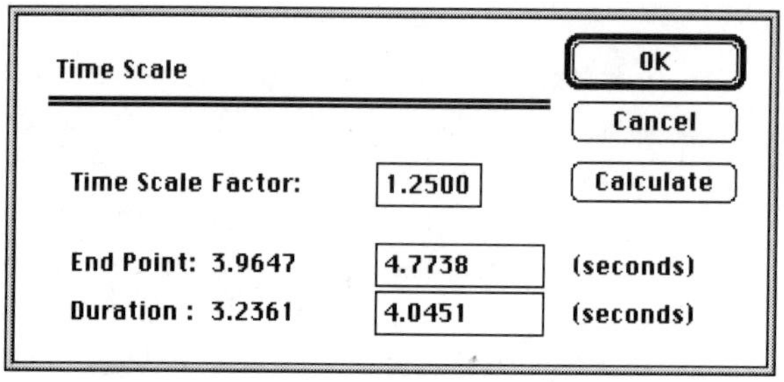

**Figure 13.13**
Alchemy's Time Scale feature lets you change the duration of a soundfile region without altering its pitch.

You can also change the pitch of any selected range, with or without changing its duration. When you choose the Pitch Shift command, a keyboard dialog box appears with a dark gray key representing the sound's current pitch (Figure 13.14). Clicking on a new key transposes the soundfile to a different pitch, while the Preserve Duration box lets you specify whether or not the shifted sound's duration will match the original.

Alchemy's documentation is exceptionally fine, marred only by the inexcusable absence of an index. Several excellent tutorials get you working with the program right away, and there are a great many pages devoted to explaining the basic concepts of sound production, digital audio, and looping.

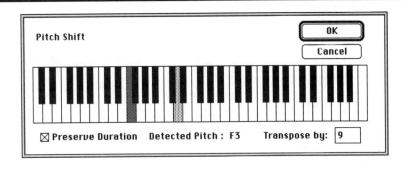

**Figure 13.14**
The Pitch Shift dialog box lets you transpose a soundfile, with or without changing its duration.

# Final Thoughts

Sound Designer II and Alchemy both provide enough high-powered editing features to handle nearly any task that might cross your path. Although they overlap each other in many ways, there are other areas in which they part company. Alchemy, for example, supports only one loop per soundfile, while Sound Designer II lets you create several. Sound Designer's harmonic display appears in 3-D but only allows viewing, while Alchemy's 2-D display is fully adjustable, allowing a range of precise, harmonic-editing options. While Sound Designer offers more kinds of EQ filtering and mixing of up to four soundfiles at once, Alchemy provides advanced amplitude and frequency-enveloping modes. And Sound Designer II comes in versions that are optimized for SampleCell and Audiomedia, while Alchemy stresses its Distributed Audio Network concept for integrating different samplers into a common editing environment. Finally, both programs are compatible with Apple's MIDI Manager and provide very good documentation.

# Chapter 14

# Digital Audio Meets MIDI

Once MIDI caught hold among musicians, it quickly evolved into a potent tool for composing and performing music in a wide variety of applications. By adding samplers and timecode devices to a setup, sound designers and postproduction professionals got in on the act and soon it seemed as if there wasn't anything that MIDI couldn't do. In fact, MIDI does have a few limitations. MIDI instruments are not especially well suited to dealing with the human voice, for instance, or with the idiosyncrasies and nuances of some solo instruments.

Many people turned to digital recording to solve these problems. But digital audio has its own limitations. Even though you can cut, copy, and paste digital soundfiles, you can't, for example, reorchestrate them or change the timing of one instrument relative to another. The complementary nature of MIDI and digital audio set the stage for a marriage that has since spawned a number of interesting hybrids. The products in this chapter take different approaches to combining digital recording with MIDI. One of them might be just right for producing your multimedia soundtracks.

## Audio Trax

Passport Designs introduced its Trax sequencer (see Chapter 6) to fill the needs of MIDI composers and multimedia producers who didn't require expensive, high-end programs to create and edit their scores. Now with

Audio Trax, Passport has taken that same sequencer and added the ability to record two channels of 8-bit digital audio in combination with up to 64 MIDI tracks.

Audio Trax uses MacRecorder, Voice Impact Pro, or the internal sound-input capabilities of the newer Macs to record its audio channels. Although this won't produce CD-quality sound, it can serve quite well for many kinds of presentations and offers the opportunity to explore the digital audio–MIDI connection without investing in expensive, additional hardware. Furthermore, Audio Trax is as simple and straightforward in its design as its MIDI-only predecessor, so it's intuitive and easy to use.

The Transport window in Audio Trax is exactly the same as the one used in Trax (Figure 14.1). It appears when you first open the program and provides the necessary controls for recording and playing back both the MIDI and audio parts of a sequence. Audio Trax also uses the same kind of Track Sheet as Trax, and it's nearly identical except for the addition of the audio tracks at the top—indicated by two small speaker icons (Figure 14.2).

**Figure 14.1**
The Transport window in Audio Trax is the same as the one in Trax.

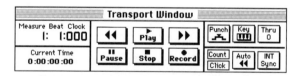

**Figure 14.2**
The Track Sheet in Audio Trax resembles its counterpart in Trax except that it adds two audio tracks at the top.

You can enable playback of any combination of MIDI and audio tracks by clicking on the corresponding triangles in the Play column. During playback you can turn any MIDI tracks on or off to hear different combinations of instruments. The audio tracks, however, must be play-enabled when you begin the sequence in order to be heard. Once you begin playback, though, you can turn the audio tracks on and off as needed.

The Record, Solo, Name, and Volume columns function the same in Audio Trax as they do in Trax. The Instrument, Channel, and Loop columns are also the same for MIDI data, but are treated differently for the top two tracks. For these tracks, the Instrument column shows the length and sample rate for each recording, and the Channel column allows you to select the left or right audio output channel. Because the single internal speaker on most Macintoshes receives only the left audio channel, you can assign both audio tracks in the Track Sheet to output to the left channel to ensure that all of your audio material is heard. To achieve true stereo playback, you must attach the output of your computer, using an adapter cable, to a stereo amplifier and speakers. Finally, the Loop column applies only to MIDI data because you can't loop the audio tracks in this program.

To make an audio recording, you simply click on the Record column in front of track 1 or 2 in the Track Sheet. A small dot appears, indicating that the track is record-enabled. When you click the Record button in the Transport window, recording proceeds until you click Stop. Audio Trax saves each sequence as a separate MIDI file, along with one or two audio files, all sharing a common prefix.

For setting additional recording parameters, the Audio Setup dialog box (Figure 14.3) lets you select one of two sampling rates and provides information on available recording time. An Input Level meter helps you optimize recording levels, and two Audio Start columns let you specify where in the sequence you want recording to begin for each track. This can eliminate long stretches of recorded silence at the beginning of a piece, which results in added noise and wasted memory. You can also use these settings to shift the audio tracks in relation to one another or to their related MIDI tracks.

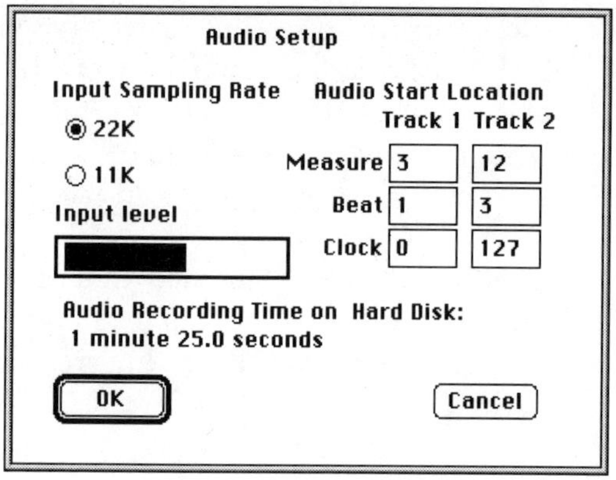

**Figure 14.3**
The Audio Setup dialog box provides additional parameter settings and information for recording audio.

Once you have recorded an audio track, you can view and edit the soundfile in the Audio window, where it appears as a waveform accompanied by several icons (Figure 14.4). In the upper-left corner of the window, the Eraser tool allows you to erase audio material by dragging across an area. Next to that, the black Speaker icon plays back the entire audio track or any selected portion of it, and the Arrow tool lets you select regions to cut, copy, and paste. With the white Speaker icon, you can change the display from one audio track to another, while the field next to it allows you to switch audio channels.

To help improve the quality of a recorded soundfile, Audio Trax provides three options on its Audio menu that you can apply to any waveform or selected region. These are all destructive edits that you can't undo, so you need to approach them with some caution.

The Normalize command increases the amplitude of a waveform to maximize its level without clipping. This can be a valuable tool for improving the sound quality of your output system, but you have to be careful when using it because Normalize multiplies any recorded noise along with the desired sounds.

The Gain command lets you increase or decrease the amplitude of a waveform by a percentage of the soundfile's current level. This is especially valuable for matching the overall levels of different sections of a waveform

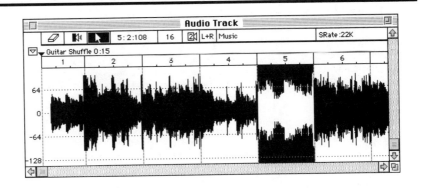

**Figure 14.4**
The Audio window provides a waveform display and several tools. It is shown here with measure 5 selected for editing.

and for adjusting entire soundfiles. When using the Gain command, you must be careful not to produce too large an increase in amplitude or it could result in clipping.

The Noise Gate command helps you eliminate the unwanted low-level noise that frequently occurs between sections of music or dialogue. With the Noise Gate dialog box, you can enter a threshold level at which the Gate effect becomes activated. Audio Trax will then eliminate any audio material that falls below that level. This can help to clean up a recording by removing distracting background sounds between pauses in a soundfile, but you must be careful not to choose a threshold that is too high or the effect will be quite noticeable.

Any sequence data, either audio or MIDI, that you record with Audio Trax can appear as one-measure units in the Song Editor window (Figure 14.5). This is the same Song Editor that Trax uses except that this display includes the two audio tracks at the top. Measures that contain MIDI data appear as small black boxes, while the audio data appears in similar boxes with a waveform drawn inside them. White boxes represent empty measures. You can select sections of the sequence for editing by dragging through both of the audio tracks or all of the MIDI tracks. You can also select individual tracks from each section, all of the tracks from both sections, or groups of MIDI tracks. Once they are selected, you can use commands such as Cut, Copy, Paste, and Delete to rearrange the structure of the sequence.

**Figure 14.5**
The Song Editor window shows the presence of both MIDI and audio data in one-measure units.

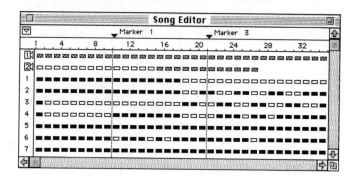

Choosing Insert Measures from the Edit menu opens a dialog box that lets you add empty measures to any track or combination of tracks (Figure 14.6). You can then fill these empty measures with data that you've copied to the Clipboard. If you paste data onto measures that aren't empty, the new material replaces the old. Using the Mix Data command, however, lets you merge the new with the old, though you can only mix MIDI with MIDI and audio with audio.

The Paste Audio From command enables you to paste audio files from other sources, such as other Audio Trax scores or 8-bit Audio IFF files from programs like SoundEdit. If the new material is longer than your sequence, the sequence will automatically expand to accommodate it. The Mix Audio From

**Figure 14.6**
The Insert Measures dialog box lets you add empty measures to any track.

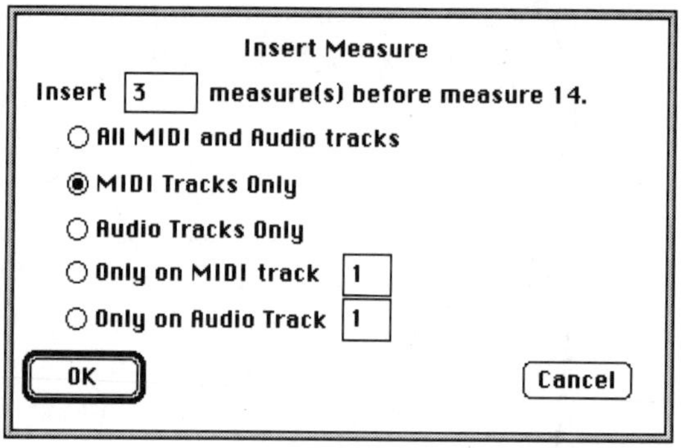

command works the same way except that the new data gets blended with the old instead of replacing it.

The MIDI-sequencer part of Audio Trax functions the same as in Trax and provides the same editing options and tools, along with an identical Step Editor window (Figure 14.7). Both programs also use the same Conductor window, but in Audio Trax if you change the tempo after recording your audio, you will lose sync between the MIDI and audio because the tempo of the audio tracks can't be changed. It's best to record the MIDI sequence first and make sure that the tempos are satisfactory before adding the audio portions. MIDI files created with Audio Trax are fully compatible with Master Tracks Pro 5 and Trax, and the audio files can be imported into other programs, such as Alchemy, for further editing.

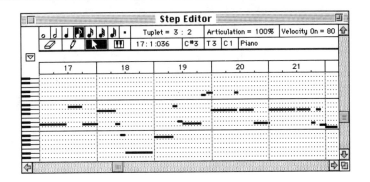

**Figure 14.7**
Trax and Audio Trax use the same Step Editor window and share the same MIDI editing options.

# Deck

Digidesign's Audiomedia card has brought digital, direct-to-disk recording within the reach of a great many Macintosh users. But in spite of its sophisticated editing capabilities and high-quality audio, it can't, on its own, satisfy the needs of a fully integrated audio-production system. To do that you'll need Deck—Digidesign's multitrack recording and playback program. With Deck you can record, process, and mix digital audio and synchronize it with a MIDI sequence to create stereo, CD-quality master recordings.

All of Deck's primary functions are handled by its main display, which fills the screen when you open the program (Figure 14.8). It is designed to look and operate like a typical four-track tape recorder, but with several significant advantages, including an automated mixer and two on-board digital effects per track. The transport controls, in the lower-right corner, work much like the buttons on a standard tape deck. Below these controls, the eight Time buttons let you store "autolocate memories," which enable you to return instantly to any specific time within the current recording—whether Deck is playing or not.

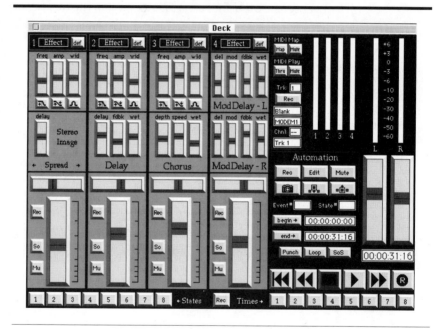

**Figure 14.8**
Deck's main window looks and operates like a four-track tape-deck/mixer combination. It is shown here in Playback mode, with a different effect selected for each track.

Above the Transport buttons, the Master Counter indicates elapsed time in SMPTE format (hours: minutes: seconds: frames), giving a resolution of one-thirtieth of a second. The Master Output faders that sit above the Counter let you control the overall output for the current recording, while the Master VU meters indicate the output levels. The four smaller VU meters display the individual output levels for each of the tracks.

The left half of the main display is devoted to these input/output modules, which represent Deck's four digital tracks. Each of the channels can operate in one of two modes: Record or Playback. In Playback mode, each module provides a Channel fader (to control playback volume relative to the other tracks), a Stereo Pan fader (to adjust the placement of the track within the stereo image) and a Solo, Mute, and Record Mode button.

At the top of each module, two boxed areas house the EQ and effects controls that you can apply to each independent track. You can elect to have two bands of parametric EQ or one band of EQ and one other effect by making a selection with the Effects pop-up menu. For each chosen effect, the display changes to provide the appropriate control sliders for setting the necessary parameters. In all cases (except the ModDelay effect, which has no EQ), the audio signal is equalized before it passes through the other effect. The Defeat button lets you turn off the effect and equalization on the corresponding track—a useful tool for making before and after comparisons.

Deck's Parametric EQ feature provides three types of filters: low-shelf, high-shelf, and notch filter. Sliders allow you to adjust the frequency range and amplitude-boost/cut range for each type. The Stereo-ize effect makes a pseudostereo image from a monaural source by creating a delayed copy of the original and letting you pan the two versions to the left and right. Deck also provides a Delay effect and a Chorus effect, as well as a Stereo Modulated Delay (ModDelay) effect, which you can use to set up a different modulated delay on each channel.

Deck applies its audio-effects processing in a nondestructive way so that the original recording is not altered. If you want the effects to become a permanent part of a track, you can "bounce" the track onto another track. When you copy a recording from one track to another, the processed sound of the first track gets recorded onto the destination track. This allows you to take the new recording and apply additional effects if you need them.

If you don't have any empty tracks, Deck can bounce a track onto itself. It can also take four tracks and bounce them down to two, allowing you to build up a recording without worrying about leaving empty destination tracks. With Deck's Bounce To Disk dialog box (Figure 14.9), you can mix tracks internally, and because everything is handled in the digital domain, there is no degradation of sound quality.

Nondestructive processing makes Deck work like an analog tape recorder/mixer combination, and it gives you the opportunity to try different effects without changing your original recording. There are times, however, when you'll want to alter the audio data on a track to improve the recording itself. To this end, Deck provides three types of destructive processes that you can apply to individual tracks. The Normalize function adjusts a recording to achieve the maximum allowable level without clipping. This can help improve the signal-to-noise ratio. The Hum Removal function filters out the 60-Hz hum that often appears in analog signals, and the Noise Gate works the same as in Audio Trax to eliminate ambient noise below a selected threshold.

**Figure 14.9**
The Bounce To Disk dialog box

```
Bounce To Disk                          [    OK    ]
                                        [  Cancel  ]

Output Format:          File Options:
  ○ Mono                  ● Whole File
  ● Stereo                ○ Region Only

Destination Tracks:     Region:
  Left/Mono:  [ 4 ]       Begin:  00:00:03:25
  Right:      [ 1 ]       End:    00:00:46:20
```

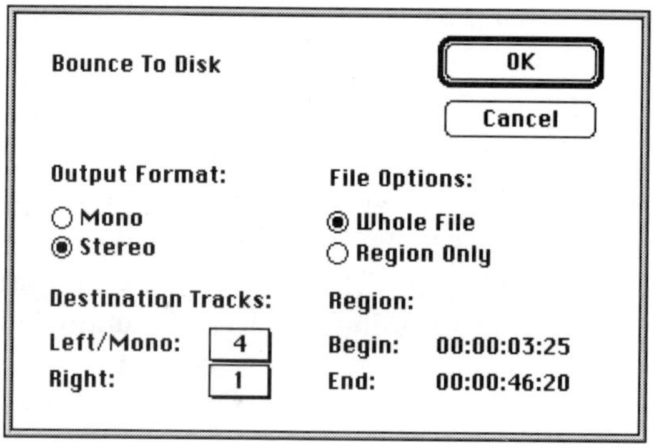

Making a recording with Deck is relatively easy because the procedure closely follows the one used with analog equipment. When you click the Record Mode button on one of the tracks, the Playback Module changes appearance and becomes highlighted, indicating that the track is ready for recording (Figure 14.10). The Channel fader and Stereo Pan fader are now used for making adjustments while monitoring the recording. In the upper half of the Record Module, an Input Level fader and VU meter enable you to set the proper recording level, and the Input Selector buttons at the top let you choose which input channel or channels will be recorded onto the track.

**Figure 14.10**
Tracks 2 and 4 are shown here in Record mode. Notice that the effects controls have been replaced by the Input Level faders.

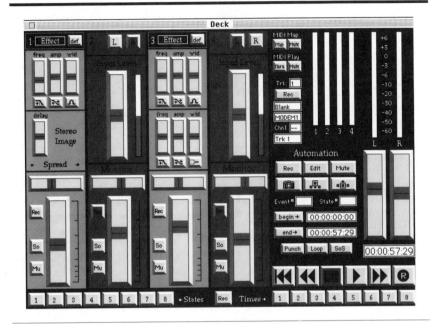

To begin recording, simply click the Record and Play buttons in the Transport panel and then click Stop when you're finished. If the recording sounds fine, you can add tracks in the same way while listening to what you've already done. If you plan to combine your digital recording with a MIDI sequence later, you must remember to use the MIDI Metronome option (Figure 14.11), so you can maintain sync between the audio and MIDI music. This will provide you with the bar and beat framework that MIDI uses and let you know the MIDI tempo as you perform.

Aside from its normal Record mode, Deck offers three additional recording options that you can access by clicking one of the buttons above the Transport controls. The Sound-on-Sound (SoS) button lets you record onto any track without replacing the original audio track. Instead, the original and the new material are mixed together with no loss of fidelity and without requiring additional hard-disk space.

With the Loop Mode button, you first designate a beginning and ending point in the counters directly above the button. Deck will then play that section over

**Figure 14.11**
The MIDI Metronome dialog box

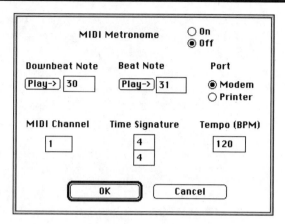

and over to allow you to rehearse a passage before recording. Combining Sound-on-Sound with Loop mode lets you make drum-machine-style recordings where you can add new audio with each pass through the area—without losing the previous recording. The third button, Automated Punch In/Out, uses the Begin and End counters to enable you to insert new audio into a specific area of a previously recorded passage.

When recording engineers mix down a multitrack recording to stereo, they use their fingers and both hands to manipulate the controls. This sometimes requires an exceptional sense of timing and coordination, and complicated mixes are often difficult to reproduce. To alleviate this problem, high-end mixing boards provide automated mixdown capabilities. On-screen mixers are even more problematic because you can only operate one control at a time with a mouse, so Deck has adopted some of the same automation features found on professional mixers.

Deck's automation process incorporates three concepts: mixer states, snapshots, and transition times. A *mixer state* is a picture of the current position of every fader on screen, including EQ, pan, level, and effects. You assign each of these mixer states to one of the eight buttons in the lower-left corner of the window. From then on, you can instantly recall the complete fader configuration of each state by clicking the appropriate button. A *snapshot* is like a mixer state that only occurs once and is not associated with one of the mixer-state buttons. Through its snapshot feature, Deck can support as many as 200 different mixer states, including the 8 assigned to buttons. *Transition times* are used to create smooth fader motions between any snapshots or mixer states.

To record an automated-mixer session, you first need to set up the most important mixer states and assign them to buttons. Then you click the Automation Record button and begin playing back your audio recording. As the recording proceeds, you can click the different mixer-state buttons at the appropriate times to create the desired combinations of fader positions. You can also include other configurations and capture them with the snapshot button. When you're through, you can go back and edit the placement of the mixer states so that they occur exactly where you want them. If the resulting fader movements seem too abrupt for your recording, you can use the Transition feature to create smoother fades between the automation events.

Deck's MIDI-handling capabilities are not at the level of a full-featured sequencer program, but Deck does offer a substantial number of basic MIDI functions, including the ability to import and export Standard MIDI Files. In most cases, the best way to use Deck for combining MIDI with digital audio is to first develop your MIDI sequence using one of the programs described in Chapters 5 and 6. Then you can import the sequence into Deck and add the audio tracks. Although Deck can't directly open dedicated MIDI sequences from programs like Vision, Master Tracks Pro 5, and Performer, these sequencers can all save their files in Standard MIDI File format, making Deck compatible with a wide range of programs.

If you first compose your MIDI music, import it into Deck, and then add the audio tracks, you can be sure that the synchronization between the two music sources will be maintained throughout the piece. If you choose to work in the other direction—recording audio first and then adding MIDI—you'll likely encounter problems unless you record your audio tracks using the MIDI Metronome to provide a tempo and reference source.

Deck's MIDI Play/Record area (to the left of the Channel VU meters) allows you to record and play back as many as 32 new MIDI tracks. With the Track Status indicator, you can choose to record, play, solo, or mute any track, and the Mute button, in the MIDI Play section, lets you mute all of the tracks at once. As in its audio section, Deck also offers sound-on-sound and punch-in/punch-out recording options for MIDI. Additional editing features, such as transposing, channelizing, and filtering MIDI data, are available in the Transform MIDI Track dialog box (Figure 14.12). Deck also lets you control its faders from an external MIDI device, like a keyboard controller, by switching to its MIDI Map mode, where you can assign individual faders to specific control sources.

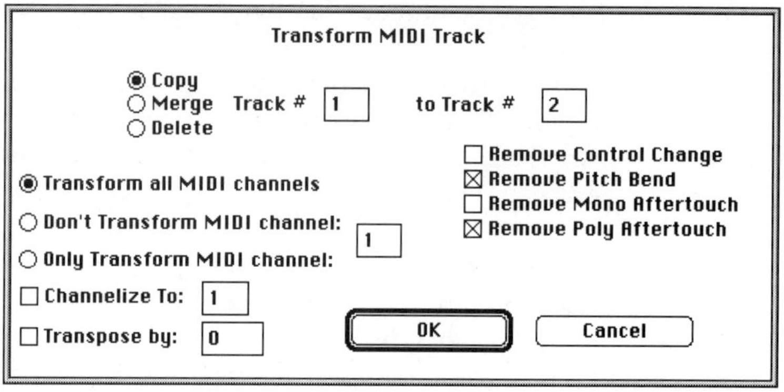

**Figure 14.12**
The Transform MIDI Track dialog box provides additional editing options.

Every time you complete and save a recording project with Deck, it saves it as a document called a Session. A Session file contains one MIDI file, one Automation file, and a list of the soundfiles for the four digital audio tracks. The Session file also retains all of the mixer state and Time button settings along with the configuration of all EQ and effects buttons and faders.

The audio soundfiles themselves reside outside of the Session file and are accessed when a Session is opened. Deck allows you to load any monophonic Sound Designer II files directly onto any of its four tracks. You can also use earlier Sound Designer files and Audio IFF files, but these must be imported into the program. This process involves making a copy of the file in the correct format, which requires additional hard-disk space and takes more time.

If lowering your storage demands is important, Deck provides a real-time 2:1 compression algorithm that reduces the amount of audio data needed during recording. Compressed Sessions, however, cannot use Deck's real-time effects and EQ processing features.

Deck and Audio Trax represent two opposite approaches to combining digital audio and MIDI. With Audio Trax, Passport Designs took a popular sequencer program and added some basic audio recording and editing capabilities. Digidesign, on the other hand, created Deck as a powerful multitrack recording program that included a number of basic sequencing features enabling it to synchronize its digital audio recordings with MIDI music.

Which of these approaches best suits your needs will depend on how much money you can afford to spend, what level of audio quality you demand, what method of composition and music production you most often employ, and how the music will eventually be distributed.

The next group of programs all take the approach of starting with a professional-level sequencer and adding advanced audio-recording and editing features.

# Studio Vision

Opcode Systems was the first MIDI software company to create a program that combined the powerful features of a high-end sequencer with the ability to record and edit CD-quality direct-to-disk audio. Developed in conjunction with Digidesign, Studio Vision uses the Audiomedia card (or Sound Tools) to perform its digital audio recording, so the sound quality, storage demands, and hardware requirements are the same (see Chapter 12). It also provides all of the same MIDI-handling capabilities as Vision, Opcode's highly successful, pro-level sequencer. In fact, the two programs are so much alike that Studio Vision comes with the Vision owner's manual and simply adds another section to cover the audio aspects of the program.

When you open Studio Vision, the same three windows appear as in Vision: the Control Bar, the Sequence window, and the File window (Figure 14.13). Only the telltale Audio heading in the menu bar reveals that this sequencer has something extra. This level of similarity between the two programs means that if you're already familiar with Vision, you'll feel right at home with Studio Vision. If you're starting from scratch, though, be prepared to spend some time with the owner's manual because this program does have a bit of a learning curve.

The people at Opcode have done an excellent job of integrating audio recording and editing into Studio Vision. As much as possible, they've maintained a consistent feel for the way that MIDI data and audio data are handled. Many of the editing operations that work on MIDI also apply to audio events, and the same editing environments that Vision offers for MIDI are available here for audio as well. For a more detailed look at the MIDI-sequencing component of Studio Vision, see the section on Vision in Chapter 5.

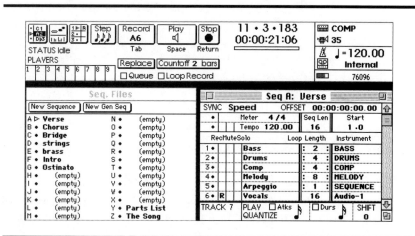

**Figure 14.13**
Studio Vision uses the same Control Bar, Sequence window, and File window as Vision.

Studio Vision incorporates audio data into a sequence just as it does with MIDI. To begin recording, you first select a track (in the Sequence window) where you want your audio data to appear and then record-enable that track by clicking in its Record box. Next you open the Record Monitor window (Figure 14.14), which provides two VU-style meters (with clipping indicators) to measure your input levels along with a Thru option that lets you listen to the audio signal as you record. To designate which audio channel to use for recording, you must click the appropriate check box under the Record heading—Studio Vision allows mono or stereo recording—and name the soundfile that will hold the audio data.

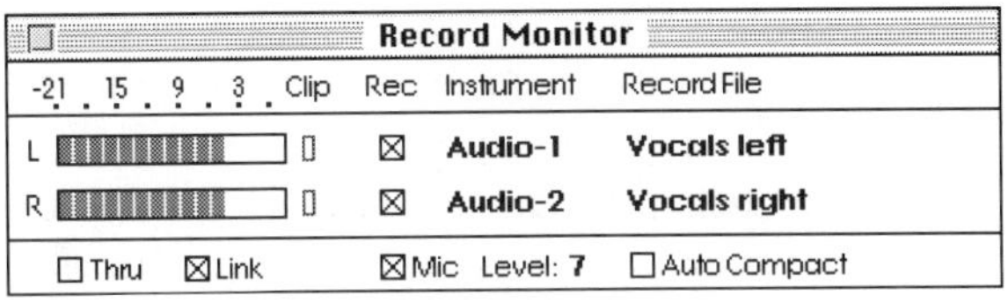

# Digital Audio Meets MIDI 259

**Figure 14.14**
The Record Monitor window lets you measure input levels and select channels for recording.

When you're ready to start, click the Record button in the Control Bar (you can use the same Replace, Punch, and Overdub modes as for MIDI) and click Stop when you're done. While making your recording, you can listen to any MIDI tracks already in the sequence, along with the metronome and any previously recorded audio material. You can also record MIDI and audio data simultaneously. If you're unhappy with your performance, you can undo the recording to reclaim the disk space and try again.

Each time you complete a recording, Studio Vision creates a waveform display that appears at the bottom of the Graphic window in what Opcode calls an "audio pane" (Figure 14.15). Since this can take several seconds to complete, you have the option to disable the waveform drawing to keep the recording session moving along. Later, when you need it for editing, you can have the program draw the waveform without any problem.

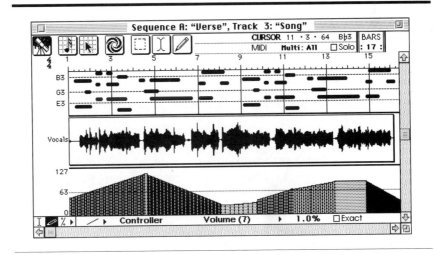

**Figure 14.15**
In Studio Vision each waveform display appears in the Graphic window just above the Strip Chart in an area called the "audio pane." This allows you to view and edit MIDI, audio, and continuous controller data simultaneously.

Studio Vision's audio pane is actually just an extension of its Graphic window, where you can view one or more "audio instruments"—a term used by Opcode to describe how audio data relates to a sequence in Studio Vision. Each recorded audio event appears in the Graphic window once you assign it a name. There are slots for up to 16 audio instruments, each of which has a volume and pan setting associated with it. Audio instruments function somewhat like separate audio tracks within a sequencer track, and each appears in a different vertical layer in the audio pane (Figure 14.16). If you record a performance in stereo and check the Link option in the Record Monitor window, the waveform display will show both channels in a single instrument layer. This indicates that they represent a single audio instrument and will therefore respond as a unit to any editing operations.

**Figure 14.16**
Each audio instrument appears on its own layer in the audio pane. Linked stereo recordings occupy a single layer.

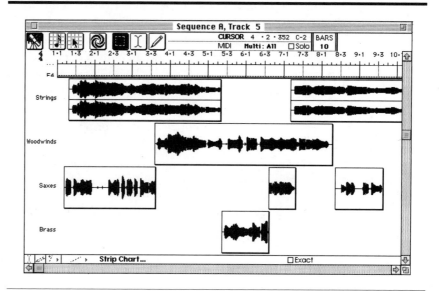

You can use any audio track in as many sequencer tracks as you like, and by using the Audio Instrument window, you can mute or solo each one individually. If you have a color monitor, you can also assign a different color to each audio instrument so that the different waveforms appear in different colors in the Graphic window. Continuous data drawn in the Strip Chart also reflects the color of the corresponding audio instrument.

All of this offers the potential for some impressive data displays, because any Studio Vision track can include multiple MIDI channels and audio instruments in a single window.

Once a waveform appears in the audio pane, you can manipulate it in a surprising number of ways. Of course, you can select all or part of any audio event's waveform and apply the usual Cut, Copy, and Paste commands, but that's only the beginning. You can easily drag any waveform to the right or left to change its start time. You can also drag an event up or down into a different layer in the window to change the instrument that's assigned to it. Then the new instrument's volume and pan settings will apply to that audio data. Option-dragging a waveform creates a copy of the event, which can occupy the same or a different instrument track.

By creating several copies of an event and overlapping, or "shingling," them on a single instrument track, you can create a stutter effect. That's because Studio Vision will play only the exposed part of each event, cutting off playback of the first event when the second event starts and so forth. You can change the amount of overlap anytime you want by dragging any of the events forward or backward.

If you want to hear two events simultaneously, you must assign them to different audio instruments; they will appear on different layers in the Graphic window. Studio Vision is limited, however, to only two playback channels, so you can only hear two audio instruments at one time. If more than two events occur in the same time range, the program will play the first two events until a third event occurs. At that point the event with the earliest start time will get cut off by the most recent event.

Studio Vision offers several ingenious methods for subdividing its waveforms. With the Retain command, you can select an area in the middle of a waveform and clear the data on either side of it, leaving only your selection. The Separate command provides two ways of splitting up an audio event into smaller parts: You can drag across a portion of the audio event and separate it from the rest of the waveform, or you can simply click at any desired locations in the waveform to create separation points. If you play an audio event right after you separate it into smaller segments, it will sound unchanged; but on the screen each segment appears in its own box, indicating that it is now a self-contained audio event that you can move and edit independently of the other segments.

Cutting into a waveform can often cause annoying clicks or pops at the edit point if you happen to catch a sound wave at a high-amplitude part of its cycle. To help reduce this problem, Studio Vision applies a zero-crossing function that nudges your selection point to the nearest zero crossing before making the separation.

The Strip Silence command, one of Studio Vision's most impressive features, lets you eliminate areas of audio that fall below a specified amplitude. It's actually a sophisticated noise gate that opens a dialog box where you enter a threshold level and a signal period. Then, when you choose Strip Silence, the program automatically clears any audio material that falls below the threshold level and lasts longer than the specified duration. Silence that lasts for a shorter time than the signal period (such as a brief pause) is left alone to prevent the audio from sounding unnatural. The remaining parts of the waveform appear on-screen as separate audio events that you can edit further (Figure 14.17).

**Figure 14.17**
A waveform shown before and after applying the Strip Silence command

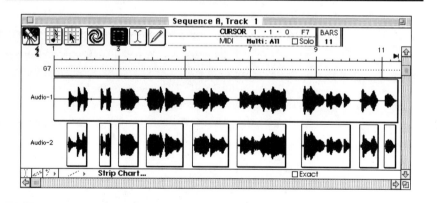

You might, for instance, record a section of narration and use the Strip Silence command to separate the waveform into the individual words and phrases. You could then rearrange the sentences, eliminate or replace certain words, and move any phrase forward or backward in time to align it with a specific musical event. Or you might record a drum part and use the

Strip Silence feature to divide it into separate beats, which you could then rearrange or move as needed. In fact, Studio Vision offers the same Quantize option for audio as it offers for MIDI, so you can align individual audio events to your MIDI music with any level of precision that you like. You can also combine the Strip Silence command with a zero-crossing option to ensure noise-free separation points.

The ability to separate audio events into segments opens the door to all kinds of postproduction possibilities. You can, for example, choose your best three or four performances of a musical passage and assign them to different audio instruments. Then you can select your favorite parts from each and assemble them into a perfect performance (Figure 14.18). Studio Vision even lets you audition your choices with its Play Selected option so that you can hear how they will sound together before you combine them into a single track.

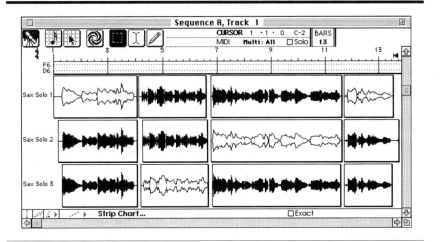

**Figure 14.18**
By selecting the best parts from different recordings, you can assemble a perfect performance. Studio Vision lets you audition your selections (shown here in white) before committing to a final mix.

It's important to note that nearly all of Studio Vision's editing operations are nondestructive. This means that no matter how often you move your audio events back and forth and no matter how many times you cut apart and recombine your waveforms, you will not alter the original soundfiles nor consume any additional hard-disk space. When you edit wave data in Studio Vision, you are not changing the raw audio data on the hard disk; you're simply providing instructions, or pointers, that tell the program which part of a soundfile to play and when to start and stop. Each time you change or add an edit, the program just issues a new set of pointers. This allows you to return to the original soundfile at any time and start all over again if you're unhappy with your results.

To change the few editing parameters not available in the Graphic window, Studio Vision provides a List window (Figure 14.19) that displays a chronological list of all audio, MIDI, and text events in a track. Audio events appear with their start and end times indicated in bars, beats, and units (or SMPTE time) along with their "velocities." Studio Vision uses the term *velocity* to maintain the analogy with MIDI data, but obviously audio events don't correspond exactly to the kind of data that originates from a keyboard controller. In this case, velocity simply refers to the initial volume level at which an audio event is played back. The events all default to the maximum value of 127, but you can easily lower this amount if necessary. The Volume data, also shown in the List window, affects the audio event continuously as it plays and allows you to fade a sound in or out. The Pan setting indicates the audio event's placement in the stereo field, and you can adjust it over time as well.

**Figure 14.19**
The List window can display both MIDI and audio data.

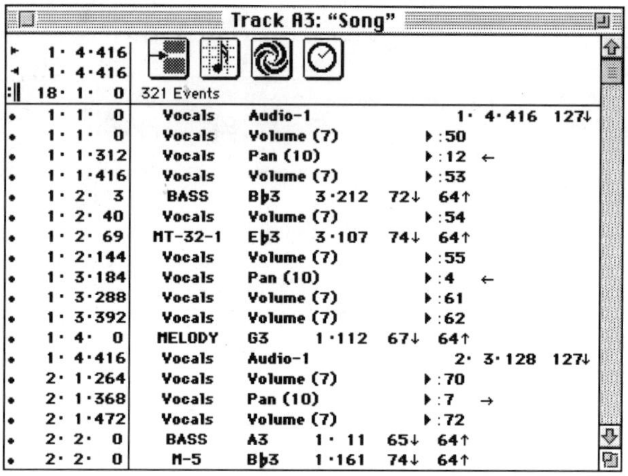

For real-time control of your audio tracks, Studio Vision provides the same Faders window that Vision uses (Figure 14.20). In Studio Vision you can assign any of the 32 faders to control either volume or panning for any of the individual audio instruments. Or you can assign faders to transmit continuous controller data to your MIDI devices.

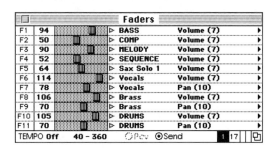

**Figure 14.20**
Studio Vision provides 32 faders for real-time control of MIDI and audio tracks.

After you've recorded several soundfiles and edited a number of audio events, you'll find it useful to organize your files and, if necessary, to free up some disk space. To help you deal with these and other tasks, Studio Vision includes the File Management window (Figure 14.21). This window displays the data that is stored in each audio file as a gray rectangular bar. The white sections represent areas of unused data—in other words, parts of the soundfile that are not referenced by the current sequence file. Along the top of each bar, a line of text provides additional information about each soundfile, such as its file type, sample rate, and size.

After examining your files, you can choose the Compact command to eliminate any audio data that is not being used. The Consolidate command takes all of the referenced data from various files and splices them together into a single audio file, and the Delete File command removes a specified file completely. Unlike the editing operations described earlier, these commands do change the audio data on your hard disk, so you should use them with some caution.

Studio Vision can import soundfiles in one of four formats: Sound Designer, Sound Designer II, Audio IFF, and Dyaxis. The program itself

**Figure 14.21**
The File Management window helps you organize your audio files and free up disk space.

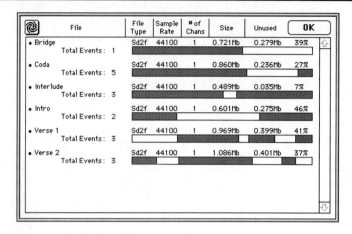

stores all of its audio files in Sound Designer II format, and it allows you to import either selected regions or playlists—without the playlist crossfades. While you're working with audio events in Studio Vision, you can, at any time, apply extensive editing operations to a waveform by using the Edit SoundFile option on the Audio menu. This links you directly to Sound Designer II (assuming that you have it), where the selected waveform will appear, ready for editing.

Unlike Studio Vision, Sound Designer's edit operations are destructive, so it's important to work with a backup copy or you may lose parts of your audio file. Also, Studio Vision records stereo sounds as two separate audio files, while Sound Designer II records the left and right channels into a single file, interleaving the audio from both sides. Although you can separate the two halves of a Sound Designer II stereo event, the procedure is not as straightforward as with a Studio Vision file. This makes it a bit more cumbersome to edit the two channels of a Sound Designer file independently.

If you need to synchronize your sequence to a tape recorder or VCR, you can use SMPTE timecode with Studio Vision along with the Lock Audio to Tape option and the Tape Calibration option. These features ensure the proper playback of MIDI and audio data in spite of minor variations in the tape speed.

Studio Vision is impressive in its power and versatility. The MIDI and audio sections can each stand alone as complete programs, and in combination with Sound Designer II, you have a postproduction environment that offers seemingly endless possibilities. The program takes some time to get used to, but in the long run you'll find it well worth the effort.

## Cubase Audio

Cubase, from Steinberg/Jones, is a complex, pro-level sequencer with something for everybody. Following the maxim that bigger is better, the program includes numerous viewing and editing windows, a drum track editor, a mixer, a music-generating function, and more. To further enlarge its list of features, Cubase has now evolved into a second version, Cubase Audio, that also offers digital audio recording and editing.

Like Studio Vision, Cubase Audio uses the popular Audiomedia card (or Sound Tools) from Digidesign. The MIDI sequencer part of the program has been somewhat beefed up, but remains largely the same as in Cubase. Because the structural and organizational aspects of this program differ from those in other sequencers, it may take a while to get used to Cubase Audio if you've been using another program. For a more detailed description of how the program handles MIDI data, see the section on Cubase in Chapter 5.

As much as possible, Cubase Audio strives to handle its audio data the same as it handles MIDI. All recording and editing operations begin with the Arrange window (Figure 14.22), which closely resembles its counterpart in Cubase. The window consists of two halves. On the left, a list of the different tracks appears along with pertinent information about MIDI channel, instrument, and output assignments. On the far left, the Info column provides a look at the current settings for any selected track. Between the Info column and the Track column, three narrow columns let you set certain characteristics of each track. In the Mute (M) column, you can temporarily stop playback of any Track. The Class (C) column lets you select any of Cubase Audio's six types of Track Classes: MIDI, Audio, Drum, Mix, Tape, and Group. Each type of Track then appears in the Class column represented by a different icon. The Time Lock (T) column lets you lock the start time of a Track to a specific SMPTE timecode location independently of the master tempo.

**Figure 14.22**
The Arrange window shows a list of Tracks—both MIDI and audio—and their associated Parts.

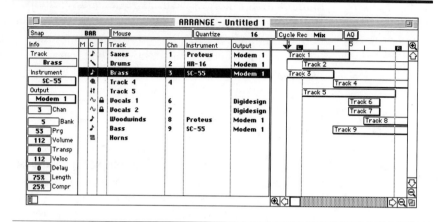

The right side of the Arrange window displays the Parts that correspond to each of the Tracks. In Cubase Audio, Parts (represented by rectangular segments) can contain either MIDI or audio data, and you can use many of the same kinds of editing operations on both. You can drag Audio Parts into new locations and onto other Tracks. You can also cut, copy, paste, snip, merge, and mix them as if they were MIDI Parts. The resulting graphic configuration provides a good overview of the sequence, which scrolls along as the music plays.

To record audio into your sequence, you first create a new Track and use the Class column to set the Track type to Audio. Next you create a Part into which the recording will go. To adjust and monitor input and playback levels, the program provides a Record Monitor (Figure 14.23), which includes two peak-hold-style VU meters, two faders, and two controls for setting the pan positions. Clicking the NewRec button prompts you to name your new soundfile.

All of Cubase Audio's recording and playback functions originate from the same Transport Bar that the MIDI-only sequencer uses (Figure 14.24). Once you've named your file and made the necessary adjustments, you click the Record button to start recording. Clicking Stop ends the recording and the program pauses briefly as it builds the waveform.

**Figure 14.23**
Cubase Audio's Record Monitor

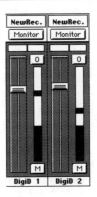

**Figure 14.24**
Cubase Audio uses the same Transport Bar as Cubase.

To view and edit your soundfile, you have to open the Audio Editor window (Figure 14.25), which shows the audio data as a waveform display. If you're importing a soundfile into the Audio Editor window, you simply choose the Pencil tool from the Tool Palette and click in the empty display area. You can then use a dialog box to select any Sound Designer II or Audio IFF files, which can then appear in the window.

Cubase Audio provides several tools for manipulating its waveform displays. The Arrow tool lets you select a waveform and change its position in time by dragging it to the left or right. The Scissors tool enables you to cut a waveform into segments. With the Snap feature active, the cut-point that you select is automatically shifted, before cutting, to the nearest specified measure subdivision—sort of like a quantize-on-cut feature. The Eraser tool lets you erase a waveform with a single click, and the Mute tool lets you mute one or more waveforms by clicking on them. Muted waveforms appear grayed out to indicate that they're temporarily disabled. To quickly preview parts of a soundfile, the Magnifying Glass tool allows you to click

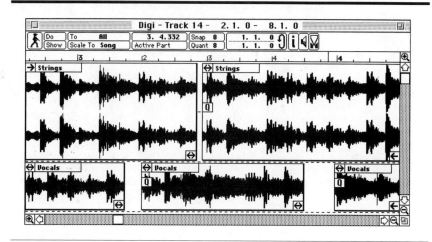

**Figure 14.25**
Waveforms can appear as stereo or mono audio events. Each has a set of arrows to increase or decrease the waveform segment's size.

anywhere on a waveform and begin playback at that point. Finally, the Kick tool lets you bump a waveform forward or backward by a specific amount.

Each waveform appears in its own rectangular box with a name label in the upper-left corner. When you cut a waveform into smaller segments, each new segment also gets its own box and label. Arrows in the upper-left and lower-right corners of the display boxes let you expand and contract the view of each waveform. Double-headed arrows indicate that some of the display is hidden from view. Since you only hear the visible part of each waveform during playback, you can easily adjust the length of each audio section by exposing more or less of the display.

Cubase Audio stresses real-time editing in its design. As a sequence is playing, you can cut, copy, paste, and manipulate the Parts anywhere in the Arrange window. During playback a moving cursor line indicates the current location in the sequence, and the window scrolls to keep up. The Score Edit and Key Edit windows (see Chapter 5) along with the Audio Editor window work the same way. You can make changes in any window while the sequence is playing and hear the results immediately. If you have a large-enough monitor, you can have the Arrange window, the Audio Editor window, and one of the MIDI editing windows all open and all indicating the current sequence position with synchronized moving cursors while simultaneously playing MIDI and audio data.

Cubase Audio is compatible with, but doesn't require, Apple's MIDI Manager. Its many features and unique approach to working with MIDI make it worth considering if you want to add digital audio recordings to your MIDI sequences.

# Digital Performer

Performer, from Mark of the Unicorn, has long been a favorite of composers and electronic-music makers of all kinds. It has continued to enjoy a high degree of success over the past several years because of its long list of features, intuitive user interface, and nice-looking graphics. With the coming of affordable digital audio hardware and growing competition from other companies, it was inevitable that this ever-popular sequencer would join the ranks of MIDI programs offering digital-recording capabilities.

The result of this audio-MIDI coupling is Digital Performer, a sequencing program that retains the look and feel of Performer while adding features that allow direct-to-disk recording and editing. If you're already familiar with Performer, you'll have no trouble adjusting to Digital Performer. The MIDI aspects of both programs are virtually identical, so experienced Performer users can skip most of the documentation and go directly to the additional section covering the digital audio features.

As much as possible, Digital Performer handles audio the same as it handles MIDI. Most of the editing operations use the same Tracks window, Graphic Editing window, and Event List window as before, only now modified to accommodate audio data. Additionally, many of the menu items apply to both MIDI and audio data. For a detailed description of Performer's various windows and MIDI editing features, see Chapter 5.

To use Digital Performer, you'll first have to install an Audiomedia or Sound Tools card in your computer. You'll also need 5 megabytes or more of RAM and a large hard disk with a 20-millisecond access time or less. The program loads and plays Sound Designer, Sound Designer II, and Audio

IFF file formats, but it always generates monaural Sound Designer II files when it records. Digital Performer treats stereo recordings as two mono recordings and does not interleave the channels as does Sound Designer II.

When you first open the program, you're presented with the same Consolidated Controls Panel (Figure 14.26) as in the MIDI-only version of Performer—identical except for the small waveform button in the lower-right corner. The transport controls and the counter display work the same, and you have the same recording options—Regular, Overdub, Punch In, and Auto Record—for audio as for MIDI. If you plan to combine MIDI data with an audio recording, it's important that you use the metronome to provide a reference tempo before recording the audio or you'll have a hard time synchronizing the two. Remember also, that if you change the tempo after recording MIDI and audio, they will no longer play together because tempo changes affect only the start times of audio events and not (as with MIDI) the actual notes that make up the audio data.

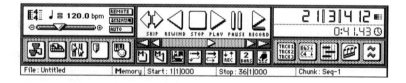

**Figure 14.26** Performer and Digital Performer share nearly identical Consolidated Controls Panels.

To begin recording, you first add an audio track to the Tracks window (Figure 14.27), assign it an input channel number (1 or 2), and record-enable it by clicking in the Record column. The standard recording mode allows you to record a single channel onto a single track. With MultiRecord you can record two channels onto two tracks or simultaneously record MIDI data onto any number of MIDI tracks along with audio on one or more audio tracks.

To help you adjust your input levels, Digital Performer provides the Audio Monitor window (Figure 14.28), which includes two VU-style meters with clipping indicators. Each time you make a recording, the program automatically opens a new file with the default name, Takefile, followed by a channel number and a take number. For example, take 1 of a recording on channel 2 would appear as Takefile 2.1. You can change the Takefile name

**Figure 14.27**
The Tracks window lets you view and edit both audio and MIDI data.

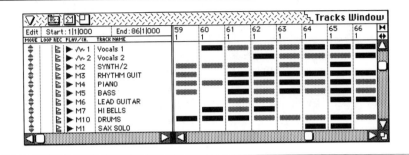

**Figure 14.28**
The Audio Monitor window provides VU-style meters to indicate recording and playback levels.

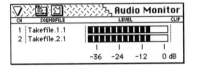

at any time, but in the meantime the automatic naming system provides each recorded pass with a separate label to help you stay organized and to prevent duplicate names. Once you complete your recording, the audio data appears on the appropriate audio track in the Tracks window.

Digital Performer allows you to import soundfiles, regions, and playlists (without crossfades) directly from Sound Designer II or Audiomedia (see Chapter 12). When you open the Soundbites window and select Add Soundbite from the pop-up mini-menu, a dialog box appears that enables you to select from the available soundfiles, regions, and playlists. If you select a playlist to import, all of its corresponding regions appear in the Soundbites window (Figure 14.29) along with the soundfile name.

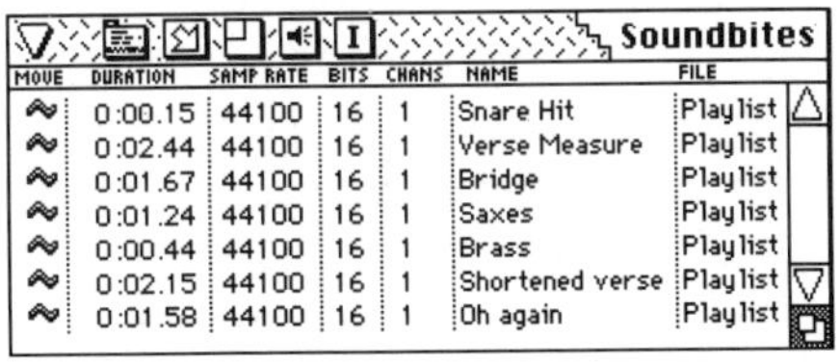

**Figure 14.29**
The Soundbites window lets you view and organize your soundfile regions.

Digital Performer refers to regions as *soundbites* to avoid confusion with its term *regions*, which describes selected areas used for editing MIDI data. Nonetheless, a Sound Designer region and a Digital Performer soundbite are the same thing—a subdivision of a soundfile. A soundbite consists of a beginning and ending location pointer that delineates a specific part of a soundfile for playback. Because it is not the actual audio data itself, you can edit a soundbite nondestructively by using many of the same editing commands that are available for MIDI data, including Cut, Copy, Paste, Erase, Repeat, Merge, Snip, Splice, and Shift.

Each recording that you make also shows up in the Soundbite window, which becomes a kind of catalog of audio data. Every entry in the Soundbite window includes a name, duration, sampling rate, resolution, and audio channel. Several file-management options allow you to sort the soundbites by name, size, or parent soundfile and let you select unused soundbites to delete. The Compact command removes (permanently) the portions of a soundfile that are not part of a soundbite and closes up the gaps between parts to form a single file. This is important if you need to reclaim storage space on your hard disk to continue making recordings.

By clicking on the Play button in the Controls Panel, you can play through all of the soundbites in a playlist. You can also click the Audible Mode button (the small speaker icon) in the Soundbites window. This lets you preview any individual soundbite by simply clicking on its name.

Digital Performer uses the same kind of Event List window (Figure 14.30) for audio data that it uses for MIDI data. Each soundbite appears in the list with its attack (start) time indicated on the left in measures, beats, and ticks. If you prefer, you can change the numbers to read in SMPTE timecode. To the right of the soundbite name, the soundbite velocity and duration appear. As in Studio Vision, "velocity" does not refer to the same parameter that you normally associate with MIDI data. In this case it is the initial volume level that the soundbite will use for playback.

The Event List lets you edit the velocity directly by clicking on the value and typing a new number. To change the duration, on the other hand, you must use Sound Designer II to readjust the region boundaries. You can also assign volume and pan data to each soundbite. Unlike velocity, which only

**Figure 14.30**
Digital Performer uses the same kind of Event List window for audio data that it uses for MIDI data.

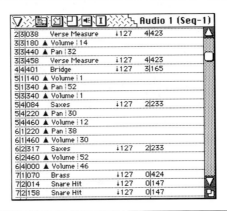

affects the beginning of the soundbite, volume and pan events function like MIDI continuous-controller events (which they aren't) to affect a soundbite while it's playing. You can also construct a panel of sliders and assign them to control the volume and pan parameters for various soundbites just as with MIDI events.

For a better view of your soundbites, Digital Performer provides an audio version of its Graphic Editing window (Figure 14.31). It omits the note grid for MIDI events, but provides a display for viewing soundbites along with velocity, volume, and pan data. When you assemble a playlist and view it in the Graphic Editing window, the waveform appears with the names of the different soundbites under the corresponding places in the display. Although the playlist will usually sound like a continuous recording, the soundbites that form it are contained in separate boxes that you can drag to new locations or delete entirely.

Both the Event List window and the Graphic Editing window share the same Audible Mode button that the Soundbites window has. When in Audible Mode, you can click on any soundbite in the display to audition it separately. The Insert button (I), also in both windows, lets you insert a soundbite wherever you want and also allows you to add volume and pan events individually. If you prefer that your soundbites "snap" to a grid location when you drag them, you must set and activate the Edit Resolution button in the upper-right corner. Otherwise, any audio event that you drag will move smoothly to any location along the display.

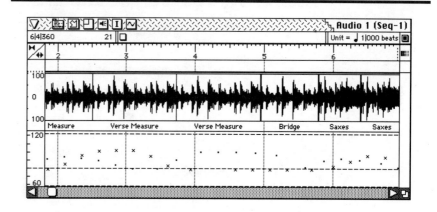

**Figure 14.31**
The Graphic Editing window shows audio data in a waveform display with the names of the individual soundbites beneath it. Volume and pan events appear in a graph-like display below.

If you select a portion of a soundbite, you can separate it from the surrounding waveform with the Split command, or you can choose Trim to eliminate parts outside of the selected area. In either case, Digital Performer automatically finds the nearest zero crossing before making the edit to reduce the possibility of clicks and pops. By option-clicking before you drag a soundbite, you can drag a copy of the soundbite to a new location without changing the position of the original.

As with Studio Vision, Digital Performer offers a Strip Silence function that acts like a noise gate to eliminate low-amplitude sections from a waveform. The Strip Silence dialog box offers parameters for setting the threshold level, attack time, and release time along with an option to activate the zero-crossing function. When you apply Strip Silence to a waveform, Digital Performer labels each of the resulting soundbites with a name that reflects their origins (Figure 14.32). The Soundbites window lets you assign another name to them at any time.

You can use most of Digital Performer's MIDI editing commands with selected audio regions as well. Commands such as Quantize, Change Velocity, Reverse Time, Retrograde, and Scale Time are available for use with soundbites, but you must keep in mind that they apply only to the placement of each audio event as a whole. When you use Quantize with a number of soundbites, only the attack times are affected, not the data within the

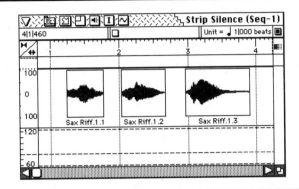

**Figure 14.32**
After applying the Strip Silence command, Digital Performer labels the resulting soundbites.

waveform. Reverse, for instance, will change the order of a group of soundbites, but the audio data within each soundbite will still sound the same.

The program also provides a Mix command that allows you to combine two or more soundbites onto a new track. To prevent the combined waveforms from clipping, the Mix dialog box offers a Normalize option that automatically keeps the amplitude within the optimum range. To apply more extensive editing operations to your waveforms, Digital Performer provides a direct link to Sound Designer II or Audiomedia. When you select a soundbite and choose the Edit in Sound Designer II command, the editing program opens with the soundbite highlighted and ready for editing.

Digital Performer has the ability to synchronize to external devices—such as tape decks and VCRs—that output SMPTE timecode. Combining MIDI with digital audio, however, poses unique synchronization problems because the two types of data respond differently to slight variations in tape speed. To overcome these problems, Digital Performer incorporates a real-time tracking function, which ensures that both audio and MIDI data are continuously synchronized with the incoming timecode—without requiring a tape calibration process or additional external hardware.

Speaking of hardware, Mark of the Unicorn offers its own alternative to Digidesign's Audiomedia and Sound Tools cards. The Digital Waveboard is designed specifically to work with Digital Performer and provides the same

CD-quality sound as the Digidesign products. The Waveboard uses only digital circuits and connections for its inputs and outputs, so you'll need to use the analog-to-digital and digital-to-analog converters in a pro-level DAT recorder, or other external converters, to record and play back your audio. If it's important to you to keep your recordings in the digital domain, this audio NuBus card is worth looking into.

The appearance of Digital Performer in the MIDI marketplace will make many longtime Performer users very happy. It retains the best features of Performer while integrating direct-to-disk recording into an audio-MIDI package with considerable appeal. For a good number of musicians and postproduction professionals, this should provide the intuitive yet effective work environment that they want.

## Final Thoughts

The products covered in this chapter all approach the task of combining MIDI with digital audio from different perspectives. This is good news for multimedia producers because it means that you can choose a program with the right balance of MIDI and audio features.

Audio Trax is the least expensive of this chapter's products, and it's also the only one that doesn't require additional hardware to use. Deck is the only one that combines true multitrack digital recording, mixing, and processing, but it emphasizes digital audio at the expense of its MIDI capabilities. Studio Vision, Cubase Audio, and Digital Performer all start with sophisticated high-end sequencers and add two-channel direct-to-disk recording to the package. Each of these products has a definite niche in the audio marketplace, and each should appeal to users with the right combination of needs.

# Chapter 15

# Adding Sound to Desktop Presentations

*I*f you're interested in producing multimedia presentations on the Macintosh, you should spend some time seriously considering the role that music and sound will play in your productions. Since music and sound always take place in time, they have the magical ability to imbue a program with a sense of immediacy and presence that more static elements lack. And since movies and other forms of animation also take place in time, the natural combination of the two can produce the proverbial marriage-made-in-heaven.

But getting this couple to the altar is another story altogether. Producing a finished product that appears organic and seamless can be a frustrating experience if you find yourself working with a program that doesn't allow for the kind of sound implementation that you need.

This chapter discusses most of the current crop of System 7-compatible animation and multimedia programs, with regard to how they incorporate music and sound into their presentations. The list is long and the range is wide, so it's likely that somewhere in this burgeoning field there's a program that's right for you.

# HyperCard

It's hard to imagine a Macintosh user who hasn't spent at least some time exploring this multifaceted program. Certainly one of the reasons for its widespread, lasting popularity is that HyperCard (Claris Corp.) is a truly universal vehicle for capturing, storing, finding, and presenting information of any kind. In other words, it's multimedia for the man on the street—accessible and adaptable. But HyperCard's power and versatility have also propelled it into the realm of professional artists and presenters, giving it a range of applications unparalleled by other products. The success of Hyper-Card can be largely attributed to its three main features: a structure based on a common, intuitive metaphor, a full-featured, integrated paint program for graphics, and a built-in, comprehensible programming language.

HyperCard stores and presents its information on *cards,* the electronic equivalent of the paper index cards in a library card catalog. Cards are grouped into *stacks,* which are usually, but not always, based on a common theme. Each stack is a separate file that appears in the Finder as a Hyper-Card icon. Stacks function much like index drawers or boxes filled with cards that cover a particular subject. When you reach the last card in a file, you automatically return to the first card, so a closer analogy might be that of a rotary card file where an endless loop of information is available and you can move in either direction to explore it.

HyperCard, however, does not limit you to only moving in two directions. Most cards have *buttons* that provide a *link* to other cards or other stacks, so the structure of a stack can be as simple or as complex as necessary to interactively supply you with the information that you seek. You might for example create an address-book stack and an appointment-book stack like the samples included with the program (Figure 15.1). With buttons to link the two, you can look up a person's name and address and with the click of a button, see your next appointment with that person. Or you can look up an appointment and see where you have to be that day. This is only a very simple example. More elaborate stacks can take you in many different directions, creating an interactive environment of text, graphics, animation, and sound.

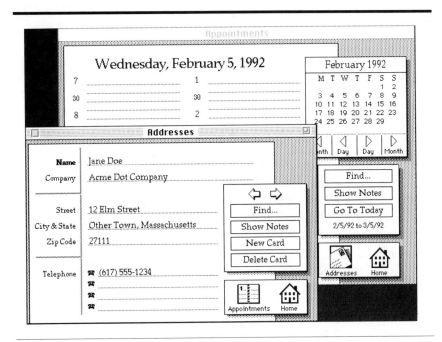

**Figure 15.1**
These two cards from different stacks have buttons that link the stacks together, allowing you to jump from one type of information to another.

## HyperTalk and Sound

To control all its features and interactions, HyperCard provides its own programming language, HyperTalk, which uses common English words to create short command sequences called *scripts*. HyperCard scripts contain the instructions that tell the different parts of a stack what to do and how to do it. Calculations, message displays, button actions, animation events, and sound are all controlled by their corresponding scripts.

HyperCard can produce two types of sounds directly from the computer. The first is the familiar Macintosh system beep, used mainly to call attention to something like a dialog box or an alert message. Although you can specify the number of times it sounds, the beep tone (or whatever Control Panel sound is assigned to replace it) only plays at one pitch and you can't change its length. If you're trying to add a tune to your HyperCard stack, the Beep command is not the way to do it. The second type of sound is much more exciting. HyperCard can play back digitized soundfiles through the Macintosh speaker (or audio output jack) at any specified pitch and tempo.

To get these sounds, you must first record them with an audio digitizer, such as MacRecorder or Voice Impact Pro (see Chapter 11). The products include software that converts the recording into a Macintosh resource file that you can add to any HyperCard stack with a resource mover utility. By using the Play command, you can play back the sound at any tempo, pitch, and rhythm, making it possible to compose a simple melody that appears at specific places in your stack. It's helpful if you have some basic understanding of musical notation because the sound parameters that you set in HyperTalk are expressed in common musical terms.

HyperCard comes with three sounds already installed: Harpsichord, Boing, and Flute. You can use the Play command with any other sounds installed as resources so long as the name attached to the resource file matches exactly the name that you use for your HyperTalk script. If you choose not to specify a tempo value, HyperCard will default to a tempo of 200 or will retain the last tempo entry until the next Play command or specified tempo.

Next you indicate the pitches that you want by specifying the names of the notes using letters: a, b, c, d, etc., and r for rest. To add chromatic scale degrees, you follow a letter with a sharp (#) or flat (b). Additionally, you need to indicate the octave that the notes will occur in. If you don't include an octave value in the Play command script, HyperCard defaults to an octave value of 4—the octave starting at middle C. When you include an octave number with a note, that octave applies to all subsequent notes in the command line until another value appears. If you prefer, you can use note numbers to indicate pitches. In that case, middle C equals note number 60, C# equals 61, D equals 62, etc. This eliminates the need for including accidental and octave parameters.

Finally, you must specify the durations of the notes by using single letters. HyperTalk allows any of the following durations: whole note (w), half note (h), quarter note (q), eighth note (e), sixteenth note (s), thirty-second note (t), and sixty-fourth note (x). To indicate a dotted note, type a period after the note's duration value (e.g., dotted quarter = q.). To indicate a triplet, add a 3 after the duration. A typical HyperTalk note entry would look like a#5e or eb4q.

To create a melody, simply type in a script that begins with the Play command followed by the name of the sound, then the tempo, and finally a string of note letters with the appropriate octave and duration values. As with octave numbers, duration values apply to all subsequent notes until a new value appears. In some cases you may want to play a sound only at its original pitch, such as when you're using sound effects or a person's voice. In these cases, simply enter the Play command and the name of the sound without any other parameters.

For HyperCard to play a melody (or any other kind of sound for that matter), it must first load the resource sound into memory. This means that there must be enough available RAM to load the sound completely before playback or you may lose part of it. Also, large resource sounds take time to load, so there may be a brief delay before playback starts the first time you load the sound into HyperCard. If you have enough RAM, HyperCard can retain the sound in memory and subsequent playback will begin without a pause. In some cases you might want to have a very large sound resource load when the stack first opens so it will be available in RAM when needed. Because it's the sound itself that demands the memory and loading time, once it's in RAM the computer can trigger different notes with very little effort.

If you don't want the music to continue after a person leaves the current card, you can include the Play Stop command in your HyperTalk script. If, on the other hand, you want the music to finish before the rest of the script continues, you can use a special version of the Wait command.

## *External Commands and Functions*

HyperTalk consists of a large vocabulary designed to meet the needs of most users under most circumstances. But there are times when special needs arise that require HyperTalk to perform tasks that exceed its usual capabilities. For these situations, HyperCard includes the ability to attach *external commands* (XCMDs) and *external functions* (XFCNs) to its stacks by using a resource editor like ResEdit. XCMDs and XFCNs are executable code resources written in one of several Macintosh programming languages, such as Pascal, C, or 68000 assembly language. They act as special-purpose code modules that allow HyperTalk to extend its range of influence to include such things as serial port input and output routines, and the ability to control external devices, such as videodisc players, MIDI instruments, and CD-ROM drives. XCMDs and XFCNs are available from a number of user groups, online services, and commercial developers.

With its external commands, HyperCard provides the opportunity to produce interactive multimedia presentations that include large amounts of CD-quality audio without the need to include massive storage within the computer. Combining MIDI with HyperCard also offers great potential for adding high-fidelity sound to presentations, again without heavy storage demands. For more on HyperCard and MIDI, see Chapter 8.

## MacroMind Director

MacroMind Director is unquestionably one of the most powerful, versatile, and fully implemented products currently available for creating animations, presentations, and interactive multimedia on the Macintosh. Its animated sequences have appeared in films and on television, and in corporate offices, schools, and retail outlets. They have also made frequent appearances in other programs, like HyperCard.

Director's popularity results mainly from its integration of three important elements: its sophisticated graphics program, its effective animation features, and its ability to incorporate a variety of different kinds of sounds into its presentations. To further extend its capabilities, Director includes its own HyperTalk-like programming language, Lingo, that enables you to create fully interactive multimedia presentations.

MacroMind Director consists of two distinct but interrelated parts: Overview and Studio. In the Studio part, you can produce high-quality animated scenes called *movies*. These movies can consist of not only animation but text, imported graphics, and sound as well. In the Overview part, you can create multimedia slide shows, which can include graphics, animated text, visual transitions, Director movies, and sound.

## Overview

To create an Overview presentation, you first open the Overview window (Figure 15.2), which includes an icon bar across the top. The icons represent the different kinds of documents and effects that you can use to compose your presentation. The document types are (from left to right) MacPaint, PICT, Glue, MacroMind Director movie, MacroMind Accelerator movie, Auto Animate, sound, timer, transition, and Overview document.

**Figure 15.2**
The Overview window lets you create presentations by linking together different kinds of icons.

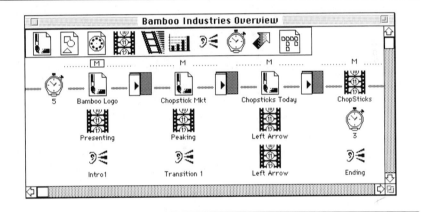

You produce an Overview presentation by dragging document and effects icons into the working area of the window, where they become linked automatically into a sequence. Each element in the sequence, called a *slide*, plays in order from left to right, creating an animated "slide show." It's important to remember that slides are not simply single-image documents. They can include sounds, movies from the Studio part of Director, and graphics from other programs, all tied together in the Overview window by a variety of special transitions (wipes, dissolves, reveals, etc.) and timer settings.

By dragging an icon below another icon in the Overview window, you can create a *compound slide*, which plays two or more elements at the same time.

In this way you can have sound play when a visual element appears in the sequence. Compound slides offer great potential for creating complex events. You might, for instance, have a graphic background appear with an animated sequence superimposed on it while a musical passage plays along.

Overview documents don't actually contain all of the pictures and sounds that make up a presentation. The Overview document is simply a list of other documents along with information concerning such things as their order, timing, and transitions. For this reason, Overview documents don't require much disk space, but they must know the locations of the other, related documents to find them when needed.

## *Sound in Overview*

MacroMind Director includes a large selection of sounds in its Sounds file. To add sound to an Overview presentation, you just drag a sound icon from the icon bar and position it under one of the slides in the window. You then assign it one of the sounds from the pull-down Sound menu (Figure 15.3) by dragging through the list until you find a suitable choice. The name under the sound icon then changes to reflect your selection.

The amount of time that a slide remains on screen depends on the setting of the timer effect, which is represented by the stopwatch icon. If you display a slide for less time than it takes for the assigned sound to play, the sound will be cut off. To solve this, you need to include a timer that's set to a time long enough to accommodate the sound effects or music.

MacroMind Director movies created in the Studio can include their own sounds. If you use one of these movies as a slide in the Overview window, you won't see a separate sound icon. The Overview window allows you to play only one sound in each slide column. If you add a sound to a column that includes a Director movie with its own sound, Overview will play only the topmost sound in the column.

You can record your own soundfiles with MacRecorder or Voice Impact Pro to extend your range of choices, and you can add sounds to the Sound menu by using the Sounds Utility that comes with Director.

# Adding Sound to Desktop Presentations

**Figure 15.3**
The Sound menu offers a good selection of sound effects and music for your presentations.

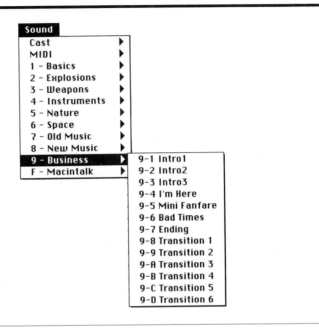

## Studio

The Studio part of MacroMind Director is where you create your animation. You can show these movies directly from Studio, or you can add them to any Overview document as part of a presentation. You can also distribute your animations by using the MacroMind Player that comes with Director.

Although there are 11 different windows in Studio to produce your animation, you only need 4 of them to create simple animated sequences. The Paint window provides the tools for drawing and editing your artwork. Its list of features rivals many standalone programs. You can create your artwork from scratch using the Paint window, or you can import your art from a variety of other sources, such as paint programs, draw programs, 3-D modeling applications, digitizers, and Scrapbook files.

When you create or import artwork, Studio automatically stores it in the Cast window (Figure 15.4). The Cast window holds your collection of art, sound, and color with each *castmember* appearing in a small numbered box.

To produce an animated sequence, you drag the castmembers onto the Stage window, which lets you view the animation one frame at a time. Studio also provides a feature that automatically places a series of castmembers into a sequence of movie frames.

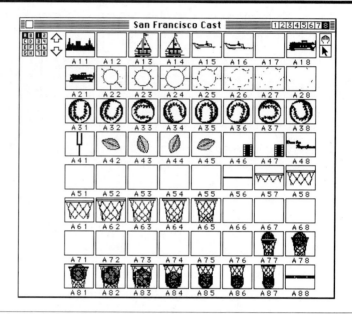

**Figure 15.4**
The Cast window holds the collection of castmembers that you use to create your animated sequence.

It's important to keep in mind that Director uses essentially the same animation techniques that traditional animators have used for years. A number of images, each with a slightly different shape or position, are assigned to individual frames and played back in succession, flip-book style. The images in each frame can be composed of several different bits of artwork, with each overlaying the other to form a composite image—for example, foreground, moving figure, moving background, and static background.

To gain a better perspective on your movie and to keep track of which castmembers appear in which frames, Studio provides the Score window (Figure 15.5). The Score helps you visualize the interrelationships of these components by displaying them on a grid that shows elapsed time in frames along the top. Each individual element, called a *cell*, appears in a small box

## Adding Sound to Desktop Presentations 291

in one of the 24 horizontal rows called *channels*. A vertical column of cells represents one frame, or in other words, everything you see on the Stage when you stop or pause a movie.

At the top of the Score window, above the 24 numbered animation channels, there are 5 channels dedicated to special effects. These are, from top to bottom, tempo, color palette, visual transitions, and two channels for sound. The sixth channel stores scripts created using Lingo.

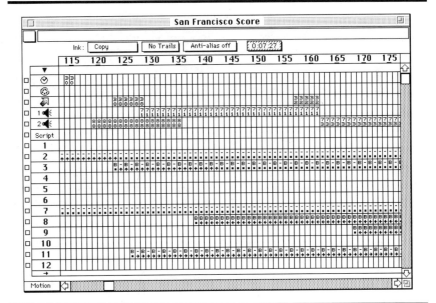

**Figure 15.5**
The Score window provides an overview of your presentation showing how the different components interrelate.

## Sound in Studio

You can add sounds to Studio in two ways. One way is to import sounds directly to the Cast window by using the Import command on the File menu. These are called *internal* sounds, and they always remain with the movie that they were imported to. You can also add sounds from the MacroMind Director Sounds file. If the available sounds aren't appropriate to your needs, you can always add others with the Sounds Utility. Sounds drawn from the Sounds file are called *external* sounds, and the file that contains them must reside in the same folder as Director or the current movie to appear on the Sound menu.

You can only use an internal sound in one movie. If you need to use that sound again somewhere else, you'll have to copy it and import it to the other movie's Cast window. In contrast, you can use external sounds in any of your movies as long as the file is in the right folder. Because digitized soundfiles are frequently large, using external sounds in a number of movies can save you considerable disk space.

To add sound to your movie, you first open the Score window and select one or more cells, in sound channel 1 or 2, by dragging across them. The highlighted cells correspond to the sequence of frames that your music or sound effects will appear with. When you choose a sound from the Sound menu, it is automatically pasted into the selected cells along with an identification number that corresponds to the sound's number in the menu.

In most cases, you'll need to assign several cells to a sound in order for it to play all the way through. If you find that part of your music, for instance, is getting cut off, you'll have to add more cells or change the tempo setting in the Tempo channel. Tempos can help you synchronize the sounds with the animation by changing the animation speed. This doesn't directly affect the sound, but it can make a specific number of frames take longer to run. A ten-frame sound that doesn't work at one tempo might work fine at another.

With its two sound channels, Director allows you to play two different sounds simultaneously. This enables you to combine sound effects with music or add background music to narration. To use the second sound channel, however, you must have a Macintosh that can output two-channel sound. You'll also need System 6.0.7 or higher or the second sound channel will appear grayed out in the Score window.

For some sound effects (such as the sound of a bouncing ball), you might want to have a sound repeat several times. To accomplish this, you must retrigger the sound by adding a blank cell before the beginning of each repetition. Be sure to allow enough cells for the sound to finish each time. You can cut, copy, paste, and clear sounds the same as with all other Score window notations. You can also use Lingo to control the volume of a sound with fade-in, fade-out, and set-volume commands.

## Music with MIDI

If you have a MIDI system hooked up to your computer, you can trigger MIDI events or sequences at specific places in your animation. Choosing MIDI from the Sound menu opens a submenu with six commands that you can use to control a sequencer. You can set a beat, song pointer, and song-select number or choose to start, continue, or stop a sequence.

There are several possible configurations for using MIDI with Director. Drum machines and some synthesizers have on-board sequencers that, although seriously limited, will work with Director as long as you can set them to wait for an external signal. A better choice would be to use one of the sequencing programs described in Chapters 5 and 6. In this case you'll have to use MultiFinder and Apple's MIDI Manager so you can run both programs at once. The most expensive solution, although perhaps the best in terms of data processing, is to add a second computer and MIDI interface to the system. Then the second computer can handle all of the MIDI responsibilities, while the main computer deals with the animation.

To add external MIDI control to an animation, you first select an appropriate cell in one of the sound channels in the Score window. From the MIDI category in the Sound menu, choose Set Beat and use the dialog box to assign a tempo to your sequence. Then select a cell immediately to the right of the beat cell and choose Start from the MIDI submenu. Finally, determine where you want the sequence to end, select a cell, and choose Stop.

For the music to play correctly, you must load the sequence into your sequencer and set it to receive an external trigger. When you return to Director and play the movie, the sequence should begin at the appropriate frame and continue until the animation reaches the Stop command. To play back a sequence from a place other than the beginning, you use the Song Pointer command to assign a measure and beat for the music to begin on. In this case, you use the Continue command instead of Start to indicate that you're beginning in the middle of the sequence. You can also use the Song Select command with drum machines and external sequencers that allow you to specify a sequence by number.

## MacinTalk

In some cases, you might want to generate speech using MacinTalk rather than digitized soundfiles. MacinTalk, which must be in the System folder to work, synthesizes speech based on what you type phonetically into the Text window. Each line in the Text window has a corresponding number that appears in the MacinTalk submenu. You can assign a statement to any frame by selecting a cell and choosing the desired text. Because MacinTalk uses a lot of processing to synthesize its speech, it may interfere with the playback of your movie when the computer speaks. It's therefore best to add MacinTalk speech where the animation has paused momentarily.

## HyperCard and Lingo

If you're working with HyperCard, you may decide to use a sound from a HyperCard stack in one of your movies. With MacroMind Director you can import SND sound resource files. Unlike soundfiles in other formats, however, sound resources don't appear with an icon on the desktop. To see the sound, you must click Resource in the Import dialog box, where it will appear in a list so that you can import it for use in a movie. You can also add a sound from Director to a HyperCard Home card or stack. Once installed, HyperCard doesn't need the Sounds file from Director to play the sound.

MacroMind Director includes its own versatile scripting language called Lingo, which can use compiled code modules called XObjects (external objects) to control external hardware devices. Director comes with several ready-to-use XObjects, including one—the AppleAudioCD XObject—that lets you play audio CD music from an Apple (or Apple-compatible) CD-ROM player.

Playing music from a CD player has an important advantage beyond the higher audio quality. Since the external device is independent of the Macintosh's normal processing, you can play continuous sound even while movies are loading into memory—something not possible with sounds played from the Sound channels. In fact, you can play back sampled sounds from the two Sound channels and from the CD-ROM player simultaneously if you want. With Lingo you can also use a large number of available Hyper-Card XCMDs and XFCNs to further extend Director's capabilities.

# MediaMaker

MediaMaker grew out of a collaborative effort between the BBC in London and Apple Computer. In 1988, two teams that were exploring the common ground between television and computers joined forces to develop a software tool that would allow people to harness the impact and effectiveness of television in a direct, creative way that anyone could apply. The result of the effort was a program called the Sequence Editor. A few years later, MacroMind entered into a partnership with the group that developed the Sequence Editor and MediaMaker was born.

With MediaMaker you can choose from a variety of media elements and quickly assemble them into presentations incorporating many different kinds of images and sounds. MediaMaker lets you create presentations from graphic and audio files stored on your Macintosh, or you can use external devices such as videotape recorders, compact disc players, and videodisc players to create elaborate multimedia productions that you can show on your computer or transfer to videotape.

## *Overall Structure*

MediaMaker refers to a piece of media information as an *element*. To create a presentation, you can combine any of six types of elements: animated sequences (such as MacroMind Director movies), videotape segments, clips from videodiscs, graphic files (such as PICT images), compact disc selections, and digitized sounds. To keep track of all these multimedia elements, MediaMaker uses visual objects called *picons* (picture icons). You can move picons around the screen as if they were documents in the Finder. You can also arrange and organize picons by selecting them individually or in groups and dragging them to other windows to make copies. You create picons in a Collection window (Figure 15.6)—a sort of multimedia library for organizing and saving picons for use in your presentations. Each picon has a *micon* (miniature icon) in its upper-left corner to identify the type of file that it represents.

To begin producing your presentation, you must first assemble a collection that contains all of the elements that you'll need to use. If you want, you can arrange the picons in the Collection window and play them back one after another by clicking on them. In most cases, however, you'll want to assemble the picons into a self-running, audiovisual presentation called a *sequence*.

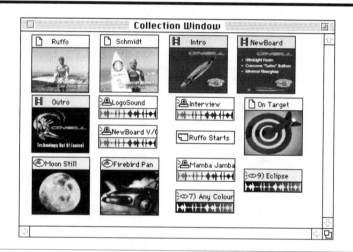

**Figure 15.6**
MediaMaker's Collection window acts as a library for organizing and saving media elements.

The Sequence window (Figure 15.7) contains separate tracks where you can arrange your multimedia elements along a horizontal *timeline* so that more than one picon can play at once and all of the elements can exist in proper relationship to one another. The width of each picon along the timeline represents the duration of that element. You can drag a picon to the right or left to change its start time, and you can extend and contract its borders to change its duration.

All of the picons that make up a sequence are dragged into the Sequence window from a Collection window. After first opening a new Collection window, you use the Elements menu to choose an appropriate element type, such as

**Figure 15.7**
The Sequence window contains separate tracks for arranging multimedia elements along a timeline.

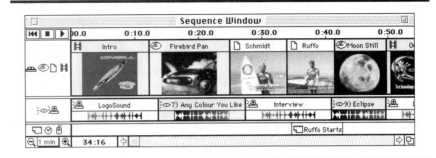

the Mac-based elements—Graphic, Animation, and Mac Sound. For Graphic and Animation, this produces a dialog box that offers a list of the available files. When you select a file, an editor window opens that provides information specific to that picon and lets you name it and set its time-related parameters. Transport controls at the bottom of the window allow you to play back the picon to preview it.

Sound picons are all assigned the same waveform image as an icon. For graphic-based picons, you can capture any frame or selected area from an element's file to represent it. If at a later time you want to change a picon's parameters (or picture), you can double-click on the picon's title bar to reopen its editor window.

## Mac-Based Sounds

If you choose Mac Sound from the Elements menu, the Mac Sound Editor window (Figure 15.8) opens immediately, providing you with the opportunity to record a new sound. If you choose not to, clicking the Source field lets you open any soundfile or sound resource on your hard disk from the dialog box that appears. The Editor window for the selected soundfile shows the name of the file at the top, next to the Mac Sound picon image. In the center of the window, two fields display the end time and duration of the sound along with arrows for adjusting them.

Mac Sounds always start from the beginning of the soundfile; the start point cannot be changed. You can make the end time earlier, which will

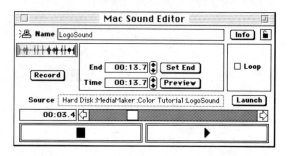

**Figure 15.8**
The Mac Sound Editor window lets you record new sounds or import soundfiles from your hard disk.

produce a corresponding change in the duration field. In the Sequence window, you can stretch or contract a Mac Sound picon to change its duration, but you can't stretch it past the actual duration as set in the Mac Sound Editor window.

The best way to adjust the end point and duration of a soundfile is by playing the sound and clicking the Stop button when you reach the appropriate place. Then you can use the Set End button to transfer the current setting (as shown in the counter next to the scroll bar) to the End field. The Time field will change automatically to reflect the new setting. Clicking the Preview button lets you hear your settings, and the up/down arrows enable you to fine-tune the numbers.

The Mac Sound Editor includes a looping function that lets you loop a sound from its assigned end point back to its beginning as many times as you want. By clicking the Preview button with the Loop box checked, a sound will play from beginning to end, looping continually until you reach the specified duration time. MediaMaker can use sounds stored as SoundEdit files, AIFF, and AIFF-C soundfiles. You can also import SND sound resources from HyperCard stacks, games, and other applications.

Additionally, the Mac Sound Editor lets you record your own sounds directly from the window if you have an external digitizer, like MacRecorder, or one of the Macintosh models with its own microphone, like the LC or IIsi. When you click the Record button, it opens the recording and playback dialog box appropriate to the driver that you're using. After you finish and save your recording, MediaMaker loads it into the Mac Sound Editor, where you can view and edit its parameters. You can also launch the sound-editing application of your choice from the Editor window by assigning it ahead of time in the Preferences dialog box. This enables you to do extensive editing of your soundfiles, at any time, by clicking the Launch button on the right side of the window. After returning from the editing program with your edited soundfile, you can click the Preview button to remove the old version of the sound from RAM and replace it with the new version.

## *External Sounds*

In addition to the three Mac-based elements listed on the Elements menu, MediaMaker offers three additional elements derived from external devices: Videotape, Videodisc, and CD Audio. The program controls these devices with software modules called XObjects (external objects). In the Preferences dialog box (Figure 15.9), you must first specify which hardware devices you have and where they're connected. MediaMaker allows you to connect a CD-ROM drive to the SCSI port. After installing the proper drivers and XObjects in the System folder, you can create picons from external sources just as with Mac-based sources.

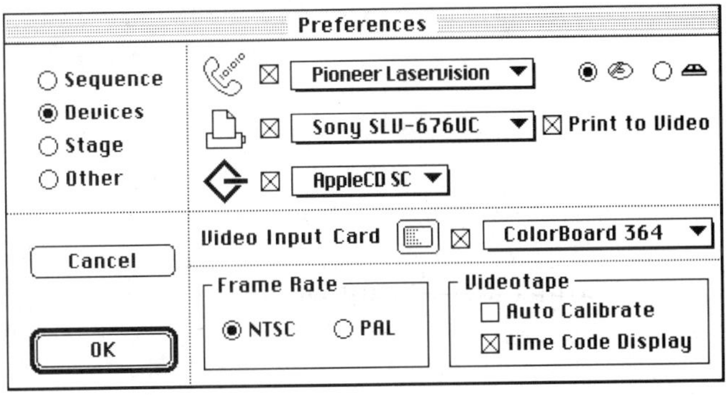

**Figure 15.9**
The Preferences dialog box lets you specify which external devices you have connected to your Macintosh.

The CD Audio Editor window (Figure 15.10) differs in several ways from the Mac Sound Editor window, although they share a number of features. The two speaker icons on the right let you select either or both of the two output channels on the CD player. The Loop function is essentially the same as described above except that with CD audio you can specify both a start time and an end time for the looped section. In some cases, there may be a slight gap when the CD jumps from loop end to loop start, so it's important to preview the sound first to see if it will work in a given situation.

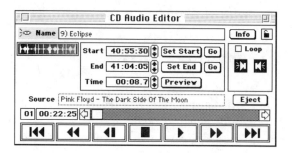

**Figure 15.10**
The CD Audio Editor window provides a full set of transport controls and several fields for setting parameters.

The CD Audio Editor window also provides a complete set of transport controls to help you locate and define segments of sound. On the far left of the scroll bar, the current track is displayed in the Track Counter box. Next to that the Frame Counter shows you the current location in minutes, seconds, and CD frames (75 CD frames per second). Once you've set all the parameters for a CD audio picon, you can save it in a Collection window, where it appears with a small disc icon in its title bar.

From there you can copy it into a Sequence window and drag it along the timeline to the appropriate point in the presentation. Moving the left or right edge of the picon adjusts its start or end time, but you must be careful not to lose track of your original settings in case you change your mind. If you choose the Separate CD option in the Preferences dialog box, you can display Mac-based audio and CD audio on separate tracks in the Sequence window. This allows you to synchronize Macintosh digitized sounds with a CD recording if, for example, you want to combine sound effects and music or music and narration.

Since videodiscs also include audio tracks, the Videodisc Editor includes two speaker icons so that you can mute one or both audio channels depending on your needs. Animation from sources such as MacroMind Director movies may also include their own sound. The Animation Editor window provides a speaker button to toggle the audio on or off. With the audio turned on, the sound attached to the animation will take precedence over the audio from a Mac Sound picon. If you turn off the animation's sound, you can play the Mac Sound audio file while the animation runs.

## *Getting in Sync*

Although the Sequence window allows you to place picons in precise locations along its timeline, the process of synchronizing audio and visuals is not an exact science. Sounds always play at the same speed, but animation can vary in speed depending on the processing power of your computer and how busy it is at the moment. If you play an animation alone, the sequence will play as fast as your computer's processor will allow. But if you play an animation along with a Macintosh soundfile, the animation may go slower because of the additional work being done. If you begin a sound after an animation has started, the animation may slow down during the audio playback.

The best way to arrive at the proper synchronization is to apply what MacroMind describes as the process of "successive approximation." In other words, you should place the picons in their approximate locations, replay the sequence, and fine-tune the positions of the picons relative to one another. Playing longer sections of the sequence each time you make your adjustments will yield more accurate results.

File loading times are another possible source of synchronization problems. If you produce a sequence built entirely on Macintosh-based elements, there may be occasional pauses when the computer tries to load one picon while playing another. Load times vary according to the processing power of your Macintosh, the size of the file involved, and the access speed of your hard disk. Combining visuals with audio can become tricky because MediaMaker will continue to play the audio tracks while it searches for and loads the corresponding visual picon. To avoid losing the synchronization of sound and visuals, you can activate the Pause for Search function in the Preferences dialog box. This causes all of the picons to wait momentarily while MediaMaker finds and loads the next picons in the sequence. The best approach is to experiment with different picon locations to arrive at a sequence configuration that works in a fluid and cohesive manner.

# Adobe Premiere

Adobe Premiere is part of the vanguard of new multimedia programs that are designed to work with Apple's QuickTime software. By using the 32-bit addressing capability of System 7, it allows you to access more than 8 megabytes of RAM, so you can manipulate large files in the computer's memory without having to continually transfer data to and from your hard disk. You can play your finished digital movie from Adobe Premiere or from within any application that supports the QuickTime format. If you prefer, you can also transfer your presentation to videotape for a more universal format.

With Adobe Premiere you assemble your movie from a variety of source material called *clips,* which can include captured video from VCRs or cameras, animations, scanned images or slides, QuickTime movies, and digitized soundfiles. The program accepts source material in seven different file formats: movies in QuickTime format, animation in PICS format, still images in the PICT and Adobe Photoshop formats, and audio in the SoundEdit, Audio IFF, and SND sound resource formats.

You can use sounds saved in the SND resource format as long as the file's creator type is "sfil." Some programs, like MacRecorder's SoundEdit, save SND resource sounds with different creator types. You can use these sounds with Adobe Premiere, but you must first change the creator type by using a program such as DiskTop. Additionally, Adobe Premiere supports only 3:1 and 6:1 compression ratios.

The first step in creating a movie is to gather together your source material by importing the various files into a Project window (Figure 15.11). The Project window acts as a reservoir of available clips for use in assembling your movie. Within the window, each clip is identified with a *thumbnail*—a rough indication of the contents of a clip using one or more frames. In the case of audio clips, the thumbnail consists of a miniature representation of a part of the soundfile's waveform.

Next to the thumbnail, each clip includes a description that provides such information as the type of clip (Movie, Still image, Background Matte, Animation, or Audio) and its duration. Audio clips include the sampling rate (5, 11, or 22 kHz), the resolution, and whether the soundfile is stereo or mono. In the third column, there are spaces to add comments for each clip.

**Figure 15.11**
The Project window shows each clip with a thumbnail picture and a description.

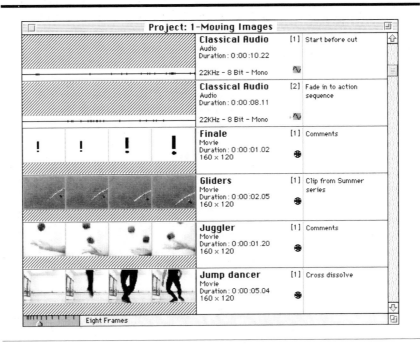

When you import movie and audio clips into the Project window, they play, by default, from beginning to end as they were originally recorded. Before you use each clip, therefore, you must edit its beginning (In) and ending (Out) points to designate the part of the clip that you want to use and to establish its duration. Double-clicking the thumbnail area of a clip opens its Clip window (Figure 15.12), which contains transport controls for playing the file, a counter display for locating specific frames, a duration display, and a viewing area for previewing the edited clip.

In the case of audio clips, the viewing area shows the soundfile waveform. Just above the counter display, a frame indicator uses two short vertical lines to show the length of a single frame ($1/30$ second) as a reference guide. To set the In and Out points for your audio clip, you can scroll through the waveform by using the slider in the lower-left corner, or you can simply play the soundfile until you reach the appropriate place and click the In button. This places a flag at the specified point in the waveform, and you can then use the same procedure for setting the Out marker. If the positions are a little off, you can fine-tune them at any time.

**Figure 15.12**
The Clip window provides controls and buttons for viewing and editing each clip.

Once you've organized your clips in the Project window and edited them with their Clip windows, you can begin to assemble your movie in the Construction window (Figure 15.13). The Construction window displays the clips in seven tracks along a horizontal *time ruler*. The tracks include two Video tracks for movie and still image clips, one Special Effects track for transitions, one Superimpose track for overlaying movie and still images, and three Audio tracks for playing digitized soundfiles.

To assemble your movie, you simply drag each clip from the Project window into the Construction window and place it in the proper track at the appropriate location along the time ruler. The program will then play all of

**Figure 15.13**
The Construction window displays the clips in different tracks along a time ruler.

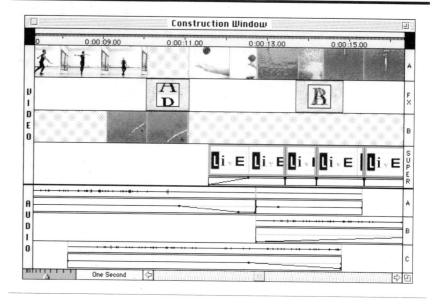

the clips in order from left to right. You can move clips around to change their start times and relationships to one another. You can also lengthen or shorten each clip's playing time by dragging on its border. This produces the same effect as changing the In and Out points in the Clip window.

Adobe Premiere lets you have up to three audio tracks playing simultaneously, and you can mix the tracks by independently adjusting the volume level of each clip. When you drag an Audio clip into the Construction window, its waveform appears in a long narrow box over a second box containing a horizontal line. This second box is called the Audio Fade control, and the line represents the volume level of the waveform.

The volume defaults to a straight, midlevel setting, but you can change the setting anywhere along the waveform. When you move the cursor into the Audio Fade control, it turns into a finger pointer. Clicking on the line adds a handle that you can use to drag the line up or down. When a handle is at the bottom of the Audio Fade control, the clip is inaudible. When it's at the top, the volume is doubled. You can add as many handles as you want to create ascending and descending lines that act like amplitude envelopes to shape and blend your audio tracks.

To add some variety to your soundtrack, Adobe Premiere provides two "filters" that you can apply to your Audio clips. These are actually not filters but would more appropriately be called effects. The Backwards filter plays the soundfile backward, and the Echo filter lets you create a number of echo effects.

The clips in Adobe Premiere are not the actual source files stored on your hard drive. They simply contain pointers to the original files. When you combine and edit your clips, you are working exclusively with these pointers and the source files are left intact. To turn your project into a QuickTime movie, you must choose Make Movie from the Project menu. The program then compiles the clips into a new file that Adobe Premiere and other QuickTime-compatible applications can play. At this point you can print your movie to video for presenting it away from the computer. The new movie file can also become a clip in another Adobe Premiere project, allowing you to assemble a larger work by first creating smaller segments.

# Animation Works

Animation Works, from Gold Disk Inc., is designed to bring the power and impact of animation within the reach of a wide group of users who may or may not have previous experience with this art form. Although the program takes a traditional approach to creating animations, it includes a number of features that allow the computer to handle many of the more tedious aspects of animating. This provides a direct, interactive quality that makes the creative process more fun and less time-consuming.

Animation Works uses the same three-step process that noncomputer animators have used for years. First you create the characters, or actors, which are drawn as a series of incremental images called *cels*. Then you create the backgrounds that form the backdrop for the different scenes in your movie. The final stage involves combining the actors and the backgrounds into a completed animation consisting of a series of frames.

To develop each of these three stages, Animation Works provides three editing environments. The Background Editor offers a full-featured color paint program that can import Scrapbook and PICT files and export Scrapbook, PICT, and PICS files. The Cel Editor enables you to create cels and group them into actors. The Movie Editor, the heart of the program, allows you to view and edit your actors and establish their movements and interrelationships.

Each frame in Animation Works consists of one or more actors in front of a background. The actors move along *paths*, which are straight or curved lines representing the position of each actor through a series of frames. An actor walking across the screen from left to right, for instance, would have a path consisting of a straight line.

The program lets you specify how many frames the completed action will take. If the sequence takes 20 frames, the path line will appear on screen with 20 points on it representing the actor's position in each frame. Using fewer frames produces faster movement; to slow down an actor, you simply add more frames. The Movie Editor automatically creates the assigned number of frames, adds the background, and cycles through the character's cels, placing each in a slightly different position along the path to simulate motion.

# Adding Sound to Desktop Presentations

The Movie Editor actually consists of four different movable windows (Figure 15.14). On the left, the Tool palette provides the tools for creating and editing paths. On the right, the Actor window lets you view the individual actors and preview their motions. At the bottom, the Player window provides transport controls that let you navigate through your movie as a scrolling frame counter indicates your present position. You view your animation in the Movie Editor window, where you also create and modify the paths that establish the movements of each actor.

**Figure 15.14**
The Movie Editor, with its four movable windows

Whereas a path occurs over a number of frames, an *event* initiates an action at a specific frame. Animation Works lets you place an unlimited number of events within a movie. Events include such things as background changes, transitions, frame rate changes, and sound. The sound capabilities in Animation Works are easy to use though rather limited. You can use any soundfiles in MacRecorder's SoundEdit format or SND sound resource format, but there are no editing options provided within the program. All sounds will play from beginning to end unless they're interrupted by another sound or unless you place the Kill Sound option in a frame to cut off the sound.

Adding sound to an Animation Works movie is easy. First, you locate the frame where you want to add sound by using the controls in the Player window. Next, you choose Sound from the Events menu to open a dialog box (Figure 15.15) that lets you select any sound in memory or lets you import sounds from your hard disk. To audition a sound, just click on its name. When you select a sound, its waveform appears on the right along with information about its duration and sample rate. Clicking the Select button installs the sound at the current frame location.

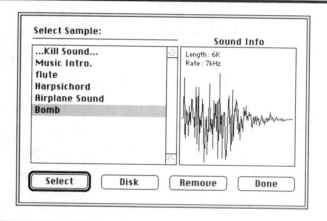

**Figure 15.15**
The Sound dialog box displays the waveform of a selected sound and lets you audition it by clicking on its name.

To give you an overview of your movie and to help you locate specific frames, Animation Works provides a Storyboard feature. The Storyboard window (Figure 15.16) displays miniature versions of the frames that make up your movie. Clicking on a frame makes it the current frame in the Movie Editor window. The Storyboard Settings window allows you to display only frames that meet certain criteria. This lets you view, for example, only the frames that have sound events attached to them. Or you might choose to view only frames with sounds or transitions.

If you want to incorporate your movies into HyperCard stacks, Animation Works comes with an XCMD that allows you to play your animated

Adding Sound to Desktop Presentations

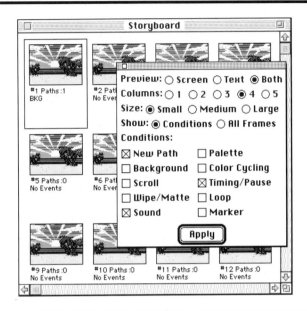

**Figure 15.16**
The Storyboard window gives you an overview of your movie and helps you locate specific frames.

sequences from within HyperCard. The XCMD comes with documentation in the form of a HyperCard stack along with several examples.

# SuperCard

SuperCard, from Aldus Corp., provides an extensive and versatile set of tools for creating custom programs ranging from simple organizers and databases to complex, sophisticated multimedia presentations. It combines the familiar Macintosh concept of windows and pull-down menus with HyperCard's highly effective metaphor of cards and stacks. In fact, you can easily import HyperCard stacks directly into SuperCard, where you can jazz them up by adding multiple windows, color, and animation.

Although SuperCard has much in common with HyperCard, it is actually a much more powerful program that allows you to have several different kinds of windows open at once along with a number of customized menus. It also provides numerous tools for creating and using a variety of buttons, text fields, and graphic images in both color and black and white. When you've completed your program, SuperCard lets you turn it into a stand-alone application that will run on any Macintosh without the presence of the SuperCard application itself.

In SuperCard a document or application is called a Project. Each Project can consist of several windows, and each window contains several cards that you see by looking through the window. The SuperCard tool kit actually consists of two separate programs: SuperEdit and SuperCard. The SuperEdit application enables you to assemble and change Projects, add windows and cards, and create graphics, text fields, and buttons. The SuperCard application runs the Projects that you produce in SuperEdit.

Any object that you create in SuperEdit can have a script that tells the computer how to respond when you click on the object. Scripts take you from one card to another, open or close windows, start animations, or play digitized sounds. SuperCard provides a scripting language called SuperTalk, which is based on HyperTalk, the language used in HyperCard. The two languages are so similar that anyone familiar with HyperTalk should have no trouble working with SuperTalk. You might think of SuperTalk as a superset of HyperTalk because SuperTalk can do almost anything that HyperTalk can do, plus a lot more. With SuperTalk commands you can manipulate Paint and Draw graphics, windows, and menus. You can cycle colors, play SND resource sounds, and display scanned images and 3-D animations created in other programs.

From the standpoint of adding sounds to your presentation, SuperCard and HyperCard are nearly identical. In fact, SuperEdit can convert a HyperCard stack into a SuperCard Project while retaining all of its original functions. If a HyperCard stack has sound resources placed in its resource file, SuperEdit will convert the sounds unaltered and immediately playable by SuperTalk's Play command. SuperEdit can also import sound resources from HyperCard stacks without necessarily converting the entire stack. And it can import sound resources from other documents and applications as well.

SuperTalk's Play command works the same as HyperTalk's, and you can construct melodies from digitized sounds by using essentially the same scripting procedures that I described earlier in the chapter. Because sounds take up a lot of RAM, it's important to check your memory requirements if you plan to distribute your completed SuperCard Project. If a computer has insufficient memory to play a sound completely, the sound won't play at all. Once the Play command triggers a sound, however, the script can go on to do other things, making it possible to have actions occur on screen while a long sound plays.

SuperEdit also makes use of XCMDs (external commands) and XFCNs (external functions), just as HyperCard does, to extend its capabilities. For audiovisual applications, XCMDs provide the opportunity to control external devices, such as compact disc players and MIDI instruments. Most of HyperCard's XCMDs and XFCNs should work with SuperCard, and you can import additional resources from other applications that use them. Furthermore, SuperCard has many of its own external commands, which are specific to its capabilities.

## Voyager CD AudioStack

If you're interested in adding CD-quality sound to your HyperCard presentations, it's not likely that you'll find a faster or easier way to do it than with the Voyager Company's CD AudioStack. This versatile set of HyperCard stacks forms a tool kit that lets you control and play audio compact discs (and the audio portions of mixed-mode CDs) from your own HyperCard stacks by using your CD-ROM drive as the playback device. In fact, you can control up to six CD-ROM drives by using different SCSI ID numbers.

CD AudioStack provides you with automatic installation of the necessary CD audio resources, a large collection of ready-made buttons to copy and paste into your stacks, ideas and suggestions for creating your own scripts, a ready-to-use remote control, and much more. Before you begin, however, you must be sure that the following files are in your System folder: Audio CD Access, Foreign File Access, and the system extension (INIT) that applies to your specific CD-ROM drive.

The first step in using CD AudioStack involves the installation of the CD audio resources: the 29 CD XCMDs and XFCNs that work behind the scenes to control your CD-ROM drive. With AudioStack's CD Resource

Installer, the process is simple and automatic, involving a couple of mouse clicks and a pop-up menu. If you install the resources into your Home stack, any other stack using that Home stack can issue CD commands if they're configured to do so. If you install the resources into a specific stack, the CD commands will follow that stack no matter where it's moved and will always work.

Once you've installed the necessary resources, you can easily add control functions to any HyperCard stack with the Ready-Made Button cards provided with CD AudioStack. These cards contain over 40 buttons of various types that you can copy and paste onto your own cards. The buttons let you quickly design custom transport panels with controls that let you play, scan, pause, skip to the next track, eject, and more.

If you're not interested in creating a custom arrangement of buttons, you can use the CD Audio Controller (Figure 15.17), which looks and works like the remote-control unit for a CD player. To add this set of controls to your stack, just click the Copy CD Controller button on the card and paste it into your stack. The controller provides buttons for Play, Scan (forward and reverse), Next/Previous Track, Pause, and Eject. Below the transport buttons, two displays indicate the current track and elapsed time, and additional buttons provide even more functions.

At the heart of CD AudioStack, the Audio Event Maker (Figure 15.18) enables you to define and control specific sections of audio data. Audio compact discs can have up to 74 minutes of sound divided into minutes, seconds, and *blocks*. A block is $1/75$ second, and CD AudioStack and its Audio Event Maker can control a CD down to that level. The Audio Event Maker lets you specify events by indicating tracks (there can be up to 99 tracks on a compact disc) and absolute time in minutes, seconds, and blocks.

To define a passage of sound as an event, you enter the appropriate address locations in the Start and End boxes. The transport controls at the bottom of the card let you navigate the CD to find the appropriate area. By clicking the pointing hands, you can automatically select the current location as the start or end point, and the plus and minus buttons let you adjust each setting. To hear your event, you can click the Play Event button.

Adding Sound to Desktop Presentations

**Figure 15.17**
The CD Audio Controller lets you play compact discs from any HyperCard stack.

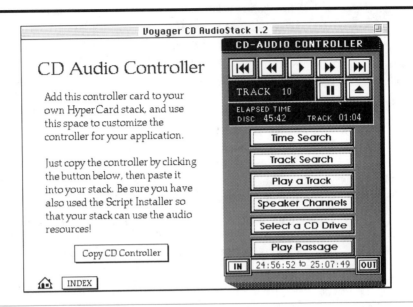

**Figure 15.18**
With the Audio Event Maker, you can create buttons that play specific segments of sound.

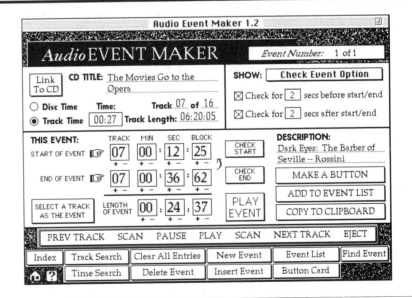

When you're satisfied with how your event sounds, you simply click on Make a Button to create a button that plays your event. The new button is pasted into the Button card, which serves as your scrapbook of buttons. Here you can customize the button by modifying and setting its font, icon, and style. Once you have a button that looks and acts the way you want it to, you can paste it into any HyperCard stack. You can also create an Event List that shows all of the events that you've described with the Audio Event Maker card. Finally, the Copy to Clipboard button lets you copy the HyperTalk script for any event to the Macintosh's clipboard so that you can add it to your own scripts.

Voyager CD AudioStack holds great potential for adding all kinds of high-fidelity recordings of music, speech, and sound effects to your HyperCard stacks. With the tools that it provides, you can easily produce elaborate interactive presentations that combine the accessibility of HyperCard with CD-quality audio.

## interFACE

InterFACE, from Bright Star Technology, is an unusual product that holds great potential for enhancing many presentations and other kinds of applications. It's designed primarily to create animated talking heads that convey information in a more effective and compelling way than by using plain dialog boxes and text fields. Having someone greet you with synchronized speech and facial movements is not only entertaining but it also adds a friendly quality to programs, improving their user interfaces and making them seem more accessible.

Each character that you see on screen consists of a group of facial images that, when combined in a series, create the appearance of movement. These collections of images are stored as files called *actors*. By animating an actor, synchronizing it with sound, and presenting it on screen, you create an *agent*. The technique of creating movement from a series of images is hardly a new one, but interFACE approaches the process of animation from a completely different angle than the traditional method. Rather than using a preset linear sequence of images, interFACE uses a type of random-access animation that Bright Star calls HyperAnimation.

To create a talking agent with this type of animation, you begin with a collection of predefined images that form an inventory of different mouth positions and facial expressions. The computer then displays each image as needed and includes it in a series that creates the appropriate movements. Random-access animation allows you to call up any image in any order for any amount of time. And because the images can be recombined and reused over and over, random-access animation reduces not only the size of the animation files but also the amount of time it takes to create them. This nonlinear approach to animation imparts an almost spontaneous quality to interFACE's agents, and it allows you to generate a seemingly endless number of variations in movement from a relatively small number of individual frames. By creating different mouth positions to represent the basic units of speech, called *phonemes,* you can have a talking agent that is capable of saying virtually anything.

## Creating Actors

InterFACE allows you to create three different types of actors that range from simple to complex. A Standard actor uses 8 Speaking Images, an Extended actor uses 15 images, and a Coarticulated actor uses 32. Using actors with more speaking positions produces smoother animation and more lifelike agents, but requires more memory. Aside from the Speaking Images, actors can also have Expression Images, which are added during pauses or when the actor isn't speaking. You can add as many Expression Images as you want to an actor until the total number of images reaches 120.

To begin creating an actor, you first enter the Dressing Room (Figure 15.19). This part of the program provides a complete set of paint tools, along with import and export capabilities, actor resizing and conversion commands, and several animation tools. The Dressing Room window houses the Easel, which appears as a blank, shadowed field when you first open the program. This is where you draw or paste the images that make up your actor.

Images can range from the simplest line drawings and cartoons to more sophisticated artwork. For even greater realism, you can use digitized pictures of actual people, who can pose with different mouth positions representing the different phonemes. Even people with little artistic skill can achieve surprisingly good results. To help you even more, interFACE

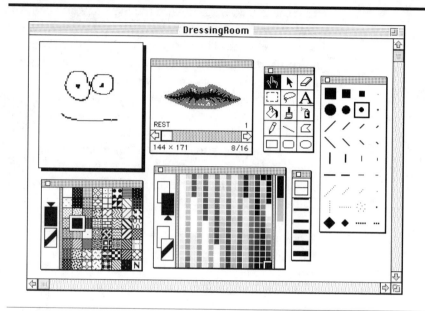

**Figure 15.19**
The Dressing Room provides a number of drawing and painting tools, an Easel, and a Control window to use as a guide.

provides a generous assortment of clip art, which includes all of the basic mouth positions along with other body parts and accessories (Figure 15.20).

To help you draw your mouth positions correctly, interFACE provides the Control window, which displays the name and number of each Speaking Image along with a pair of lips to use as a guide. The lips display the Key Image, which you can change by cycling through the different mouth positions with the scroll bar in the window. As each Key Image changes, the actor image in the Easel changes with it, allowing you to view and compare your drawings. If you want, you can also add some Expression Images, like blinks and smiles, to enhance the actor's appeal.

When you're finished in the Dressing Room, you next move on to the Stage to test the speaking animation of your actor. In the Stage window (Figure 15.21), you can type (phonetically) anything you want your actor to say. When you choose Talk, interFACE automatically generates the appropriate speech—using MacinTalk—and simultaneously accesses the corresponding Speaking Images to create a fully synchronized talking head. You can test your Expression Images in the Express window by typing in the appropriate commands in RAVE, interFACE's scripting language. If the actor's speech is too slow or the pitch is too low, you can change both parameters in the MacinTalk window and the actor will stay synchronized.

**Figure 15.20**
InterFACE supplies a good assortment of clip art to help you create your actors.

**Figure 15.21**
The Stage lets you test your actors with MacinTalk. The digitized actor shown here is one of several that come with interFACE.

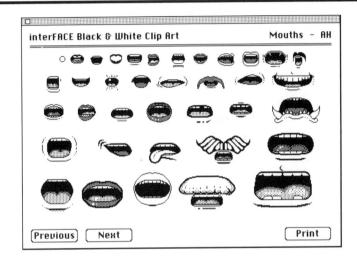

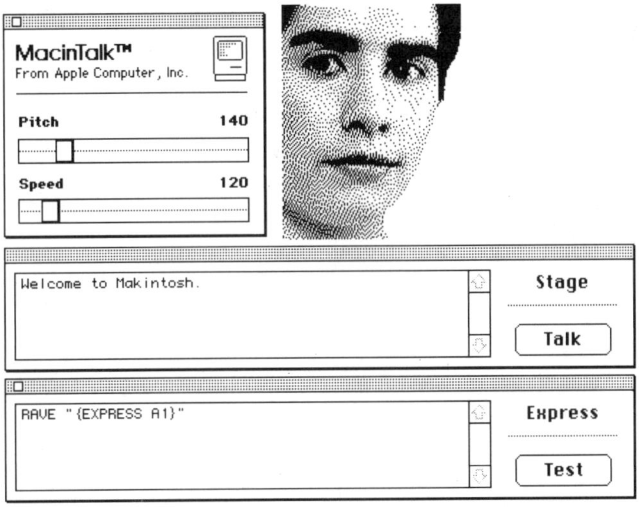

At this point in the process, you could just stop and still have a perfectly usable agent that could talk your ear off about anything, whenever you type the corresponding text into the program. But anyone who has heard MacinTalk knows that it does not produce the most elegant or mellifluous-sounding speech. In fact, by today's standards, it sounds too much like a robot and not enough like a real person. So, in most cases, most people will want to proceed to the next step, which takes place in the Speech Sync section of interFACE.

## Speech Sync

Speech Sync lets you synchronize your actors to digitized recordings of actual people. This not only allows an agent to speak with a natural-sounding voice but you can derive your recordings from a variety of sources, such as the head of a company, a famous actor, or your best friend. In fact you can have your agent sing a song or speak with several different voices, or in different languages if you want.

The process of synchronizing animation and sound in interFACE involves four steps. The first step is to acquire the necessary sound. You can import sounds from a variety of applications, or you can make your own recordings from within Sound Sync. InterFACE includes its own MacRecorder window (Figure 15.22), which lets you make recordings without leaving the program. After plugging in your MacRecorder, you simply select a sampling rate, set the recording time, and click the Record button. As you speak, a thermometer-style Record Time Bar indicates the elapsed time until you click the mouse to end the recording. When you stop, the new recording becomes the current sound and interFACE automatically saves it for you.

Once you have a voice recording that you like, you can proceed to the next step in the synchronization process. This involves entering text into Speech Sync that represents the words that are spoken in the sound that you've just recorded or imported. The words that you type into the Text window are used as a guide to the spoken words in your recording.

You initiate the third step in the process by clicking the Convert button in the Text window. InterFACE then breaks the text into its phonetic elements and displays them as a RECITE command in the Recite window

# Adding Sound to Desktop Presentations

(Figure 15.23). RECITE is a special RAVE command that plays a sound along with a sequence of images.

The RECITE command represents speech as a series of phoneme labels and numeric values called a Phonetic/Timing Value String. The word *welcome* would be broken down into the following phonemes: W, EH, L, K, AH, M. These correspond to the Speaking Images that you created for the

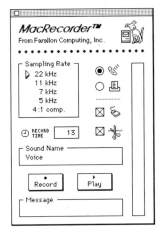

**Figure 15.22**
With the MacRecorder window, you can make recordings without leaving the program.

**Figure 15.23**
In Speech Sync you break down the spoken text into its phonetic elements.

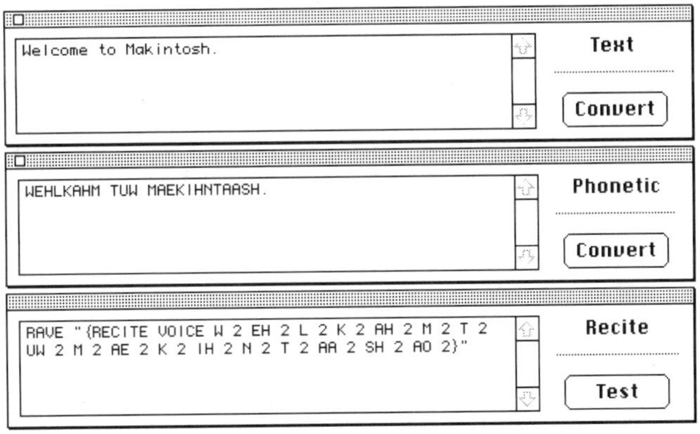

current actor in the Dressing Room. Between each phoneme, a number (representing one-sixtieth of a second) indicates how long each image appears on screen. The RECITE command causes the sound to play while simultaneously starting the animation specified by the Phonetic/Timing Value String.

Although your actor may be perfectly synchronized when speaking with MacinTalk, it's unlikely that it will still be in sync when you switch to a recorded sound. Because people have different idiomatic speaking styles and use different cadences when they talk, you'll have to adjust the animation to fit the recorded voice. The final step, therefore, in synchronizing your images to sound involves increasing or decreasing the timing values in the RECITE command to accommodate the recording. You can also change the phoneme labels, if necessary, and add Expression Images where appropriate. Since this step involves a fair amount of trial and error, it will likely be the most time-consuming.

Once your agent is complete, you can import it into HyperCard or a number of other applications to use in things like online help systems, advertising, telecommunications, education, and entertainment. You're also not limited to using interFACE for only animating talking heads. You can use the same animation tools to produce a wide variety of animated sequences. Agents aren't limited to just talking either. They can play musical instruments and use sound effects as well. The interFACE package includes a large assortment of ready-made actors both drawn and digitized, in color and black and white. The online help, easy tutorial, and thorough documentation make the program enjoyable to use.

## *At Your Service*

At Your Service (also from Bright Star) offers an excellent glimpse into the potential for using interFACE agents as part of your daily routine. This standalone desk accessory uses an actor named Phil to greet you when you start up or shut down your computer. But Phil can do much more than that. If you're using Microsoft Mail 3.0 or CE QuickMail, Phil can come on screen to announce the arrival of electronic mail and offer you the option of reading it now or later.

Phil also keeps an eye on your health. The Health Watch Service Panel lets you specify how long you want to work before taking a break. Phil then monitors your activity level and if you exceed the Activity Limit, he pops up to remind you of the dangers of repetitive strain injury and offers advice on treatment and prevention.

One of Phil's most useful jobs is to remind you of appointments, birthdays, meetings, deadlines, and things to do. The Reminder Service Panel (Figure 15.24) offers to alert you to a number of different types of occasions and lets you specify how often they occur. At the appropriate time, Phil politely interrupts to call your attention to each important event.

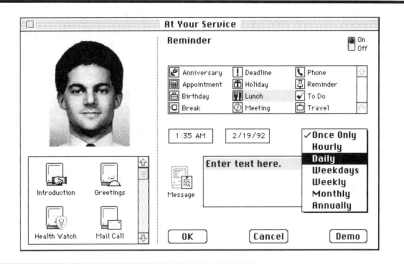

**Figure 15.24**
By using the Reminder Service Panel, you can have Phil alert you to a variety of important events.

At Your Service provides four versions of Phil, each requiring a different amount of memory. You can choose either a drawn or digitized version in black and white or color. If you get tired of Phil or just want a change of gender, Bright Star sells additional actors in a variety of types. My current favorite is Gabrielle, who greets me in the morning with a pretty smile and a French accent.

# MediaTracks

MediaTracks, from Farallon Computing, provides the tools necessary to create a variety of interactive presentations that work extremely well as training programs, guided tours, desktop help systems, product demonstrations, and tutorials. It does this by allowing you to record the Macintosh's screen activity and then edit and save the recording for later replay as a standalone presentation or from within HyperCard or other applications.

The MediaTracks package actually consists of three component parts. ScreenRecorder is a desk accessory that lets you record the screen activity of a Macintosh session, in real time, and save it as a file called a *tape*. The MediaTracks editor allows you to modify and combine tapes and add sound to transform them into finished presentations. And the MT Player is a separate application that plays the tapes created with ScreenRecorder.

You begin recording your session by choosing ScreenRecorder from the Apple menu, which produces a small control panel with transport-like buttons on it. Clicking Record opens a dialog box that prompts you to name the recording. When you type in a name and click Save, the dialog box and control panel disappear and recording begins immediately, evidenced by the tiny tape-cassette icon in the menu bar. From that point on, all screen activity will be recorded (in black and white), including such things as pointer and cursor movements, menu choices, window openings, icon selections, warning beeps, and specific activities within an application.

When you have a tape that you like, you can close ScreenRecorder and begin refining your recorded session by opening the MediaTracks application, with its MediaTracks Presentation window (Figure 15.25). The Presentation window displays your tape as a strip of film across the middle of the window, just below a time ruler that indicates elapsed seconds. At the bottom of the window, there are several Edit buttons and a scroll bar. Above these controls a narrow strip—the Sound track—lets you add sounds to your presentation.

The first step in turning your ScreenRecorder tape into a MediaTracks presentation is to subdivide the tape into smaller segments called *clips*. By

# Adding Sound to Desktop Presentations

using the Mark button on the Playback Control Panel (Figure 15.26), you can convert the tape into a series of clips, which you can then cut, copy, paste, and delete as needed. Later you can also add sound, graphics, text, color, and interactive buttons to the clips.

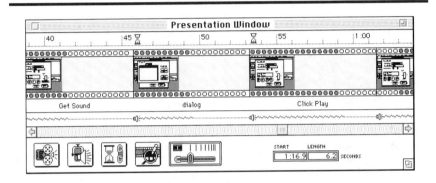

**Figure 15.25**
The MediaTracks Presentation window, showing several clips with sounds attached

**Figure 15.26**
With the Mark button on the Playback Control Panel, you can subdivide a tape into a series of clips.

Creating clips is simple: Just play the tape and click the Mark button at key locations or transitions. Each clip appears in the Tape track with a miniature screen shot called a *still*, followed by a section of gray to indicate the total length of the clip. To help identify each of the clips, you can add descriptive labels below them, and if you have a color system, you can also assign them different colors.

When you finish making and editing your clips and you're satisfied with the visuals, you can add sound to enhance the presentation. There are several ways of adding sound to a MediaTracks presentation and a number of options that enable you to synchronize the sound to the visuals. If you have a MacRecorder digitizer, you can record directly into MediaTracks by using the Record Sound dialog box (Figure 15.27). Before recording, you can choose one of four sampling rates—22, 11, 7, and 5 kHz—and one of four optional compression ratios—3:1, 4:1, 6:1, and 8:1. The Record Limit pop-up menu lets you specify the maximum amount of memory devoted to the recording, so the soundfile won't get too large for some end-users.

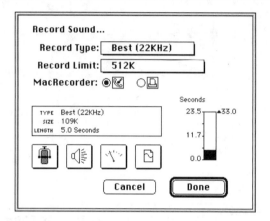

**Figure 15.27**
The Record Sound dialog box lets you record and import sounds for your presentation.

The first three buttons in the Record Sound dialog box are for recording, playing, and setting input levels. The fourth one—the Get Sound button—enables you to import sounds from other sources. MediaTracks lets you use any sounds saved in the Audio IFF and SoundEdit file formats as well as SND sound resource files, such as those used in HyperCard or other MediaTracks presentations. Additionally, you can copy sounds from the Clipboard or from MacRecorder's SoundEdit application directly to the Presentation window.

When you attach a sound to a clip in the Presentation window, a small speaker icon appears in the Sound track with a waveform-like line to the right of it representing the length of the sound. If you need to, you can cut, copy, and paste sounds from clip to clip. In some cases a segment of dialogue or music may last longer than the clip it goes with. To keep things synchronized, and to prevent sounds from overlapping into the neighboring clips, MediaTracks provides two options for adjusting the playback timing of individual clips. You can use the Playback Speed dialog box to increase or decrease the playback speed of any clip (or group of clips), or you can use the Actions dialog box to introduce a pause during a clip's playback. To pause playback of a clip, you first open the Actions dialog box (Figure 15.28) and then choose For Sound from the Pause menu. MediaTracks will then cause that clip to wait until the attached sound has finished playing before it moves on to the next clip. If you prefer, you can specify a number of seconds to pause playback instead.

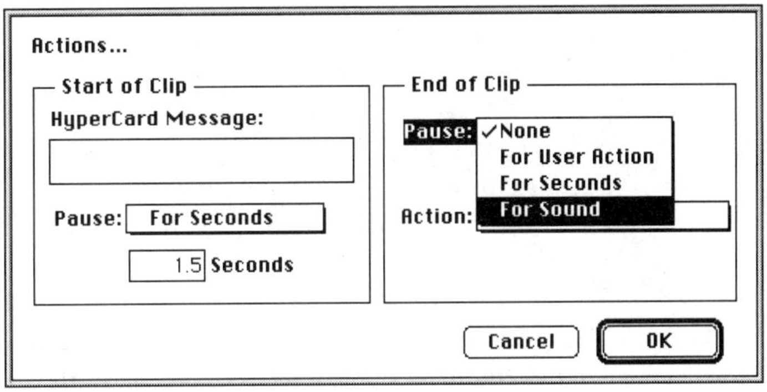

**Figure 15.28**
With the Actions dialog box, you can make a clip wait for its attached sound to finish.

To further enhance your projects, MediaTracks provides a Drawing window, which offers several common drawing tools, along with the ability to add colors, text, boxes, arrows, and other graphics. Of particular importance in the use of sound, the Drawing window lets you create buttons and assign specific actions to them. By selecting the Button tool, you can quickly and easily create a button anywhere in the Drawing window. You then use the Button Info dialog box to determine the button's appearance and to assign it an action. If you choose Play Sound from the Action menu, clicking the button will play the sound attached to that clip as long as the clip is in progress. You can also have Pause and Continue buttons to allow the user to set the pace while viewing the presentation.

Because MediaTracks and HyperCard are a natural combination for multimedia, Farallon includes an MTPlay XCMD that lets you play your tapes from within HyperCard. By using the MTPlay HyperCard Installer stack, you can add buttons to any HyperCard stacks or write your own HyperTalk scripts to play your MediaTracks presentations.

# Paracomp Magic

Paracomp Magic is part of the gaggle of popular animation and multimedia programs currently offered by MacroMind/Paracomp. Unlike Director, however, Magic is better suited to users with little prior multimedia experience and more modest needs for creating original artwork and animation. Its graphic approach to assembling presentations combined with its ability to import artwork and animation from other sources will, nonetheless, make this program appealing to a great many people of all levels.

To help you conceptualize its structure, Paracomp Magic uses the metaphor of a theater. Graphic elements and text are called *actors* and the display area, called the *stage*, presents the actions and artwork in distinct *scenes*. To begin forming a presentation, therefore, you must first create or import the actors and place them on the stage in the current scene.

For developing and assembling your scenes, you begin in Draw mode, where the program provides a large Stage window and several movable palettes (Figure 15.29). The Tool palette in the upper left provides several common tools for creating graphics out of shapes, lines, and text. The Costume palette, directly beneath the Tool palette, lets you assign each actor a fill pattern with a different foreground and background color. You can also change the line width, pattern, and color and set the transparency level for each actor.

Clicking the large button at the top of the Tool palette lets you select one of several additional modes for developing your visuals. The Shape mode enables you to modify an actor's appearance by altering its outline. In the Move mode, you can draw simple paths for animating the different actors using the same shapes and lines that you use in Draw mode. The Pan and Mask modes apply to imported graphics.

To view the interactions of the actors on the Stage, you can use the Control palette to play through the scene. It provides a frame counter and several buttons to play in forward and reverse, to step through frames one at a time, or to skip to the beginning or end of the scene.

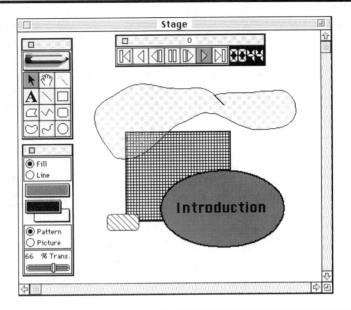

**Figure 15.29**
You use Paracomp Magic's Stage window to create, modify, and animate graphic elements called actors.

After you've created all of the actors in a scene and you've established their positions and movements, you can open the Cue palette to further control and synchronize your graphic elements. The Cue palette (Figure 15.30) is actually a window that provides a *timeline* along the top showing elapsed time in 10-frame increments. At the bottom of the window, all of the actors in the current scene are listed opposite their *lifespans*—thin rectangular bars that show when, and for how long, each actor appears on the Stage.

You can select any actor by clicking on its lifespan, which turns from white to gray, indicating that it is the current selection. Each actor can have one or more of six attributes, which consist of animation effects, transitions, and sound. When you select an actor, the attributes associated with that actor appear as gray bars in the upper half of the Cue palette. The Move attribute bar, for instance, shows when the actor begins to move and how many frames it takes to complete its motion. The Fill In/Out attribute refers to how and when one of several transitions will affect the appearance or disappearance of the actor's filled area. Line In/Out works the same way. When you create a new scene, all of the lifespans and attribute bars are given a

**Figure 15.30**
The Cue palette shows each actor and its corresponding attributes along a timeline marked in frames.

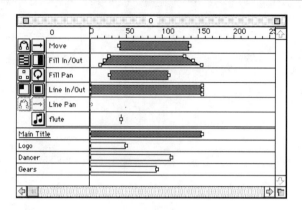

default value of 50 frames, which you can increase or decrease by dragging the grab handles on the bars. You can also fade in and fade out attributes and move actors and their attributes to new locations along the timeline.

Sounds are treated as attributes and attached to individual actors in the Cue palette. Sound attributes, however, appear as only a single grab handle, which indicates the starting point of the sound in relation to the timeline. You can import any SND sound resource file with the Import command and add the sound to the Sound List. Once the sound appears in the Sound List, you simply attach it to the current actor by clicking on the Sound attribute icon in the Cue palette and selecting it from the pop-up menu.

You can also copy sounds to and from the Scrapbook and paste them into the Sound List for selection. If you have MacRecorder or a Macintosh with built-in recording capability, you can record your own sounds to add to the Sound List. Paracomp Magic provides a simple sound-recording dialog box that lets you make recordings up to 10 seconds long and add them directly to the Sound List.

Once you've attached a sound to an actor, you can move the sound to any position along the timeline. The sound will then play from that point until it's finished or until another sound interrupts it. Because Paracomp Magic only allows you to play one sound at any given time, a more recent sound, even from across scenes, will cut off and replace an earlier sound's playback.

One additional feature worth noting is Paracomp Magic's ability to create *links* between scenes. By using the Link palette, you can create buttons, or turn any existing actors into buttons, that link the current scene to any other specified scene in the presentation. This enables you to produce fully interactive presentations that let you navigate from scene to scene in a nonsequential order by clicking the appropriate buttons.

Each link can have a transition like those in the Cue palette. But these are full-screen transitions that gradually replace the current scene with the destination scene using one of several effects. The Link palette also offers an additional transition option called Movie. Choosing the Movie option lets you import an animated sequence to use as a transition.

Paracomp Magic includes an application called QuickPICS that compresses and enhances the playback of animations in the PICS file format. QuickPICS works well for use in interactive productions because its unique compression scheme improves animation speed and reduces RAM requirements by allowing playback directly from your hard disk. QuickPICS enables you to import PICS format animations from a variety of sources and use them as transitions between scenes. You can even save animated sequences from Paracomp Magic itself to use as transitions in the same presentation or elsewhere.

QuickPICS lets you include a soundfile with the graphic information in a movie (Figure 15.31). You can create the sound with MacRecorder's SoundEdit application or any program that supports the SoundEdit file format. The sound that you attach to a QuickPICS movie starts when the animation begins and plays until the end of the soundfile or until the animation finishes—whichever comes first.

To resolve the problem of mismatched sound and animation lengths, QuickPICS provides a feature that adjusts the playback of the animation to accommodate the sound. Choosing the Frame Rate Based on Sound option automatically adjusts the animation's frame rate so that the sound and visuals will begin and end together. Without this feature, finding the appropriate frame rate could involve much trial and error.

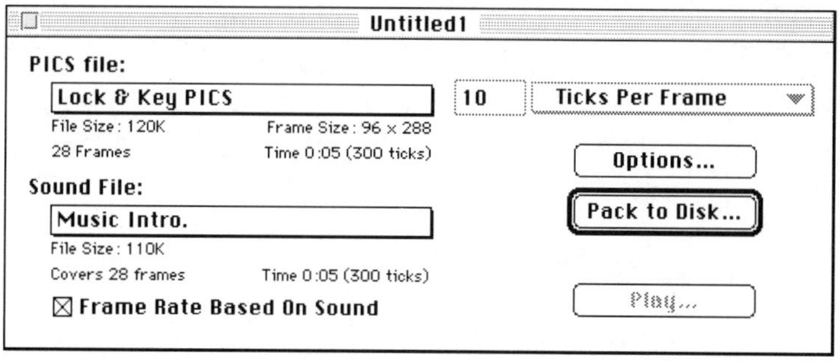

**Figure 15.31**
QuickPICS lets you include a soundfile with an animation file.

Finally, in an effort to make Paracomp Magic immediately usable, MacroMind/Paracomp includes several additional disks with tutorial files, business presentation templates, and samples of backgrounds, animations, sounds, and 3-D models. These extra materials should give you a head start in exploring the program's potential, especially for producing corporate-style presentations.

# HookUp!

HookUp!, from VPL Research, Inc., is a unique and creative piece of software. Designed as a programming construction kit, it lets you create your own software for animation, music, and sound. The great appeal of this product lies in the fact that people with no knowledge of programming techniques can produce applications ranging from very simple to quite elaborate.

Rather than typing lines of code, you drag graphic icons from a toolbox and connect them with software "wires." The result looks much like a schematic flowchart, with graphics and icons representing standard programming operations involving clocks, counters, switches, sequences, arithmetic, and logic operators (Figure 15.32). HookUp! is fully interactive and functions in real time. Its inputs can be from the mouse (click and/or position), MIDI devices, software buttons, and sliders.

**Figure 15.32**
HookUp! uses graphic icons and software "wires" to create real-time interactive animations.

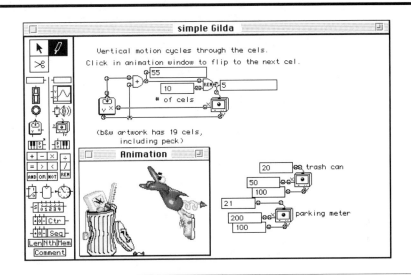

In its current release, HookUp! is limited to importing documents from early versions of MacroMind Director (or VideoWorks II) as its source of animation. To use sounds other than those that come with HookUp!, you must use the Sound-to-Video II utility that came with the earlier versions of Director. You can then import SND sound resource files into the HookUp! directory and include them in your animations.

Sounds are started by a trigger input to a sound icon, which in turn can be controlled by other operations in the schematic. You can use MIDI devices to input and generate music, although only note on, note off, and velocity messages are recognized. Combining MIDI with graphics in an interactive environment provides an opportunity for some very creative programming. Animated figures and graphics can change in response to pitch or velocity output from a keyboard. Or sounds from a MIDI device can respond to animation, which itself is being manipulated in real time by the end user. HookUp! includes a library of digitized sounds and some samples of animation to get you started.

VPL Research has also developed a high-end version of HookUp!, called Body Electric, which includes real-time 3-D animation capabilities and allows you to import PICS files. Body Electric comes as part of a virtual-reality hardware/software package that also includes enhanced audio capabilities.

## Studio/1

Studio/1, from Electronic Arts, is a full-featured black-and-white graphics program with animation capabilities. The animations are created as a sequence of images in the traditional flip-book style, and Studio/1 lets you place any Type 1 SND resource sound on any frame in the sequence.

The procedure is very simple: Locate the frame where you want the sound to occur, and click the Sound button in the Control Panel (Figure 15.33). This opens the Load a Sound dialog box, which lists the available sounds. Clicking on the names in the list lets you audition them. When you've made a selection, click the Load Sound button to place that sound in the current frame. The Control Panel then displays the sound's name next to the Sound button. The procedure for adding subsequent sounds is very similar.

**Figure 15.33**
Studio/1's Control Panel provides a Sound button that lets you attach a sound to a specific frame.

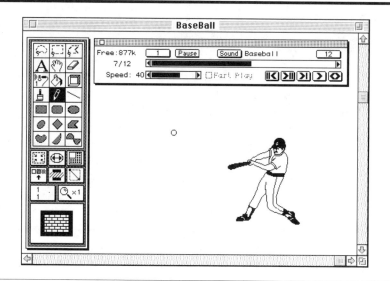

In Studio/1, a sound is linked to a specific frame so that the sound plays as the frame plays. You can add sounds to as many frames as you like, but only one sound per frame. Studio/1 ignores pitch setting and looping information and does not play stereo or compressed sounds.

A sound will play until it ends or until the next frame with a sound interrupts it. For best results, Electronic Arts recommends that you use sound effects with quick attacks and releases. They also point out that having too many digitized sounds in a single document may slow down the playback speed of a Studio/1 animation. Studio/1 is HyperCard-compatible.

## PROmotion

PROmotion, from Motion Works, is a sophisticated and versatile animation program that makes the process of animation accessible to the average user without sacrificing power or flexibility. With PROmotion you can create text, graphics, and animation, and combine them with imported still video, full-motion video, 3-D images, and sound to produce fully interactive multimedia presentations.

A PROmotion animation consists of a number of elements. The movable objects that appear in the foreground are called *actors*, and each actor is composed of a series of individual images called *cels*. To cause an actor to move, you assign it to an animation *path*, a series of points that the actor follows. Each point along the path represents the actor's position in that frame. By displaying the actor's cels in sequence along the series of points in a path, you create the illusion of movement. The speed of an actor depends on the number of points in a path and how far apart they are. Background objects, called *props*, consist of single cels and provide the stage settings for the actors. Once they become part of an animation, you can assign transitions and visual effects to props.

When you first open a new animation screen in PROmotion, a large window appears, accompanied on the left by a movable palette called the Media Controller (Figure 15.34). This acts as the control center for your animations by providing a set of transport buttons and several icons that enable you to create, edit, and manipulate the actors, props, sounds, and other elements that form your animation.

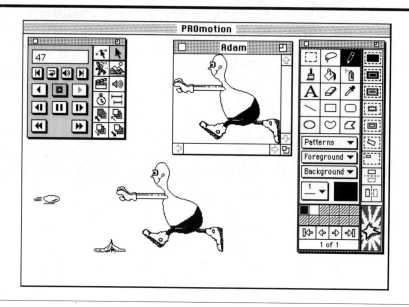

**Figure 15.34**
PROmotion provides its Media Controller for controlling and editing animations. The Paint palette supplies tools for creating and modifying actors and props.

For creating and modifying your actors and props, PROmotion provides a full-featured 24-bit color paint program, which includes a Paint palette with several standard tools and a number of additional icons for producing special effects and transformations. Along the bottom of the palette, a row of arrows lets you cycle through an actor's cels.

You can add an SND resource sound to any frame in your animation by clicking the Add Sound icon (the small loudspeaker) on the Media Controller. This opens the Select a Sound dialog box (Figure 15.35), which lists the available sounds. On the right the selected sound appears as a waveform display with relevant information about the sound below it. If the Preview option box is checked, you can hear each sound when you click on it. The Import button lets you add sounds from other programs, and the remaining buttons let you duplicate, rename, and remove sounds.

PROmotion also lets you make your own recordings to include in your animations. If you have a recording device such as MacRecorder or Voice Impact Pro, or you own one of the Macs with built-in recording capabilities, you can click on the New button. This opens a standard recording dialog box, like the one described in Chapter 16. With the controls in the dialog box, you can

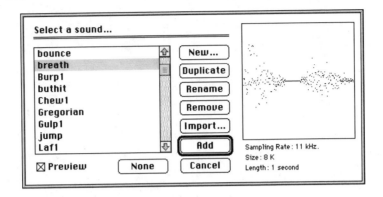

**Figure 15.35**
The Select a Sound dialog box lists available sounds and shows their waveforms.

make a recording and add it to the list of available sounds. Once you have the sound that you want—whether by importing it, recording it, or selecting it from the available sounds—you can add it to any frame in the current animation.

Clicking the Add button opens the Sound Information dialog box (Figure 15.36), which lets you adjust any sound that you've added to your animation. The name of the sound appears at the top of the dialog box next to the Sound Selection icon. To change sounds, you can click on the icon, which reopens the Select a Sound dialog box enabling you to make a new selection. Each sound appears with its playing time shown in seconds and in number of frames.

Using the Start Frame and End Frame fields, you can change where the sound occurs and how long it plays. When you first add a sound, the start frame defaults to the frame that the animation was on at the time the sound was added, and the end frame defaults to the end of the animation. A sound will begin playing at the start frame and continue until it's finished or until it reaches the end frame. If a sound is shorter than its assigned animation segment, you can select the Repeat Sound option to loop the sound over and over until the end frame arrives. You can also fade in and fade out a sound and set its overall volume with a pop-up menu.

With PROmotion you can have as many as 100 sounds in an animation, with up to 16 sounds occurring at once. Whether or not your particular

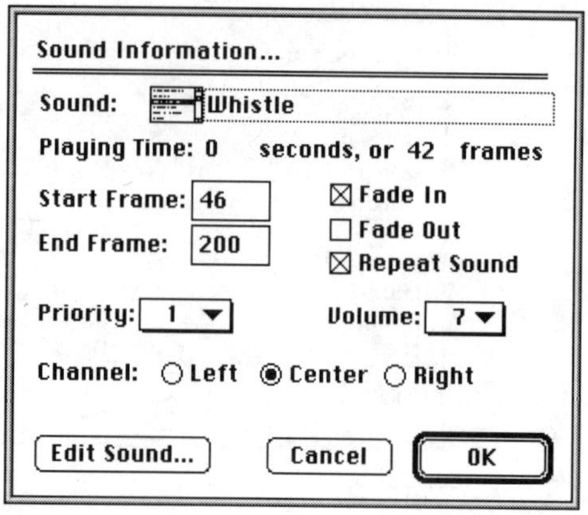

**Figure 15.36**
The Sound Information dialog box lets you set a sound's parameters.

Macintosh will handle 16 sounds simultaneously depends on the model that you have and its available memory. Because of this, if you produce an animation on one model of computer and play it back on another, you may lose some of the sounds.

To give you more control over this potential problem, PROmotion provides a Priority pop-up menu, which lets you assign a priority setting (from 1 to 16) for each sound that you add to an animation. This ensures that a more important sound won't get cut off by a background sound if the Mac has reached its limit. If, for example, you have five sounds assigned to play on a particular frame and your Macintosh only supports two channels of sound, the two sounds with the highest priority will be heard. The Channel selector lets you choose which of the Mac's audio output channels the sound will play through. All Macs can play through the left channel, but only Macs with stereo capability can also access the right channel.

Once you've assembled your animation and added sounds, timings, cues (see below), and other elements, you can view all of these objects together in the TimeLines window (Figure 15.37). This gives you an overview of the presentation and lets you perform certain editing functions. Each object in the presentation appears on the left with a descriptive icon and a name. To the right of each name, a *timeline* shows the number of frames used by each object and when the object appears in the animation.

# Adding Sound to Desktop Presentations

**Figure 15.37**
The TimeLines window gives you an overview of your presentation.

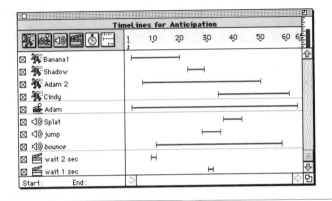

You can drag sounds and other elements to new positions along the timeline, and you can stretch or shrink the timelines to change their durations. Clicking on a sound opens its Sound Information dialog box, allowing you to make changes to the sound's parameters. The icons along the top of the window let you select which elements will appear in the TimeLines window, and you can turn objects off and on with the check boxes on the left.

In addition to its other sound-handling features, PROmotion provides extensive editing capabilities from within the program. Clicking on the Edit Sound button in the Sound Information dialog box opens the Edit Waveform dialog box (Figure 15.38). It displays the sound as a waveform that you can view and edit in a variety of ways by using the buttons below the scroll bar.

The Zoom In button gives you a closer look at the waveform, while the Zoom Out button provides a better overview. The Louder and Softer buttons change the amplitude of the waveform (or a selected portion) in steps. The Echo button repeats the waveform or selected area with a decay, and the Backward button simply plays the sound in reverse. The Play button plays the entire sound or its selected region.

Option-clicking the first four buttons provides additional functions. The Zoom buttons become Lower Hz and Raise Hz buttons, enabling you to change the frequency of a sound. The Louder and Softer buttons become

**Figure 15.38**
PROmotion provides a number of sound-editing capabilities with its Edit Waveform dialog box.

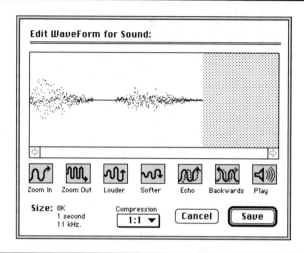

Ramp Up and Ramp Down buttons, which let you fade a selected area in or out. Finally, the Compression pop-up menu at the bottom of the dialog box lets you apply 3:1 or 6:1 compression to a sound when it's saved.

To create a fully interactive presentation, PROmotion provides *cues* to trigger additional actions. Using cues, you can make actors and props behave like buttons and, by sending Apple Events to other applications, PROmotion enables you to control external devices, like CD players, videodisc players, and MIDI instruments. In addition to its ability to import and export PICT and PICS files, PROmotion can also turn its animations into QuickTime movies, or it can play QuickTime movies from within a PROmotion presentation. Additionally, PROmotion allows you to print your animations to video.

If you do a lot of work with HyperCard, you might want to consider ADDmotion II, another product from Motion Works. ADDmotion II is very similar to PROmotion except that it's fully integrated with HyperCard and allows you to create and play your presentations from within your HyperCard stacks.

# Final Thoughts

The products covered in this chapter illustrate well the tremendous wealth of software that exists for creating desktop presentations on the Macintosh. The available choices range from simple animation programs with limited sound capabilities to powerful high-end multimedia packages that can access external devices, MIDI instruments, and multiple internal sound sources.

All of the animation programs mentioned here can include 8-bit digitized sounds, but how the programs implement sound and how much flexibility they provide varies considerably from one product to the next. Many of the products are so idiosyncratic in their design that they may appeal to you on that basis alone. It's important, however, to keep in mind the overall audio-visual balance when you evaluate a program's potential.

You also have to take into account what the final form of your project will be. Some of the low-end programs might work just fine for presentations that you'll distribute on a floppy disk. On the other hand, for full-blown multimedia in front of a live audience, there is no question that the ability to include audio from CD players, MIDI instruments, and other high-fidelity sources will add considerably to the impact and effectiveness of your presentations.

a. No. 5, "Eusebius"

# Chapter 16

# Sound and the System

Most Mac users would certainly agree that computers and sound were meant to go together. Sound can be much more than just fun; it can add an important new dimension to working with a keyboard and monitor. The original design teams that developed the Macintosh knew this to be true, and Apple has wisely continued its support for sound by continually evolving the Mac's system software to accommodate bigger and better audio capabilities.

Now that multimedia has burst upon the scene, the magic of sound has been thrust from the background into the limelight. Software developers from all over are finding ways to put the Macintosh's built-in audio skills to good use for enhancing presentations. In this chapter I'll examine how the Macintosh system software handles its audio responsibilities and helps presentations to come alive with sound.

## ▣ Sound Manager

From the very start, Macs have had the ability to play back digital audio without the need for additional hardware. In fact, this is one of the things that has distinguished the Macintosh from other, more mundane, computing platforms. The Sound Manager (which replaces the now obsolete Sound Driver) is a collection of routines that allows applications to create, modify, and play sounds directly from the Macintosh's speaker or through the output jack on its rear panel.

The Sound Manager is responsible for providing a long list of important audio functions, including playing simple sequences of pitches, playing and recording sampled sounds, and producing alert sounds. An enhanced Sound Manager that has been in use with system versions 6.0.7 and later adds several additional features, including the ability to mix and synchronize multiple channels of sampled sound, the ability to play sounds stored on disk while other processing continues, and the ability to compress and decompress sounds.

## Sounding Off

The Macintosh creates sound when the Sound Manager sends the appropriate data to the on-board digital-to-analog converter, which translates the digital data into an analog audio signal for playback (see Chapter 10). The Mac II family of computers and the more recent models also have a second D/A converter chip to provide stereo output as well as an Apple Sound Chip, which provides enhanced audio output characteristics.

One of Sound Manager's capabilities involves designing and controlling complex synthesized sounds. With the right application, you can play a series of pitches with different durations to create a musical sequence. You can change the timbre of the sounds and play them simultaneously on multiple channels. You can also speed up or slow down sounds, change their volume levels, and pan them to the right or left in real time.

## Multiple Channels

The ability to produce sampled sound on multiple channels is one of the most useful new features in the enhanced version of Sound Manager. In the past, Sound Manager could only play a single channel of sampled sound at one time. If the software called for a system alert sound while another sampled sound was playing, you wouldn't hear the alert sound. More importantly, you couldn't layer your multimedia soundtracks to produce a more professional-sounding mix by combining, for example, narration and music, or music and sound effects.

With the more recent version of Sound Manager, you can have several channels of sampled sound output simultaneously to the Mac's speaker or audio jack. The number of possible channels and the quality of sound output depend on the model of Macintosh used and specifically on the internal hardware configuration and the processing speed. A Mac IIcx or IIsi, for example, can support several channels without difficulty, while a Mac Plus can only support a single channel before having its processing speed adversely affected. Furthermore, the current Sound Manager only allows you to have multiple channels of sampled sound on models that incorporate the Apple Sound Chip.

## MACE

Another important feature recently added to Sound Manager is the ability to compress and decompress sounds to conserve valuable disk storage space. Known as Macintosh Audio Compression and Expansion (MACE), this feature provides data compression and expansion capabilities to all models of the Macintosh from the Mac Plus on. MACE can perform its services in real time with either of two compression ratios: 3:1 and 6:1. Although this can save you a considerable amount of disk space, it comes at the cost of noticeably lower sound quality. You should therefore reserve the use of compression for situations where optimum sound quality is not essential.

## Recording Sounds

Since all Macs come with a digital-to-analog converter as standard equipment, playing back sampled sounds has never been a problem. To record your own sounds, however, you'll also need an analog-to-digital converter. All of the recent Macintosh models, such as the LC, the IIsi, and the Quadra, come with a built-in analog-to-digital converter and a small button-shaped condenser microphone that plugs into an audio input jack. If you don't have one of the Macs with on-board recording hardware, you can still record your own sounds by using an external digitizer like MacRecorder or Voice Impact Pro (see Chapter 11).

The enhanced Sound Manager provides a new and improved Sound control panel that lets you record sounds and add them directly to the list of alert sounds. With System 7 you just double-click the Sound icon in the Control Panels folder. The Sound control panel (Figure 16.1) displays a list of available alert sounds and a volume control. When you install a driver for a recording device, an icon appears in a separate display below the list of alert sounds. If you have one of the newer Macs, you'll see a button-microphone icon labeled *Built-in*. If you're using an external digitizer, you'll see an icon for each device driver that is currently installed in the system.

To make a recording, you first select your input device and click the Add button. This opens a standard record dialog box with a basic set of transport controls (Figure 16.2). You can monitor your input levels by watching the number of simulated sound waves that emanate from the loudspeaker icon. If you're using the built-in microphone, you adjust the volume by speaking or playing louder or softer or by repositioning the microphone. External digitizers usually have a volume control.

**Figure 16.1**
The Sound control panel, with several recording device drivers installed

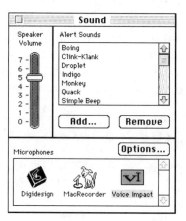

**Figure 16.2**
The standard record dialog box

A thermometer-style display and a digital readout in the dialog box indicate the elapsed time—you can only record for up to 10 seconds. When you're finished, you name the sound and click OK. The Sound Manager then saves the recording as an SND sound resource file and adds it to the list of available alert sounds.

The standard record dialog box is often used from within various kinds of applications. When used in this way, the applications often provide the opportunity to record for periods of time longer than the 10-second limit. They also typically offer the option of recording with a sampling rate lower than the Macintosh's 22-kHz (actually 22.254-kHz) output rate. Additionally, many programs allow you to take advantage of the Sound Manager's compression and expansion capabilities to reduce file size. Aside from SND sound resources, applications can use the Sound Manager to store sounds in Audio IFF and Audio IFF-C file formats.

# QuickTime

When Apple introduced QuickDraw and the PICT file format several years ago, it ushered in a new era of desktop publishing by enabling Macintosh users to paste graphics easily into virtually any text document. With the introduction of QuickTime, in January of 1992, Apple has taken another quantum leap—this time into the world of multimedia. QuickTime represents a major step in the ongoing evolution of the Macintosh system by allowing users to integrate time-based data into mainstream applications as easily as they now do with still graphics and text. Time-based data, or *dynamic data* as it's often called, is data that is stored and retrieved as values over time, such as video, animation, and sound.

## How It Works

QuickTime is actually an extension of the Macintosh's system software that lets you store, exchange, and manipulate this dynamic data in the same ways as with other standard elements in the Macintosh environment. It also provides a uniform means of connecting applications to a variety of media-related hardware, like CD-ROM players, videodisc players, VCRs, and audio NuBus cards.

The time-based data, drawn from its various sources, is integrated into a single file format called a *movie*. QuickTime movies consist of one or more tracks, each containing information that pertains to a specific type of dynamic data. A simple movie might have only a video and an audio track, while more complex movies (planned for future releases) could have several tracks.

Although each track handles a particular type of data, it doesn't actually contain the data itself. Instead, it identifies and points to where the data is stored and retrieves it for playback at the appropriate time. To accomplish this, the track must specify the order in which segments of data are to be played, how long each segment will last, what its playback speed will be, and other characteristics that relate to the type of media being addressed. QuickTime then takes this information and correlates the different time scales used by the individual tracks and synchronizes all of the data to create the finished movie (Figure 16.3).

**Figure 16.3**
A QuickTime movie typically appears in a small window with a few transport controls and a scroll bar. The speaker icon lets you set the volume level.

A QuickTime Movie file acts much like a clearinghouse for data that is stored in RAM, on hard disks, on CD-ROMs, or elsewhere. As Apple puts it, "The movie is not the medium; it is the organizing principle." This modular structure means that the large data files needed for playback can be stored separately, in appropriate media, allowing the movie files themselves to remain small. This fact, along with QuickTime's full support by the Clipboard and Scrapbook, makes it practical to cut, copy, and paste movies between documents the same way you do with still images.

The QuickTime movie format also specifies two features to help identify and organize movies. A *poster* is a single frame image used as a thumbnail to identify a movie file visually. A *preview* is a short excerpt from a movie, typically no more than 3 to 5 seconds long, that provides a glimpse into the movie's contents.

QuickTime adds three new *managers* to the Macintosh System. The first of these, the Movie Toolbox, provides developers with software routines that enable applications to create, store, retrieve, edit, and manipulate Quick-Time movies. Using the tools provided with the Movie Toolbox, programmers can add Copy, Paste, Resize, and Play commands to existing applications.

The Image Compression Manager provides a set of routines that compress and decompress high-resolution color images or sequences of graphic images to reduce their storage requirements. QuickTime includes three kinds of image compressors: one for photo images, one for video data, and another for animation files. Others will be added as future needs arise.

The third QuickTime manager is called the Component Manager. The Component Manager lets programmers define and register the capabilities of external resources, such as digitizer cards, VCRs, and system software extensions. While a program is running, it can gain access to specific components (software modules) by referring to the Component Manager, which acts as an interface between the external resources and the application. This makes the hardware transparent to use and allows developers to include access to new devices without having to modify their applications.

QuickTime also adds an important new development for handling graphics. The new Movie format extends the PICT file format to handle compressed still images. Any program that can now open a standard PICT file can use QuickTime to open compressed PICT images. There's also another PICT extension that supports previewing of images with small thumbnail versions that you can use for browsing through collections of files.

## *Synchronization and Sound*

The problem of synchronizing audio and video has been a gadfly buzzing around the heads of multimedia producers for a long time now. The trouble comes from two sources. The first problem arises when you create a presentation on one model of Macintosh and play it back on a different model, or one with a faster or slower hard disk, or a different screen redraw rate. If you change the hardware parameters, your presentation will surely be played back at a different speed than when it was originally created, and the audio that goes with the visuals will almost immediately fall out of sync.

Second, there is the question of what constitutes real time in a computer presentation. In some presentations it's clear when the playback speed is correct because people seem to move in a normal way and the movements of physical objects appear to obey the natural laws of gravity. But what is real time for a flying logo, or an animated bar graph, or a horizontal wipe transition? And how do you tell if the playback speed has changed and the original durations of your video segments are no longer the same?

QuickTime solves these problems by defining a *time coordinate system* that anchors movies and their tracks to a common reference. Since the tracks in a movie derive their timing from the operating system, everything stays in sync no matter what computer model you use for playback. When a movie contains both audio and video tracks, QuickTime defaults to using the sound track as the master timing reference and slaves the video to the audio. This ensures that the audio will always be played back correctly regardless of the computing environment. If, on a particular computer, the video track can't keep up with the audio playback rate, QuickTime will selectively drop occasional video frames to keep the two tracks progressing together. The reasoning behind this arrangement comes from the fact that when audio playback slows, its pitch drops and it sounds terrible. The video, on the other hand, can lose an occasional frame and still work reasonably well.

The sound that QuickTime uses is the same 8-bit digital audio that all Macintoshes currently use. Apple plans to add MIDI capabilities in future releases through the integration of MIDI Manager (see below) and Quick-Time. Opcode Systems has already written a QuickTime driver into Max, its real-time, graphic-based MIDI programming environment.

## Requirements

To use QuickTime you must have a Macintosh with a 68020, 68030, or 68040 processor, a color display, and a hard disk. Although QuickTime will run in 2MB of RAM, at least 4MB is highly recommended. In most cases you'll also need a CD-ROM player. Apple recommends a drive with an average seek time of less than 400 milliseconds.

# MIDI Manager

If you've been using, or exploring the possibility of using, MIDI software during the past year or so, you no doubt have encountered Apple's MIDI Manager. Most MIDI programs available today are at least compatible with MIDI Manager and many of them require it. Throughout this book, the name MIDI Manager pops up in conjunction with sequencers, universal editor/librarians, and other MIDI applications. But many people still don't know what MIDI Manager is and why it exists.

## *What It Does*

MIDI Manager allows different MIDI programs and hardware devices to coexist peacefully and to communicate with one another without causing system conflicts. Although MultiFinder made it possible to run several programs at once, it wasn't much use for MIDI applications until MIDI Manager appeared. Before MIDI Manager, if you put your sequencer into Play or Record and then tried to switch to a different program or choose a desk accessory from the Apple menu, you couldn't do it. You first had to stop the sequencer to open another program.

This is because MIDI sequencers need to access the built-in high-resolution timer that is part of the inner workings of the Macintosh. And sequencers also tie up one or both of the serial ports to communicate with your MIDI interface. If another program tries to access the timer or the serial ports while the sequencer has them busy, a conflict will occur and problems will arise.

To prevent this, MIDI programs in the past were forced to commandeer the serial ports and set up the timer for their own needs. If you were running two MIDI programs under MultiFinder and you wanted to switch between them, the active program would disconnect itself when switched to the background and would later have to reconnect when made active again.

Clearly, this arrangement was not conducive to MIDI multitasking and the real-time exchange of data, because only the currently active application could send and receive MIDI messages.

## How It Does It

To resolve this problem, Apple created a single driver that several applications could share so that each program wouldn't have to monopolize the hardware with its own driver. With the birth of MIDI Manager, multiple MIDI programs could send and receive data on the modem and printer ports. Furthermore, MIDI Manager allows you to connect the output from one program to the input of another through its *virtual ports.* You can have as many as 16 ports (input, output, and timer combined) for each application.

MIDI Manager actually consists of three parts: MIDI Manager, the Apple MIDI Driver, and PatchBay. The MIDI Manager part is a start-up document that goes in the System Folder. The Apple MIDI Driver also goes in the System Folder and allows access to the modem and printer ports when an application signs in to MIDI Manager. PatchBay is the application that lets you connect MIDI programs graphically with on-screen "patch cords" that connect the various MIDI Manager ports (Figure 16.4).

While most MIDI products are compatible with MIDI Manager, some products, like Digidesign's SampleCell (see Chapter 12), absolutely require it. Through MIDI Manager, you can send MIDI messages directly to the SampleCell NuBus card without using a MIDI interface or MIDI cables.

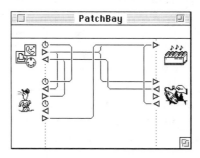

**Figure 16.4**
PatchBay lets you connect MIDI hardware and software graphically with on-screen "patch cords."

Most of the programs covered in Chapters 5, 6, and 14 will work with MIDI Manager as well.

## How It Affects Performance

There's one drawback, however, to using MIDI Manager: It slows down your computer. When it's active, MIDI Manager is very busy handling large amounts of data and timing information in an effort to service the connected MIDI devices and applications. MIDI Manager gives priority to MIDI timing to ensure that recording and playback remain consistent in spite of the extra processor load. This results in a sometimes noticeable slowing in the speed at which the Macintosh performs certain other tasks.

If you have a Mac II or faster model, it probably won't cause much of a problem. On the slower models (Plus, SE, Classic), performance speed may lag too much to be acceptable. To a great extent, it depends on the programs you're running and the demands you place on them. In any event, avoid using versions of MIDI Manager prior to version 2.0. These earlier releases were notoriously buggy and problematic.

## One Last Thought

Perhaps the most amazing thing about MIDI Manager is that it exists at all. By creating MIDI Manager, Apple Computer has not only acknowledged the importance of MIDI music but has supported its inclusion into our total computing experience. What a country!

# Chapter 17

# Hardware

The Macintosh is a terrific computer for multimedia production, but it can't be all things to all people. Each person has to add the necessary hardware that will make the system work for him or her. When it comes to sound and music, there are many options available for expanding the Macintosh's capabilities. I've discussed many of these products in detail in the previous chapters. In this chapter I'll explore in greater depth some of the hardware options that I touched on briefly in Chapters 2, 3, and 7.

## ≡ Sound Modules and More

If you've been in almost any large music store lately, you know that the world is awash in a sea of sound modules, keyboards, and MIDI devices of every type and description. Amazingly enough, most of these products are actually quite good. Certainly some instruments sound worse than others, but then they generally cost less as well. Some devices may have fewer features than others, but then they may be easier to use.

Overall, most products maintain a good balance between their positive and negative qualities and you'll find avid fans of nearly every MIDI contraption ever made. When shopping for MIDI instruments, it's best to know what your particular requirements are and then take into account each instrument's cost, available sounds, and specific features in making a final assessment.

Clearly, it would be impractical for me to list and describe every sound module on the market today. So I've chosen several that I consider noteworthy from the standpoint of creating an integrated desktop presentation system. These include a number of components from Roland that are designed as computer peripherals, several high-quality sample-playback units from E-mu, and a couple of General MIDI–compatible modules from Yamaha and Korg.

## *Roland*

Responding to the ever-growing interest in computer-based multimedia, Roland Corp. has introduced a line of music peripherals designed specifically to interface with desktop computer systems. This is noteworthy because it means that one of the world's largest manufacturers of electronic musical instruments has recognized the importance of the growing market for multimedia sound production and has committed itself to an extensive product line that enables users to create high-fidelity, professional-sounding music directly from the desktop.

Many of the products described below are based on Roland's highly successful LA synthesis technology and have existed in previous incarnations as some of its most popular general-purpose electronic-music instruments. But the components here (with a couple of exceptions) reveal their intended use through several unique and telling design characteristics.

First, they're all housed in platinum-colored plastic cases that coordinate well with the look of the current Macintosh models. Second, the sound modules are sized and shaped to fit neatly under a Mac Plus, SE, or Classic (much like an external hard drive) to give the appearance of an integrated, desktop sound-production system. And finally, the sound modules are nearly devoid of front panel controls. Each unit has a power switch, a volume control, and nothing else. This design is based on the assumption that since these modules are to be part of a computer music system, you'll accomplish all parameter setting operations through your software (see Chapter 9). Although this design cuts costs and creates a sleek-looking box, some users may be somewhat troubled by this lack of direct access.

### CM-32L

To form the core of its computer-music product line, Roland offers a choice of several music sound modules that you can interconnect to expand the system as needed. One module that makes a good first choice for an inexpensive, basic setup is the CM-32L—a synthesizer module utilizing Roland's proprietary LA (linear/arithmetic) technology.

Internally similar to the popular MT-32 music module, the CM-32L offers improved signal-to-noise ratio and significantly expanded memory, enabling it to include numerous additional sound effects that increase its suitability for multimedia presentations and postproduction sound. The CM-32L has 32-voice maximum polyphony and nine-part multitimbral capability consisting of eight synthesizer parts and one rhythm part. This enables you to combine sounds from 128 internal synthesized tones, 30 percussion sounds, and 33 sound effects to produce musical arrangements with a fair degree of complexity and texture in a good variety of styles.

Rounding out the list of features, a built-in digital reverb adds a sense of realism and spatial placement to the sounds. The CM-32L is currently compatible with several popular entertainment software packages that incorporate orchestral soundtracks and creative sound effects into their adventure games.

## CM-32P

If you're seeking to expand your palette of musical sounds, Roland offers a sample-playback module—the CM-32P. Almost identical to the CM-32L in appearance, this module uses resynthesized PCM sampled sounds, stored in ROM, as preset tones. It has 31-voice maximum polyphony, six-part multitimbral capability, and 64 internal preset tones. Since the CM-32P represents an improved version of Roland's earlier U-110 PCM sound module, it can accept, in its front-panel card slot, the extended library of sounds available on ROM cards for the U-110. This expandability, combined with the on-board digital reverb, makes the CM-32P an ideal module to use for adding high-quality, sampled sounds to a musical score.

## CM-64

The CM-64 looks like a clone of the CM-32P but contains within the same housing all of the capabilities of the CM-32P and CM-32L. This unit boasts a very impressive 63-voice maximum polyphony (32+31) along with

15-part multitimbral capability, a digital reverb, and a front-panel ROM card slot. If you're looking for a desktop orchestra-in-a-box for your presentations, this music module is worth considering.

## SC-55

As the final details of the General MIDI Standard were being hammered out, Roland was hard at work preparing for the release of the SC-55 Sound Canvas—the first General MIDI–compatible sound module. The SC-55 (Figure 17.1) incorporates Roland's GS Standard format, a superset of General MIDI that follows all of the protocols and sound maps of the General MIDI Specification while adding more controllers and sounds.

**Figure 17.1**
The Roland SC-55 Sound Canvas

The SC-55 also represents a significant improvement in sound quality, synthesis techniques, and editing capabilities over the first-generation computer-music modules described above. Roland plans to gradually phase out its earlier LA synthesis modules as the new GS Standard takes hold. Many of the producers of sequenced MIDI music mentioned in Chapter 7 now support General MIDI and a few have sequences specifically arranged for the SC-55. These sequences take advantage of the SC-55's additional capabilities, but they should also work fine with other General MIDI sound modules.

Because there is still a very large installed base of users with MT-32/CM-32L–compatible products, Roland wisely included a subset of the SC-55's sounds that re-creates the 128 patches in the MT-32/CM-32L along with the corresponding Program Change numbers. This means that games and third-party sequences designed to go with the MT-32/CM-32L can still work, although the SC-55 won't recognize system-exclusive messages for these earlier instruments.

Although, technically speaking, the SC-55 is not part of Roland's computer-music peripherals collection, its support of General MIDI combined with its wireless remote control and small, half-rack size make it highly appropriate for desktop presentations.

The SC-55 has a generous 315 sounds along with nine drum sets to cover a variety of musical needs. It offers 16-part multitimbral operation with a maximum 24-voice polyphony. You can further enhance the sounds with the on-board digital reverb and chorus effect.

The front panel provides an array of buttons that let you assign instruments, adjust level and pan, apply reverb and chorus, select MIDI channels, and more. Settings and other information are clearly shown on a large LCD screen that includes a real-time bar-graph display of the output levels for each Part. Additionally, two audio-input jacks on the rear panel let you mix stereo audio signals from an external source, like a tape deck, mixer, or hi-fi, with the SC-55's internal sounds.

## SC-155

The SC-155 Sound Canvas is a tabletop sound module that is largely the same as the SC-55 except that it adds some important new internal and external features. It offers 317 instrument sounds, nine drum sets, and the same built-in reverb and chorus effects. It also provides an MT-32 compatibility mode and the same General MIDI and GS Standard characteristics as the SC-55. It has 16-part multitimbral capability, 24-voice polyphony, and a real-time LCD bar-graph display.

The big difference between the SC-155 and the SC-55 is the presence, on the SC-155, of nine slider controls (eight Parts plus one master control). By using the Part sliders, you can adjust the volume level and pan position of up to eight Parts simultaneously. When you play back a sequence, these sliders let you control the different instrument sounds as you would with an audio mixer. You can assign the sliders to control Parts 1–8 or 9–16, and you can store the instrument sound assignments and the corresponding level and pan settings in the SC-155's memory.

The sliders can also send MIDI data to a sequencer. Using the MIDI Send function, you can record level and pan data in real time into your sequencer to provide automated mixing capabilities. You can also assign the sliders to control other sound parameters, like modulation, vibrato, cutoff frequency, resonance, reverb, and chorus.

The SC-155 has several features that let you create "music-minus-one" performances. You can play back any sequence and mute an individual Part so you can play it yourself. Or you can select a specific Part and listen to it alone. The SC-155's Minus One function makes it easy to include yourself in a MIDI performance. You simply connect the sequencer output to MIDI In 1 and the keyboard to MIDI In 2. When you select a Part for muting, that Part won't sound. Instead, the notes that you play will replace it in real time without changing the original sequence. The SC-155 also provides the same audio-input jacks for mixing stereo external sources with the SC-155's on-board sounds.

## CM-300

The CM-300 (Figure 17.2) represents the second generation of Roland's computer-music sound modules. Internally it is virtually identical to the SC-55, but comes housed in the same platinum-colored case that the CM-32L uses. It has all of the SC-55's internal sounds, including the nine drum sets and the built-in reverb and chorus effects. It also provides the same 16-part multitimbral capability and 24-voice polyphony. With the CM-300, you give up the SC-55's front panel buttons and LCD display in exchange for a less expensive, sleek-looking box that matches your other computer accessories. The CM-300 is, in essence, the GS Standard/General MIDI version of the CM-32L.

The CM-300 includes 192 sounds that emulate the tone assignments in the CM-64, so you can play back sequence data that already exists for the MT-32, CM-32L, and CM-64 without modification. The CM-300, however, does not respond to system-exclusive messages for these other sound modules and may not always provide the same polyphony as the CM-64.

**Figure 17.2**
The Roland CM-300

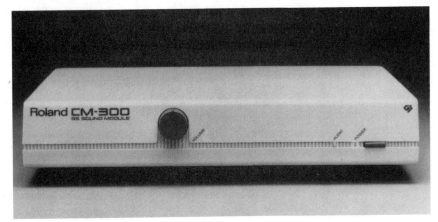

The CM-300 sports the same audio-input jacks that the other modules provide. With these jacks you can connect another sound module to the CM-300 and combine the two sound sources without using a mixer.

## CM-500

For those computer users who want the best of both worlds, Roland offers the CM-500—a combination of the CM-32L and the CM-300 in a single case. The CM-500 includes 317 GS-compatible sounds and 128 LA-synthesis sounds for an impressive 445 available Tones. There are also 64 user-programmable Tones in the LA section. The LA section has a built-in reverb effect, and the GS section offers reverb, digital delay, and chorus. With the GS section, you can play with 16-part multitimbral capability and 24-voice polyphony. In the LA section, you have 8-part multitimbral capability and 32-voice polyphony, giving you the ability to play up to 56 notes at one time.

You can configure the CM-500 in four different modes, which allow you to play the GS section alone or in combination with the LA section. In CM-300 mode, the CM-500 can play any GS-compatible data without modification. In the CM-64 Simulation mode, there are nine channels of LA sounds and six channels of simulated PCM sounds. This makes the CM-500 compatible with games and other software that use MT-32 system-exclusive messages.

With either of these modes, you can play back sequence data created for the MT-32, CM-32L, CM-32P, CM-64, and any other GS-compatible sound modules. The other modes offer preset or selectable combinations of the two sounds. The CM-500 does not provide the audio-input jacks that the other modules have; the remaining controls and connections are the same.

## PC-200

To produce musical sounds from these modules, you'll first have to connect a MIDI input device. This can be any kind of MIDI controller, but the most common type is a piano-style keyboard. As I explained in Chapter 3, MIDI keyboard controllers look like synthesizers, but do not produce any sounds of their own. Instead they transmit MIDI note on/off messages to a MIDI-equipped sound module or computer.

As part of its computer music series, Roland offers the PC-200 MIDI Data Keyboard. This inexpensive, compact device can be powered by batteries or an AC adapter. Although its MIDI implementation is somewhat limited and its range (four octaves) is rather small, it may still satisfy the requirements of those who only need an inexpensive, basic MIDI keyboard.

The PC-200—unlike its predecessor, the PC-100—sends MIDI velocity data, which allows you to add dynamic expression to your music. You can also send program changes on all 16 MIDI channels with its MIDI/Select button. The PC-200 provides a data-entry slider that you can use to adjust volume, stereo panning, and velocity range. The bender/modulation lever lets you send continuous controller messages to add such things as pitch bend and vibrato to your performances.

Experienced players and those with more demanding requirements would do well to consider some of the professional-level controllers that are currently on the market. These keyboards, offered by Roland, Yamaha, Kawai, and others, provide (at much greater cost) extensive MIDI implementation, better keyboard feel, and a wider range.

## CA-30

By now you may be thinking, "I want one of those sound modules, but I only had two years of piano lessons as a kid and I don't have a clue about how to write a musical arrangement." Fortunately for you and the many other amateur musicians in the world, Roland has created the CA-30 "Intelligent Arranger." This unassuming, membrane-paneled rectangle is actually a sophisticated music-generating device.

Styled to match the other components in the Roland computer music series, it sits perfectly on top of the sound modules and creates, from the simplest input, a full-fledged musical arrangement. A MIDI keyboard plugs into the CA-30, which in turn plugs into a sound module (either the CM-32L or the CM-64). After that, you simply play chords in the appropriate zone of the keyboard so that the unit knows what harmonies you want. If your keyboard skills are not up to par, a "chord intelligence" function enables you to play one- and two-note reductions of chords, which the "arranger" transforms into full harmonies.

The CA-30 automatically accesses the appropriate instruments from the sound module and produces a surprisingly musical combination of sounds, rhythms, and textures. There are 32 musical styles built into the unit (including rock, reggae, Dixieland, country, polka, samba, and fusion, to name a few), and you can expand this list via the ROM-card slot on the rear panel and Roland's "Style Card Library."

Each arrangement consists of a drum part, a bass part, and two or three accompanying instrumental parts, which all vary according to the style selected. Each style has an original version and a variation, as well as a basic and advanced arrangement. All of this, combined with breaks, fills, intros, and endings, provides enough raw material to create accompaniments that sound both interesting and musical. Of course you won't be putting Henry Mancini or Quincy Jones to shame, but you can assemble, quickly and easily, a good generic background accompaniment to play against a soloist or under narration.

By entering your chord changes and melody line into a sequencer, which then transmits the data to the CA-30, your arrangement can be triggered by the appropriate presentation software (see Chapter 15). More advanced MIDI users may be frustrated by this unit's need to do things its own way, but fortunately you can send the MIDI output of the CA-30 to a sequencer, where you can perform more complex editing operations on its musical parts.

The primary drawback of this product is its infectious nature. More addictive than opium, you'll find this little box so entertaining that once you start using it, your family may begin to wonder why they don't see you so much anymore.

Although the CA-30 is designed to go with the LA synthesis sound modules, it can also work with any of the GS-compatible modules. It won't, however, take advantage of the improvements and new features that are unique to these instruments. According to Roland, it's likely that the CA-30 will someday be replaced by another unit that is designed to go with the GS Standard instruments.

## E-mu Systems

When E-mu first released its Proteus sound module a few years ago, it was an overnight success. Store owners couldn't keep them in stock and everyone was talking about this new MIDI instrument. The reason for all this attention was that the Proteus offered, at a reasonable price, a 16-bit, rack-mountable, stereo, sample-playback module with excellent sound quality and a long list of features.

The Proteus has since grown into three different models, each with one or more variations. All of the Proteus sound modules get their samples from the famous Emulator III sound library and store the sounds in ROM for instant access. Although these modules are not designed specifically for multimedia, their compact size, high fidelity, and flexibility make them ideally suited to many kinds of desktop presentations and music applications.

### Proteus/1

The Proteus/1 provides 192 performance patches, which it calls *presets*. The presets are constructed from its list of internal sounds called *instruments*, which are stored in 4 megabytes of ROM (expandable to 8 megabytes). The instruments are built from 125 waveforms in various types consisting of sampled sounds and several smaller waveforms, including single-cycle waveforms (sampled and synthesized), multicycle waveforms, and harmonic waveforms.

A preset corresponds to one MIDI channel and can consist of either one or two instruments, each with its own key range, tuning, volume, pan position, chorusing, and modulation. If you have two instruments in a preset, you can crossfade or switch between them using key ranges, velocity, or foot-switch triggers. Presets respond to pitch bend, aftertouch, and up to four user-selected MIDI controllers. Additionally, you can combine, or "link," up to four presets to create even more complex sounds. The Proteus/1 allows you to choose one of six tuning scales for each preset. Aside from the standard equal-tempered scale, there are four alternate scales available internally and one user-defined scale. From the total number of available presets, 64 are user-programmable, allowing you to create new sounds by combining different waveforms to produce new instruments.

The Proteus/1 has 16-part multitimbral capability and a maximum 32-voice polyphony. On its back panel there are three pairs of audio outputs, labeled Main, Sub1, and Sub2. You can configure these to provide three separate stereo outputs (or six mono outputs), and you can also use the Sub jacks as sends and returns for external effects devices.

The front panel of the Proteus is simple and clear in its design. Selecting presets and changing most parameters is straightforward and logical. The 16-bit, 39-kHz sampled sounds are very clean and for the most part quite realistic. In the Proteus/1, they are primarily oriented toward rock, pop, and other commercial styles of music. There is a good assortment of acoustic and electric keyboards, synthesizers, basses, and guitars, along with some brass, a few woodwinds, strings, and choirs, and many drum and percussion sounds.

The Proteus/1 also comes in a Proteus/1 XR version, which provides room for 256 user presets but is otherwise the same. Digidesign is currently marketing a Proteus/1 on a NuBus card, called MacProteus. It will work with any Mac II and a sequencer that supports Apple's MIDI Manager (see Chapter 16). The MacProteus card provides only one set of stereo outputs and it can't have its ROM expanded.

## Proteus/2

The Proteus/2 is virtually identical in appearance to the Proteus/1. Internally, the two are also very similar. They use the same structures involving instruments and presets and provide the same editing, modifying, and performance setup capabilities. The internal samples and most of the additional waveforms, of course, are different in the Proteus/2, which requires 8 megabytes of ROM to store its sounds. This is an orchestrally oriented sound module that nicely complements the Proteus/1. There is little overlap between the two, and the Proteus/2 supplies many of the sounds missing in the Proteus/1 that are important to composers working in the field of film and video scoring.

The Proteus/2's list of sounds includes a good assortment of stringed instruments—both plucked and bowed—in solo and various ensemble combinations. There is also a collection of orchestral brass—both solo and ensemble—and an excellent assortment of very fine woodwind sounds. The percussion sounds are primarily symphonic in nature, but the keyboard sounds lean heavily toward synthesized timbres and electronic organ sounds. Additionally, there are a few basses and a number of atmospheric sound effects. The Proteus/2 also comes in a Proteus/2 XR version, which adds more user-preset locations.

## Proteus/3

The Proteus/3 is the newest member of the Proteus family. It uses the same 16-bit stereo technology to store its sounds in 4 megabytes of ROM. As with the other units, it provides 32-voice polyphony, 16-channel multitimbral capability, and six audio outputs. The Proteus/3 is filled with interesting and unique sounds from around the world. In its collection you'll find such unusual sounds as Aboriginal Digeridoo, Arabian Mizmar, French Troubadour Harp, and African Udo Drum. Other instruments from the British Isles, India, Cuba, Japan, South America, the Middle East, Africa, and Europe contribute to an assortment of sampled sounds that is exciting in its musical potential. You can use the Proteus/3 to create ethnic compositions or combine the instruments to form new timbres for sound effects and soundtracks. The Proteus/3 also comes in an XR version.

# *Yamaha*

Yamaha markets an extensive line of electronic musical instruments and accessories, including MIDI controllers, effects processors, synthesizers, and sound modules too numerous to mention. One of its newest sound modules, however, should be of particular interest to desktop multimedia producers. The **TG100** (Figure 17.3) is Yamaha's first General MIDI–compatible sound module. This low-cost sample-playback unit comes with 200 sounds stored in ROM—192 instrument voices and eight drum kits. There are also 64 user-programmable voices in RAM. The TG100 provides 16-part multitimbral capability, a maximum 28-note polyphony, and an on-board reverb effect.

**Figure 17.3**
The Yamaha TG100

As with the Roland sound modules, the TG100 provides a stereo audio-input connection so you can mix the output from an external sound source with the TG100's sounds. The Yamaha instrument, however, carries the audio-input implementation one step further by also including an input level control and an LED to serve as a signal-level peak indicator. The front panel also includes several buttons for accessing editing parameters and playback settings, a large volume control, and a small, one-line LCD display.

Of particular note, the TG100 provides a dedicated To Host connection on its back panel, which lets you connect the module directly to your computer without the need for a MIDI interface. In fact, with the TG100 configured in this way, it can act as a MIDI interface itself, allowing you to attach other MIDI instruments to it. In addition to this connection, the TG100 also has the usual MIDI In, Out, and Thru ports, so you can use it with a standard MIDI interface in the more typical way. If you're looking for an inexpensive General MIDI sound module with front panel controls and several unique features, the TG100 is worth considering.

## Korg

Like Roland and Yamaha, Korg also produces a long line of highly regarded synthesizers, sound modules, effects processors, and MIDI accessories. With the introduction of its **03R/W Synthesis Module** (Figure 17.4), Korg has embraced the General MIDI Standard with a one-rack-space sound module that has a great deal to offer.

**Figure 17.4**
The Korg 03R/W Synthesis Module

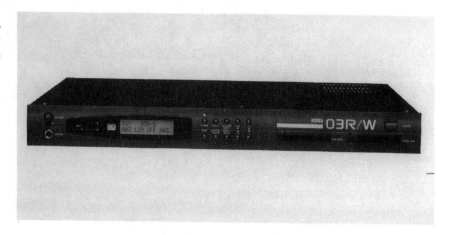

The 03R/W borrows many features from Korg's powerful 01/W synthesizer, including the Advanced Integrated Synthesis System, which uses PCM sampled sounds for its source material. The 03R/W's tone generator comes with 255 multisampled instrument sounds and 114 drum sounds. These are used as the starting point of a multistage synthesis process that includes oscillators and variable digital filters and amplifiers.

To further enhance its sounds, the 03R/W provides a dual-system multieffects processor that lets you choose from 47 different effects, including reverb, digital delay, chorusing, flanging, and myriad other options and variations. If you want to expand your available palette of sounds, the 03R/W can use PCM cards from the 01/W Series sound library, which plug into a slot in the 03R/W's front panel.

The 03R/W provides 16-part multitimbral capability and a maximum 32-voice polyphony. In addition to its internal RAM area, which can store up to 100 programs and 100 combinations, the 03R/W includes a ROM area with 128 General MIDI instrument sounds and a drum set configured to meet the General MIDI Standard. The front panel includes two card slots (PCM Data and Program Data), several buttons and LED indicators, and a two-line LCD display. The back panel provides four audio-output jacks and a controller jack for the optional RE1 remote editor unit.

## MIDI Interfaces

As I discussed in Chapter 3, you'll need to get a MIDI interface if you want to connect MIDI instruments to your Macintosh. Unlike some computers, the Mac has no built-in MIDI ports, so the MIDI interface attaches to the Mac's rear panel and provides the missing MIDI In and Out connections.

MIDI transfers data serially, which means that its data bits are sent and received one at a time. MIDI interfaces incorporate a chip called a UART (universal asynchronous receiver/transmitter) that can read the incoming serial data and send it out. Because the Macintosh modem and printer connections are serial ports, the MIDI interface has the simple job of reading the data, converting it into a form that the Macintosh can handle, and sending it on its way.

The only problem that exists in getting a Mac to speak MIDI lies in the disparity between the Mac's data transfer rate and MIDI's. The Mac's serial ports are controlled by the computer's internal clock, which operates at speeds quite different from that of MIDI. To bring the ports into line with MIDI's transfer rate, therefore, the MIDI interface must include an external clock to control the speed of the Macintosh's serial ports.

None of this, however, is terribly important to the typical MIDI musician, who only wants to plug in an instrument and make music. In fact, using a MIDI interface is, for the most part, extremely simple and entirely transparent to the end user. The only real questions arise when it's time to purchase an interface for a desktop studio. Then you'll have to decide how many inputs and outputs you're likely to need in the future, how much money you want to spend, and whether you want the additional features (like SMPTE timecode support) and associated complexity of a high-end, pro-level unit. Here are some examples of the currently available choices for MIDI interfaces.

## Good

The simplest MIDI interface that you can have is a plain box with an input and output for MIDI and a serial connection for the Macintosh. This is exactly what Apple Computer offers with its **Apple MIDI Interface.** This 1-In, 1-Out device comes in a small plastic box about the size of a cigarette pack and requires no external power supply. You just plug it into either the modem or the printer port and attach your MIDI instruments.

Many people may find this back-to-basics design a bit limiting for their tastes. By adding more outputs to an interface, you can connect several MIDI devices directly to the MIDI interface, thereby eliminating the need to daisy-chain your sound modules. Several companies, recognizing this advantage, offer MIDI interfaces that are still very simple but provide additional outputs.

Opcode's **MIDI Translator** is typical of these. It provides one MIDI In and three MIDI Outs from a small gray plastic box that requires no external power. Altech Systems offers two similar interfaces. Its **MIDIFace LX,** a 1-In, 3-Out unit, comes in a metal box with an LED to indicate MIDI activity. It also offers a more expensive version, the **MIDIFace EX,** that adds LEDs and a serial Thru switch so that you can use your serial port without disconnecting the interface. Passport's **MIDI Interface for the Mac** is another inexpensive 1-In, 3-Out unit, in a plastic case with flashing LEDs to indicate the presence of MIDI activity. JLCooper Electronics offers yet another variation on the same theme with its **MacNexus** interface, a 1-In, 3-Out device.

## Better

All of the interfaces described above allow you to send and receive data on MIDI's 16 available channels. Since the Macintosh has two serial ports, you could, if you wanted to, attach an interface to each port and double the number of available MIDI channels. A much better solution, however, is to buy one of the midlevel interfaces that attach to both the printer and modem ports and provide 32 MIDI channels in a single unit with several additional benefits.

The most common configuration is represented by Opcode's popular **Studio Plus Two.** It connects to both Macintosh ports simultaneously and provides two MIDI Ins and six MIDI Outs. With its front-panel switch, you can assign three outputs to each input or have all six outputs connected to a single port.

Because the MIDI interface ties up both the modem and printer ports, the Studio Plus Two provides connections for these peripherals on its rear panel, with bypass switches on the front to disengage the MIDI interface when it's not in use. The front panel also includes LED activity indicators that show the presence of MIDI data at the input and output connections for each serial port. The entire unit is housed in a metal case that can sit under a Mac Plus, SE, or Classic like an external hard drive.

## *Best*

If you're planning to work with film or video, you should consider one of the professional-level MIDI interfaces. These not only provide inputs to and outputs from both serial ports but they also include hardware that lets your computer read and write SMPTE timecode (see Chapter 18). JLCooper offers a relatively inexpensive pro-level interface called **Sync/Link** that comes in a compact, half-space rack-mountable case with LED indicators. It provides a MIDI In and a MIDI Out for each serial port and supports all SMPTE formats through its Sync/Link software.

With Opcode's **Studio 3,** you get two independent MIDI Ins and six MIDI Outs, which are assignable in any combination. To use the Studio 3, you first install the Studio 3 Desk Accessory. This lets you set up your outputs in any combination, such as 3+3, 4+2, 5+1, etc. The desk accessory also lets you choose the SMPTE format that the interface will read, and it lets you output timecode to record on tape when necessary. The Studio 3 comes in a single-space rack-mount case with an AC power cord and two

12-foot serial cables. The front panel provides numerous LEDs to show MIDI activity and includes bypass switches for the printer and modem ports.

## Better Than Best

Although most multimedia artists will never need a MIDI interface with more features than those mentioned above, there may be a few of you who like living at the very top of the high end. The top-of-the-line, pro-level interfaces offer an even greater number of inputs and outputs, full SMPTE support, MIDI patchbay/merging capabilities, and additional features to satisfy the needs of those with elaborate MIDI systems.

The first of these extended pro-level interfaces is from Mark of the Unicorn. Its **MIDI Time Piece** provides eight independent MIDI inputs and outputs in a single-space rack-mount unit. By treating its connections as separate "cables," it lets you assign them any of the 16 MIDI channels, which in turn provides you with control of up to 128 discrete channels. For a really enormous system, you can network up to four of these boxes for a grand total of 512 MIDI channels!

Because you can route any of the eight MIDI Ins to any of the eight MIDI Outs, the MIDI Time Piece can serve as a versatile MIDI patchbay that provides the opportunity to merge, mute, or rechannelize any MIDI data. It also reads and writes all formats of SMPTE timecode and comes with a desk accessory that lets you route MIDI channels and set up synchronization parameters.

The **Studio 5**, Opcode's top-of-the-line MIDI interface, offers an impressive 15 MIDI Ins and Outs for an amazing 240-channel capability. It too combines the functions of a MIDI interface, MIDI patchbay, MIDI processor, and SMPTE synchronizer into a (somewhat larger) rack-mount unit. Its front panel supplies LEDs for MIDI activity as well as a digital display for showing the program number of the current setup. The Studio 5 comes with OMS (Opcode MIDI System) software, which allows you to configure your system in a number of ways using its icon-based graphic displays.

# ▤ Speakers

The speaker that comes with your Macintosh works fine for system beeps, alert messages, and voice-mail annotation. But when it comes to multimedia, using only the built-in speaker for your soundtrack can make your presentation seem smaller and less substantial. Many producers spend so much time and energy creating dazzling graphics and visual effects that they forget how much poor sound quality can undermine the impact of a presentation. Now that Macintosh multimedia can include not only 8-bit digital audio but also 16-bit audio and direct output from MIDI instruments, it pays to upgrade your desktop speaker system.

If you typically present your programs in large auditoriums or lecture halls, you'll need a serious amplifier and a powerful loudspeaker system. But most presentations are aimed at individuals or relatively small groups in conference rooms, classrooms, and retail outlets, and at trade shows. For these situations there are several kinds of compact speaker systems that are designed specifically to sit on the desktop next to your Macintosh and provide it with greater volume and noticeably better sound quality.

The speakers mentioned in this chapter have several traits in common that make them suitable for use with desktop computer systems. For starters, they all have magnetic shielding, which prevents stray magnetism from distorting the images or colors on your monitor if the speakers are placed close by. Second, they all have built-in amplifiers that boost the volume level of the Macintosh's audio output without the need for additional hardware that clutters the workspace. And third, they are all compact, easily mountable, and easy to carry from one location to another.

## *Roland CS-10*

As part of its Desktop Music System, Roland offers two compact speaker systems that blend well with its other components. The CS-10 (Figure 17.5) is a stereo speaker system in a single unit that fits neatly under a compact Macintosh or one of the sound modules described above. On each side of its front panel, there are small forward-facing speakers that handle high- and midrange frequencies, while a single downward-firing woofer projects low frequencies from beneath the case.

**Figure 17.5**
The Roland CS-10

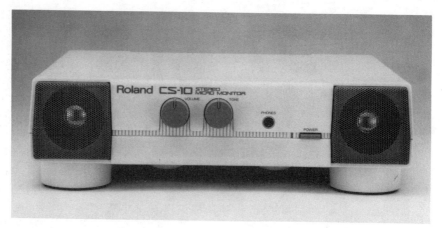

Between the right and left speakers, there are volume and tone controls and a headphone jack that takes a ¼-inch stereo plug. The back panel provides two sets of stereo inputs to accommodate the computer output or any sound modules, tape decks, or other devices.

The CS-10 is compact and simple in design, but it's also limited in many ways. The 5-watt amplifier does not offer enough volume to make it suitable for group listening. The fixed positions of the speakers and the lack of a balance control make it hard to establish the correct sense of stereo sound placement. Nonetheless, the CS-10 does improve the Macintosh's sound by allowing stereo playback, and it offers an easy way to hook up a MIDI sound module for small-room listening.

## *Roland MA-12C*

Roland's MA-12C speaker system (Figure 17.6) costs a little more than the CS-10 but provides much better sound quality and greater power from its 10-watt amplifier. It comes as two independent 4-inch speakers housed in high-quality, compact cases. Each speaker has a high-boost and low-boost EQ control and a volume control on the front panel.

The rear panel provides three separate inputs: microphone, instrument, and line-level. You can use any combination of these inputs to mix sounds simultaneously through the amplifier. The MA-12C is more suitable for

**Figure 17.6**
The Roland MA-12C

musical applications than the CS-10 because of its greater carrying power, flexibility in speaker placement, and higher-fidelity audio output.

## MacSpeaker

MacSpeaker, from Monster Design Group, is similar in some ways to Roland's MA-12C. It also incorporates a 10-watt power amplifier into each compact speaker housing. But MacSpeaker (Figure 17.7) offers several unique features that make it worth looking into. Its two-way "high-resolution" speaker design provides a respectable 75 Hz–18 kHz frequency response, and its lightweight enclosures make it possible to mount the speakers directly to the sides of your monitor for proper close-range placement with zero footprint.

The side of one speaker provides controls for adjusting volume and bass, and a small jack on the back panel lets you bypass the external speaker so you can listen on headphones. MacSpeaker also includes a unique Sonic Imaging Control, which provides a stereo image even if the audio signal coming from your Macintosh is monaural. A control on the side of the speaker lets you adjust the amount of stereo separation from close-in for one

**Figure 17.7**
MacSpeaker from Monster Design Group

or two people to a wide-field effect that can work reasonably well for small groups. For extended bass response, Monster Design Group also offers an optional subwoofer system that allows you to reproduce frequencies down to 40 Hz.

## Powered Partner 570

The Powered Partner 570 (Figure 17.8) represents a significant step up in both sound quality and power over the speaker systems described above. Manufactured by Acoustic Research, it retails for more than twice as much as MacSpeaker or Roland's MA-12C. Acoustic Research has long enjoyed a reputation for producing excellent-sounding high-quality speaker systems, and the Powered Partner carries on the tradition.

**Figure 17.8**
The Powered Partner 570 from Acoustic Research

It consists of a two-way acoustic suspension system that provides high-fidelity sound from its compact, wedge-shaped, aluminum-alloy enclosures. With a 35-watt power amplifier in each speaker, it is substantially more powerful than the other speaker systems in this chapter. This makes it especially appropriate for small- to moderate-sized groups and explains its popularity for trade show demonstrations and exhibits.

The Powered Partner can operate on either AC or DC electricity, and there are a number of adapters and optional accessories available. Each cabinet includes a single RCA-type input jack and a volume, treble, and bass control. By mounting the wedge-shaped speakers in a corner, you can further enhance their bass response.

# Chapter 18

# Adding Sound after Transfer to Video

Every producer of multimedia must decide at some point what the final format will be for his or her presentation. One very popular approach to creating a finished product is to use the Macintosh to develop the animation, graphics, titles, text, charts, slides, and other visual elements and then transfer the whole shebang onto videotape. This is especially good for product demonstrations, even products that run on the Mac itself. That's why companies like Apple, Microsoft, Adobe, and Digidesign have distributed videotape demos to showcase their products.

## Video Pros and Cons

The advantages of videotape as a final format are clear. For one thing, it's a far more universal format than computer-based media. In recent years, VCRs have become as ubiquitous as the common household telephone. In fact, even outside the home, in places like trade shows, schools, and retail outlets, you're more likely to find a VCR than a functional computer. Once you capture your presentation on tape, you can display it on a much larger color monitor than most Macintoshes offer. And by assembling a presentation in sections, you can create a program that is considerably longer than most computers can hold in memory.

Of course, there are disadvantages. Videotape cassettes are more difficult and expensive to reproduce, package, and ship than floppy disks. And, most important, one very significant aspect of multimedia is unavailable from videotape: interactivity. Video presentations don't allow a user to interact with a program, such as a training video for instance, the way the Macintosh does. With many animation and presentation applications offering more features designed to exploit the potential for interactive multimedia, you may not be willing to sacrifice this aspect.

Nevertheless, if you decide to work with videotape, you'll gain some additional benefits with regard to sound. Using a VCR instead of a computer to play back a presentation eliminates the audio-visual synchronization problems that often plague computer-based programs. Since all VCRs play back at the same number of frames per second, you can rest assured that your animation will progress at the proper speed and the audio track will stay in sync no matter what machine it's played on. Additionally, you can draw from a variety of sources for sound effects, music, and dialog, and the final audio quality will be better than the internal 8-bit audio that comes from the Mac.

After you transfer your presentation to videotape, you use the same basic process for building the soundtrack that is used in postproduction for television, movies, and commercial videos. I'll begin by focusing on music—where to get it and how it's synchronized to the visuals.

## ▤ Production Music Libraries

The quickest and easiest way to provide music for a video presentation is to use one of the many *production music libraries*. These collections of compact discs contain a wide variety of musical styles designed specifically as background, main-title, and theme music (see Chapter 19). Although the compositional quality may vary from piece to piece and company to company, the recording and overall sound quality are generally very high.

Libraries are usually arranged according to musical styles. Within each style there are frequently a variety of formats, such as 30-second and 60-second pieces for commercials, short "stings" for logos and introductions, and longer selections of 2 to 4 minutes. Because these libraries are designed for production use, you don't have to worry about copyright hassles once you've paid the appropriate usage fee. This makes them easy and convenient to use for a wide range of situations.

The big advantage of prerecorded music is, of course, that it's prerecorded, and this gives you the opportunity to hear several pieces and reflect on the suitability of each before committing to one for your project. The big disadvantage of prerecorded music is, of course, that it's prerecorded and will, therefore, never perfectly fit your presentation if you're adding the music after the visuals are completed. This lack of what I call "aesthetic resonance" often gives a video soundtrack that "canned music" quality, and, in the extreme, this can ruin an otherwise fine presentation.

Almost any piece of prerecorded music will occasionally line up with events on screen, just as a broken clock will occasionally show the right time. But if you find that the visuals and the music are strolling along their separate ways and acting as if they don't know each other, it's time to put more effort into making your musical selections or, perhaps, consider the next option: original music.

## Original Music

In the hands of a good composer, original music can match your visuals precisely. A well-constructed musical score can support, enhance and even create a sense of architectural form in your presentation. This alone can significantly improve audience involvement by carrying viewers from section to section as the program unfolds. Specific events on screen can be emphasized musically within the fabric of the ongoing score and thereby highlight key points in the presentation. Want a cymbal crash and brass fanfare every time your company logo appears on screen? No problem! Want a timpani roll and orchestral flourish for each new product announced? No problem! The tight bonding of music to visuals grabs the viewer's attention and creates a more absorbing and professional presentation.

Lack of time and money are the two most common concerns about working with a composer. Certainly, you should allow a little extra time, and perhaps some additional money, to have custom music written for your presentation. But you may be surprised to find that the time and money issues are not the problems that they were just a decade ago. Recent developments in the areas of electronic music equipment and computer-integrated postproduction systems have created a proliferation of small music studios, often called *project studios,* that can offer a reasonably priced, high-quality alternative to prerecorded music. To make effective use of this new technology, you'll need a general understanding of how a small studio operates and what is expected of you as the producer of a video presentation.

Project studios use many of the products that I've described in earlier chapters of this book. In a Mac-based studio, you'll typically find an assortment of MIDI synthesizers, sound modules, effects processors, and other music accessories. There will be a video recorder that uses either ½-inch tape (VHS) or ¾-inch tape and a television set or video monitor for playback. The computer in this type of audio-for-video studio always runs one of the high-end sequencer programs (see Chapter 5) because they provide an essential feature for working with video: the ability to read SMPTE timecode.

## SMPTE Timecode

SMPTE (pronounced "simpty") stands for the Society of Motion Picture and Television Engineers, which adapted the timecode standard (from one originated at NASA) in 1969. Unlike film, where each frame is clearly visible, videotape doesn't allow you to see its individual frames directly. But video consists of frames just as film does, and just as film identifies each frame with an edge number, video uses a time-based code to identify each of its frames. The system that SMPTE uses for marking video locations consists of an eight-digit number based on a 60-minute clock. The timecode locations appear as four sets of two numbers representing hours, minutes, seconds, and frames. An individual frame indicated by a SMPTE number might appear as 06:37:14:25.

Actually there are two kinds of SMPTE code currently in use: *longitudinal time code* (LTC) and *vertical interval time code* (VITC, pronounced "vitzy"). Longitudinal timecode uses an audio tone to carry its stream of data, which you record onto an audiotape or onto one of the audio tracks of a videotape. When you play back your video, the channel with the timecode signal gets routed to the audio-in jack of your MIDI interface. All pro-level interfaces (see Chapter 17) can read and write SMPTE code and provide an audio input jack for this purpose. The MIDI interface then translates the code into a form that the computer can handle and the sequencer program can follow (Figure 18.1). By setting the sequencer to sync to an external source, the sequencer can "lock to picture," allowing the composer to work directly with the video.

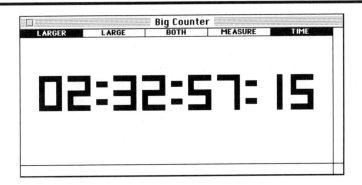

**Figure 18.1**
Master Tracks Pro 5's enlarged timecode display lets you read the SMPTE numbers from across the studio.

Vertical interval timecode is integrated into the video signal and recorded onto an unused portion of the videotape. This frees up an audio track and allows you to know exact frame numbers even when the tape is paused. But VITC reading and writing devices are considerably more expensive and less common than LTC devices. In either case, the timecode itself is the same.

Unfortunately, SMPTE code comes in several frame rates just to keep things confusing. Originally, video timecode was based on a rate of 30 fps (frames per second). But when the video standard changed from black-and-white to color, the 30-fps rate had to be adjusted slightly to 29.97 fps. Today most audio-only applications and black-and-white video use 30 fps, while all broadcast and cable television and all color video productions use 29.97 fps. There are also several other frame rates and variations, but fortunately all of the pro-level MIDI interfaces and sequencer programs recognize the major types.

If you just record timecode onto a videotape, there's no guarantee that the timecode numbers will align perfectly with the actual video frames. To sync the code directly to the frames, you'll have to use a process called *genlocking*. Your video editing facility can do this for you. They can also create a work print for you that shows the timecode on screen in a rectangular window. This is called a *window dub,* and it allows you to see the SMPTE numbers fly by as you view the tape.

Before you finish your Macintosh presentation, it's a good idea to add some temporary sound effects and dialogue to use as a reference for the composer. You can mix these down to mono and record them onto one of the audio tracks when you transfer your work to video. The composer can use this temporary track as a guide to where the dialogue and sound effects are placed, and he or she can then write the music around them to avoid clashes.

At this stage in the process, you should have a window-dub work print with temporary sound effects and dialogue on one audio channel and SMPTE timecode on the other. Be sure to find out what videotape format your composer prefers for the work print. In the past, ¾-inch tape was always the norm, but these days, as VHS tape decks become more sophisticated and acquire more editing features, many small studios are forgoing the expense of ¾-inch equipment and turning to ½-inch instead.

## Working with a Composer

Once you have your work print in hand and you've arranged a schedule with the composer, it's time for the *spotting session.* This is where you and the composer sit down together to view the video and discuss the kind of music that you have in mind. The window dub enables you to point out exact start and stop times for segments, called *cues,* as well as points of interest to emphasize musically. The composer's notes, with their timing references, form the *cue sheet,* which the composer uses as a guide when he is back in the studio.

Next the composer takes the work print and generates matching timecode, which he records onto one of the tracks of his audiotape. This is called *striping* the tape with timecode. It's important for the composer to ask the video editing facility what track format, tape size, and speed they prefer for the final music mix. Is this to be mixed down to a mono or stereo recording? Can they use ¼-inch or ½-inch audiotape for the final master? What tape speed do they prefer: 7½, 15, or 30 ips (inches per second)? Which track should the timecode be on? These questions can be cleared up immediately with a single phone call by the composer to the video editor or recording engineer.

When the music is finished, the audio master tape with its matching timecode is locked to the video master tape by using a device called a *synchronizer*. The recording engineer then adds the music to the final video in the *layback* process.

MIDI studios can create scores that sound traditional and orchestral or modern and electronic, but it's important to find a composer who fits your particular needs. Request a demo tape or ask for references. A good composer, once found, is a valuable resource for future projects and can provide useful input for improving your presentations.

## Other Sounds

To add sound effects to a video presentation, you follow a procedure very similar to the one described above. Instead of a composer, you meet with a sound-effects editor or a sound designer in a separate spotting session. For low-budget productions, you might find a composer who can also provide you with sound effects since much of the equipment in an audio-for-video project studio can serve dual purposes. To add narration, you'll need a voice-over artist, a script with timing guidelines, and a recording studio. For productions with all three sound elements, the different master recordings are transferred to a multitrack tape deck, where they can then be mixed and adjusted during the layback process. Even with low-budget productions, the final results should sound clean and professional if you pay attention to details and don't underestimate the importance of a good soundtrack.

a. No. 5, "Eusebius"

# Chapter 19

# Production Music and Sound-Effects Libraries

Although I often encourage multimedia producers to work with composers whenever they can, I also realize that there are times when this may be impractical. The symbiotic relationship between composers and producers is usually a beneficial one to both parties, but many producers may be unable to establish this relationship because of various circumstances.

Many people naturally turn to recordings by their favorite rock groups or jazz ensembles for theme and background music. If you're one of these people, you're most likely breaking the law. Whereas the copyright laws generally tolerate some recording of copyrighted material for personal use, adding commercially released music to a corporate presentation or a multimedia trade show display is not considered personal use. Generally speaking, if you're using someone else's music in your presentation and the copyright holder isn't receiving royalties from it, you're guilty of copyright infringement.

When you work with a composer, you can avoid this trouble by arranging to acquire the rights to the composition when it's complete. This arrangement, called a *buyout*, gives you the rights to use the music whenever you want. If you aren't hiring a composer, however, there's another alternative: production music libraries.

Production music libraries are the audio equivalent of film stock footage houses. They act as repositories of prescored music composed, produced, and edited specifically to provide a range of styles, tempos, moods, and textures for productions of all kinds. In previous years, the music was stored on tape or records, but these days, compact discs are considered the industry standard. Most libraries are continually growing, providing fresh material and current styles for ad agencies, editing facilities, and postproduction houses around the world.

Aside from offering a wide assortment of musical material, production music libraries allow you to use finished recordings without the problem of first obtaining copyright clearances. Some libraries have a buyout policy, which lets you purchase a CD and then use its contents more or less freely. With other libraries, you purchase or lease the rights to use a CD collection, and then pay a *needle drop*, or per-use fee, each time you use a cut in a presentation.

Because the libraries are aimed primarily at the film and broadcast industries, the music comes in various lengths, such as 60, 30, and 10 seconds, to reduce editing time. Most pieces also come in full-length versions and often include an alternate mix. This typically includes the background tracks without the melody to avoid interfering with narration.

Sound effects are usually handled in a way similar to music. In fact, a large number of music libraries also offer sound-effects libraries and, as with music, compact discs are considered the norm. The following list of music and sound-effects libraries is by no means exhaustive, but it does give a good cross-sectional view of what's out there.

# Music and Sound Effects on Compact Disc

**AirCraft Music Library**
77 N. Washington St.
Boston, MA 02114
(800) 343-2514

AirCraft offers a 50-CD collection covering a range of styles. The music comes in full-length versions with alternate mixes, 60-, 30-, 20-, and 10-second cuts, and repeating loops and short logos. Each CD focuses on a topic such as comedy, action, or instruction. Within each topic there are several appropriate musical styles. AirCraft supplements its collection with about ten new discs a year.

**Associated Production Music**
6255 Sunset Blvd., Suite 820
Hollywood, CA 90028
(800) 543-4276

APM offers four separate libraries with an impressive combined total of over 600 CDs and with over 120 new discs released each year. The music comes in a wide range of categories, including Americana, children's music, comedy, country and western, drama, holidays, industry, jazz, jingles, ethnic, classical, rock, sports, warfare, and romantic. Many pieces come in full-length versions as well as 29- and 59-second cuts. APM also offers an extensive sound-effects library, with over 60 CDs covering a wide range of sounds.

**Audio Action**
4444 Lakeside Dr.
Burbank, CA 91505
(800) 533-1293

This is a large library with approximately 200 CDs in a variety of categories, including pop, jazz, classical, industrial, ethnic, solo, period, comedy, and drama. Each CD contains one category and includes full-length versions, jingle versions in 30- and 60-second lengths, alternate versions, and stings. Audio Action also offers a ten-CD collection of sound effects.

**Capitol Production Music**
6922 Hollywood Blvd., Suite 718
Hollywood, CA 90028
(800) 421-4163

Capitol offers over 60 CDs in its library called The Professional. It's divided into five color-coded categories grouped by style and extensively cross-referenced. The Blue line has high-tech themes and background variations. The Red line has contemporary pieces, including rock, new age, Latin, and dance. The Purple line has specialized material, including comedy, drama, and travel. The Green line has classical works for large and small ensembles. The Golden line has vintage jazz, satirical pieces, and country and western. New CDs are issued regularly.

**Creative Support Services**
1950 Riverside Dr.
Los Angeles, 90039
(800) 468-6874

This collection consists of 11 libraries on 39 CDs. There are dynamic themes, 5–7 minute cuts, historical, period, and patriotic music, classical music, motivational pieces, panoramic music, and corporate cheers and jingles. CSS also offers a collection of approximately 400 real sound effects and 200 electronic effects.

**DeWolfe Music Library**
25 W. 45th St.
New York, NY 10036
(800) 221-6713

DeWolf offers approximately 150 CDs with around 30 categories of music, including classical, opera, corporate, high-tech, pastoral, pop, children's, ethnic, romantic, period, and vocal. These come in full-length versions and in some cases shorter cuts, such as 30- and 60-second lengths. DeWolf also offers an 11-CD sound-effects library providing general-purpose effects for a variety of situations.

**Hollywood Film Music Library**
11684 Ventura Blvd., Suite 850
Studio City, CA 91604
(818) 985-9997

This 32-CD collection is organized into 22 musical style categories. There are full-length cues with multiple endings, stings, and 10-, 29-, and

59-second formats. Some of the categories are industrial, pop rock, nature, romantic, classical, novelty, comedy, mystery, country, and big-band jazz.

**Killer Tracks**
6534 Sunset Blvd.
Hollywood, CA 90028
(800) 877-0078

The Killer Tracks Multimedia Library consists of three CDs, entitled Sales, Training, and Education. Each CD includes more than 30 selections of music divided into several categories: rock, urban, semiclassical, high-tech, comedy, mellow, industrial, and new age. Aside from the music, each CD contains several sound effects and production elements designed for desktop presentations. Killer Tracks also offers a complete library of standard production music on 48 CDs in full-length versions with alternate mixes and 30- and 60-second cuts. Two CDs are devoted to stings, sweeps, links, bridges, and other elements. The remaining discs include categories such as blues, drama, fantasy, high-tech, new age, orchestral, rock, sports, mellow, and holiday.

**Manhattan Production Music**
311 W. 43rd St., Suite 702
New York, NY 10036
(800) 227-1954

Each of the 38 CDs in this collection is broken down into 12 themes consisting of underscores, rhythm tracks, and 60-, 30-, 20-, and 10-second lengths, in addition to longer lengths of 2 to 15 minutes. The musical categories include pop, rock, sports, news, symphonic, industrial, classical, marches, new age, comedy, and more. There is also a five-CD collection with 495 sound effects designed for radio, television, and film production.

**Metro Music Productions**
645 West End Ave.
New York, NY 10025
(212) 799-7600

This is a small collection of eight CDs consisting of over 200 titles in mixed styles ranging from urban high-tech rock to jazz fusion, new age,

R&B, jazz, and blues. Titles are offered in full-length versions and 60-, 30-, and 10-second cuts.

**Network Music**
11021 Via Frontera
San Diego, CA 92127
(800) 854-2075

Network offers several music and sound-effects libraries. Its Production Music Library contains over 105 CDs with categories that include business, sports, contemporary, solos, orchestral themes, specialty, seasonal, and comedy. Its Primrose Music Library features over 45 CDs with categories that include music from the Middle Ages, Renaissance, and Baroque periods, children's music, and slapstick, pop, industrial, and environmental music. Both libraries are updated each month. Network also offers a 50-volume sound-effects collection containing over 4000 effects of various types. Another seven-CD set includes a variety of production elements for presentations of all kinds.

**Omnimusic**
52 Main St.
Port Washington, NY 11050
(800) 828-6664

The Omnimusic Library consists of 56 CDs with full-length musical themes. Each CD contains an average of 18 themes with additional underscores and alternate mixes. The categories include technology, sports, drama, classical, rock, country, industrial, new age, and specialty. The Professional Broadcast Library of 17 CDs contains contemporary pieces with 30- and 60-second cuts, along with stings, logos, and other musical effects. Omnimusic also offers the Omni-FX Library, a 12-CD collection of sound effects of different kinds for video and small studio applications.

**SoperSound Music Library**
P.O. Box 498
Palo Alto, CA 94301
(800) 227-9980

SoperSound offers a sixteen-volume collection of production music, of which nine volumes are available on CD. Of these, one is a collection of sci-fi sound effects. The other CDs have a variety of musical styles, such as orchestral, contemporary, new age, fusion, jazz, exotic, sports, and high-tech. These are available in differing formats, such as extended-length, 30-, and 60-second cuts.

**Sound Ideas**
105 W. Beaver Creek Rd., Suite 4
Richmond Hill, ON L4B 1C6, Canada
(800) 387-3030

Sound Ideas is best known for its extensive and popular sound-effects library, which is divided into six collections. The original 1000 and 2000 series provide a total of over 5000 sounds on 50 CDs. The 3000 series offers ambience and background sounds on 12 CDs. The Hollywood series provides 5 CDs of sounds designed for cartoons and movies. The Wheels series has 24 CDs with car and truck sounds. The Lucasfilm Sound Effects Library contains 6 CDs produced by sound designers at Skywalker Sound and by Sound Ideas for use in movies. Sound Ideas also offers a production music library designed for a variety of commercial purposes. Full-length themes are provided with alternate mixes and 30- and 60-second versions where appropriate.

**TRF Production Music Libraries**
1619 Broadway
New York, NY 10019
(800) 899-MUSIC

TRF offers an enormous number of musical selections from its nine different full-sized libraries, which total approximately 400 discs. The selections range from full-length pieces to jingle-length versions, including openings, transitions, dissolves, stings, and fanfares. Instrumentation ranges from full orchestra to small groups and solos. Its numerous libraries offer music in many categories, including industrial, new age, period, rock, atmospheric, comedy, electronic, jazz, sports, jingles, classical, ethnic, and Americana.

**27th Dimension**
2312 S.E. 29th St.
Okeechobee, FL 34974
(800) 634-0091

Dimension offers three libraries of production music totaling 30 CDs designed to fill a variety of needs. The music comes in several tempos and categories, such as country, industrial, ethnic, rock, high-tech, children's music, classical, sports, new age, and jazz. Some pieces come in full-length versions with alternate mixes, as well as 30- and 60-second cuts. Dimension also offers its Holophonic Sound Effects library, containing 1001 digitally recorded holophonic effects from around the world, and its Tech Effects library, containing 241 high-tech audio logos. For MIDI users, Dimension offers a collection of MIDI files. Additionally, Dimension's HyperFEX collection offers sound effects for Macintosh applications.

**Valentino**
151 W. 46th St., Suite 803
New York, NY 10036
(800) 223-6278

The Valentino Production Music Library consists of approximately 75 CDs designated by tempo and/or category. Some of the categories are contemporary, easy listening, industrial, specialty, sports, new age, and classical. The pieces come in full-length versions and 60- and 30-second cuts. Valentino's Sound Effects Library contains approximately 50 CDs of general-purpose sound effects grouped by category for easy reference.

# Music and Sound Effects on CD-ROM

If you want to incorporate production music into a desktop presentation, you'll first have to record the music with a digitizer or sampler and save it in an appropriate file format. If the music needs editing, you'll also need to use an editing program to make the necessary adjustments.

It wasn't long after multimedia began to take off that a number of people realized that producers of desktop presentations could benefit substantially by having their music and sound effects ready to go in a usable file format. Recently, a number of products have appeared that use CD-ROM technology to store sounds in digital form for direct importation into presentations or editing applications. The following are a few of this new breed of music and sound-effects libraries aimed specifically at Macintosh users.

**Digidesign, Inc.**
1360 Willow Rd., Suite 101
Menlo Park, CA 94025
(415) 327-8811

The Clip Tunes CD-ROM was produced by Digidesign in collaboration with Prosonus. It contains 300 megabytes of stereo CD-quality soundfiles stored in Sound Designer II format, so you'll need an Audiomedia card or Sound Tools (see Chapter 12) to use this library. The collection contains 22 musical pieces in lengths ranging from less than 30 seconds to almost 3 minutes. The selections are grouped into folders by musical style, such as jazz, rock, new age, country, etc. A sound-effects section contains a variety of general-purpose effects and a number of medium-length ambience sounds for backgrounds. The disc also includes a number of audio test signals from the Prosonus Studio Reference Disc. These are helpful for testing and calibrating your audio system.

**Olduvai Corp.**
7520 Red Rd., Suite A
S. Miami, FL 33143
(305) 665-4665

The DTP & Multimedia CD mentioned in Chapter 7 includes a Sound Clips section with approximately 8 megabytes of sound effects. These are stored as SND sound resources in a number of HyperCard stacks. Each stack displays the sounds as buttons that you can click for previewing. The sounds cover a wide range of types and are especially suitable for Hyper-Card, SuperCard, and other compatible programs.

**Optical Media International**
180 Knowles Dr.
Los Gatos, CA 95030
(408) 376-3511

Optical Media, a well-known leader in CD-ROM technology, has released two collections of sounds for the Macintosh. The Multimedia DeskTop Sounds disc offers more than 400 sound effects from around the world. These are stored in Apple SND sound resource format and catalogued in HyperCard. You can import the sounds into a variety of Macintosh applications, as well as HyperCard, SuperCard, and other presentation programs. The Digital Sound Series consists of two discs with a total of 2762 sounds. These are high-quality soundfiles stored in Sound Designer format. The collection contains mostly sound effects along with percussion and instrument sounds.

**Passport Designs, Inc.**
625 Miramontes St.
Half Moon Bay, CA 94019
(415) 726-0280

The Sound Magic CD-ROM (produced jointly with Prosonus) offers thousands of samples and sound effects for use with Alchemy (see Chapter 13). Most of the sounds are samples of instruments, both acoustic and electronic, that you can edit and export to the sampler of your choice. There are also approximately 30 sound effects that you can use for animations or presentations.

# Chapter 20

# Just for Fun

As I've mentioned earlier, the great thing about sound is how it can add another level of involvement to what might otherwise be a simple display of visuals. Although graphics, text, and animation are themselves quite compelling, with the addition of sound, they can blossom into something altogether different. It's true that sound is often used to convey specific information, but sound very readily lends itself to another equally important task—it makes things fun! The following programs illustrate how the addition of sound effects, speech, and music can raise a piece of software to a position above the prosaic. They use sound to draw you into their world of pictures and animation and make you smile in the process.

## ▤ After Dark

Every Mac user needs a screen saver. When you leave your computer screen on for an extended period of time, the static image can destroy the screen's phosphor coating, resulting in a permanent ghost image called *burn-in*. The solution is simple: Replace the static image with a changing display. This makes screen savers a natural place to apply the art of animation in a utilitarian manner that can benefit the computing world at large. But this doesn't mean that screen savers have to be dull—*au contraire*! After Dark (from Berkeley Systems) has elevated the art of screen saving to a new high. It offers over 30 different display modules that you can choose individually or in combination, and a second volume—More After Dark—adds another 25 to the list.

After Dark uses beautiful, sometimes mesmerizing, often whimsical, and always entertaining animations that are both colorful and inventive. And best of all they use sound. Many of the modules have digitized sound that greatly enhances these mini-presentations and boosts the level of whimsy accordingly. The famous Flying Toaster module (Figure 20.1) lets you set how dark your toast will be and provides the sound of flapping wings as the toasters fly by. The much-beloved suboceanic module called Fish! lets you choose the kinds of sea creatures that swim across your screen while the sound of bubbling water creates just the right ambience. The sounds of thunder and lightning, bouncing balls, munching worms, shooting stars, dripping drops, and ticking clocks each contribute to the overall sense of fun that these modules bring and help combat boredom at the same time.

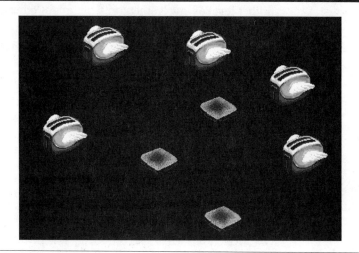

**Figure 20.1**
The famous Flying Toasters save your screen with flapping wings and sound effects.

You can also save your screen with a company logo, a scrolling message, or a random combination of your favorite displays. To choose or modify a module, you open the After Dark control panel (Figure 20.2). On the left you'll find a list of the available displays, and on the right there are several controls that affect the currently selected module. If a module has sound, you'll see a speaker icon next to the Demo button. By clicking on the speaker's up and down arrows, you can set the volume level or turn off the sound.

After Dark uses beautiful, sometimes mesmerizing, often whimsical, and always entertaining animations that are both colorful and inventive. And best of all they use sound. Many of the modules have digitized sound that

Just for Fun

**Figure 20.2**
The After Dark control panel

box. Additionally, a System IQ feature monitors disk access and CPU load as well as activity levels on the printer and modem ports to determine when it's appropriate to engage the screen saver. Note: Some MIDI programs access the serial ports in nonstandard ways, so MIDI activity alone from these programs may not stop After Dark from activating.

After Dark offers numerous ways to customize your displays. The Randomizer lets you select any combination of After Dark modules and display them in random or sequential order. You can set the length of time that each module is displayed before it's replaced by the next one. The Logo module lets you use your own graphic, pasted from the clipboard, to create a custom screen-saver image. The Picture Frame module allows you to use any color PICT file as a screen saver, and the Message module lets you create lines of moving text. With the PICS Player, you can use animation files created in other applications to produce animated displays. The multi-module lets you combine several displays on the screen simultaneously in a number of ways.

The After Dark documentation also includes a thorough programmer's manual that details how to write your own graphics modules. After Dark supports SND sound resources and lets you specify a Volume value from 0 to 7.

Many of the algorithmically generated displays are simply amazing, others have a calming effect, and still others bring a smile to your face even after a hard day of computing. My biggest complaint about After Dark is that I frequently find myself watching my screen saver for long periods of time instead of getting back to work. Such are the hazards of combining function with fun.

# Kid Pix

Kid Pix (from Broderbund Software) is an exceptional program that brings the joys of creating computer art to kids of all ages. It was designed so that children who aren't old enough to read can use it with ease and fully explore its many hidden treasures. Late at night, when the kids are asleep, the adults can sneak over to the computer and do a little doodling of their own. Be sure to turn the volume down a bit because Kid Pix comes with a surprising assortment of sound effects and speech that turns this inventive painting environment into a veritable fun house of animated shapes and textures. From its crazy sound effects and patterns that burst into color to its wacky brushes and mystery tools, the program invites exploration and discovery.

The Kid Pix Drawing Screen (Figure 20.3) starts out like a blank sheet of paper, which is entirely visible when you open the program. This eliminates the need for scroll bars and lets you see what you'll get if you print out your picture. The drawing tools appear on a vertical palette to the left of the screen—there are no confusing menus or dialog boxes needed to get started.

Each tool comes with its own set of options that appear along the bottom of the screen. To get to work, you just select a tool and start clicking and dragging around the screen. When you select a new tool, the tool options below the screen change to offer a wide assortment of choices that control such things as line width and pattern, drawing styles, and eraser effects. If you're using a color system, a color palette appears on the left beneath the tools. The currently selected color appears in a box at the top of the palette and indicates the color that the current tool will produce. Some of the tool options produce multicolored effects.

Just for Fun

**Figure 20.3**
The Kid Pix Drawing Screen is shown here with just a few of its many creative options.

Most of the tool options are available in several banks that you can cycle through with the arrow button on the right. The Wacky Brush tool, for example, comes with a number of entertaining options. The Leaky Pen option creates ink blotches whenever the pen stops moving. The Northern Lights option creates colorful horizontal and vertical aurora borealis patterns. The Drippy Paint option creates lines that have paint drips running from them, and the Connect-The-Dots option lets you create your own dot-to-dot pictures—automatically numbered, with or without the lines.

The list goes on and on. There are bubbles, dots, and zigzags, kaleidoscopes, magnifying glasses, and echoes, spray paint, pine needles, and much more. You can create Jackson Pollock effects, generate "fractal" trees, or produce a galaxy of stars. When you tire of your picture, you can use the Electric Mixer tool to transform the whole display into something entirely different. Or you can use the Eraser tool with its hilarious options, or the Rubber Stamps, Text, or Moving Van.

As if the graphics weren't enough, this whole cavalcade of creativity comes complete with a dazzling array of sound effects. Paint gurgles as it pours, pens drip, the letters speak their names (in either English or Spanish), firecrackers explode, sliding doors clatter as they open, the eraser makes a rubbing sound, the truck screeches to a halt, and pictures and symbols fall into place with a definitive click. Kids find these effects enormously entertaining, and the sounds further stimulate creativity as they reinforce learning.

Kid Pix also lets you record your own sound effects, music, or speech if you have MacRecorder or a Macintosh with built-in recording capability. To record your sounds, choose Record from the Goodies menu. This opens a standard recording dialog box like the one described in Chapter 16.

When you have a recording that you like, you simply click Save and the sound is attached to your drawing. If you decide to save your drawing to disk, you have the option of saving it with or without the sound. Pictures saved with a recorded sound automatically play the sound upon opening. After that, you can hear your sound by choosing Play from the Goodies menu. To speed up the sound, click the Option key. To slow down the sound, press the spacebar.

Kid Pix rightly captures the true essence of multimedia by combining sound, graphics, text, and animation into an inexpensive program that frees the artist within us all. With Kid Pix there is no right or wrong; there is no better or worse. The creative process is its own reward, and sound makes it all the more memorable.

## Talking Moose

Are you feeling kind of lonely lately? Need some company while you're chained to that keyboard? Maybe you should consider a talking moose. The first Talking Moose began appearing on Macintosh screens in 1986 as a shareware desk accessory. It gained widespread popularity through bulletin board services and shareware distribution outlets and eventually went through several revisions. Now it has been transformed into a full-color Control Panel device with improved animation and a complete Cartoon Carnival of strange and amusing characters. In its new, commercially released version from Baseline Publishing, Talking Moose comes with a variety of tools and applications that let you customize the program and experiment with the characters and what they say. But what exactly is Talking Moose?

Talking Moose and his Cartoon Carnival are an assortment of animated characters that pop up on your screen, for various reasons, and talk to you. Sometimes what they say is helpful, sometimes it's funny, and sometimes it's just annoying. The Talking Moose (Figure 20.4) greets you when you start your computer and says good-bye when you shut down. Between times he may pop up to remind you to get back to work if the computer has been idle too long. Or he may drop by to deliver some sarcastic remark or one-liner.

**Figure 20.4**
The Talking Moose

As you work, the Moose (or one of his pals) speaks the names of menu options when you choose them or tells you the names of windows when they open. He also reads and speaks the messages in dialog boxes and alerts. If you get tired of the Moose, you can use the Choose a Picture window (Figure 20.5) to select one of the other Cartoon Carnies to replace him—only one character at a time can be active.

Talking Moose uses MacinTalk to generate its speech. The program comes with an enhanced version of MacinTalk that is more compatible with System 7 than earlier versions and offers additional features such as the ability to interrupt the speech quickly with a mouse click. Talking Moose also comes with a complete utility program that lets you edit and personalize the spoken phrases. You can add your own moose jokes or change the greetings to suit your taste. With the Preferences dialog box (Figure 20.6), you can determine when the Moose will appear and how he will behave. Additionally, with the optional Cartoon Creator application, you can produce your own animated characters and install them into the Talking Moose program.

**Figure 20.5**
The Choose a Picture window lets you select a replacement for the Talking Moose.

**Figure 20.6**
The Talking Moose Preferences dialog box

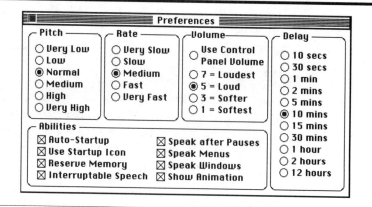

If you've ever wanted to fool around with MacinTalk, this program is a good place to start. It comes with a Phonemes Reference desk accessory that provides a quick guide to the phonetic spellings used by MacinTalk to generate speech from text. The Moose Proof desk accessory reads any text that you've typed into your favorite word processor. Just select a block of text and copy it to the clipboard. Then paste it into Moose Proof and the Moose will read what you've written. If you want it to sound right, use the Phonemes Reference to help you change the text to the appropriate phonetic spellings. The documentation includes lots of advice on using MacinTalk.

If you want to use Talking Moose with other applications, the program includes a stack that makes Talking Moose compatible with HyperCard and another stack that lets you modify programs to work with Talking Moose. The Moose Goes Hyper stack provides XCMDs that allow you to control Talking Moose from within HyperCard stacks, and the Advanced Moose stack covers ResEdit and how to use it to customize applications for the Talking Moose.

## Adventures in Musicland

Certainly one of the most appropriate and worthwhile reasons to combine sound, graphics, and text is for the teaching of music. The Macintosh is especially well suited for creating entertaining environments that children of all ages can use to explore the intricacies of music and its elements. Recognizing this fact, Dr. T's Music Software has released Adventures in Musicland—an inexpensive introduction to music that teaches with animation and digitized sounds. Adventures in Musicland is a collection of four musical games that anyone can enjoy even if they don't have any musical background or previous musical experience. The colorful animations are based on the John Tenniel illustrations from Lewis Carroll's classic story, *Alice's Adventures in Wonderland.* Most of the games require no spelling or typing skills, so even very young children can play, although it helps to have a grown-up handy to read the White Rabbit's comments and to enter occasional text. Each game has numerous answers that appear in different combinations to provide the right blend of exploration and repetition. The games also have different levels of difficulty to maintain the sense of challenge and to let adults get in on the act. With the help of the Mad Hatter, the White Rabbit, the King and Queen of Hearts, the Cheshire Cat, and Alice, you can learn to identify musical instruments and sounds, symbols and terminology, and famous composers.

All four games have a similar user interface, the same menu items, and a similar set of buttons and dialog boxes. The White Rabbit stands to the left and issues instructions, makes suggestions, and offers encouragement. You can use the Hint and Show Answer buttons if you get stuck, but you'll lose some points.

In the Picture Perfect game (Figure 20.7), you try to guess the name of a composer, an instrument, or a musical symbol that is revealed to you one piece at a time. Whenever you click the More Picture button, another piece of the puzzle appears. The White Rabbit will give you a clue if you click the Hint button. When you're ready to guess, you can type in the answer and click the Check My Answer button.

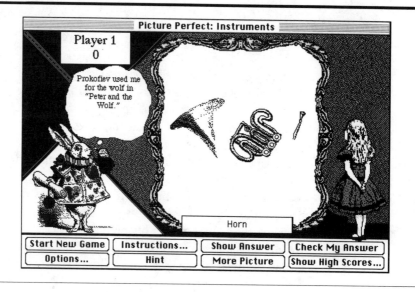

**Figure 20.7**
The Picture Perfect game teaches you about composers, instruments, and musical symbols.

The Melody Mixup game (Figure 20.8) develops melody recognition and memory skills by asking you to re-create an ever-growing pattern of notes played by the on-screen characters. First one of the characters plays a note. When you click on that character, he plays back the note. Then the first character and a second character play notes that you must duplicate in the proper sequence. The melody continues to grow until you reach the length set in the Options dialog box (5, 10, 15 notes or infinite) or until you make a mistake.

You can choose one of three groups of characters, each of which have different numbers of performers that play different scales. The trumpeters play the notes in a major chord, the bell ringers play a pentatonic scale, and the cats meow the notes of a complete major scale. The difficulty setting determines the amount of helpful animation that accompanies each performance.

## Just for Fun

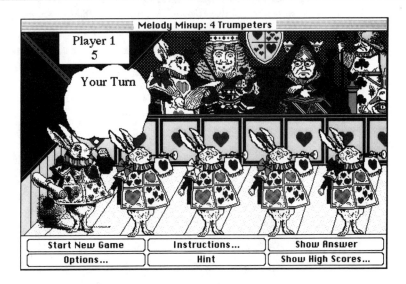

**Figure 20.8**
The Melody Mixup game develops melody recognition and memory.

The Sound Concentration game (Figure 20.9) is an aural memory builder. Each time you click on a top hat, a rabbit pokes its head up and makes a sound. You then click a second hat and listen to that rabbit's sound. If the two sounds match, the rabbits pop out of the hats and you earn points. If the sounds don't match, the rabbits return into their hats and you try again to find a matching pair. The sounds can be anything from a tuba or a piano to a frog or a bird. Some of the sounds are actually a series of two or more notes that form intervals, triads, or scales.

The final game, Music Match, is another recognition and memory builder. This time the elements are visual, and they can consist of music symbols, notes and rests, instruments, notes in treble clef, and notes in bass clef. Several playing cards are displayed facedown. When you click on one, it flips over, revealing a symbol or picture. You then click a second card and try to make a match. Each time you match a pair, you gain points. If the pictures don't match, the cards flip back and you can try again. The Options dialog box lets you determine the number of cards used in the game and how long the pictures remain visible before flipping back.

Adventures in Musicland turns music education into a lively exploration of sounds and symbols. The fun and challenge of solving the puzzles serves to maintain your level of interest as you develop new skills. This combination of sound effects, music, text, and animation effectively illustrates multimedia's great potential for teaching.

**Figure 20.9**
The Sound Concentration game awards points for matching sounds.

# Appendix A

# Glossary

***aftertouch***   A type of MIDI controller data that indicates how hard a key is pressed after it is struck and before it is released.

***algorithm***   A set of digital instructions or a pattern of information used in implementing a specific task or function.

***aliasing***   The phenomenon that results when false frequencies (lower harmonic multiples of the frequencies above the Nyquist limit) enter a digital recording, causing harmonic distortion.

***amplitude***   The strength of a sound or audio signal—perceived by the listener as volume.

***analog***   An electrical signal that varies continuously in strength and frequency in a direct relationship to sound waves or other variable parameters.

***analog-to-digital converter***   A circuit that changes the continuously fluctuating voltages from an analog source into digital information for processing and storage in a computer or other digital device.

***attack***   The beginning of a sound.

***Audio IFF***   Audio Interchange File Format; also abbreviated AIFF. A standard audio file format supported by many applications, including Alchemy and Sound Designer II.

***compressed sound***   A digital sound that has been altered so that it requires less memory—at the expense of lower sound quality.

***continuous controllers***    A set of MIDI messages, typically coming from a device such as a thumb wheel, lever, slider, or pedal, that represents dynamic or continuously varying performance data. These are most often used to add expressive content to MIDI music.

***cue***    A scene or section of a scene from a film or video that requires sound effects or music. Cues can range from a few seconds to several minutes, and the music can be as little as a single note or as much as a complex orchestral score. The specific on-screen event that initiates a cue is sometimes referred to as *hit point*.

***DAT***    Abbreviation for digital audiotape; a storage medium for digital audio data, which uses a small cassette resembling a miniature video cassette.

***dB***    Abbreviation for decibel; a unit of measurement used to indicate sound level differences; also used to indicate a signal's amplitude.

***decay***    The decrease, over time, of a sound's volume. Typically used to describe the change in amplitude that occurs as a sound progresses from one segment of its envelope to a segment with a lower amplitude level.

***digital***    Using binary operations to acquire, store, retrieve, and modify information. The opposite of analog, digital circuits assign discrete values to variable events which can then be edited through software.

***digital-to-analog converter***    A circuit that changes digital information into a continuously fluctuating voltage that can be sent to an amplifier to produce sound.

***DSP***    Abbreviation for digital signal processing. A method of manipulating audio data through the use of algorithms.

***envelope***    A shape representing the changes in a sound's overall signal level as a function of time. Most envelopes consist of at least four stages: attack, decay, sustain, and release. These are commonly referred to as ADSR envelopes.

***envelope generator*** A circuit or its software equivalent that changes a sound's parameters over time. Most often used to affect a sound's volume as the sound progresses from beginning to end; also called a *contour generator*.

***equalization*** The selective alteration of an audio signal's frequency spectrum; abbreviated EQ.

***filter*** A circuit or its software equivalent that removes or attenuates certain elements in the audio frequency spectrum.

***hertz*** The standard unit of measurement for frequency; abbreviated Hz. It is equivalent to cycles per second.

***keyboard controller*** A piano-like keyboard used to send MIDI data to a sound module or computer.

***layback*** The process of rerecording the mixed audio tracks back to the edited master videotape.

***layering*** Triggering two or more independent sounds from a single key depression.

***LFO*** Abbreviation for low-frequency oscillator; a circuit or function that generates an alternating subaudio frequency (usually in the 1–15 Hz range) for creating effects such as vibrato, tremolo, and wahwah.

***loop*** A portion of a sound or a section of music that repeats over and over when played. In sequences, a loop is typically a musical phrase. With sampled sounds, a loop allows a sound of fixed length to last as long as the key that triggers it is depressed.

***MACE*** Abbreviation for Macintosh Audio Compression and Expansion; a set of Sound Manager routines that allows an application to compress and decompress audio data.

***MIDI*** Pronounced "middy"; abbreviation for Musical Instrument Digital Interface. The standardized language and protocol that enables synthesizers and other electronic devices to communicate with one another regardless of manufacturer or synthesis system used. MIDI is a serial interface with a transmission rate of 31.25 kBaud.

***MIDI channel*** One of the 16 numerical data designations that allow you to independently address several instruments over a single MIDI cable. In a MIDI system the different instruments can be set to respond to specific channels while ignoring others.

***MIDI interface*** A hardware device that attaches to one or both of the Macintosh's serial ports and translates MIDI data into a form that the computer can understand. This allows you to connect MIDI instruments to your computer for recording, playing, and editing MIDI performances and compositions.

***modulation*** The process of varying one signal with another. Typically this involves introducing a control signal to alter the characteristics of a sound.

***monophonic*** Capable of playing only one note at a time.

***multitimbral*** Pronounced "multy-tambrul"; having the ability to produce more than one instrument sound at a time. Synthesizers having this capability can generate instrumental ensembles (such as a woodwind quintet or jazz combo) in real time when controlled by a sequencer.

***Nyquist limit*** The highest frequency—equal to $1/2$ the sampling rate—that you can record digitally without causing aliasing.

***oscillator*** A circuit or its software equivalent that generates audio signals.

***parameter*** A variable characteristic, value, or element.

***patch*** A set of synthesizer parameters that produce a specific sound; sometimes referred to as a *program*.

***PCM*** Abbreviation for pulse code modulation; a method used for encoding and storing sampled sounds.

***pitch bend*** A type of continuous controller that momentarily raises or lowers the frequency of a sound, usually through the movements of a wheel or lever.

***polyphony*** The production of more than one note at a time. A flute or clarinet is monophonic, whereas a piano or harp is polyphonic. A synthesizer with 8-note polyphony can produce up to 8 notes simultaneously in either a chordal or contrapuntal setting. Most modern synthesizers are capable of at least 16-note polyphony.

***postproduction*** The period of development for a film or video that occurs between the completion of photography and the acceptance of the final release print.

***program change*** A MIDI message that causes an instrument to change from one sound (patch) to another.

***quantization*** The process of measuring the levels of an analog signal at specific points in time and assigning the signal a series of numerical values that represent its continuously fluctuating voltages as discrete steps. Also referred to as *digitization*.

***quantize*** In a MIDI sequencer program, to correct rhythmic inaccuracies by aligning notes to specific rhythmic divisions or subdivisions.

***real time*** The actual time in which something takes place. With sequencers it refers to a method of recording MIDI data where the notes and other events are entered into the computer at a speed roughly proportional to the playback speed—the opposite of step time.

***release*** The final stage of an envelope, following a note-off message, during which the signal typically returns to a zero value.

***sample*** A digitally recorded sound.

***sampler*** An electronic keyboard instrument that takes short digital recordings of sounds and, after editing and processing, uses them as the basis for creating its musical tones. A sampler is to music what a scanner is to visual art, in that it relies on preexisting sources for its input. Samplers excel at reproducing harmonically rich acoustic timbres.

***sampling rate*** The number of times per second that an incoming analog signal is examined during the process of converting it into digital form. Typical sample rates range from 11 kHz to 48 kHz. The higher the sampling rate, the better the sound.

***sawtooth wave*** A waveform that has a jagged appearance resembling the teeth of a saw. It consists of a fundamental and all of its harmonics. Sawtooth waves produce a bright, brassy sound.

***semitone*** A chromatic interval or half step; the difference in pitch between two adjacent keys on a piano.

***sequencer*** A software program that records a musical performance in the form of a series of MIDI events and messages, such as note on, note off, velocity, aftertouch, etc. Aspects of the performance can then be edited in detail or with global commands.

***serial*** A type of connection that transfers data one bit after another rather than several bits at a time.

***sine wave*** A simple waveform consisting of a single frequency with no overtones. Sine waves produce a pure, somewhat muted sound.

***SMPTE*** Pronounced "simpty"; abbreviation for Society of Motion Picture and Television Engineers. A standard-setting professional organization.

***SMPTE timecode*** A timing reference based on the concept of hours, minutes, seconds, and frames. When timecode is recorded onto the audio track of a videotape, each frame is given its own specific identifying number. This allows precise location and synchronization anywhere on the tape.

***sound module*** A synthesizer that lacks its own attached keyboard. It is essentially the sound-producing component of a synthesizer or sampler and requires input from an external controller via MIDI to produce its sounds.

***sound resource*** A file format (SND) supported by the Macintosh system software and HyperCard.

***soundfile*** A type of file, such as Audio IFF or Sound Designer II, that is used to store sound data.

***spotting session*** The meeting between a composer and a film or video director where decisions are made—while viewing a work print—about the type and placement of music. Also applies to narration and sound effects.

***square wave*** A waveform that consists of a fundamental and its odd-numbered harmonics. Square waves produce a hollow, sometimes reedy sound.

***stack*** A HyperCard document consisting of one or more *cards*.

***step time*** A method of entering MIDI data one event at a time as opposed to recording in real time.

***sting*** A single musical chord or note used for dramatic effect in a film or video scene.

***stripe*** To record a timecode signal onto a tape track.

***sustain*** The part of a sound's envelope where the level remains constant for a period of time.

***synchronizer***   A device that reads timecode from two or more tape transports (audio or video) and coordinates their operation with a common timing reference.

***synthesizer***   An electronic musical instrument that generates sounds through its audio signal-processing circuitry. Currently there are many systems of synthesis in use: additive, subtractive, frequency modulation, linear arithmetic, and others. Unlike samplers, synthesizers do not rely on outside sources for their sounds.

***system exclusive***   A type of MIDI message that is specific to one instrument or family of instruments and whose format is defined by the instrument's manufacturer.

***tempo***   The rate of speed at which a piece of music is played; typically indicated in beats per minute.

***timbre***   Pronounced "tambur"; the quality of a sound, resulting from its harmonic content, that distinguishes one instrument or sound from another at the same pitch and volume. Often referred to as *tone color*.

***timecode***   *See* SMPTE timecode.

***transpose***   To change a piece of music from one pitch or key to another.

***tremolo***   A common type of amplitude modulation.

***triangle wave***   A waveform with a relatively pure sound and a somewhat muted quality similar to a sine wave, but with some additional weak overtones.

***velocity***   A MIDI message that indicates how fast a note is played or released.

***vibrato***   A common type of frequency modulation used for musical expressiveness.

***waveform***    A visual representation of a sound.

***window dub***    A video work print with a rectangular window superimposed on the video image, which displays the SMPTE timecode numbers as they change. This allows the editor and composer to watch the minutes and seconds flash by as the video progresses.

***XCMD***    Abbreviation for external command; a command written in a programming language other than HyperTalk that extends HyperCard's built-in command set.

***XFCN***    Abbreviation for external function; a function written in a programming language other than HyperTalk that extends HyperCard's built-in command set.

***zero crossing***    The point at which a digital waveform crosses the center line between its range of possible positive and negative values.

# Appendix B

# List of Companies

**Acoustic Research**
330 Turnpike St.
Canton, MA 02021
(617) 821-2300

**Adobe Systems, Inc.**
1098 Alta Ave.
Mountain View, CA 94039
(415) 961-4400

**Aldus Corp.**
411 First Ave. South
Seattle, WA 98104
(206) 622-5500

**Altech Systems**
122 Faries Industrial Park Dr.
Shreveport, LA 71106
(318) 868-8036

**Apple Computer, Inc.**
20525 Mariani Ave.
Cupertino, CA 95014
(408) 996-1010

**Articulate Systems, Inc.**
600 W. Cummings Park, Suite 4500
Woburn, MA 01801
(617) 935-5656

**Baseline Publishing, Inc.**
1770 Moriah Woods Blvd., Suite 14
Memphis, TN 38117
(901) 682-9676

**Berkeley Systems, Inc.**
2095 Rose St.
Berkeley, CA 94709
(510) 540-5535

**Bright Star Technology, Inc.**
1450 114th Ave., SE, Suite 200
Bellevue, WA 98004
(206) 451-3697

**Broderbund Software, Inc.**
P.O Box 6125
Novato, CA 94948
(415) 382-4700

**CD Technology, Inc.**
766 San Aleso Ave.
Sunnyvale, CA 94086
(408) 752-8500

**Celestial Wind Carillons**
Route 1, Box 32, Hwy. 23 South
Eureka Springs, AR 72632
(501) 253-7319

**Claris Corp.**
5201 Patrick Henry Dr., Box 58168
Santa Clara, CA 95052
(408) 727-8227

**Digidesign, Inc.**
1360 Willow Rd., Suite 101
Menlo Park, CA 94025
(415) 327-8811

**Dr. T's Music Software**
124 Crescent Rd., Suite 3
Needham, MA 02194
(617) 455-1454

**Dynaware USA, Inc.**
950 Tower Lane, Suite 1150
Foster City, CA 94404
(415) 349-5700

**EarLevel Engineering**
21213-B Hawthorne Blvd., Suite 5305
Torrance, CA 90509
(310) 316-2939

**Educorp**
7434 Trade St.
San Diego, CA 92121
(619) 536-9999

**Electronic Arts**
1450 Fashion Island Blvd.
San Mateo, CA 94404
(415) 571-7171

**E-mu Systems, Inc.**
1600 Green Hills Rd.
Scotts Valley, CA 95067
(408) 438-1921

**Farallon Computing, Inc.**
2000 Powell St., Suite 600
Emeryville, CA 94608
(415) 596-9100

**Five Pin Press**
P.O. Box 550363
Dallas, TX 75355
(214) 328-2730

**Gold Disk Inc.**
5155 Spectrum Way, Suite 5
Mississauga, Ontario L4W 5A1
(416) 602-4000

**Greytsounds Sound Development**
8700 Reseda Blvd., Suite 101
Northridge, CA 91324
(818) 773-7327

**International MIDI Association**
5316 W. 57th St.
Los Angeles, CA 90056
(310) 649-6434

**JLCooper Electronics**
12500 Beatrice St.
Los Angeles, CA 90066
(310) 306-4131

**Kawai America Corp.**
2055 E. University Dr.
Compton, CA 90220
(213) 631-1771

**Korg, Inc.**
89 Frost St.
Westbury, NY 11590
(516) 333-9100

**MacroMind/Paracomp, Inc.**
600 Townsend St., Suite 310W
San Francisco, CA 94103
(415) 442-0200

**Mark of the Unicorn, Inc.**
222 Third St.
Cambridge, MA 02142
(617) 576-2760

**McGill University Master Samples**
555 Sherbrooke St. West
Montreal, Quebec H3A 1E3
(514) 398-4548

**MIDI Inn**
Box 2362
Westmont, IL 60559
(708) 789-2001

**MIDI Manufacturers Association**
5316 W. 57th St.
Los Angeles, CA 90056
(310) 649-6434

**Monster Design Group**
274 Wattis Way
South San Francisco, CA 94080
(415) 871-6000

**Motion Works**
1020 Mainland St., Suite 130
Vancouver, B.C. V6B 2T4
(604) 685-9975

**Mus-Art Productions**
P.O. Box 680664
Orlando, FL 32868
(407) 290-MIDI

**New Sound Music**
P.O. Box 37363
Oak Park, MI 48237
(313) 355-3643

**Olduvai Corp.**
7520 Red Rd., Suite A
South Miami, FL 33143
(305) 665-4665

**Opcode Systems, Inc.**
3641 Haven Dr., Suite A
Menlo Park, CA 94025
(415) 369-8131

**Parker Adams Group**
12335 Santa Monica Blvd., Suite 124
Los Angeles, CA 90025
(310) 454-1192

**Passport Designs, Inc.**
100 Stone Pine Rd.
Half Moon Bay, CA 94019
(415) 726-0280

**PG Music, Inc.**
111-266 Elmwood Ave.
Buffalo, NY 14222
(416) 528-4897

**Phil Wood Consulting**
3450 Granada Ave., Suite 50
Santa Clara, CA 95051
(800) 484-1096 ext. 3525

**Prosonus**
11126 Weddington St.
North Hollywood, CA 91601
(818) 766-5221

**Roland Corp.**
7200 Dominion Circle
Los Angeles, CA 90040
(213) 685-5141

**Sound Quest Inc.**
66 Broadway Ave., Suite 1207
Toronto, Ontario M4P 1T6
(416) 322-6434

**Steinberg/Jones**
17700 Raymer St., Suite 1001
Northridge, CA 91325
(818) 993-4091

**Tran Tracks**
133 West 72nd St., Suite 601
New York, NY 10023
(201) 383-6691

**Trycho Music International**
2166 W. Broadway St., Suite 330
Anaheim, CA 92804
(800) 543-8988

**Voyager Co.**
1351 Pacific Coast Hwy.
Santa Monica, CA 90401
(310) 451-1383

**VPL Research, Inc.**
656 Bair Island Rd., 3rd Floor
Redwood City, CA 94063
(415) 361-1710

**Works Music Productions, Inc.**
P.O. Box 22681
Milwaukie, OR 97222
(503) 659-3964

**Yamaha International Corp.**
6600 Orangethorpe Ave.
Buena Park, CA 90620
(714) 522-9011

a. No. 5, "Eusebius"

# Appendix C

# Bibliography

## Books

Anderton, Craig. *MIDI for Musicians.* New York: Amsco Publications, 1986.

Apple Computer, Inc. *Inside Macintosh, Volume VI.* Menlo Park, Calif.: Addison-Wesley Publishing Company, 1991.

Bryan, Marvin. *Introduction to Macintosh System 7.* San Francisco: SYBEX, 1991.

Carlin, Dan, Sr. *Music in Film and Video Productions.* Boston: Focal Press, 1991.

Casty, Alan. *Development of the Film: An Interpretive History.* New York: Harcourt Brace Jovanovich, 1973.

Giannetti, Louis D. *Understanding Movies.* Englewood Cliffs, N.J.: Prentice-Hall, 1972.

Goldberg, Michael. *The Ultimate Home Studio.* Menlo Park, Calif.: Digidesign, 1991.

Goodman, Danny. *The Complete HyperCard 2.0 Handbook.* New York: Bantam Books, 1990.

Heid, Jim. *Macworld Complete Mac Handbook.* San Mateo, Calif.: IDG Books Worldwide, 1991.

Hubatka, Milton C., Frederick Hull, and Richard W. Sanders. *Audio Sweetening for Film and TV.* Blue Ridge Summit, Penn.: Tab Books, 1985.

Huber, David M. *Random Access Audio.* Menlo Park, Calif.: Digidesign, 1990.

McClelland, Deke. *Macintosh System 7: Everything You Need to Know.* San Francisco: SYBEX, 1992.

Milano, Dominic, ed. *Mind Over MIDI.* Milwaukee: Hal Leonard Books, 1987.

Mott, Robert L. *Sound Effects: Radio, TV, and Film.* Boston: Focal Press, 1990.

Pohlmann, Ken C. *Principles of Digital Audio.* Carmel, Ind.: Howard W. Sams & Co., 1989.

Weis, Elisabeth and John Belton, eds. *Film Sound: Theory and Practice.* New York: Columbia University Press, 1985.

Yelton, Geary. *Music and the Macintosh.* Atlanta: MIDI America, 1989.

## *Periodicals*

*Computer Pictures.* White Plains, N.Y.: Montage Publishing.

*Electronic Musician.* Emeryville, Calif.: Act III Publishing.

*Film & Video.* Los Angeles: Optic Music.

*Home & Studio Recording.* Chatsworth, Calif.: Music Maker Publications.

*Keyboard.* San Francisco: Miller Freeman Publications.

*MacUser.* New York: Ziff-Davis Publishing Co.

*Macworld.* San Francisco: Macworld Communications.

*New Media Products.* Los Altos, Calif.: New Media Research.

# INDEX

## A

Actions dialog box (MediaTracks), 325
actors
    with Animation Works, 307
    with interFACE, 314-318, 320-321
    with Paracomp Magic, 326-328
    with PROmotion, 333
ADDmotion II program, 338
Adobe Premier program, 302-305
Advanced Integrated Synthesis System sound module, 366-367
Advanced Moose stack, 405
Adventures in Musicland program, 405-408
After Dark screen saver, 397-400
aftertouch data, 20-21
agents in interFACE, 314
AIFF. *See* Audio Interchange File Format
AirCraft Music Library, 386-387
Alchemy sample-editing software, 230-241
Algorithm stack (HyperMIDI), 143-144
aliasing, 172-173
amplitude, 170-171
    with Alchemy, 234-235
    with Voice Impact Pro, 192
analog audio, 169
Analog Interface (Sound Tools), 210
analog-to-digital (A/D) converters, 171, 343
animation
    with Adobe Premier, 302
    with Animation Works, 306-309
    with interFACE, 314-321
    with MacroMind Director, 286, 289-294
    with MediaMaker, 301-305
    with Paracomp Magic, 329
    with PROmotion, 333-338
    with QuickTime, 346
    with SOUNDtraK, 142
Animation Works program, 306-309
anti-aliasing filters, 173
Apple MIDI Driver, 350
Apple MIDI Interface, 368
Arrange window
    with Cubase, 83
    with Cubase Audio, 267-268, 270
Arrangement window (EZ Vision), 100
articulation, 69
assembling sequences, 43
Associated Production Music library, 387
At Your Service (interFACE), 320-321
Attached Patch feature (Galaxy Plus Editors), 159
Audible Feedback option (EZ Vision), 99
audio
    for multimedia presentations (*See* multimedia, sound for)
    sources of, 13-14 (*See also* libraries)
    for video, 15
Audio Action library, 387
Audio Editor window (Cubase Audio), 269-270
Audio Event Maker (CD AudioStack), 312-314
Audio Fade control (Adobe Premier), 305
Audio Instrument window (Studio Vision), 260
Audio Interchange File Format (Audio IFF), 186, 196
Audio Monitor window (Digital Performer), 272-273
audio panes with Studio Vision, 259-261
Audio Setup dialog box (Audio Trax), 245-246
Audio Trax system, 243-249
Audio window (Audio Trax), 246-247
Audiomedia system, 14, 200-210
    with Cubase Audio, 267
    with Digital Performer, 271

with SampleCell, 212–213, 219–220
with Studio Vision, 257
Auto control (Master Tracks Pro 5), 65
autolocate memories, 250
automation with Deck, 254–256
Auto-Return feature (Ballade), 106

## B

Bach Songbook sequences, 130
Background Editor (Animation Works), 306
Background Rhythm Patterns sequences, 120–121
background sounds, 11
Backwards filter (Adobe Premier), 305
Ballade sequencing software, 104–109
Band-in-a-Box program, 122–124
bandwidth and sampling rate, 172
banks
    with MIDI Quest, 161–162
    with patches, 150
    with SampleCell, 213–214, 217–219
Bargraph display (Cubase), 87
Barron, Louis and Bebe, 5
Beep command (HyperCard), 283
Bender effect (MacRecorder), 182–183
benshi, 4
Beyond sequencing software, 73–82
bidirectional MIDI data flow, 19, 25
Blend & Mingle command (X-oR), 156
blocks
    with CD AudioStack, 312
    with EZ Vision, 100
Body Electric (HookUp!), 331–332
Boing sound (HyperCard), 284
Book of MIDI stack, 145–146
Bounce To Disk dialog box (Deck), 252
Bridge display (Beyond), 79
Bundle window (Galaxy Plus Editors), 157–158
burn-in, screen saver for, 397–400
Button Info dialog box (MediaTracks), 325
buttons with HyperCard, 282
buyouts, 385–386

## C

cables for MIDI, 18
Capitol Production Music library, 387–388
cards with HyperCard, 282
Cartoon Carnival, 402–403
Cast window (MacroMind Director), 289–292
CA-30 sound module, 360–362
CD Audio Controller (CD AudioStack), 312–313
CD Audio Editor window (MediaMaker), 299–300
CD AudioStack program, 311–314
CD players (MacroMind Director), 294
CD-ROM libraries, 392–394
    with CD AudioStack, 311–314
    for music, 14
    with SampleCell, 212–213
    for voices, 11
cells in MacroMind Director, 290–291
cels
    in Animation Works, 306
    in PROmotion, 333
chaining modules, 26–27
Change Duration dialog box (Performer), 53
Change Filter feature (Master Tracks Pro 5), 72
Change menu (Master Tracks Pro 5), 72
Change Velocity dialog box (Performer), 53–54
channels
    with DeluxeRecorder, 109
    with MacRecorder, 181
    with MacroMind Director, 291
    with Master Tracks Pro 5, 66–67, 70
    for MIDI, 19–20, 127
    with PROmotion, 336
    with Sound Manager, 342–343
    vs. tracks, 37–38
Chaplin, Charlie, 4
Choose a Picture window (Talking Moose), 403–404
Choose command (MIDI Quest), 162–163
Chord display (Cubase), 88

Chord Embellishment option
    (Band-in-a-Box), 123
Chorus effect (Deck), 251
Chromatic harmonizing (Beyond), 81
Chunks window (Performer), 53
circuits, sample-and-hold, 170–171, 174
Clair, René, 5
Click button (Master Tracks Pro 5), 65
Clip Tunes CD-ROM, 393
clipping, 179–180
clips
    with Adobe Premier, 302–305
    with MediaTracks, 322–324
clock messages, 21
CM-32L sound module, 127, 354–355
CM-32P sound module, 355
CM-64 sound module, 127, 355–356
CM-300 sound module, 358–359
CM-500 sound module, 359–360
Coarticulated actors (interFACE), 315
Collection window (MediaMaker),
    295–296, 300
color
    with Audiomedia, 203
    with EZ Vision, 98
    with Vision, 56
comments
    with Performer, 46
    with SOUNDtraK, 139
Compact command
    with Digital Performer, 274
    with Studio Vision, 265
compact discs (CDs)
    libraries on, 386–392
    sampling rates for, 173
compact speakers, 371–372
Compare Patches command (X-oR), 156
Component Manager (QuickTime), 347
composers, working with, 379–380,
    382–383
composing
    with MIDI, 24
    with Performer, 52–53
compound slides, 287–288

compression
    with Adobe Premier, 302
    with Audiomedia, 207–208
    with Deck, 256–257
    with MacRecorder, 178
    with Paracomp Magic, 329
    with PROmotion, 338
    with QuickTime, 347
    with Sound Designer II, 230
    with Sound Manager, 343
    with Voice Impact Pro, 189, 192
Connect-the-Dots option (Voice Impact
    Pro), 193–194
connections for MIDI, 18–19
Console window (DeluxeRecorder), 109
Consolidate command (Studio Vision), 265
Consolidated Controls Panel
    with Digital Performer, 272
    with Performer, 49
Constrained Random option (Galaxy Plus
    Editors), 161
Construction window (Adobe Premier),
    304–305
continuous data, 20–21, 76–77
control bars and windows, 38
    with DeluxeRecorder, 109
    with interFACE, 316
    with Paracomp Magic, 326
    with Performer, 47, 49
    with Studio Vision, 257
    with Studio/1, 332
    with Vision, 57–58
controller windows
    with Cubase, 89
    with Master Tracks Pro 5, 70
copyright clearances, 385–386
Costume palette (Paracomp Magic), 326
Count In button (Master Tracks Pro 5), 65
counter displays, 38–39
    with Beyond, 80
    with Performer, 48–49
    with SOUNDtraK, 141
    with Vision, 58
Creative Support Services library, 388

crossfade feature
    with Alchemy, 234, 238
    with Audiomedia, 204
    with Sound Designer II, 229
CS-10 speakers, 371–372
Cubase Audio system, 267–271
Cubase sequencing software, 82–93
cues and cue sheets
    with Beyond, 79
    for composers, 382
    with Paracomp Magic, 327–329
    with PROmotion, 338
Cursor Locator icons (Alchemy), 233

## D

DAT (digital audiotape). *See* digital audio
Data Base feature (MIDI Quest), 164
Deck system, 249–257
delay effects
    with Deck, 251
    with Voice Impact Pro, 192
Delete File command (Studio Vision), 265
DeluxeRecorder sequencing software, 109–113
demos for ed/lib programs, 151
desktop speakers, 24
destructive editing, 203–204
Device menu (Master Tracks Pro 5), 66
DeWolfe Music Library, 388
Digidesign library, 220–221, 393
digital audio, 169–170
    Audiomedia, 200–210
    high resolution, 199
    with MacRecorder, 177–188
    with MIDI systems
    Audio Trax, 243–249
    Cubase Audio, 267–271
    Deck, 249–257
    Digital Performer, 271–278
    Studio Vision, 257–267

Mitshiba StereoRecorder, 196–197
    playing back, 174–175
    quantization for, 171
    recording, 171–174
    Sound Tools, 210–211
    Voice Impact Pro, 188–196
Digital EQ dialog box (Alchemy), 239–240
Digital Interface (Sound Tools), 210
Digital Performer system, 271–278
digital signal processing (DSP), 189, 225
Digital Sound Series library, 394
Digital Waveboard (Digital Performer), 277–278
digital-to-analog (D/A) converters, 174, 342
DIN connectors, 19
Display List window (Beyond), 77–78
Display Options command (MacRecorder), 179
Display Scale icon
    with Audiomedia, 203
    with Sound Designer II, 227–229
distortion
    from clipping, 179–180
    from quantization, 171
    and sampling rate, 172
Distributed Audio Networks (Alchemy), 231
downsampling with MacRecorder, 178
Drawing window (MediaTracks), 325
Dressing Room window (interFACE), 315–316
drivers
    Apple Midi Driver, 350
    for ed/lib programs, 150–151
    with Galaxy Plus Editors, 161
    with MIDI Quest, 161, 164–165
    with X-oR, 156
drum machines and sequences, 31–32, 88–89, 124
DTP & Multimedia CD sequences, 130
duration of notes, 40
dynamic data with QuickTime, 345
dynamic range, 171

## E

Easy Configuration feature (Galaxy Plus Editors), 157
echoes
    with Adobe Premier, 305
    with MacRecorder, 181
    with X-oR, 154
editing and edit windows
    with Animation Works, 306–307
    with Ballade, 108
    with Beyond, 75, 80
    with Cubase, 86–88, 90
    with Cubase Audio, 269–270
    with DeluxeRecorder, 111–113
    destructive and nondestructive, 203–204
    with Encore, 114
    with EZ Vision, 98–99
    with MediaMaker, 297–301
    with Performer, 52
    with PROmotion, 337
    with SampleCell, 213–219
    with sequencers, 40
    with SOUNDtraK, 140–142
    with Voice Impact Pro, 190–191, 196
editor/librarians, 149–151
    Galaxy Plus Editors, 97, 156–161
    MIDI Quest, 161–165
    X-oR, 152–156
ed/libs. *See* editor/librarians
education
    Adventures in Musicland for, 405–408
    sound effects for, 12
    speech synthesizers for, 11
Effects menu (Deck), 251
elapsed time. *See also* SMPTE timecode
    with Deck, 250
    with DeluxeRecorder, 110
    with Master Tracks Pro 5, 65
    with Performer, 47–48
Electric Mixer tool (Kid Pix), 401
elements with MediaMaker, 295–299
E-mu sound modules, 362–364
Encore sequencing software, 113–115
envelope effects and windows
    with Alchemy, 235
    with Galaxy Plus Editors, 160
    with MacRecorder, 182
    with SampleCell, 219
    with X-oR, 155
E-oR Profile Development System, 156
EQ with Deck, 251, 257
Eraser tool (Master Tracks Pro 5), 71
events and event list windows, 41
    with CD AudioStack, 312–314
    with Cubase, 86
    with Digital Performer, 271, 274–275
    with Master Tracks Pro 5, 69
    with Performer, 49, 51
    with Studio Vision, 261–262, 264
    with Vision, 62–63
Expand SubSections function (Beyond), 79
expanding MIDI systems, 26–30
Export card (SOUNDtraK), 142
Expression Images (interFACE), 315–317, 320
Extended actors (interFACE), 315
external commands and functions for HyperCard. *See* XCMDs and XFCNs
external sounds
    with MacroMind Director, 291–292
    with MediaMaker, 299–301
EZ Vision sequencing software, 97–101

## F

faders and fade effects, 29–30
    with Adobe Premier, 305
    with Alchemy, 234, 238
    with Audiomedia, 204
    with Ballade, 106–107
    with Beyond, 81
    with Cubase, 90
    with Deck, 250–252, 254
    with EZ Vision, 101
    with MacRecorder, 182

with MacroMind Director, 287–288
with Performer, 55
with SampleCell, 217
with Sound Designer II, 229–230
with SOUNDtraK, 140–141
with Studio Vision, 264–265
with Vision, 62–64
with Voice Impact Pro, 192
Fast Fourier Transform (FFT) display
with Alchemy, 238
with Audiomedia, 207
with Sound Designer II, 230
feedback with Vision, 62
FFT display. *See* Fast Fourier Transform display
File Management window (Studio Vision), 265
File window
with Studio Vision, 257
with Vision, 59
films. *See also* animation; movies
aliasing in, 173
early, 4–5
filters
with Adobe Premier, 305
with Alchemy, 238
with Deck, 252
low-pass, 173–174
with MacRecorder, 182–183
with Master Tracks Pro 5, 69, 72
with Performer, 50
with Sound Designer II, 229
with Voice Impact Pro, 192
Find command (X-oR), 153–154
Fish! screen saver module, 398
Flanger effect (MacRecorder), 181
Flute sound (HyperCard), 284
Flying Toaster screen saver module, 398
FM (frequency modulation) synthesis, 22, 181, 235
*Forbidden Planet*, 5
frequency and frequency response, 170, 172–173
frequency modulation (FM) synthesis, 22, 181, 235

Frequency profiles (Alchemy), 236
Functions bar (Cubase), 85

## G

Gain command (Audio Trax), 246–247
Galaxy Plus Editors, 97, 156–161
Gate button (SampleCell), 218
General Find dialog box (Galaxy Plus Editors), 157–158
General MIDI Standard, 125–129
generated sequences, 60
genlocking process, 381
Ghost Notes window (Master Tracks Pro 5), 70
graphic display windows, 41–42
with Digital Performer, 271, 275–276
with Performer, 50–52
with Studio Vision, 259–261, 264
with Vision, 58, 60–61
Graphic EQ feature
with Audiomedia, 206–207
with Sound Designer II, 229
Greytsounds library, 221
Grid Edit window (Cubase), 86–88
Group Tracks (Cubase), 84
Guess Durations command (Encore), 115

## H

hardware
for HyperCard, 137–138
MIDI interfaces, 367–370
sound modules, 353–367
speakers, 371–375
harmonic distortion, 172
Harmonic Spectrum Display window (Alchemy), 238–239
harmonizing with Beyond, 81
Harpsichord sound (HyperCard), 284
Health Watch Service Panel (interFACE), 321
Hitchcock, Alfred, 5

Hollywood Film Music Library, 388–389
Holophonic Sound Effects library, 392
HookUp! program, 330–332
Hum Removal function (Deck), 252
humanize function, 40
HyperAnimation (interFACE), 314
HyperCard stacks
    with ADDmotion II, 338
    with Animation Works, 308–309
    with Audiomedia, 209–210
    Book of MIDI for, 145–146
    with CD AudioStack, 311–312
    hardware and software for, 137–138
    HyperMIDI for, 143–145
    HyperSound, 186–188
    with interFACE, 320
    with MacroMind Director, 294
    with MediaTracks, 325
    for sound, 282–286
    for Sound Clips library, 393
    SOUNDtraK for, 138–142
    and SuperCard, 309–311
    with Talking Moose, 405
    with Voice Impact Pro, 196
    for wind chimes, 12–13
HyperFEX library, 392
HyperMIDI software, 143–145
HyperSound stack, 178, 186–188
HyperTalk language, 283

## I

I-beam tool
    with EZ Vision, 99
    with Vision, 61
Image Compression Manager (QuickTime), 347
Import command
    with MacroMind Director, 291
    with Paracomp Magic, 328
Insert Event button (Vision), 62–63
Insert Measures command (Audio Trax), 248
Instrument format (MacRecorder), 186

Instrument Patch Map (General MIDI), 127–128
instruments and instrument windows
    with Beyond, 81–82
    with Proteus/1, 362
    with SampleCell, 214
    with Studio Vision, 260
    with Vision, 57
Intelligent Arranger sound module, 360–362
Intelligent harmonizing (Beyond), 81
Interactive Phrase Synthesizer (Cubase), 91
interFACE program, 314–321
interfaces for MIDI, 21, 27–28, 367–370
internal sounds with MacroMind Director, 291–292
Interpreter module (Cubase), 91
IPS (Cubase), 91

## J

Jazz Swing style (Band-in-a-Box), 123
Jazz Through MIDI sequences, 121
Jump feature (X-oR), 155

## K

Key Edit window
    with Cubase, 85–86
    with Cubase Audio, 270
Key Groups (SampleCell), 215–216
Key Images (interFACE), 316
Key Pressure window (Master Tracks Pro 5), 70
Key Strummer stack (HyperMIDI), 143–144
keyboards, 22
    with Master Tracks Pro 5, 69
    for MIDI, 25–26
    transposing, with Performer, 54
Kid Pix program, 400–402
Killer Tracks Multimedia Library, 389
Korg sound modules, 366–367

## L

LA (linear arithmetic) synthesis, 22
labels with SOUNDtraK, 139
layback process, 383
layering, 17
libraries
    with CD AudioStack, 311–314
    on CD-ROM, 392–394
    on compact disc, 386–392
    and copyright clearances, 385–386
    with MIDI Quest, 162
    for music, 14, 129–133, 378–379
    with SampleCell, 212–213, 220–222
    for sound effects, 13, 386, 393–394
    for videotape, 378–379
    for voices, 11
    with X-oR, 153
lifespans in Paracomp Magic, 327
line mixers, 28
linear arithmetic (LA) synthesis, 22
linear-style sequence structuring, 43
Lingo language, 286, 291, 294–295
links
    with HyperCard, 282
    with Paracomp Magic, 329
    with Studio Vision, 260
List windows
    with Studio Vision, 264
    with Vision, 58, 62–63
Load a Sound dialog box (Studio/1), 332
Lock Audio to Tape option (Studio Vision), 266
Logical Edit display (Cubase), 90
Logo module (After Dark), 399
longitudinal time code (LTC), 380
looping
    with Alchemy, 237–238
    with Beyond, 81
    with Deck, 253–254
    with MacRecorder, 184
    with Master Tracks Pro 5, 66
    with MediaMaker, 298, 300
    with Sound Designer II, 227–229
    with Vision, 58
low-pass filters, 173–174
LTC (longitudinal time code), 380
Lucasfilm Sound Effects library, 391

## M

Mac Sound Editor window (MediaMaker), 297–299, 301
MACE (Macintosh Audio Compression and Expansion), 343
MacinTalk
    with interFACE, 316–318
    with MacroMind Director, 294
    with Talking Moose, 403–404
Macintosh Audio Compression and Expansion (MACE), 343
MacNexus MIDI interface, 368
MacProteus sound module, 13, 363
MacRecorder, 14, 177–178
    with Audio Trax, 244
    HyperSound stack in, 186–188
    with interFACE, 318–319
    with MacroMind Director, 288
    resolution of, 171, 178
    SoundEdit application in, 179–186
MacroMind Director, 286
    Overview part of, 286–289
    Studio part of, 289–295
MacSpeaker, 373–374
Mac-to-Sampler icon (Sound Designer II), 226
Magnifying Glass tool (Cubase Audio), 269–270
Manhattan Production Music library, 389
mapping with samplers, 30
Marquee tool
    with EZ Vision, 99
    with Vision, 61
Master Tracks Pro 5 sequencing software, 64–73
Matrix Modulation window (SampleCell), 217–218
MA-12C speakers, 372–373
McGill University library, 221–222

Media Controller (PROmotion), 333-334
MediaMaker program, 295-301
MediaTracks program, 322-325
melody
   in HyperCard, 285
   in music sequences, 130
Melody Mixup game (Adventures in Musicland), 406-407
memory
   for Audiomedia, 200
   for Digital Performer, 271
   for HyperCard, 285
   for MacRecorder, 178
   for music sequences, 119
   for SampleCell, 212
   for samplers, 31
   for speech synthesizers, 10
   for SuperCard, 310-311
   and videotape, 377
Merge command (Audiomedia), 205
messages with MIDI, 20-21, 29
Meter display (Beyond), 79
Metro Music Productions library, 389-390
metronome options, 39
   with Cubase, 84
   with Deck, 253
   with Performer, 48-49
micons with MediaMaker, 296
microphones, 343-345
MIDI (Musical Instrument Digital Interface), 18
   channels for, 19-20, 127
   connections for, 18-19
   with digital audio
      Audio Trax, 243-249
      Cubase Audio, 267-271
      Deck, 249-257
      Digital Performer, 271-278
      Studio Vision, 257-267
   expanding, 26-30
   General MIDI Standard, 125-129
   with HyperCard (*See* HyperCard stacks)
   interfaces for, 21, 27-28, 367-370
   keyboard controllers for, 25-26
   and Macintosh, 21
   with MacroMind Director, 293
   messages with, 20-21, 29
   mixers with, 28-30
   modes for, 20
   music sequences for (*See* music and music sequences)
   ports for, 18-19, 350
   and samplers, 30-32
   sound modules for, 14, 22
   speakers for, 23-24
   systems for, 24-25
   with Vision, 56
MIDI Hits sequences, 130-131
MIDI Inn sequences, 131
MIDI Input module (Cubase), 91
MIDI Interface for the Mac, 368
MIDI Jukebox sequences, 131
MIDI keyboards
   with DeluxeRecorder, 110-111
   with Master Tracks Pro 5, 69
   with Sound Designer II, 230
MIDI Manager, 349-351
MIDI Metronome option (Deck), 253
MIDI monitors and windows
   with Audiomedia, 205
   with Beyond, 77
   with Cubase, 91-92
   with EZ Vision, 98
   with Master Tracks Pro 5, 70
   with MIDI Quest, 163-164
   with Performer, 55-56
   with Sound Designer II, 230
MIDI 1.0 Specification, 17-18
MIDI Quest editor/librarian, 161-165
MIDI System Exclusive (sys/ex) commands, 149-150
MIDI Thru channels and connectors, 18, 80
MIDI Time Piece interface, 27, 370
MIDI Translator interface, 368
MIDIclips sequences, 131-132, 142
MIDIFace LX interface, 368
MIDIFile Tunes sequences, 132
MIDIKeys feature (Vision), 63-64
Milestone, Lewis, 5

Misc window (SampleCell), 217
Mitshiba StereoRecorder system, 196–197
mixer states, 254, 256
mixing and mixer windows
    with Audio Trax, 248–249
    with Audiomedia, 206
    with Ballade, 106–107
    with Deck, 252, 254, 256
    with Digital Performer, 277
    with EZ Vision, 101
    with MacRecorder, 185–186
    with MIDI, 28–30
    with MIDI Quest, 161–163
    with Performer, 55
    with Sound Designer II, 230
    with Voice Impact Pro, 191
ModDelay effect (Deck), 251
modes for MIDI, 20
Modulation window (Master Tracks Pro 5), 70–71
Mogrify button (Vision), 61–62
Monitor window (X-oR), 152
Mono mode (MIDI), 20
Moose Goes Hyper stack, 405
Moose Proof desk accessory (Talking Moose), 404
More After Dark screen saver, 397
MouseKeys window (Galaxy Plus Editors), 159
MousePlay feature (X-oR), 154
Movie Editor window (Animation Works), 306–307
Movie Toolbox (QuickTime), 347
movies. *See also* animation; films
    aliasing in, 173
    early, 4–5
MT Player application, 322
MTPlay stack, 325
MT-32 sound module, 127, 129, 355
Multi-Channel Record option (Master Tracks Pro 5), 67
multimedia, sound for, 1, 9. *See also* presentations
    Adobe Premier, 302–305
    Animation Works, 306–309

CD AudioStack, 311–314
HookUp!, 330–332
HyperCard, 282–286
interFACE, 314–321
MacroMind Director, 286–295
MediaMaker, 295–301
MediaTracks, 322–325
Paracomp Magic, 326–330
PROmotion, 333–338
Studio/1, 332–333
SuperCard, 309–311
Multimedia Artists Sequences, 131
Multimedia DeskTop Sounds library, 394
MultiMedia HANDisc sequences, 132
Multiple Take mode (Beyond), 81
multiple-track displays in EZ Vision, 98–99
MultiRecord mode (Digital Performer), 272
multisamples, 211
multitimbral capability, 22–23
Multitrack page (Beyond), 74
Multi-Track Record option (Master Tracks Pro 5), 67
Mus-Art Productions sequences, 132
music and music sequences, 119
    background, 120–122
    Band-in-a-Box, 122–124
    cards for, 13
    drums, 124
    General MIDI, 125–129
    libraries for, 14, 129–133, 378–379
    original, 379–380, 382–383
    in presentations, 13–14
    with sound effects, 2–3
Music Match game (Adventures in Musicland), 407
Musical Instrument Digital Interface. *See* MIDI

# N

needle-drop fees, 386
Network Music library, 390

noise and noise gates, 171
    with Audio Trax, 247
    with MacRecorder, 180
    with Studio Vision, 262
nondestructive editing, 203–204
Normalize commands
    with Audio Trax, 246
    with Deck, 252
Notation Editing window (Performer), 52
notation windows, 42–43
Note Editor window (Beyond), 75, 80
note events and messages, 20, 41
note scrubbing with Vision, 62
note-entry mode (Master Tracks Pro 5), 69
Numbered Marker feature
    with Audiomedia, 203
    with Sound Designer II, 227
Nyquist theorem, 172–173

## O

Olduvai Corporation library, 393
Omni mode (MIDI), 20
Omnimusic library, 390
OMS (Opcode MIDI System), 56, 156–157
OMS Setup procedure (Galaxy Plus Editors), 157
Opcode MIDI System (OMS), 56, 156–157
Open Instrument command (SampleCell), 214
Open Special command (Alchemy), 231–232
Optical Media International library, 394
Output module (Cubase), 92
output sample-and-hold circuits, 174
Overview display (Audiomedia), 202
Overview part and window (MacroMind Director), 286–289

## P

Paint Brush tool (Cubase), 86–87
Paint palette (PROmotion), 334
Paint window (MacroMind Director), 289
Paracomp Magic program, 326–330
Parametric EQ feature (Deck), 251
Parts (Cubase), 83–85, 88
Passport Designs, Inc. library, 394
Paste Audio From command (Audio Trax), 248
Patch Talk language, 161
PatchBay application, 350
patches and patch windows
    with ed/lib programs, 150
    with Galaxy Plus Editors, 158–159
    with MIDI Quest, 164
    with Vision, 59
    with X-oR, 155–156
paths
    with Animation Works, 306
    with PROmotion, 333
Pattern button (Sound Designer II), 230
pattern-song sequence structuring, 43
PC-200 sound module, 360
Pencil tools and icons
    with Alchemy, 236
    with Audiomedia, 203
    with Beyond, 75, 80
    with Cubase, 86–87
    with EZ Vision, 100
    with Master Tracks Pro 5, 69, 71
    with Sound Designer II, 227
    with Vision, 62
    with Voice Impact Pro, 191
Percussion Key Map (General MIDI), 127, 129
Performance window (X-oR), 152
Performer sequencing software, 45–56
Phase Input module (Cubase), 91
phonemes
    with interFACE, 315, 320
    with Talking Moose, 404
Phonetic/Timing Value Strings (interFACE), 319
piano-roll display, 41–42
picons with MediaMaker, 295–297
PICS Player (After Dark), 399
Picture Frame module (After Dark), 399
Picture Perfect game (Adventures in Musicland), 406

Ping Pong effect (MacRecorder), 181
pitch and pitch bend, 21
    with Alchemy, 240–241
    with Beyond, 76
    with HyperCard, 284
    with Master Tracks Pro 5, 70–71
    with SampleCell, 217
Play command (SuperCard), 310
Play Selected option (Studio Vision), 263
Playback Speed dialog box (MediaTracks), 324
player pianos, 35–36
Player window (Animation Works), 307
Playlist window (Audiomedia), 204–205
Poly mode (MIDI), 20
polyphony, 23, 134
ports, MIDI, 18–19, 350
Post Record dialog box (DeluxeRecorder), 111
posters with QuickTime, 346–347
Powered Partner 570 speaker, 374–375
Preferences dialog box
    with MediaMaker, 299–301
    with Talking Moose, 403–404
prerecorded sounds. *See* libraries
Presentation window (MediaTracks), 322–324
presentations, 9. *See also* multimedia, sound for
    music in, 13–14
    sound effects in, 11–13
    voice in, 10–11
presequenced MIDI music. *See* music and music sequences
presets
    with ed/lib programs, 150
    with Proteus/1, 362–363
pressure data, 20–21
previews
    with QuickTime, 347
    with SOUNDtraK, 140
priorities with PROmotion, 336
Pro 5. *See* Master Tracks Pro 5
Process icons (Alchemy), 233
production music. *See* libraries
Professional, The, 388
Professional Analog Interface (Sound Tools), 210
Profile Development System, 156
Profiles (X-oR), 152
program change messages, 21
Program Number feature (Master Tracks Pro 5), 66–67
Program setting (Vision), 58–59
project studios, 380
projects and project windows
    with Adobe Premier, 302–304
    with SOUNDtraK, 142
    with SuperCard, 310
PROmotion program, 333–338
props with PROmotion, 333
Prosonus library, 222
Proteus sound modules, 31, 362–364
protocols, 18

# Q

quantization, 171
    with Ballade, 108
    with Beyond, 81
    with Encore, 113
    with EZ Vision, 98
    with Performer, 53–54
    with sequencers, 40
    with Studio Vision, 263
    with Vision, 60, 62
Queue mode (Vision), 59
QuickPICS program (Paracomp Magic), 329–330
QuickTime program, 302, 305, 345–349
QuikTunes sequences, 132–133

# R

radio, 3
randomize features
    with After Dark, 399
    with X-oR, 156
RAVE command (interFACE), 319

real-time recording, 39
RECITE command (interFACE), 318–320
Record Mode button (Master Tracks Pro 5), 65
Record Monitors
    with Cubase Audio, 268–269
    with Studio Vision, 258–260
Record Sound dialog box (MediaTracks), 324
Recording Workshop button (Audiomedia), 209
Redmon, Nigel, 143
regions, 274
Reminder Service Panel (interFACE), 321
Remote Controls window (Performer), 47–48
Replacement mode (Vision), 58
Resample command (Voice Impact Pro), 192
resolution
    of Alchemy, 231
    of Audiomedia, 171, 200
    of Ballade, 104, 108
    of Beyond, 80
    of DeluxeRecorder, 109
    of Encore, 114
    of EZ Vision, 97
    of MacRecorder, 171, 178
    of Master Tracks Pro 5, 64
    of MIDI Manager, 349
    of Performer, 48
    of SampleCell, 212
    of sequencers, 38–39
    of Trax, 102
    of Vision, 56, 60
    of Voice Impact Pro, 189
Retain command (Studio Vision), 261
Reverb effect (MacRecorder), 183
reverse feature
    with Adobe Premier, 305
    with Digital Performer, 277
    with Voice Impact Pro, 192
Rhythm Track editor (Ballade), 108
Roland
    sound modules by, 107, 127, 354–363
    speakers by, 371–373

## S

sample-and-hold circuits, 170–171, 174
SampleCell system, 212
    editor for, 213–219
    sampling with, 219–220
    sounds for, 220–222
sample-editing software, 225
    Alchemy, 230–241
    Sound Designer II, 226–230
sample-playback modules, 31
samplers, 211
    and MIDI, 30–32
    SampleCell, 212–222
sampling rates, 171–174
    with Alchemy, 231
    with Audiomedia, 200, 205
    with Voice Impact Pro, 189
SC-55 Sound Canvas sound module, 127, 129, 356–357
SC-155 Sound Canvas sound module, 357–358
Scale Paste command (DeluxeRecorder), 112
scenes in Paracomp Magic, 326–329
Scissors tool (Cubase), 84
score viewing and editing
    with Ballade, 105–106, 108
    with Cubase, 88
    with Cubase Audio, 270
    with MacroMind Director, 290, 292
screen savers, 397–400
ScreenKeys feature (X-oR), 153–154
ScreenRecorder (MediaTracks), 322
scripts
    with HyperCard, 283–284
    with MacroMind Director, 291, 294–295
Scroll window (Voice Impact Pro), 191
scrubbing features
    with Cubase, 84
    with EZ Vision, 99
    with Sound Designer II, 230
    with Vision, 62
searches
    with Galaxy Plus Editors, 158–159
    with SOUNDtraK, 138–139

Sections window (Beyond), 77–78
Select a Sound dialog box (PROmotion), 334–335
Selection icons
  with Audiomedia, 203
  with Sound Designer II, 227
Separate command (Studio Vision), 261–262
sequencers. *See also* sequencing software
  editing with, 40
  event list windows for, 41
  graphic display windows for, 41–42
  with MediaMaker, 296
  moving around with, 38–39
  notation windows for, 42–43
  parts of, 37–40
  and player pianos, 35–36
  structuring by, 43
sequences, viewing and editing. *See also* music and music sequences
  with Galaxy Plus Editors, 160
  with MediaMaker, 295–298, 300–301
  with Studio Vision, 257
  with Vision, 58–60
sequencing software. *See also* sequencers
  Ballade, 104–109
  Beyond, 73–82
  Cubase, 82–93
  DeluxeRecorder, 109–113
  Encore, 113–115
  EZ Vision, 97–101
  Master Tracks Pro 5, 64–73
  Performer, 45–56
  Trax, 101–104
  Vision, 56–64
Set Colors command (Audiomedia), 203
Set Pitches command (MacRecorder), 184
Shade Two option (Galaxy Plus Editors), 161
Show Editing option (Voice Impact Pro), 196
Show Velocity feature (Master Tracks Pro 5), 67–68
Shuffler option (Galaxy Plus Editors), 161
Shuttle button (EZ Vision), 99–100
silent movies, 4
sliders. *See* faders and fade effects
Smith, Dave, 17
smoothing
  with Alchemy, 237
  with Audiomedia, 205
  with MacRecorder, 181
  with Voice Impact Pro, 192
SMPTE timecode, 15, 27
  with Ballade, 104, 107, 109
  with Beyond, 80
  with Cubase Audio, 267
  with Deck, 250
  with Digital Performer, 274, 277
  with Master Tracks Pro 5, 65
  with Performer, 47–48
  with SOUNDtraK, 141–142
  with Studio Vision, 266
  on videotape, 380–382
Snap feature (Cubase Audio), 269
snapshots, 254–255
songs
  with Audio Trax, 247–248
  from Band-in-a-Box, 122–123
  with Beyond, 81
  with EZ Vision, 100
  with MacroMind Director, 293
  with Master Tracks Pro 5, 73
  with Performer, 53
  with Trax, 102–103
Sonic Imaging Control (MacSpeaker), 373
Sonogram effect (MacRecorder), 184–185
SoperSound Music Library, 390–391
sound
  for multimedia presentations (*See* multimedia, sound for)
  sources of, 13–14 (*See also* libraries)
  for video, 15
Sound Checker feature (MIDI Quest), 163, 165
Sound Clips library, 393
Sound Concentration game (Adventures in Musicland), 407–408
Sound control panel (Sound Manager), 343–344

Sound Designer II system, 211, 220, 226–230, 266
Sound Editing window (Voice Impact Pro), 190–191
sound effects, 2–3
    with Kid Pix, 402
    libraries of, 13, 386, 393–394
    with MacroMind Director, 292
    in presentations, 11–13
    for videotape, 383
Sound Ideas library, 391
Sound Information dialog box (PROmotion), 335–337
Sound List (Paracomp Magic), 328
Sound Magic CD-ROM, 394
Sound Manager, 341–345
Sound menu (MacroMind Director), 288–289, 293
sound modules, 14, 22, 353
    chaining, 26–27
    E-mu, 362–364
    Korg, 366–367
    Roland, 107, 127, 354–363
    Yamaha, 364–366
Sound Priority slider (SampleCell), 217
Sound Sync (interFACE), 318
Sound Tools system, 210–211
    with Digital Performer, 271
    with SampleCell, 219–220
SoundAccess application (Audiomedia), 209–210
Soundbites window (Digital Performer), 273–275
SoundEdit application (MacRecorder), 178–186
SoundEdit format (MacRecorder), 186
Soundfile window (Audiomedia), 202–203
SoundMan application, 197
Sound-on-Sound button (Deck), 253–254, 256
Sounds file (MacroMind Director), 288
Sounds Utility (MacroMind Director), 288
SOUNDtraK stack, 138–142
Soundtracks for MIDI sequences, 121–122
SoundWave application (Voice Impact Pro), 189–194

SoundWave format, 196
sources of sounds, 13–14. *See also* libraries
Speaker icon (Sound Designer II), 226, 228
speakers, 23–24, 371–375
Speaking Images (interFACE), 315–316, 319–320
Specific Find dialog box (Galaxy Plus Editors), 158–159
Spectrogram effect (MacRecorder), 184–185
spectrum displays
    with Alchemy, 238–239
    with MacRecorder, 179, 184
    with Voice Impact Pro, 192–193
Speech Sync (interFACE), 318–319
speech synthesizers, 10–11
Speed scroll bar (Voice Impact Pro), 191–192
Splice Mode icon (Alchemy), 237
Splice transitions (Audiomedia), 204
Split Channel command (DeluxeRecorder), 109
splitting events (Studio Vision), 261–262
spotting sessions, 382
SR Convert command
    with Audiomedia, 205
    with Sound Designer II, 230
stacks. *See* HyperCard stacks
Stage windows
    with interFACE, 316–317
    with Paracomp Magic, 326–327
Standard actors (interFACE), 315
Standard MIDI Files, 125–126
    with Galaxy Plus Editors, 160
    with MIDI Quest, 163–164
Step Editor windows
    with Audio Trax, 249
    with Master Tracks Pro 5, 67–68, 70–71
    with Trax, 102–103
step entry, 39
step recording
    with Ballade, 105, 108–109
    with DeluxeRecorder, 113
    with Encore, 114
stereo
    with Deck, 251

digital, 196–197
   with EZ Vision, 101
stills with MediaTracks, 323
Storyboard windows (Animation Works), 308
Strip Charts
   with EZ Vision, 98, 100–101
   with Studio Vision, 260
   with Vision, 62
Strip Silence feature
   with Digital Performer, 276
   with Studio Vision, 262–263
striping videotape, 382
structuring by sequencers, 43
Studio 5 MIDI interface, 370
Studio/1 program, 332–333
Studio part (MacroMind Director), 286, 289–295
Studio Plus Two MIDI interface, 369
Studio Setup window (Vision), 56–57
Studio 3 MIDI interface, 369
Studio Vision system, 257–267
stutter effect (Studio Vision), 261
StyleMaker feature (Band-in-a-Box), 123
SubSections (Beyond), 78–79
Subsequences (Vision), 59
successive approximation synchronization, 301
SuperCard program, 309–311
SuperEdit program (SuperCard), 310
SuperTalk language, 310
Swap Channels effect (MacRecorder), 181
synchronization, 11–12
   with interFACE, 318–320
   with MediaMaker, 301
   with QuickTime, 347–348
   and videotape, 378, 383
Sync/Link MIDI interface, 369
synthesizers, 17
sys/ex messages, 21
system extensions in Vision, 56
System IQ feature (After Dark), 399
system software
   MIDI Manager, 349–351
   QuickTime, 345–349

Sound Manager, 341–345
system-exclusive messages, 21

## T

Talking Moose program, 402–405
Tap Tempo feature
   with EZ Vision, 100
   with Performer, 55
Tape Calibration option (Studio Vision), 266
Tape Deck Panel (Audiomedia), 201, 203
Tech Effects library, 392
television, 5
templates
   with ed/lib programs, 150–151
   with Galaxy Plus Editors, 160–161
   with X-oR, 155–156
tempo display and effects
   with Beyond, 79
   with EZ Vision, 100
   with Master Tracks Pro 5, 66, 71
   with Performer, 55
   with Voice Impact Pro, 192
Text Markers
   with Audiomedia, 203
   with Sound Designer II, 227
Text window (MacroMind Director), 294
TG100 sound module, 365–366
Threshold Bars icon (Alchemy), 234
through-composed sequence structuring, 43
Thru options and channels, 18, 80
   with Master Tracks Pro 5, 65
   with Studio Vision, 258
   with Vision, 58
thumbnails in Adobe Premier, 302
Tile Windows command (Voice Impact Pro), 193
Time Compression/Expansion window
   with Audiomedia, 207–208
   with Sound Designer II, 230
time coordinate systems, 348

time rulers and scales
    with Adobe Premier, 304
    with Alchemy, 239–240
    with Performer, 47
timecode. *See* SMPTE timecode
timelines
    with MediaMaker, 296
    with Paracomp Magic, 327
    with PROmotion, 336–337
timing resolution. *See* resolution
tone generators
    with MacRecorder, 181
    with MIDI Quest, 164
    with Voice Impact Pro, 193–194
tool palettes and menus
    with Alchemy, 231–232
    with Animation Works, 307
    with DeluxeRecorder, 112
    with Paracomp Magic, 326
Trace Envelope icon (Alchemy), 235
tracks and track windows, 37–38
    with Audio Trax, 244–245
    with Beyond, 74
    with Cubase, 83
    with Cubase Audio, 267
    with DeluxeRecorder, 109, 111
    with Digital Performer, 271–273
    with EZ Vision, 98–99
    with Master Tracks Pro 5, 66–67
    with Performer, 46, 49
    with QuickTime, 346
    with SampleCell, 218–219
    with Trax, 102
Tran Tracks sequences, 133
Transform MIDI Track dialog box (Deck), 256
transition times, 255
transport windows and controls
    with Audio Trax, 244
    with Ballade, 106
    with Cubase, 84–85
    with Deck, 253
    with DeluxeRecorder, 110
    with Master Tracks Pro 5, 64
    with Trax, 103

transpose function, 40
Transpose Map command (Performer), 54
Trax sequencing software, 101–104
TRF Production Music Libraries, 391
Truncate button (SOUNDtraK), 142
Trycho Tunes sequences, 133
27th Dimension library, 392
260 Instant Drum Patterns sequences, 124

# U

UART (universal asynchronous receiver/transmitter), 367
universal editor/librarians. *See* editor/librarians
Universal Synthesizer Interface, 17
Use Select command (MIDI Quest), 162

# V

Valentino Production Music Library, 392
velocity
    with Beyond, 75
    with Master Tracks Pro 5, 67–68, 71
    with MIDI, 20–21
    with Performer, 53–54
    with SampleCell, 215–216
    with sequencers, 40
    with Studio Vision, 264
vertical interval time code (VITC), 380–381
video and videotape
    audio for, 15
    with MediaMaker, 299
    music libraries for, 378–379
    original music for, 379–380, 382–383
    pros and cons of, 377–379
    SMPTE timecode on, 380–382
Videodisc element with MediaMaker, 299–300
View Filter (Performer), 50
View Memory buttons (Alchemy), 232
virtual ports with MIDI Manager, 350

Vision sequencing software, 56–64
VITC (vertical interval time code), 380–381
vocals in music sequences, 130
Voice Impact Pro system, 188–196
    with Audio Trax, 244
    with MacroMind Director, 288
    SoundWave application in, 190–194
    Voice Record application in, 195–196
voice in presentations, 10–11
volume messages, 29
Voyager CD AudioStack program, 311–314

## W

wagon-wheel effect, 173
waveforms
    with Alchemy, 232
    with MacRecorder, 179–181
Wedding Package sequences, 131
Welles, Orson, 5
window dubs, 382
wires with HookUp!, 330–332
Works Music Productions sequences, 133

## X

XCMDs (external commands) and XFCNs (external functions), 285–286
    with Animation Works, 308–309
    with Audiomedia, 209
    with CD AudioStack, 311–312
    with HyperMIDI, 143
    with HyperSound, 188
    with MediaTracks, 325
    with SuperCard, 311
    with Talking Moose, 405
    with Voice Impact Pro, 196
XObjects
    with MacroMind Director, 294
    with MediaMaker, 299
X-oR editor/librarian, 152–156

## Y

Yamaha sound modules, 364–366

## Z

zero crossing with Alchemy, 238
03R/W Synthesis Module, 366–367
zooming
    with Alchemy, 232
    with Audiomedia, 202
    with PROmotion, 337
    with Sound Designer II, 227
    with Vision, 60
    with Voice Impact Pro, 196

# Selections from The SYBEX Library

## APPLE/MACINTOSH

### Desktop Publishing with Microsoft Word on the Macintosh (Second Edition)
**Tim Erickson**
**William Finzer**
525pp. Ref. 601-4

The authors have woven a murder mystery through the text, using the sample publications as clues. Explanations of page layout, headings, fonts and styles, columnar text, and graphics are interwoven within the mystery theme of this exciting teaching method. For Version 4.0.

### Encyclopedia Macintosh
**Craig Danuloff**
**Deke McClelland**
650pp. Ref. 628-6

Just what every Mac user needs—a complete reference to Macintosh concepts and tips on system software, hardware, applications, and troubleshooting. Instead of chapters, each section is presented in A-Z format with user-friendly icons leading the way.

### Encyclopedia Macintosh Software Instant Reference
**Craig Danuloff**
**Deke McClelland**
243pp. Ref. 753-3

Help yourself to complete keyboard shortcut charts, menu maps, and tip lists for all popular Macintosh applications. This handy reference guide is divided into functional software categories, including painting, drawing, page layout, spreadsheets, word processors, and more.

### Introduction to Macintosh System 7
**Marvin Bryan**
250pp; Ref. 868-8

An engaging, plain-language introduction to the exciting new Macintosh system, for first-time users and upgraders. Step-by-step tutorials feature dozens of screen illustrations and helpful examples drawn from both business and personal computing. Covers the Desktop, working with programs, printing, customization, special accessories, and sharing information.

### Mastering Adobe Illustrator
**David A. Holzgang**
330pp. Ref. 463-1

This text provides a complete introduction to Adobe Illustrator, bringing new sophistication to artists using computer-aided graphics and page design technology. Includes a look at PostScript, the page composition language used by Illustrator.

### Mastering Microsoft Word on the Macintosh
**Michael J. Young**
447pp. Ref. 541-7

This comprehensive, step-by-step guide shows the reader through WORD's extensive capabilities, from basic editing to custom formats and desktop publishing. Keyboard and mouse instructions and practice exercises are included. For Release 4.0.

### Mastering PageMaker 4 on the Macintosh
**Greg Harvey**
**Shane Gearing**
421pp. Ref.433-X

A complete introduction to desktop publishing—from planning to printing—with emphasis on business projects. Explore the tools, concepts and techniques of page design, while learning to use PageMaker. Practical examples include newsletters, forms, books, manuals, logos, and more.

### Mastering Ready, Set, Go!
**David A. Kater**
482pp. Ref. 536-0

This hands-on introduction to the popular desktop publishing package for the Macintosh allows readers to produce professional-looking reports, brochures, and flyers. Written for Version 4, this title has been endorsed by Letraset, the Ready, Set, Go! software publisher.

### PageMaker 4.0 Macintosh Version Instant Reference
**Louis Columbus**
120pp. Ref. 788-6

Here's a concise, plain-language reference, offering fast access to details on all PageMaker 4.0 features and commands. Entries are organized by function—perfect for on-the-job use—and provide exact keystrokes, options, and cross-references, and instructions for all essential desktop publishing operations.

### Up & Running with the Mac Classic
**Tom Cuthbertson**
160pp; Ref. 881-5

A fast, breezy introduction to computing with the Mac Classic. In just 20 steps, you get the fundamental information you need—without the details you don't. Each step takes only 15 minutes to an hour to complete, making this book a real timesaver.

### Up & Running with Macintosh System 7
**Craig Danuloff**
140pp; Ref. 1000-2

Learn the new Mac System 7 in record time. This 20-step tutorial is perfect for computer-literate users who are new to System 7. Each concise step takes no more than 15 minutes to an hour to complete, and provides needed skills without unnecessary detail.

### Up & Running with PageMaker on the Macintosh
**Craig Danuloff**
134pp. Ref. 695-2

Ideal for computer-literate users who need to learn PageMaker fast. In just twenty steps, readers learn to import text, format characters and paragraphs, create graphics, use style sheets, work with color, and more.

### Up & Running with Norton Utilities on the Macintosh
**Peter Dyson**
146pp. Ref. 823-8

In just 20 lessons, you can be up and running with Norton Utilities for the Macintosh. You'll soon learn to retrieve accidentally erased files, reconstruct damaged files, find "lost files," unformat accidentally formatted disks, and make your system work faster.

### Using the Macintosh Toolbox with C (Second Edition)
**Fred A. Huxham**
**David Burnard**
**Jim Takatsuka**
525pp. Ref. 572-7

Learn to program with the latest versions of Macintosh Toolbox using this clear and succinct introduction. This popular title has been revised and expanded to include dozens of new programming examples for windows, menus, controls, alert boxes, and disk I/O. Includes hierarchical file system, Lightspeed C, Resource files, and R Maker.

# WORD PROCESSING

## The ABC's of Microsoft Word (Third Edition)
**Alan R. Neibauer**
461pp. Ref. 604-9

This is for the novice WORD user who wants to begin producing documents in the shortest time possible. Each chapter has short, easy-to-follow lessons for both keyboard and mouse, including all the basic editing, formatting and printing functions. Version 5.0.

## The ABC's of Microsoft Word for Windows
**Alan R. Neibauer**
334pp. Ref. 784-6

Designed for beginning Word for Windows users, as well as for experienced Word users who are changing from DOS to the Windows version. Covers everything from typing, saving, and printing your first document, to creating tables, equations, and graphics.

## The ABC's of WordPerfect 5
**Alan R. Neibauer**
283pp. Ref. 504-2

This introduction explains the basics of desktop publishing with WordPerfect 5: editing, layout, formatting, printing, sorting, merging, and more. Readers are shown how to use WordPerfect 5's new features to produce great-looking reports.

## The ABC's of WordPerfect 5.1 for Windows
**Alan R. Neibauer**
350pp; Ref. 803-3

This highly praised beginner's tutorial is now in a special new edition for WordPerfect 5.1 for Windows—featuring WYSIWYG graphics, font preview, the button bar, and more. It covers all the essentials of word processing, from basic editing to simple desktop publishing, in short, easy-to-follow lessons. Suitable for first-time computer users.

## The ABC's of WordPerfect 5.1
**Alan R. Neibauer**
352pp. Ref. 672-3

Neibauer's delightful writing style makes this clear tutorial an especially effective learning tool. Learn all about 5.1's new drop-down menus and mouse capabilities that reduce the tedious memorization of function keys.

## The Complete Guide to MultiMate
**Carol Holcomb Dreger**
208pp. Ref. 229-9

This step-by-step tutorial is also an excellent reference guide to MultiMate features and uses. Topics include search/replace, library and merge functions, repagination, document defaults and more.

## Encyclopedia WordPerfect 5.1
**Greg Harvey**
**Kay Yarborough Nelson**
1100pp. Ref. 676-6

This comprehensive, up-to-date WordPerfect reference is a must for beginning and experienced users alike. With complete, easy-to-find information on every WordPerfect feature and command—and it's organized by practical functions, with business users in mind.

## Mastering Microsoft Word on the IBM PC (Fourth Edition)
**Matthew Holtz**
680pp. Ref. 597-2

This comprehensive, step-by-step guide details all the new desktop publishing developments in this versatile word processor, including details on editing, formatting, printing, and laser printing. Holtz uses sample business documents to demonstrate the use of different fonts, graphics, and complex documents. Includes Fast Track speed notes. For Versions 4 and 5.

# FREE BROCHURE!

Complete this form today, and we'll send you a full-color brochure of Sybex bestsellers.

**Please supply the name of the Sybex book purchased.**

_____

**How would you rate it?**

_____ Excellent  _____ Very Good  _____ Average  _____ Poor

**Why did you select this particular book?**

_____ Recommended to me by a friend
_____ Recommended to me by store personnel
_____ Saw an advertisement in _____
_____ Author's reputation
_____ Saw in Sybex catalog
_____ Required textbook
_____ Sybex reputation
_____ Read book review in _____
_____ In-store display
_____ Other _____

**Where did you buy it?**

_____ Bookstore
_____ Computer Store or Software Store
_____ Catalog (name: _____ )
_____ Direct from Sybex
_____ Other: _____

**Did you buy this book with your personal funds?**

_____ Yes  _____ No

**About how many computer books do you buy each year?**

_____ 1-3  _____ 3-5  _____ 5-7  _____ 7-9  _____ 10+

**About how many Sybex books do you own?**

_____ 1-3  _____ 3-5  _____ 5-7  _____ 7-9  _____ 10+

**Please indicate your level of experience with the software covered in this book:**

_____ Beginner  _____ Intermediate  _____ Advanced

**Which types of software packages do you use regularly?**

_____ Accounting        _____ Databases           _____ Networks
_____ Amiga             _____ Desktop Publishing  _____ Operating Systems
_____ Apple/Mac         _____ File Utilities      _____ Spreadsheets
_____ CAD               _____ Money Management    _____ Word Processing
_____ Communications    _____ Languages           _____ Other _____
                                                        (please specify)

## Which of the following best describes your job title?

_____ Administrative/Secretarial   _____ President/CEO

_____ Director   _____ Manager/Supervisor

_____ Engineer/Technician   _____ Other _____

(please specify)

**Comments on the weaknesses/strengths of this book:** _____

_____

_____

_____

_____

**Name** _____

**Street** _____

**City/State/Zip** _____

**Phone** _____

PLEASE FOLD, SEAL, AND MAIL TO SYBEX

**SYBEX, INC.**
Department M
2021 CHALLENGER DR.
ALAMEDA, CALIFORNIA USA
94501

SYBEX

SEAL

## About the Companion Disk

The Companion Disk contains music and sounds that are especially well suited for desktop presentations and multimedia applications. They are provided in a way that lets you play them even if you haven't yet purchased an animation program or a MIDI sequencer.

## Contents and Requirements

The Companion Disk includes 13 Standard MIDI Files—in a number of lengths and musical styles. There are four classical pieces as well as several examples of contemporary production music. These professionally performed and edited works represent music libraries from Dr. T's Music Software, Opcode Systems, the Parker Adams Group, and Passport Designs.

If you have a General MIDI sound module, a MIDI interface, and HyperCard 2.0 or higher, you can play these music files directly, without additional software, by using the SOUNDtraK Demo stack put together by Kord Taylor and provided by Opcode Systems. If you don't have a General MIDI sound module, I've included a MIDI setup document so that you can use any multitimbral synthesizer or sound module with the SOUNDtraK demo. If you don't have HyperCard 2.0 or higher, but you do have a sequencer program, you can import these files into your sequencer for editing and playback.

All of Passport's QuikTunes MIDI files also come in digital audio versions, so I've attached a few of these to a HyperCard stack. If you have HyperCard 2.0 or higher, you can preview these files directly from the stack by clicking the provided buttons. If you don't have HyperCard 2.0 or higher, you can import these resource sounds into a great many applications of all types. For instance, if you don't have an animation program with sound capability, but you do have Microsoft Word 5.0, you can create a new document and use the Voice Annotation command on the Insert menu to audition any of the sounds.

I've also included a few musical sound effects from the MultiMedia HANDisc from CD Technology. These sounds are also contained in a HyperCard stack, and you can treat them the same as the digitized QuikTunes examples mentioned above.

Please read the documentation that's included on the disk. It contains important information about the examples that appear in this collection. Note: The two Parker Adams MIDI files have a few measures of lead-in time before the music begins.

## Installation

The contents of this disk were compressed using Compact Pro by Bill Goodman. To uncompress the disk, you'll need a hard drive with about 1.3 megabytes of available space. Just double-click the icon labeled *Audible Mac Companion,* and designate your hard drive as the location for the uncompressed folder to appear. The rest is automatic.